The Huks: Philippine Agrarian Society in Revolt

Eduardo Lachica

The Praeger Special Studies program—utilizing the most modern and efficient book production techniques and a selective worldwide distribution network—makes available to the academic, government, and business communities significant, timely research in U.S. and international economic, social, and political development.

The Huks: Philippine Agrarian Society in Revolt

PRAEGER SPECIAL STUDIES IN INTERNATIONAL POLITICS AND PUBLIC AFFAIRS

Framingham State College
Framingham, Massachusetts

Praeger Publishers New York Washington London

PRAEGER PUBLISHERS
111 Fourth Avenue, New York, N.Y. 10003, U.S.A.
5, Cromwell Place, London S.W.7, England

Published in the United States of America in 1971
by Praeger Publishers, Inc.

All rights reserved

Library of Congress Catalog Card Number: 77-171236

Printed in the United States of America

DS
686.5
L23
1971b

To the memory of my father

Contents

Maps, Charts and Figures

The Huks: Philippine Agrarian Society in Revolt

Acknowledgments

This book began as a journalistic enterprise; early in 1969 Philippines *Herald* managing editor, Antonio Escoda, commissioned a "task force" to investigate Huk activism in Central Luzon. This was a fairly ambitious project for there was not much to start with.

Just as important to our purpose was to demonstrate what could be done with "task force" or group reporting. Three of the *Herald's* Central Luzon correspondents got marching orders to scout for possible leads; the Department of National Defense reporter was asked to relay to us the Army and Philippine Constabulary side of the story and I, as Senior Writer, was to collate all these into a comprehensive whole.

It took us nearly five months to complete the assignment for the distractions of daily journalism do not permit the luxury of extended research on a single subject. The result was a series of seven articles on the newly-risen New People's Army (NPA) of Commander Dante and what looked then like his fateful partnership with the Maoists. This was the most extensive treatment on the Huks in years, and there were requests in the Philippines and from abroad for back copies of the *Herald* series. When the *Herald* stories won the Rotary Club Award for Distinguished Investigative Reporting, a new task presented itself: the authors were asked to prepare their work for book publication.

Now that it had to go between firm covers, our modest journalism had to be a respectable history as well. The material needed not only updating but backdating as well, for the Huk movement can be traced to the last World War, and its doctrinal and spiritual roots even further back. Since Dante was known to have been a protege of Commander Sumulong, the parent Pampanga organization had to be investigated as well. To identify its specific strain, the Huk movement had to be compared with the pathology of insurgency and dissidence elsewhere in the world.

With its expanded scope, the enterprise therefore became more difficult. It grew by accretion — and sometimes by substitution — as new facts displaced outdated ones. In its present form, this book is certainly not the last word on the Huks, for the narrative continues to unfold further and threatens to outdate portions of this book even before publication.

A major burden of this work was the scarcity of unbiased witnesses. Those who *do* know the inner workings of the Huk movement are too compromised to be completely truthful, or they are afraid to talk.

There were some compensations, however. Once the propaganda channels were bypassed, once the natural reserve was breached, information became readily available.

The "field work" in Central Luzon was only mildly dangerous. The Huks respect the Manila press and there has been not one case of a non-Pampango journalist suffering the vengeance of the movement. The only possible peril was being mistaken by one of the competing groups as a "spy" of their rivals. To make our identity clear to everyone, we drove around Pampanga and Tarlac in a vehicle with *Herald* markings. This was when the Monkees and the Beatles were hot after each other; when even a passing army vehicle got fired upon with a M-79 grenade-launcher. We felt safer without a military escort.

This book could not have been possible without the collaboration, advice and encouragement of many. My primary indebtedness is to my associates in the original *Herald* task force report: Amante Reyes, who covers Tarlac, contributed much to the chapter on Commander Dante; Ramiro Mercado, based in Angeles City, covered Pampanga and Ben Maglaque filed out of Camp Olivas, the headquarters of the First Philippine Constabulary zone; TV 13 cameramen, Vernie Razon, a native Tarlaqueño, was my constant companion and guide. Subsequently, Andy Morales, another old Central Luzon hand, joined the team. Being native Pampangos and living out there where the action is, they took more physical risks than any *Herald* taskforcer based in Manila.

Some of the credit for the original *Herald* series should go to our hard-working City Desk, particularly to news editor Jose Pavia and assistant news editor Alberto K. Corvera.

I am grateful to Luis Taruc not only for going over the drafts but also for contributing rich anecdotal detail to the recounting of the Socialist movement and the building of the Huk organization. Alfredo Saulo, another former Huk activist and John Alan Larkin whose revised history of the Pampango society extends to the outbreak of World War II, provided me with backgrounders.

Ambassador Rafaelita Hilario Soriano, Sen. Benigno Aquino Jr., Carlos and Mila Albert, and Rep. Emilio Espinosa also assisted me with extended interviews. The San Miguel Corporation Public Relations Department — Jose Carpio and Nanerico Santos especially — backstopped the *Herald* team with additional research.

Frank Denton, a Rand Corporation researcher, and Mary Hollnsteiner, director of the Institute of Philippine Culture of the Ateneo de Manila University, Marina Dayrit, director of the University of the Philippines Library (and a native of Angeles), introduced me to source materials.

W. Scott Thompson, a visiting Professor from the Fletcher School of Law and Diplomacy in Tufts University, and David Joel Steinberg, a Philippine specialist from the University of Michigan, gave me invaluable advice on style and organization.

I am also obligated to Manuel Manahan, Frances L. Starner, Ruben Santos-Cuyugan and Josefa Saniel of the University of the Philippines Asian Center; to Macario Peralta, Luis Alfonso, and the staff of the Asia Reading Room of the Ramon Magsaysay Awards Foundation.

The Armed Forces of the Philippines was also most helpful. Hon. Alejandro Melchor, then Undersecretary of National defense, gave his blessings from the very start. General Manuel Yan, AFP chief of staff, declassified several Defense College papers. Col. Fidel Ramos, AFP intelligence chief, also gave background briefings. Commodore Rene Lavadia, president of the National Defense College of the Philippines, Brig. Gen. Rafael Ileto, Philippine Army commanding general; Brig. Gen. Felizardo Tanabe, 1st PC zone commander, Col. Roso Saballones, then Task Force Lawin commander; Lt. Col. Bienvenido Castro, 10th BCT commanding officer, and Maj. Vicente Custodio, 1st PC zone intelligence officer, all gave generously of their time.

Leonardo Siguion Reyna and Saklolo Leaño helped with legal advice.

I would also like to acknowledge the research assistance of Yolanda Faylona, Lucita Salmorin and Carlos Josue of the *Herald* Library Staff. Lina Cruz, *Herald* editorial secretary, and her assistants typed the manuscript in record time.

Our greatest debt is to Andres Soriano, Jr. who thought up the idea of enlarging the *Herald* series into this book and who was a constant source of encouragement and support.

Eduardo Lachica

Manila, December 1970

Introduction

PURSUING AN INVISIBLE ARMY

The Second World War was the portent of many of the dissident movements of Southeast Asia. It broke up the head office-and-branch relationships between the Western nations and their colonial outposts and gave the hitherto underground communist parties, nationalist cabals and other anti-Establishmentarians an opportunity to organize and arm themselves for the post-victory struggle for independence. Nguyen Ai Quoc, or Ho Chi Minh as he styled himself, fashioned the wartime Viet Nam Doc-Lap Dong Minh (Vietminh) into the precursor of what would be the 20th century's most dogged and self-sacrificing national liberation movement, next to the ultimately successful Chinese Red Army. Out of the ruins of the French colonial administration in Indochina sprang the Lao Issara (Free Laos) which later became the Pathet Lao of more recent years. Postwar Burma was afflicted with the insurrections of three separate forces — Thakin Soe's Communist splinter faction called the Red Flag, Thakin Than Tun's reestablished Communist Party of Burma called the White Flag and a rebel militia called the People's Volunteer Organization (PVP) — plus the depredations of thousands of Karen and Shan insurgents.[1] From the wartime Malayan Race Liberation Army sprung the postwar guerrilla movement that took the British Army 40,000 regular troops, 25,000 regular police, 50,000 special constables and 250,000 "home guards" to contain.[2]

The Huks belong to this war-born generation of dissident bands. They were mustered into service in 1942 when the Philippines was experiencing the humiliation of Japanese

---

[1]Brief histories of these Southeast Asian dissident movements appear in studies by Bernard B. Fall ("The Pathet Lao: A 'Liberation' Party"), John H. Bagley ("The Communist Parties of Burma") and John C. Donnel ("North Vietnam: A Qualified Pre-Chinese Position") collected in *The Communist Revolution in Asia: Tactics, Goals and Achievements,* edited by Robert A. Scalapino, (Englewood Cliffs, N.J.: Prentice-Hall, 1965).

[2]D. E. Kennedy, *The Security of Southern Asia* (New York: Praeger, 1965).

Army occupation and they resisted the interlopers along with other Filipino guerrilla organizations, legitimate or otherwise. After the American liberation, the other guerrilleros disbanded; the Huks did not fully. Under communist leadership, they saw a chance to seize national power at a time when the newly-proclaimed Philippine Republic was in obvious distress as a result of a monetary crisis, graft in high office and mounting peasant unrest.

In 1949, the Huks were a formidable army of 12,000 regulars with the proven support of over a hundred thousand peasants in Central Luzon. The security forces were undermanned and demoralized. The Lava brothers, who dominated the Politburo, saw the whole rotting bourgeois structure of the post-colonial Philippines crumbling under the advance of the proletariat. But they miscalculated the odds; a dynamic Filipino leader, Ramon Magsaysay, rose and turned the government battalions into an effective counter-insurgency force and with timely United States aid (materials but not troops) crushed the rebellion.

Since their defeat in the field, the Huks have lapsed into an ambivalent state of outlawry and reform advocacy. They are now in such greatly reduced numbers that they cannot conceivably pose another threat to the central government. But remarkably enough, they have persisted through all these years. Nearing their third decade, they are among the oldest dissident groups still extant today. It is their continued survival, long after their nearly total defeat in the field, that has brought about much perturbation and misapprehension about the nature of this phenomenon. To be quite truthful, the confusion is most pronounced right at home.

The Huks had ceased to be critically and intelligently reported on for more than a dozen years when they seemed not revolutionarily active during that period. It was only in the last year or so that the "resurgent" Huks began to draw more than routine attention from journalists and scholars. In the interim, the Huks were the almost exclusive property of the myth-makers, the rather complacent Manila press and the oversolicitous Armed Forces.

Guerrillas? Outlaws? Robin Hoods?

Thus, the old imagery of the Huks still prevails in the public imagination, though it may no longer reflect the reality. They have been variously called guerrillas, dissidents, communists, bandits and Robin Hoods. Not one of these descriptions fit, though there conceivably may be a bit of each in all Huks, or some Huks may deserve a specific label more than others. But they definitely are not guerrillas — at least not since the Japanese occupation and for a brief spell during the 1950 rebellion.

The common understanding of a guerrilla force is of one totally committed to wearing down the armed strength of the government by sabotage and terrorism, by hit-and-run warfare, by continually seeking to expand its bases of effective operation. Almost by definition, guerrillas are full-time fighters, their normal pursuits abandoned for their cause, living in the hills or in the countryside ready to strike at the enemy when his guard is down.

This is the image which appeals best to Westerners, particularly the incurable romantics who imagine the classic guerrilla to be somebody fitting the mock-heroic description of Col. Napoleon Valeriano and Lt. Col. Charles T. R. Bohannan: "He is the essence of individuality, in a state-ridden, automaton-threatened world; the hunted man whose lonely courage appeals deeply to the outsider — particularly to the nostalgic sophisticate in his armchair, denied physical courage and the romantic ideal of 'the frontier'."[3]

Some Huks are enamored with the romance of perilous existence, as we shall see from the nature of their breeding. But, disillusioning as it may be, only a score or so of the top leaders with five-digit prizes on their heads are really in full flight from the law and even they are not inclined to fire a shot in anger except when trapped by pursuers or in the process of liquidating a specific enemy who is more often civilian than military. Most of the supernumeraries listed in the AFP's "order of battle" are "12-hour Huks," on call by their superiors for specific missions but otherwise enlisted in normal occupations and are farmers, mechanics or municipal policemen.

What commonly eludes non-Filipinos is the relatively small scale of the Huk movement in terms of bodies. The estimated hard-core usually runs from 200 to 800 (not counting the civilian supporters which involves a higher calculation). This is about 1/10,000 of the population in the four provinces affected by Huk dissidence. And the whole region has only 1/36 of the total population of the Philippines. Numbers, of course, are deceptive. Fidel Castro started with only a score or so comrades and in a few years he was dictator of Cuba. The Philippines, however, has still far to go before it can resemble Cuba before the fall of Batista. What makes the Huks even less of a threat to national security is the fact that the Armed Forces outnumber them by at least four to

---

[3]Valeriano and Bohannan, *Counter-Guerrilla Operations: The Philippines Experience* (New York: Praeger, 1961).

one in Central Luzon and by 40 to one in the entire country.

If a Manilan does not read the newspapers, he would never suspect that a dissident struggle was going on in the countryside only 50 kilometers north of the capital. Most Manilans go through their daily rounds, hustling for a living, enjoying their little pleasures, completely unaffected by what is going on in Central Luzon. A tourist can drive over the asphalt and concrete highways of Pampanga and Tarlac without noticing any evidence that Central Luzon is different from the rest of the Philippines except for the slightly more visible military presence. One sometimes wonders indeed whether the Huks are not just a convenient invention of the Armed Forces for purposes of raising their own budget.

The references being made to the "budgetary Huks" are not entirely jocular. Armies are often criticized by civilian dissenters for magnifying the strength and intentions of their official enemies. The Vietnam war provides an analogical situation on a far larger scale. The American "military-industrial complex" is the villain of the piece, and in the New Left view it intentionally promotes the slaughter of Asians for the sake of building its war machine and rolling up stock values on Wall Street.[4]

The perceived Huk problem has contributed greatly to the expansion and prosperity of the Armed Forces of the Philippines, though the country has no comparable industrial complex with an investment stake in national defense. In 1949, the year the Lavas declared a "revolutionary situation," the AFP had a budget of ₱54 million. In 1954, when the Huk rebellion was ebbing, the Armed Forces budget was ₱147 million. It has since been raised to ₱593 million pesos in 1970, despite President Ferdinand Marcos' pledges of "fiscal restraint." The budgetary increments have been due to other factors, too, such as the need to modernize equipment and reduce AFP dependence on U.S.-supplied weapons and materiel, the worsening of the "peace and order" situation in other (non-Huk) provinces, the AFP's share in the total growth of the Philippine bureaucracy and inflationary pressures on the peso. But much of the public tolerance of increasing militarism is due to the AFP's brief on national security, and the Huks are a convenient excuse.

A case indeed can be made for the Huks being in one sense a "constituency" of the military establishment. The Department of National Defense is the only legitimate source of day-to-day information about the Huks and one of the few

---

[4]As though to reenforce the New Left view of a Pentagon-Wall Street conspiracy, stock values took a tumble following President Nixon's phased Vietnamization program.

agencies officially quotable on the subject. Politicians occasionally make pronouncements on the Huks which tend to balance off the AFP's institutional biases. But by the sheer volume of press releases, official interviews and briefings, it is the AFP position that tends to predominate in the Manila press.

Peculiarly enough, the Huks make "news" in few other instances than when the Philippine Constabulary or the Army goes into action against them. The Huks thus carry on a strange twilight existence on the front pages based almost entirely on what the AFP claims they are doing.

At the other extreme of the perceptual range are the so-called "committed" writers who see the Huks as the champions of the poor and downtrodden and the "fascistic" government as their unjust oppressors. Reformed dissidents like Luis Taruc and Alfredo Saulo are generally sympathetic to the Huks in their writings. They, moreover, had the advantage of having lived with the Huks, so they are perhaps more competent to dissect the movement than some of the armchair ideologues who have addressed themselves to the same subject.

Popular perceptions of the Huks vary widely. Angeles city officials openly sympathize with them. The typical man-in-the-street comment is that the Huks are not the nicest of people but they are at least better than some outright gangsters trying to move into Central Luzon.

Some politicians, student leaders, even some minor bureaucrats believe the Huks are sincere reformers. What undermines the credibility of this sanguine view is the likelihood that the ones expressing it are probably beholden in some way to the movement. The scion of a rich Pampanga family who had some good words to say about Sumulong sought the Huk leader's support for his uncle in the 1969 elections.

"The Huks are peaceful. They do not milk the population. They do not extort. They are Robin Hoods." These statements were made in an earnest manner by a ranking official of Angeles city. They could carry some weight if the speaker was not known to have unofficial contacts with Sumulong's organization.

A ranking Tarlac politician was convinced Dante was a dedicated and honest do-gooder. This would be a strong endorsement were it not for the likelihood that the politician— and which practical Tarlac politician doesn't? — had some personal dealings with this young hero.

Contrasting with these favorable views are the findings of the Rand Corporation. The Huks were seen by most respondents as an "unappetizing organization." About two-thirds of all groups did not think they were "men of justice."

A significant number said the Huks were "brutal" and a surprisingly low number of tenants regarded the Huks as their deliverers.[5]

This conflict of perceptions is not easy to resolve. Rand's myth-shattering judgments are based to a large extent on quantitative data and are difficult to challenge. Against its views are the grassroots feelings about the Huks which tend to be more sympathetic than critical. Few Pampangos are willing to talk openly about the Huks and only those identified in one way or another with contending factions were. Pampanga is perhaps too divided against itself to have a clear consensus about its dissident problem.

It is proper then for this work to concern itself initially with an approximate cosmology of the Huk world. Who are the Huks? How do they function? Where did they spring from? What do they stand for and what are their goals? There are many constraints against arriving at the truth. Not the least is the ambiguities of language. The basic documents on the Huks are mainly in English; there are a few in Pilipino (Tagalog), the national language; there are fewer still in Pampangueño (also called *Capangpangan),* the dialect of most of the dissidents. The major commentators who write in English tend to fit the perceived phenomena into western constructs which cannot be expected to convey the most accurate sense of what the movement is about. Guerrillas, dissidents, insurgents — these words communicate varied meanings to different readers.

Those who have spoken for the movement — Jose Lava, Luis Taruc, and recently "Amado Guerrero" — are not themselves rank-and-file Huks. Dante, the most hunted of the Huk leaders, has never made himself available for interviews in the bougeois media. He writes and speaks largely in *Capangpangan.* So do the great majority of the peasant-born dissidents. Much of the essence of "Hukism" is lost in the translation; the real Huk literature is oral. It seems to be something derived from the heart rather than from the intellect. That alone may provide a clue to the degree of alienation between the Huks and the miscomprehending outside world.

What may also complicate the analysis is the long time span of actual Huk history — 28 years to date. What was true at one time — e.g., the Huks being the military arm of the Communist Party of the Philippines — may not be so

[5]H. A. Averch, F. H. Denton and J. E. Koehler, *A Crisis of Ambiguity: Political and Economic Development in the Philippines* (Rand Corporation, Sta. Monica, Calif., 1970), pp. 217-218. Subsequently cited as the Rand report.

anymore. The Huk chronology and chart in the book may help the reader sort out the ups and downs of the movement since 1942.

Finally, there is the matter of personalities. It is an impressive cast — from the Lavas and the Tarucs of the late forties, to Sumulong, Alibasbas and Dante of the sixties, and to the newly-risen commanders only now surfacing. One can use a historian's sense in sorting out the actors and placing them in their proper hierarchical niches. But it is tentative work at best and must be forgiven for lapses. A few of the actors may die before this work sees print; this would not necessarily mean the end of the movement.[6] Alibasbas and Sumulong; the Lavas and "Amado Guerrero"; Delio, Freddie and Dante seem to be cast in "roles" — the professional revolutionary, the hard-as-nails pragmatist, the starry-eyed idealist-reformer. There is always someone to fill the roles.

Brig. Gen. Felizardo Tanabe, 1st PC Zone Commander, testified to the prompt succession of Huk leadership in his appearance before a Congress subcommittee hearing. "After a commander has been killed a subordinate commander takes the place of the slain commander and after a few weeks he gains control of the area." Whether this was his intent or not, General Tanabe pointed out the futility of trying to extinguish the movement with gunfire and the iron heel.

---

[6]Two weeks before the final manuscript was ready for the press, Commander Sumulong was captured in Angeles City, making necessary some changes in the copy.

[7]Renze L. Hoeksema, *Communism in the Philippines, A Historical and Analytical Study of Communism and the Communist Party in the Philippines and Its Relations to Communist Movements Abroad,* an unpublished doctoral thesis submitted to the Department of Government, Harvard University, 1957.

Chapter One

THE NATURE OF THE HUK

"Huk" is a generic name for the various orders of armed dissidents claiming descent from the *Hukbo ng Bayan Laban sa Hapon* (Army of Resistance Against Japan) or its postwar successor organization the *Hukbong Magpapalaya ng Bayan* (People's Liberation Army). Their habitat is Central Luzon where certain social and cultural conditions create a hospitable environment for their movement. The Huks are distinct from ordinary bandits in that they invariably identify themselves with the redress of agrarian grievances.

The Huks belong to several organizations. There are three, to be exact, according to the field guide issued by the AFP. In direct line of succession from the HMB is the Pampanga organization based in Angeles City. A group of younger Huks led by Commander Dante broke off from the Pampanga organization and established itself as the New People's Army (NPA). The AFP recognizes a hazy formation called *Army ng Bayan* (Army of the Nation), led by Commander Diwa and presumed to be linked with the "traditional" Communist Party of the Philippines (CPP).[1]

Two of the Huk factions have staked out their territories; the HMB in western Pampanga and parts of Bataan and Bulacan, the NPA in southern Tarlac and southwestern Nueva Ecija The *Army ng Bayan* has no clearly defined hegemony. The Huk factions share a common lineage and generally the same corporate objectives, but that is about all. They are as much at odds with each other as they are with the AFP which

---

[1]The nomenclature and some of the basic information about the three contemporary Huk factions are taken from the "So The People May Know," a series of mimeographed documents prepared by the AFP General Headquarters. In these AFP documents and in other writings, the CPP is sometimes rendered in Pilipino as *Partido Komunista ng Pilipinas* (PKP). The AFP designates the Maoist camp as MA-MAO, a psycho-war dig at the Huks, since *mamao* in the dialect means a frightful spectre. Subsequently cited as AFP documents.

gives chase to all three of them. Territorial claims are jealously protected. The geographical centers of their domains are secure but overlapping boundaries are sometimes no man's land.

Huk history is rife with factionalism.

Each self-proclaimed Huk leader surrounds himself with his own henchmen and imparts his own style to the governance of his territory. Sumulong claimed to be an agrarian reformer from the Pampanga-based Socialist Party of prewar vintage, but behaved more like an old-fashioned entrepreneur living off his "investments" in the commercial life of Angeles. By contrast, Dante made his name as a young, incorruptible peasant leader with a considerable grasp of grassroots ideology.

Neither of these two contemporary leaders acknowledged any special debt to Luis Taruc or the Lava brothers. It is doubtful whether Pedro Taruc and Sumulong legally inherited the HMB; rather, they claimed salvage rights to the old Pampanga apparatus destroyed during the rebellion. They were on record as having supplanted the old HMB with the *Bayung Fuerza Democratica ding Memalen* (New People's Democratic Force) which is strikingly reminiscent of the old Democratic Alliance. The DA served as the parliamentary arm of the post-liberation Huks. If the *Bayung Fuerza* does exist — the Angeles-based Huk leaders were the only source of this information — it would be the link between the old and the new Pampanga organizations.[2]

When Dante was in league with the student radicals, his propagandists condemned the Tarucs and the Lavas as "revisionist renegades."[3] With these peasant bands in Central Luzon claiming the one and true line, not to mention two Communist Party factions still at loggerheads in the city, a remerger of the Huk factions and their sympathizers is possible only with the demise of key leaders or a *coup* by one of the major power-wielders.

Factionalism is not confined to the Huks and other Filipino radical elements; it is part of the style of Philippine politics. A non-Filipino who tries to interpret the bewildering shifts of political alliances on the basis of party labels or verbalized or written platforms would despair of ever understanding what is going on.

Similarly, it would be impossible to comprehend the factional strife of the Huks without looking beyond the neat language of ideology. The personal relations among the Huk

[2]Alfred B. Saulo, *Communism in the Philippines. An Introduction* (Manila: Ateneo de Manila University, 1969).

[3]AFP documents.

and Communist leaders, their quarrels and ambitions, their generational differences, are extremely relevant to a true understanding of the phenomenon.

Huk Numerology

The AFP's assessments of Huk strength are "guesstimates" at best, obtained from field intelligence units and a network of informers whose reliability is of a mixed quality. The Huks certainly do not stand still long enough to be nose-counted. But since secrets are hard to keep in Central Luzon barrios, it is possible for an intelligence officer to collate a rough census of the Huk population at any one time.

Huk-strength estimates are usually given in three (and sometimes four) separate figures, corresponding to the different layers in the so-called Huk "pyramid." At the top are the Huk "regulars" or "hardcore." They are the generals and foot soldiers of the movement, all of them well-armed, committed full-time to the cause and organized into operational units. Then there are the "combat support," or as Col. Saturnino S. Indiongco describes them, the "12-hour Huks" (civilians by day, Huks by night).[4] They are also armed and usually "provide security for the regulars and carry out punitive assignments." An extra category sometimes included in Huk estimates is the "service group" or "legal cadres," made up of barrio captains and other petty officials operating in the open. They do not go out on armed missions; instead, they serve as couriers, spies, provisioners and tax collectors. At the bottom of the pyramid is the "mass base" — that part of the civilian population materially supporting the movement. The Rand Corporation, however, has a less sanguine definition of the mass base: "As practiced, mass base means the total number of people who live in the area that is defined as controlled by the HMB."[5]

Table 1 shows the rise and fall of Huk strength in the 28-year period since the founding of the organization in 1942. Unfortunately, the graph is based on no firmer figures than those offered by the AFP and other indirect sources. But they are the best that can be obtained with the marginal reporting facilities available to the researcher.

---

[4]Lt. Col. Saturnino S. Indiongco, (GSC) PC, *Reexamination of the Movement,* an unpublished thesis submitted to the National Defense College of the Philippines, Fort Bonifacio, Rizal, December, p. 207.

[5]Rand report, p. 207.

TABLE I

Estimates of Huk Strength Reported

By Various Sources, 1942-1970

Year	Regulars	Combat Support	Mass Base
Feb. 1942	300[a]		
Sept. 1942	3,000[b]		
1944	2,000[a]		
	(10,000[c])		(100,000[c])
1946	10,000[d]		
1950	12,800[b]		54,000[b]
Oct. 1952	4,000[a]		30,000-40,000[a]
1956	660[d]		
1960			9,000[a]
May 1965	75[e]	685[e]	5,000[e]
1966	256[e]		25,000[e]
1967	156[e]		
1968	300[e]		32,000[e]
1969	400[e]	500[e]	30,000-80,000[e]
1970	765[e]	730[e]	121,000[e]
NPA	400	400	41,000
AB	100	130	37,000
HMB	265	200	43,000

Legend:
a. Hoeksema
b. Handbook on the Communist Party of the Philippines, J-2, GHQ, AFO, 1961.
c. Guerrilla Resistance Movements in the Philippines, GHQ, Southwestern Pacific Area, USA, March, 1945.
d. Committee on Anti-Filipino Activities, Congress of the Philippines, 1957.
e. Armed Forces of the Philippines

The Huks began with a modest-size guerrilla band of 300 in February, 1942 and multiplied tenfold in only seven months. Renze Hoeksema believes that the wartime formation never surpassed 2,000 fully-armed and full-time guerrillas, though General MacArthur's Southwestern Pacific command intelligence estimated the Huk "members" to be as many as 10,000. The Huks reached their numerical peak in 1950 when they had 12,800 under arms. A succession of defeats cut down the force to 4,000 by October, 1952 (the estimate of the late President Ramon Magsaysay). The Huk ranks were further decimated by capture, death or desertion all through the late fifties and early sixties, until they came to near-extinction in 1965 when the dissidents numbered no more than 75. But from that year on the Huks have been steadily gaining in membership with a sharp increase reported between 1968 and 1970.

The AFP General Headquarters reported the NPA as the biggest of the three Huk factions today with 400 regulars, 400 combat support and a mass base of 41,000. Sumulong had the next largest force with 265 regulars, 200 combat support and a mass base of 43,000. The comparative figures for the *Army ng Bayan* were 100, 130 and 37,000.[6]

The lists of Huk enemy and the awards posted for their killing, capture or surrender announced by the AFP since 1959 are another basis for analyzing the growth of the Huk movement (see Annex A). On July 31, 1959, the AFP posted awards for only three identified fugitives led by Jesus Lava. Minor awards were offered for 23 classes of Huks whose names were unspecified. On October 11, 1965, there were four identified fugitives — ₱130,000 for Communist Party Secretary-General Jesus Lava, and ₱50,000 each for the HMB Military Commander Casto Alejandrino and his No. 2 man Silvestre Liwanag (Linda Bie). Minor awards ranging from ₱1,500 to ₱200 were offered for 23 classes of Huks with their individual names unspecified. On October 11, 1965, there were four names in the list — ₱45,000 for Pedro Taruc, who succeeded to the Huk leadership following the capture of Lava, ₱30,000 each for Commanders Sumulong and Alibasbas and ₱15,000 for Commander Freddie.

By February, 1967, the AFP awards list had expanded to 36 names with the prizes for the heads of Pedro Taruc and Sumulong raised to ₱100,000 and ₱80,000. The July 23, 1969 awards list had 83 names topped by Pedro Taruc, Sumulong and Commander Dante, all worth ₱150,000 each. There were 11 other lesser commanders with five-digit prizes. The most recent list of awards, issued on March 16, 1970, carried 243

---

[6]James Wilson, chief-of-mission of the U.S. Embassy, testified in the Fall of 1969 that the three Huk groups are "estimated to number some 400 regular armed men at the present time; 500 armed combat support personnel; 3,000 to 40,000 unarmed general support personnel; and a mass base estimated to number between 3,000 and 35,000 people. Some would take this mass figure at times as high as 80,000." — Hearings before the Subcommittee on United States Security Agreements and Commitments Abroad of the Committee on Foreign Relations, United States Senate, 91st Congress, Part 1, September 30, October 1, 2 and 3, 1969, pp. 226-227.

names. The prizes totalled a record ₱1,724,100 with the Huk trinity of Taruc, Sumulong and Dante wanted for ₱150,000 each, Gregorio Ocampo (Sumulong's No. 2 man) raised from ₱80,000 in 1969 to ₱100,000, and 29 other commanders in demand for prizes ranging from ₱40,000 at ₱10,000.

There are three obvious conclusions that can be drawn from this comparison. AFP intelligence is getting better every year so that more of the enemy are known. The AFP is simply getting richer in terms of awards money and can afford increasingly higher awards for their wanted men. The Huk movement has been growing steadily since 1959, its numbers indicated by the lengthening awards lists. Consequently, the growing difficulty experienced in capturing or killing them is reflected in the inflationary trend in awards money.

However, a perceptive thesis presented to the National Defense College of the Philippines by Lt. Col. Saturnino S. Indiongco cautions against interpreting the increase of Huk "activism" as a sign that the movement is growing. A salient analytical point follows:

> Huk resurgence is misleading. The Huk reservoir of strength is such that it can react to any situation forced on him. His strength is elastic. He need not go on recruiting. The force is there lying "peacefully." He can "activate" a dormant Huk in the barrio, town or city as the need arises. He needs but a few men in the field, for his purpose today is different from that of yesterday. He increases or decreases his strength as called for by the situation. The degree of activities is dictated on him by his enemies.

Col. Indiongco's model of Central Luzon's "passive" dissidence is strongly persuasive. Arithmetical calculations of Huk strength can indeed be deceptive. The potential for dissidence is always there, irrespective of the number of commanders in the field. The Huk force grows or diminishes according to the felt need for it. During the Japanese occupation, there was a nation-wide summons to resist the Japanese and thousands of Pampangos took to arms and joined their comrades in militia-like formations. Again there was a call to battle during the post-Liberation struggle against the central government followed by a waning of numerical Huk strength in the aftermath of military defeat. The survivors hoped that the government would do better; it was no longer necessary to take arms.

By the same token, the Huk movement is perceived to be "growing" once more because of the failure or slowness of reform in Central Luzon. Taking to the hills has become fashionable once again. This has a chilling implication in so far as the AFP's anti-Huk operations are concerned. The enemy cannot be defeated by attrition. Killing more Huks will not do because others would simply take the places of the slain comrades. In Central Luzon as well as in Vietnam, the body count is often meaningless.

What is meant then by a Huk "resurgence"? If it cannot significantly relate to Huk numerical strength, it may be more credibly explained in terms of *countermeasures* against the Huks. Figure 1, prepared by the AFP General Headquarters, purports to show the relative rise and fall of Huk activism in terms of killings, injuries and kidnappings attributed to the Huks.

The Huks were rather inactive from 1962 to 1965. In 1966, their homicidal proclivities took a sudden jump, maintaining more or less an annual strike rate of 60 to 80 up to 1968. In 1969, the Huks went on a rampage, inflicting 198 casualties. Can these Huk strikes be related to other factors besides the numerical growth of the Huk formation? Indeed, they can. What is also correlatable are the indicated years.

The other variable that the AFP seemed to ignore was the relative degree of military action against the Huks. Between 1961 to 1965, the AFP relaxed their pressure on the Huks. President Diosdado Macapagal, a native Pampango, did not like to persecute his own people. His Secretary of National Defense, Macario Peralta, recalled that he just "sat on the Huks so that they could not move."[7] In 1965, when certain AFP units actually fraternized with Huk commanders, there were only 17 recorded incidents perpetrated by the Huks.

In 1966, the first year of President Marcos' campaign, the battle orders were changed. The Huks became anathema to the new President, particularly since they campaigned for his opponent in the 1965 elections.[8] The AFP was directed to hit the Huks as hard as they could. On August 14, 1966, President Marcos loftily rejected a proposal to offer amnesty to the Huks, although had he done so there could have been better than fair chances that many dissidents would have given themselves up.[9]

An altogether different thesis presents itself. Huk violence rose in 1966, not because the dissidents simply felt like being more aggressive but in reprisal for increasing violence against them.

---

[7]Interview, July, 1970.

[8]Pampanga was also the only Luzon province to vote heavily for President Macapagal.

[9]Philippines *Herald,* August 15, 1966.

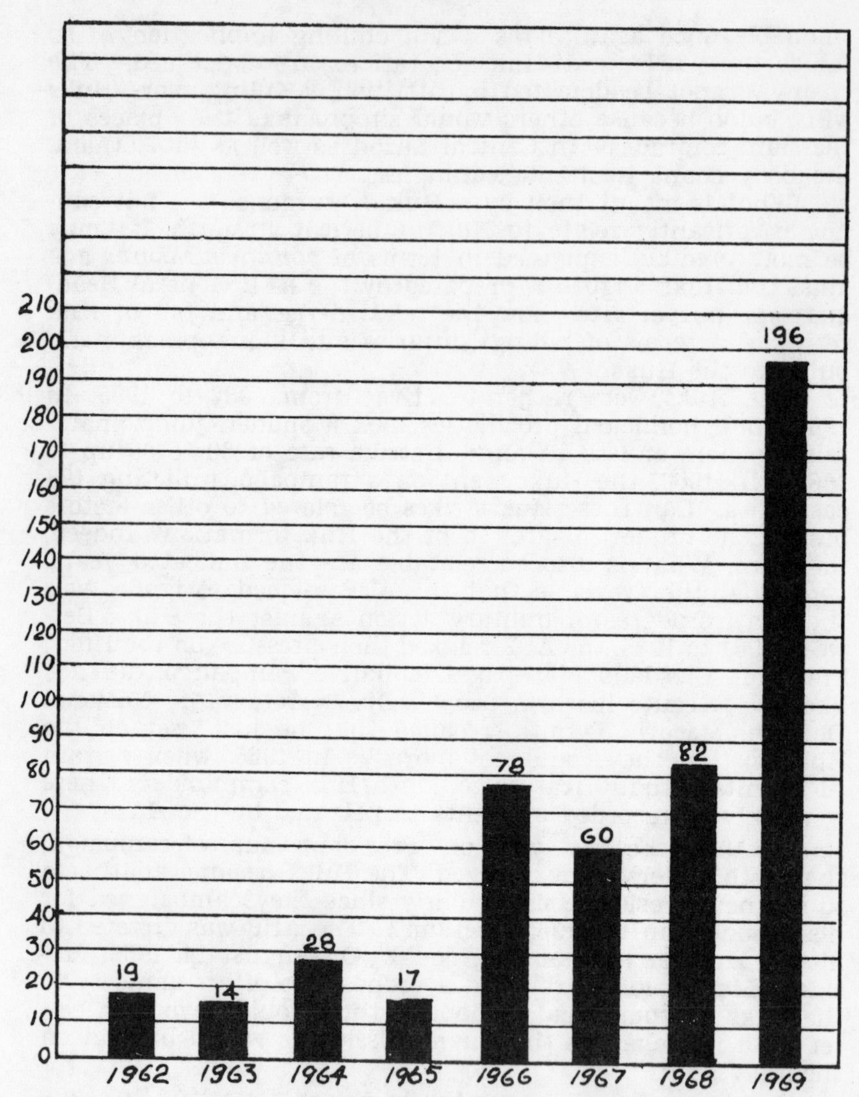

Figure 1: Annual incidence of violence attributed to the Huks, 1962-1969.

Vertical column indicates the number of "victims" of Huk violence. The horizontal columns are the years from 1962 to 1969. Figures from 1962 to 1968 are attributed to the HMB alone. The 1969 figure combines incidents charged to both the HMB and the NPA. The figures exclude persons wounded and kidnapped, "believed to have been liquidated but whose deaths could not be confirmed." From the Armed Forces of the Philippines.

The AFP campaign picked up in 1968 with one of the AFP's most efficient Huk-fighters, General Emilio Zerrudo, directing operations. In 1969, Huk activism more than doubled, but this again is explained by the fact that an intensified anti-Huk drive was undertaken against Dante's New People's Army, now proscribed as a threat to the safety of the Republic.

Huk activism, the kind that results in publicized casualties, is thus more aptly described as a reaction to suppression rather than the product of the initiative of the Huks themselves.

The Imperative to Survive

The Huks bear only a superficial resemblance to the Vietcong, the Algerian rebels of the 1950's and Al Fatah. The Filipino dissidents shy away from contact with the AFP. There is nothing in their behavior — as opposed to their captured propaganda materials — which suggests an objective of breaking out of their Central Luzon confines and attacking military or civilian installations elsewhere. The Huk is indeed a very passive dissident; his *modus vivendi* is convincingly described by Col. Indiongco.

> A Huk today no longer roams wearily and in hunger the jungles, the mountains and the swamps. In fact, he seldom moves around except when he has a mission to perform. He has been accepted as part of the daily existence of our people, particularly those in the rural areas. He lives in the barrios, sometimes in the towns or even in the city. He is one of the "peaceful" citizens there, who does not go to the Mayor but can command the Mayor to come to see him. He is known to the residents, but unknown to the military forces. Seen by the inhabitants, he is faceless to the hunters.

Wearing this magical cloak which makes him visible to his own kind but invisible to the pursuing PC, the Huk coexists with his Central Luzon community.

The primary concern of the Huks is to survive by not tempting fate, by not overreaching themselves, by not provoking repressive actions by the government forces. They thrive, as Col. Indiongco observes, in a lull when they are left to their own devices. Their day-to-day activities include propagandizing wavering barrios, placing their own men in local office, collecting their "share" of rice harvests, and running bingo games.

But they are tough; in the field they are frighteningly efficient. The average Huk packs as much firepower as his opposite number in government uniform, barring the mortars, machineguns and helicopters available to the AFP trooper.

Huk commanders and their bodyguards each carry an M-16, the standard U.S. infantry weapon, and the M-14, (both Vietnam-proven weapons are popularly known throughout the Philippines as "Armalites"). Many of these modern weapons are smuggled in from Saigon; some are spirited out of Clark air force base, close to Angeles City. In at least two recent ambushes perpetrated by the Huks, they used an M-79 grenade launcher. In still another incident near Murcia, Capas, Tarlac, the Huks showed devastating firepower. They blew a vehicle out of the road, killing all four PC troopers in it.

These deliberate attacks come rarely; they are apparently motivated not so much to inflict a tactical defeat on government forces as to wreak vengeance for some previous outrage. More typically, the Huks go out in force to execute someone on their hate list — a particularly obnoxious landlord, an uncooperative politician, or an identified PC informer. This is pretty small change as guerrilla operations go.

The Huks do fight when they have to. This happens mostly when a ranking commander and his men are caught in a PC cordon and there is no other recourse. The large toll they have exacted on the government side attests to their valor and skill.

Are the Huks Communists?

The AFP's inclination to regard the Huks — or some of their factions — as Communist-oriented is not entirely imaginary. In two separate episodes in their history, sizeable Huk groups were under communist leadership. The original organization was the wartime product of the merged Communist Party of the Philippines and the Pampanga-based Socialist Party. The Politburo directed Huk operations from behind the wings during the Japanese Occupation and openly assumed command in the late forties when an armed confrontation with the Philippine Republic became imminent.

The Huks slipped away from communist control in the late fifties — its assumed leader, Jesus Lava, was a lonely, hunted man without any effective operational control of the Huk remnants. In late 1968, Commander Dante's breakaway faction fell in with Maoist organizers from Manila and for almost a year the Tarlac commander accepted the political direction of the "ideologues."

These circumstances are damning, indeed. Presented with this evidence, public opinion would be led to believe the Huk conspiracy theory. But this is too pat an answer to the Huk enigma. Even at the height of the communist-inspired rebellion in 1950, many Huk commanders did not belong to the party and the overwhelming majority of the rank-and-file were not. In the strongly pro-Huk barrios where an underground civilian council usually organized support for the movement, "there were only a sprinkling of communists, none in a great many barrios."[10] Most of the Huks were fighting for particular reforms and not for the aggrandizement of the Communist Party.

Communist leadership came from outside the Huk milieu — the Central Luzon countryside — and not from within their ranks. Though there were superficially compatible elements in communist advocacy and the peasant grievances, the partnership fizzled. Jesus Lava, Mateo del Castillo, Casto Alejandrino and the professed communists could not hold on to power. "Amado Guerrero", the chairman of the "reestablished" CPP, later fell out with Dante.[11]

Huk Leadership

Written platforms are often insignificant as sources of information about the nature of Philippine political organizations. It is more revealing to judge organizations by the character of their leaders and their demonstrated behavior. The real leaders sprang from the very soil that still gives sustenance to the movement. Pedro Abad Santos, the ascetic philosopher from San Fernando, was one of the true leaders. Pedro Taruc, Sumulong and many of the contemporary Huk activists still swear by him. Luis Taruc, Eusebio Aquino and Silvestre Liwanag were the leaders the Pampanga peasants remained loyal to — not the haughty intellectuals that dominated their highest councils.

When he was running his Angeles organization, Sumulong was something of an aberration. He was in many ways a product of his environment, the commercialization of Angeles City.

---

[10]Indiongco, as cited.

[11]The active partnership between Dante's Huks and the Maoist students was reported to have broken up early in 1970. These accounts could not be absolutely verified but there is corroborative evidence: there has been a sharp drop in Maoist propaganda from Tarlac, there was no visible Huk support for radical student demonstrations in Manila from January to March, 1970. The "Maoist" army the PC was pursuing at this time was virtually non-existent.

But there is another older type of Huk leader. He is a reformist, a sentimentalist and a romantic. The mold, it seems, was set by the first and probably still the greatest of the Huk leaders, Luis Taruc. He chose not to conform to the Leninist mold of a professional revolutionary and was an essentially non-violent agitator whose passion for reform was stirred by the sufferings of his fellow Pampangos. For deviating from the party he was stripped of top command by his more steely Politburo colleagues.

In his "true" autobiography, "He Who Rides the Tiger," Taruc relates his almost idyllic retreat in the mountains. The passage describes the sentimental nature of Taruc better than anything ever written about him.[12]

> Often, I would start from camp with the intention of hunting deer, wild pigs, wild chickens, or wild cats, but would end up hunting plants and insects instead. I love to search for the Waling-waling orchid, the most beautiful of our wild orchids, and our famous Philippine butterflies, which are found in the vastness of the Sierra Madre mountains, in Southern Luzon.
>
> My hunting trips were especially frequent in 1949.
>
> During that year I never missed going out at least once a week. I would stay out alone the whole day, deep in the heart of the forest.
>
> No matter how late in the day I stayed, I seldom grew hungry. Sometimes I was lucky and bagged a wild chicken or a big bird, which I would pluck then roast over a bonfire. . . I would sit on a flat, moss-covered rock and lean against the cool side of another, camouflaged by the lush vegetation that grew all around me. There I felt at peace with the world. I would stay for hours, munching my roast chicken to the last scrap, feasting my eyes on the wonders of nature.

Taruc drew the ire of his colleagues for communing with nature while the revolution was in full swing. But it was Taruc, not the Lavas, who captured the imagination of the Central Luzon peasantry. Though Taruc is now a pardoned man and peacefully propagandizing for reform as a spokesman of the Christian Social Movement (CSM), he could well

---

[12]*He Who Rides the Tiger* (New York, Praeger, 1967) is substantially the writing of Luis Taruc during his prison term. He mailed the manuscript to Douglas Hyde, the reformed English Communist who scrupulously retained the essential Taruc. The earlier Taruc book, *Born of the People,* is considered the less representative of the man's true feelings. It was generously edited by Jose Lava and some ideological portions were actually written and inserted into the text by William Pomeroy, an American Communist who joined the Huk rebellion.

be more of a "true Huk" than the other Politburo members still in prison.

The breed has been represented in the sixties by Huk commanders like Delio (Zacarias de la Cruz), Freddie (Efren Lopez) and Dante (Bernabe Buscayno). They shared essentially the same characteristics. They were peasant-born and strongly identified with their class. They stuck to the straight and narrow in their office, declining personal enrichment and the comforts of accommodation.

The breed is in great danger of extinction. Delio and Freddie were killed in a little over a year's time under strangely similar circumstances. They were trapped by the PC in Bataan while trying to organize a potential opposition to Sumulong's empire in Angeles City.

In 1969 and 1970 Dante was the most hunted fugitive. It seemed almost a matter of time before he too shared the fate of Delio and Freddie. His crime for the record was illegal association with declared revolutionaries. But one suspects that his real transgression was in defying the self-aggrandizing political forces in Central Luzon — both within and without the movement.

The Huk Followership

While some sparks of ideological motivation can be seen in Huk leaders, the rank-and-file is expertly assessed as a motley and generally uninspiring lot. Alfredo Saulo, former Education Department chief, described the Huks in 1967 as a "strange conglomeration of oldtime idealist reformers, communists, farmers who are so poor they have decided to join the movement to assure themselves of three meals a day, persons with pending criminal cases in court and plain gangsters who have found it extremely profitable to operate their protection rackets in the name of the Huk organization."[13]

A well-decorated PC provincial commander, Lt. Col. Jose B. Gutierrez, had an even more unedifying regard for the common Huk recruits. In his response to Col. Indiongco's survey questionaire, he described them as "a mixture of the unemployed, disgruntled and dissatisfied peasants, fugitives of the law, opportunists and adventurers who seek the joy and thrill of living on somebody's work and perspiration...

[13]"The Huk Movement — A Historical background and Its Present Status," written for *The Challenge of Central Luzon*, a Report by the Committee on National Defense and Security submitted by Senator Manuel Manahan to the Senate during the Second Regular Session, Sixth Congress of the Philippines, May, 1967, p. 8. Subsequently cited as the Manahan report.

unprincipled men whose primary mission is not to sacrifice personal convenience and luxuries for the sake of a legitimate cause but to promote selfish personal ends at the expense of the less fortunate."

Many Huks, undoubtedly would answer to Col. Gutierrez's scathing description. But some would not; the Huks who fell with Freddie knew how to die. Outnumbered and outgunned, they fought with their doomed leaders rather than surrender.

Many of those in the field today are extremely young, some in their teens. Some are "second-generation" Huks whose fathers or older relatives were members of the organization.

As Sen. Benigno Aquino, Jr. brought out at a recent Senate hearing, the Huks tend to fit five descriptions: they are jobless, fugitives from the law for varying reasons — not necessarily political — relatives or *kababaryo* (barriomates) of former Huks, with grievances against the authorities, and Pampangos.[14]

A University of the Philippines scholar attempted to break down the Huk membership according to the motivational types suggested by Max Webber.[15] This was a reference to the 1950 Huks, but there is no evidence that the types of Huk rank-and-file active today have substantially changed.

Very few followers fell under the "value-national" category which comprises those with full understanding and conviction of Communist principles. There were probably more followers who can be properly classified as "emotional-affectual" — those responding to motives of vengeance and personal attachments. A large number were in the "traditional" group who might not have any personal score to settle or convictions of righteousness, but were following in the footsteps of fathers, brothers and other relatives. Dante himself might have been originally a "traditional" follower since his father was a Huk. Simbulan offers the examples as well of Eusebio Aquino, a distant nephew of a Philippine Revolution general who, together with his four sons, joined Luis Taruc.

The Huk 'Ideology'

There are no convincing arguments in support of the suspicion that the Huk membership responds to doctrinaire com-

[14]Hearings of Senate ad hoc committee investigating peace and order in Central Luzon, July 28, 1970. See also Chapter 12.

[15]Dante Simbulan, *The Socialist Movement in the Philippines,* an unpublished Master of Arts thesis submitted to the University of the Philippines, Quezon City, Philippines, September 30, 1960.

munism. Huks are commonly recruited from the barrios where the average educational attainment is in the early grades. It takes a fairly sophisticated man to comprehend the fundamental principles of Marxism-Leninism.

Dominador Garcia, alias Commander Ely, stopped formal schooling at Grade One because of the war and poverty. He claimed he had discovered the Communist character of the movement only shortly before his capture. He believed that the movement was "nationalistic" and that open warfare with the government was to be avoided while it was still trying to win mass sympathy.[16]

Luis Taruc had obviously poor expectations of ideological responsiveness from his own men. "There is not even one percent who have Communist mentality in them," he said.[17]

Captured Huks seem to understand Communism mainly in terms of the confiscation of land from oppressive landlords and its distribution to the tenants and the destruction of "imperialistic" and "foreign" elements in the country.

"Our Basic Program," an educational tract put out by the Lavas' organization in 1952, indicates the rudimentary level on which the movement was trying to indoctrinate its members.[18] "What is our program? Firstly, the rural program is revolutionary. The first objective is to liquidate all big landlords who own vast lands and who mercilessly oppress the peasants." The lesson discriminated between those whose lands were to be confiscated and those exempt from the fiat.

Lands to be seized included whose owned by "imperialists," be they "Americans, Spaniard, Chinese and others," those belonging to the "enemies of the people, whoever they are," friar lands, lands more than 10 hectares in size, and "all uncultivated lands after one year we assume to power." To be spared from confiscation were "all lands belonging to those who help satisfactorily the successful prosecution of the revolution, all lands belonging to schools and hospitals" and "all lands less than 10 hectares" provided they are cultivated.

The primary concern of this agrarian movement was with land, understandably enough. There were apparently as many personalistic and vindictive motives in deciding the future disposition of land as there were those acceptably ideological. When the apparent contradiction between the Huk policy of "land for the landless" and that of collective ownership was brought to the attention of Jose Lava, he replied, "Since the peasants do not understand the benefits of collec-

---

[16]The Manahan report, p. 19.

[17]Quoted by Simbulan, cited work.

[18]Fortunato L. Crisologo, *The Present Educational Practices of the Huks,* an unpublished M. Ed. thesis submitted to the University of the Philippines Graduate School, March, 1963.

tive ownership you have to cater to their backward thinking."[19]

In 1969, Rand Corporation researchers interviewed 12 captured Huks to determine their motivation and their understanding of their mission and organization. The responses were obviously not very helpful. All the subjects, for instance, claimed they received only food and a cigarette allowance of 29 pesos (about $7) a month from the organization. "It seems unlikely that 29 pesos would be enough of a motive for anyone to risk his life and freedom," Rand commented skeptically.

"Typical quotations" from four of the subjects included the following:

> We have group meetings and in said meetings, were lectured to by the commander. We were told that the Philippine Government is not bad, and it is only the administrators of said government that ought to be changed. Changes could be affected either by elections or violence if need be.
>
> ...the main enemies of the HMB's are, first: the local exploiters who suck the blood of the common *tao* so as to enrich themselves; the people in the government who commit graft and corruption and all sorts of anomalies just to entrench themselves in power; those people who serve as stool-pigeons for the above-mentioned personalities, and secondly, those foreigners who drain our rich natural resources, export it to other countries and bring it back as finished products and sell it beyond the reach of the common people. Most of these aliens are the Americans. They were what we called American imperialists.[20]

Rand observed that though the statements resembled those in early Vietcong documents, they uniquely do not attack the government as an institution. "Only the people in the institution are attacked," according to Rand. These observations are reminiscent of the admissions of Luis Taruc and Jose Lava that the ideological grasp of the Huk rank-and-file was scanty. The doctrine handed down to these Huks by their commanders is apparently a watered-down version of socialism, tailored to appeal to their personal grievances.[21]

---

[19]Quoted by Crisologo, cited work.

[20]Rand report, pp. 217-218.

[21]It must be noted that all but three of Huks interviewed by Rand were from the command of Freddie, the most celebrated young "ideologue" in the movement before he was killed and his intellectual's role taken over by Dante. This would suggest that the better indoctrinated Huks were somewhat overrepresented by the interviews. The Huks loyal to Sumulong might have responded quite differently.

A clearer picture of the Huks thus emerges but to complete the profile it is important to investigate the environment in which the Huks operate.

Chapter Two

THE ECOLOGY OF DISSIDENCE

Like estimates of Huk manpower, most calculations of the Huk mass base are highly conjectural. Only the most powerful politicians and the least intimidated citizens can express themselves freely on this sensitive subject. This constraint, however, has not discouraged the PC from making periodic estimates of the Huk mass base.

According to Table 1, the mass base has been increasing since 1965 roughly in proportion with comparative increases of the Huk regulars, (for every Huk regular there are indicated from 100 to 150 mass base supporters).

In October 1969, the *Herald* correspondents drew a rough chart of barrios and towns influenced by the Huks. It was empirically constructed, from talks with barrio captains and manifestations of Huk activities, and with the help of PC intelligence. The map showed almost three-fourths of Pampanga barrios, two-thirds of Tarlac and smaller proportions of Nueva Ecija and Bulacan settlements under "Huk influence." Huk "control" was harder to determine for it leaned heavily on the relative balance of forces between Huk sympathizers and the government.[1]

Judging from the *Herald* estimates, the Huk "invisible government" is supported by a popular base as large as 85,000 –– about one-seventh of the total number of voters in Nueva Ecija, Tarlac and Pampanga.[2]

---

[1]The Rand Report defined a "controlled" barrio as one "where full time HMB are reported frequently and where they are willing to sleep." An "influenced" barrio is where the HMB are frequently seen but where they do not sleep. p. 204.

[2]The Huk mass base might have been significantly reduced in early 1970 due to the creation by the AFP of "barrio self-defense units" in the formerly Huk-controlled villages. "Control" seems to be an ephemeral thing based on the strength of the AFP or the Huks in the locality at any one time.

Col. Bienvenido Castro, comanding officer of the 10th Battalion Combat Team, told the author that Calulut, a barrio of San Fernando, Pampanga, used to be "150 percent" Huk while Commander Canor ruled the roost there. When Canor and his superior, the even more dreaded Commander Tapang, were killed within two days, the barrio "went to our side completely."

One-seventh is small compared to the rest of the voting population of Central Luzon. From this proportion, it can be assumed that the great majority of residents in those three provinces are either indifferent or opposed to the Huk movement, which make the Huks and their sympathizers a minority in their own areas.

The 14 percent Huk sympathy in Central Luzon — granting the reasonable correctness of this estimate — is comparable to measured support across the nation for "radical politics." A survey commissioned by Sen. Helena Benitez revealed that 9.93 percent of Filipinos were receptive to reform through violence. The respondents in that category broke down into 15.82 percent of all Filipino students, 17.81 percent of Greater Manila residents, and 11.37 percent of all residents outside Manila.[3] It would seem that Central Luzon's tendency to play host to radical movements is not unusual since a comparable degree of discontent is palpable in other areas of the Philippines. The difference in Central Luzon is that unrest takes an active, violent form which is not perceptible elsewhere.

The Huk "base" includes peasants exposed to dissident influence, professionals such as doctors and lawyers who offer their services free to members of the movement, petty politicians and even some big ones who exchange their patronage for Huk "endorsement" at the polls.

The typical peasant contribution is one cavan of rice (worth about ₱15 or $2.50) every harvest. A calesa driver chips in a humble five centavos (less than one cent) a day. But there are tens of thousands of such farmers and workers within the Huk finance system and all those centavos amount to a pretty figure at the end of the year.

Huk influence has spread to the middle and upper classes of Central Luzon. Helping finance the Huk "understructure" are business firms, certain subdivision operators, landlords and nightclub, bar and jeepney drivers associations.

Communal and Kinship Ties

The Huks derive their strongest support from their own kin, neighbors and barriomates. This system of mutual dependency is a traditional function of the Philippine social structure. It is nowhere more true according to Col. Indiongco, himself a native of Pampanga, than in the Huk areas. In the barrios, people have learned to build up personal bases

[3] Jose P. de Jesus and Jose C. Benitez. *Sources of Social Unrest*, The Citizenship and Research Foundation, Inc., Manila, 1970, p. 108.

of cooperation. To plant rice seedlings, to harvest the grain, to transfer a nipa shack, to obtain credit, one needs the help of kith and kin. In Central Luzon, which has been continuous agrarian strife since the 1920's, the barrio ties are more crucial to life and survival.

The Huk-supporter relationship is innately fraternal; they call each other *kapatad* (brother) or *kayabe* (comrade), titles with powerful emotional charge. The man who does not involve himself, or give aid and comfort to the Huks denies the value of communal life.

By the *Herald's* estimate in late 1969, seven out of 10 residents in Huk-controlled barrios had the "Huk spirit."[4] The Huk spirit is basically an "us against them" identification. "They" are the PC, the city-slicker land reformists, do-gooders trying to win peasant favor, and the rest of the "outsiders" who continue to "misunderstand" Central Luzon.

Another factor helps explain the steadfast support the HMB enjoys from the rural populace. A simple-minded barrio dweller considers it a great honor to be of service to the dissidents. "If it were not a privilege to see and talk with top Huk commanders, Manila newsmen would not be outdoing each other trying to talk first with Commander Sumulong," said an Angeles City councilor.

Being a trusted member of the circle of "Huk friends," the civilian enjoys a sense of personal power and a psychological leverage over other citizens who do not have Huk connections.

"Why can't the Armed Forces get this group of 300 or so hardcore Huks and solve the Central Luzon problem once and for all?" people ask. That is impossible, a Huk sympathizer explained, "because the military authorities and their agents do not even know these Huks and would not be able to identify them."

Then who knows the Huks? Who could identify them? Only the members of the mass base support — the village dwellers and trusted leaders of the Huk-controlled commu-

---

[4]This again is admittedly a "guesstimate." No known methodology has been devised to measure accurately the popularity or unpopularity of the Huks in the Central Luzon barrios. The Rand Corporation used exclusively Filipino interviewers from the Asia Research Organization in polling its Central Luzon sample barrios but this did not apparently reduce the likelihood of "respondent bias."

It is possible that the simple farmer regards anybody asking questions and noting answers down on a clipboard as "from the government." He may then slant his responses according to what he thinks the interviewer likes to hear.

nities — know the wanted Huks. Those who know the Huks and who tell on them usually pay with their lives.

No barrio captain has yet tried to turn Dante in. In late May, 1970, the AFP went over every inch of ground in Capas and Concepcion with helicopters and armored cars, but Dante gave them the slip each time (if he, indeed, was in the area). A mere hint from any of the Tarlacqueños in the area might have given the youthful Huk leader away. But none did.

The inviolability of the fraternal bonds between the Huks and their neighbors explains why Huk commanders rarely assume territorial responsibility outside of the places where they were born and raised — e.g., Sumulong in the Porac-Angeles area, Dante in Capas-Concepcion-La Paz. Outside of their normal haunts, they are not safe.

A case in point is Comamnder Zaragoza (Hermogenes Buco) who was captured in front of the Pasig (Rizal) cathedral on Sept. 15, 1970 after eluding a PC dragnet in his native eastern Pampanga.[5]

The Aggrieved

At the root of the dissident problem, deeper even than any ideology, is anger over accumulated grievances. The court records do not even begin to indicate the breakdown of human relations in these provinces. In February, 1967, according to the Manahan report, there were 650 agrarian cases in Nueva Ecija, 391 in Bulacan, 205 in Tarlac, 178 in Pampanga, 188 in Pangasinan and 74 in Bataan. There were 9,345 criminal and civil cases pending before 29 judicial salas.

The *Herald* team was told that many grievants no longer bothered to seek justice in court. Pampanga's crime dockets are surprisingly empty although for a long time, in the late 1960's, people were getting killed every week.

Out of frustration, some peasants take their complaints to the Huks since their justice is faster. Many sympathizers are personally obligated to the Huks in one way or another. According to a former Huk, the organization has "adjudicated" hundreds of cases brought to them by the peasants. They include tenancy problems, theft, landlord abuses, marital difficulties, banditry, and seduction and rape.

A fraction of Huk support has a score to settle against the military. They or their kin have been brutalized, terrorized and tortured. They want their vengeance.

Down some village streets of Central Luzon, men are huddled by the barrio stores over bottles of gin or jars of tuba (native wine). They talk in whispers.

---

[5]Philippines *Herald*, Sept. 18, 1970.

In the group is one man who dominates the discussion. He usually talks of how hard life has been for those poor people, of the poor harvest, of the irrigation pump that was promised but never delivered, of the pre-fab school that was also promised but was never built. That man is a Huk agitator. The menfolk gather around him as he narrates a litany of government failures and explains why the poor will remain neglected and abandoned for the rest of their lives. He also attacks the crooks in the government.

Soon the group will be adding their own sad experiences with the shortcomings of democracy. The speaker says that unless this established order is toppled and a new system of government replaces it, nothing good will ever come to the poor. "But if we fight, we can achieve our rightful share of this rich country," the man perorates.

In Central Luzon there are hundreds of this kind of agitator, and the mass believes him.

Thousands of barrio poor now speak in this manner. They dream — foolishly perhaps — of a new social order in which all citizens will be equally poor or equally rich.

This fantasy of a new life, a better social order, has become the defense mechanism of the rural nightmare of poverty. The Huks are cleverly giving that vision a form.

The Fearful

Though not necessarily sympathetic to the Huks, many barrio folk lack the courage to defy the agitators. The PC troops come and go; the Huks stay in the barrio.

The Huks project their organization as more efficient, stable and enduring despite frequent changes in the HMB leadership. "The government sends us barrio workers and other teams. It sends all the land reform and agricultural agents. In one day they are pulled out," said a barrio captain. "But the Huks remain with us."

The military is convinced that various business enterprises in Central Luzon are victims of Huk taxation. A local businessman explains why: "When agents of the government who are supposed to protect your interest become the very extortionists, you must look for protection elesewhere. The Huks provide that protection."

In Manila and elsewhere, businessmen complain about abusive exactions of Bureau of Internal Revenue examiners. In contrast is the fact that no businessman in Central Luzon has raised a voice against BIR or Bureau of Labor inspectors. The reason is clear: Government collectors are afraid of swift Huk reprisals.

Asked what he thought of a people's revolution, an Arayat peasant said in the dialect: "It is like a trail in that Arayat mountain, at first there was no trail, but when we started walking on it, the path came into existence."

When the PC is not using counter-terror tactics to reduce Huk influence, the Central Luzon countryside is generally peaceful. Petty criminality and hooliganism — police problems in big cities — are rare in the Huk-infested provinces outside of Angeles City, which is normally a swinging and busy place as any R and R town. Robbers, pick-pockets, extortionists, gangsters and misbehaving ex-convicts are picked up by the Huks for "rehabilitation."

Sources in several Pampanga barrios report that after the first "night trial," recidivists mend their ways quickly. A typical rehabilitation starts with the rousing of the suspect from his house. He is taken to a secluded field where an open grave awaits. The Huks make him kneel before the gaping hole where two shovels are visible. He is ordered to swear not to repeat his violation. Another would lead to his "liquidation."

There are no rules of court to complicate adjudications. Every trial is simplified by the "yes" or "no" verdict of the civilian jury, composed of elders and the officials of the local cadres.

Government as Scapegoat

The revolutionary pride of former Huk commanders (circa 1950) discouraged civilians from receiving government-sponsored barrio projects. Having learned from past mistakes, the movement now tells the populace to take advantage of what the government is offering. It even helps prepare plans to get these quickly. It is believed that in Tarlac and Pampanga, the Huk organizations even provide "counterpart" manpower and money for self-help projects or grants-in-aid given by government agencies to the barrio councils.

While there is no sustained effort by the government to win over the masses, the Huks carry on a ceaseless psywarfare among the barrio people who are convinced that without the dissidents, not a single bridge or road would be constructed in their places. If the Huks commit anarchy, this is all to their advantage.

Riding on this propaganda bandwagon, the Huks get the credit for all government-sponsored projects in the barrios. Thus people think the land reform program was born because of Huk insurgency.

A priority plan of the dissidents is to uplift the living standards in the barrios and to increase the income of the farmers. The Huks in Pampanga encourage the peasants to avail of the services of farm management technicians and government credit officers.

This is apparently intended to boost farm income and consequently, the tax return to the Huk organizations. No farmer, however, will admit giving a share of his harvest to the Huks.

The Huks involve civilians in decisions affecting popular welfare. That is the real strength of the HMB organization among the residents. Will the town celebrate its fiesta this year, or will it undertake a *pabasa* (prayer meeting)? Which of the profferred development projects will they have first — the school building or the roads? Will they like the construction of the bridges first or the irrigation ditches? "We want to have all of these," the barrio captains tell the dissidents, "but the agencies concerned can not provide all of them at the same time."

"All right, let us draw up a plan," the Huk commander tells the mayor.

Surprisingly, without delay, provincial officials, other town mayors, and government agency heads appear on the scene to make a survey of priority projects. They talk with the civilian and barrio officials.

True to expectations, succeeding events see the fulfillment of all projects. In the first week, a prefab school building is put up. Labor is provided by barrio residents with the aid of the dissidents who also help raise the cash.

The next week, as projected, a feeder road is built. In another barrio, an irrigation system is started. Meanwhile, productivity experts and credit officials are helping hundreds of farmers prepare their farm plan budgets and loan schedules.

The succeeding days bring Army medical and health teams. The army dentist fixes the broken denture of a hardcore Huk while the barrio residents stand by watching in good humor.

Not all the barrio people, of course, take the Huk exactions in good spirit. A councilman of a BSDU protected barrio in Magalang told former Defense Undersecretary Alejandro Melchor why he resented the Huks. "We work hard and the Huks do not. When they come, they want the best food — chicken and eggs and not just the *gulay* (vegetables) and sardines that is our usual food. We have to give what they ask because we cherish our lives. When election time comes they ask us to vote for whoever gives them money," the councilman said.[6]

Dynamics of Huk Control

The Rand Corporation conducted an interesting study to determine what variables contribute most to Huk "control" of barrios. The variables examined included current Huk-related incidents, land ownership, the presence of sugar cultivation and the fraction of Pampangos in the barrio populations. Tenancy was not established as a significant variable. Contrary to Huk mythology, Rand suggested that barrios with a large fraction of their land devoted to sugar plantations have a "lower probability of being controlled than other barrios."

Rand concluded that Huk dissidence continues to exist because of a "self-perpetuating organization." "Perhaps the orignal reasons for its geographical location were social and economical but, given a cohesive organization, we argue that the coercion and terror account for HMB presence and control, and not social unrest."

Using simultaneous estimation techniques, Rand pinpointed HMB operations and liquidations in a time series on a map of Central Luzon and came up with an "expanding doughnut" model (see Figure 2). Between 1961 and 1964, most of the HMB incidents occurred in a 30-kilometer radius from the Arayat-Angeles area, which was assumed to be the center of Huk activity. In the following two years, 1965-67, the larger portion of the incidents were traced in a belt 40 kilometers away from the center. The center and the areas beyond the belt were relatively free of incidents. In 1967-68, the incidence-prone belt was extended to 50 kilometers away. The model suggests that HMB-induced violence occurs only when an area is being disputed and that the incidence belt expands outward from the already "controlled" areas.[7]

The nature of the Huks is now beginning to emerge. The Huks do not constitute a communist conspiracy, nor are they an insurrectionary band out to topple the government. They assume dissident roles only in their own terrain, in most cases the barrios and immediate neighborhood where they were born. They do not normally overextend beyond these sanc-

[6]The then Defense Undersecretary Melchor helicoptered to barrio San Isidro, Magalang, to inspect its self-defense unit. The councilman spoke at a reception in his honor, with officers of the 10th BCT present. The councilman might not have been able to speak otherwise.

[7]Rand report, pp. 208-214.

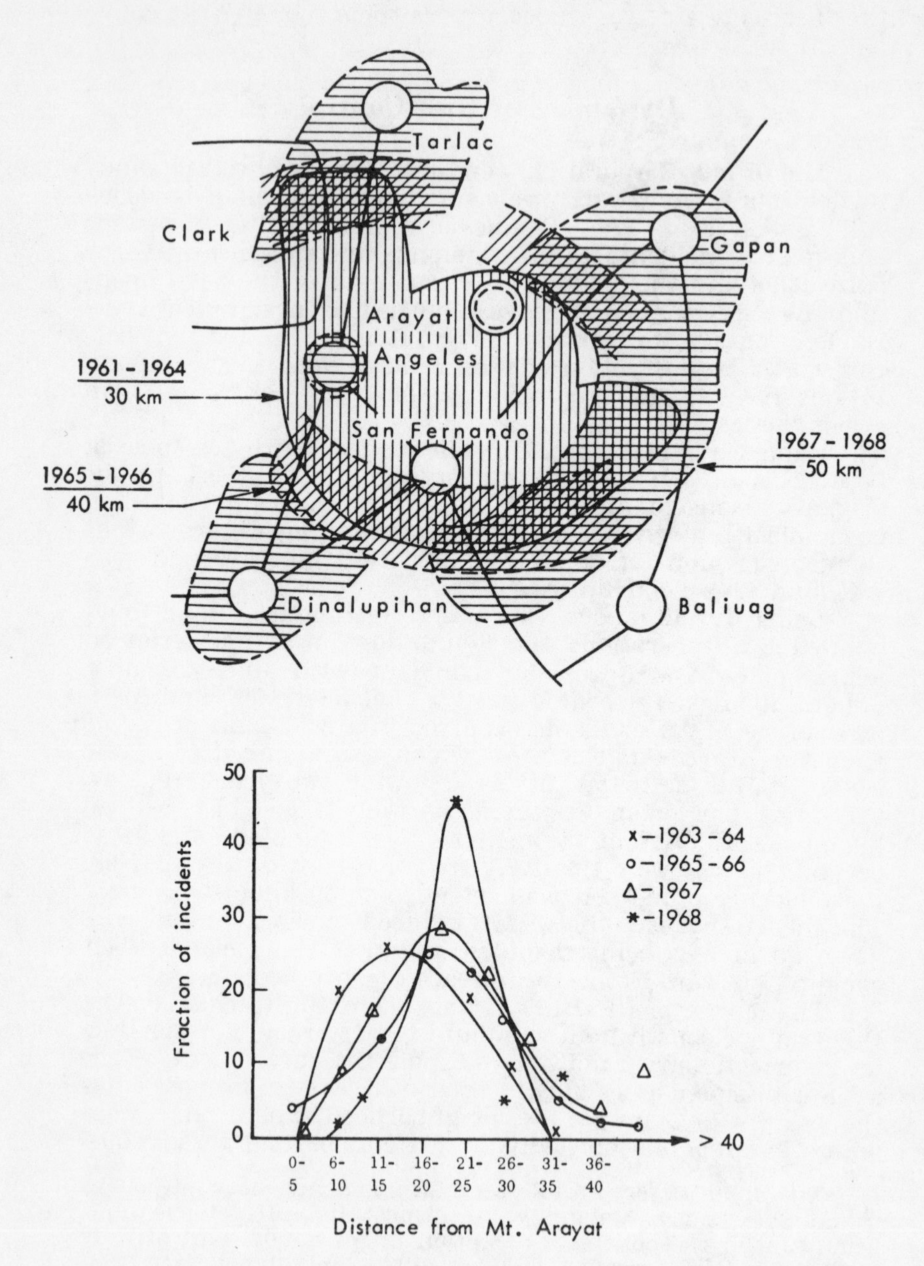

Figure 2: Pattern of Huk liquidations, the "expanding dough-nut" model from the Rand Report.

tuaries unless there are native-born leaders there ready to take charge. Given these constraints, the Huks are not an expansionist force which has to be "contained."

The Huks exist because the conditions that make their brand of dissidence possible still exist — marginal security in the barrios, alienation of the peasants from established authority, constant failures of the government. But a most important observation is that the Huks are almost exclusively found in the Pampango-speaking areas.

Chapter Three

THE BREAKDOWN OF AN AGRARIAN SOCIETY

The areas of Huk influence are almost entirely within the agricultural lands settled by the remarkable Pampangos. This dissidence does not extend into the first district of Tarlac which is predominantly Ilocano, or deeper into the mountains of Zambales where Aetas and Ilocanos live, or far south into Bulacan where Tagalog is mainly spoken. Elsewhere, there is little or no Huk-style dissidence. Elsewhere, the contagion does not "catch" except momentarily.

The Huks or their promoters have tried many times to multiply their numbers in non-Pampango-speaking areas. During World War II, they tried to invade the Ilocano and Tagalog municipalities but failed to make any significant gains. During the 1950 rebellion, the Huks sent their agit-prop units as far north as Ilocos Norte and Cagayan, and as far south as Panay island. They were reportedly active in Abra, Ilocos Sur, Isabela, La Union, Nueva Vizcaya and the Mountain Province in the north; in Bataan, Batangas, Cavite, Rizal, and Quezon in the Tagalog region and in the Bicol province of Camarines Sur.[1]

Even then, their proselytizing failed and the Huks were forced to retreat to their native habitat. They encountered the traditional obstruction of regionalism. While the Philippines is ethnically homogenous, there are eight or more major lingual groups and there are other distinct variations in social customs, traits and attitudes. This may partly account for the failure of Pampango-speaking agitators to win over the *sacadas* in Negros and, except in isolated instances, the Tagalog-speaking barrio folk in Laguna and Batangas.

This astonishing symbiotic relationship between the dissidents and their home base is the focus of this study. There must be something in their native ecology that sustains them, some baleful combination of geography, language and social history that makes that region dissident-prone.

What is that determinant?

This is a question that should be more thoroughly ex-

---

[1]Saulo, as cited, p. 57.

plored.[2] Unfortunately, there is a scarcity of comparative data relevant to this inquiry. To construct a formal body of knowledge on dissidence in the Philippines, it may be gainful to look at the Central Luzon problem afresh and dig into its history, its geomorphology, social organizations and leadership potential for more helpful clues.

The persistent unrest in Central Luzon has inspired an impressive outflow of journalism, contemporary history and social commentary in the past two decades. This literature has advanced various reasons for the phenomenon, most of which tend to be intuitive and experiential in nature.

Much of the literature on the Huks has been written from unavoidably limited viewpoints. The military chroniclers record battles won and lost, Huk commanders killed and captured, the tactics and strategies employed by the combatants. The academic specialists have dug into their own "bags."

Some admirable first-hand accounts have been written by reconstructed former Huks, the most notable being Luis Taruc and Alfredo Saulo. Both address themselves to a political cause that failed. The marches and retreats of communism and socialism resound through their works, as if indeed Central Luzon merely provides a stage on which the essential Marxist drama is enacted.

The most informed writings on Central Luzon tend to overplay the role of politics or the deterministic circumstances of the "land problem." These interpretations are quite relevant indeed, but to attribute the Central Luzon to either or even to both alone may discourage further investigation into other precipitating causes.

Saulo, for instance ascribes Huk dissidence to that one cause:

> The Huk problem is none other than the land problem. It is truly the problem of the century because ever since the Spaniards in the 17th century instituted their *encomienda* system whereby large tracts of land were given to individual Spaniards in the Philippines in recognition of their services to the Spanish crown, Filipino farmers have been agitating and petitioning the government to give them lands. When in the latter part of the Spanish rule the *encomiendas* were broken up into haciendas in recognition of the growing power of the landed gentry,

---

[2]The Rand Corporation study attributes Central Luzon dissidence to a "self-perpetuating organization" but is does not go one step further to explain why Huk-style organizations have not prospered in other areas outside of Central Luzon

there arose an increasing clamor for the expropriation of big landed estates and their distribution to bonafide tenants.[3]

Luis Taruc, a true champion of the Pampango masses, makes a similar brief:

> Thus, for centuries, "land for the landless" has been the peasants' cry, and the peasants' hunger for land has been our nation's most pressing problem. This has led to the common saying among our people that social justice can be achieved only by one of two ways: either a land reform or revolution. Our history of the past four centuries is one of successive uprisings and their basic cause has always been the peasants' hunger for land.[4]

It is understandable that Taruc's and Saulo's perceptions of their society should be shaped by their experiences and deeply held political convictions. The political-reformist bias is indeed almost typical of the special pleaders who have taken to the press and the journals in behalf of Central Luzon.

It has already been seen how communism as an expansionist ideology could not have had more than an incidental role in the shaping of Central Luzon dissidence. There is need in fact to reassess the importance given by Western scholars to the so-called "communist threat" in Southeast Asia.

Western impressions of dissident movements in Asia could well be biased by the demonstrated success of the Chinese war of national liberation. If Mao's revolution could convert China into the largest Communist country in the world, its export to the neighboring Southeast Asian countries could well have the same devastating effect. Chinese scholars, however, are careful about advancing any single preemptive cause for the Chinese revolution. It is not simply a "rural revolution," as Roy Hofheinz suggests. It is part bandwagon, part demonstration, part mobility opportunity, part a path of least frustration — with half the credit going to the Communists themselves.

Preconditions to Social Unrest

The land tenure system is probably the most compelling of the perceived reasons for Pampango unrest. Its roots go back to the 19th century when the expansion of population and farmsteads permitted "the acquisitive, the knowledgeable and the privileged" to use the civil power to legitimize

[3]Manahan report, p. 9.
[4]As cited, p. 12.

landholdings.[5] Though there were sporadic and half-hearted attempts by the American regime and the Philippine Commonwealth government to help the landless, the tenancy rate increased sharply in the 20th century — from 38 percent of Central Plain farms in 1903 to 54 percent shortly before World War II and to 60 percent in 1948. By 1948, some 36 percent of Pampango farms were under some system of tenancy.[6]

The population in the five Central Luzon provinces increased from slightly over one million in 1903 to almost three and a half million in 1960. Unlike the Ilocanos and the Cebuanos, the Pampangos and other Plain people showed no marked tendency to migrate to the urban areas and the less populated lands in Mindanao. Largely, they stayed in their native region, preferring the proven security of their kinship and group relationships to hustling for a living in Manila or the uncertainties of pioneer life in the South.[7]

The population growth had the effect of reducing farm sizes from a cultivated land per capita average of 0.9 acre in 1918 to less than 0.5 acre in 1948.[8]

Figure 3, reprinted from David Reeves Sturtevant's unpublished dissertation, shows the comparative prevalence of tenancy in Central Luzon and surrounding provinces in 1939. Nueva Ecija had the highest percentage of tenancy (67.8 percent), followed by Pampanga (67.0 percent), Bulacan (66.5 percent), Cavite (58.5 percent), Tarlac (52.4 percent), Batangas (47.8 percent), Bataan (46.7 percent) and Laguna (44.0 percent).

The chart indicates a high correlation between tenancy and Huk activism. Four of the five provinces with the highest tenancy rates were in Central Luzon, the cradle of agrarian unrest. Bataan and Laguna, which had moderately high tenancy, had histories of Huk infestation and are still reported to be the objects of politicizing by various radical groups. By comparison, relatively Huk-free areas like the Ilocos, Mountain Province, Quezon and Bicol had substantially lower tenancy rates than Central Luzon.

[5]Frederick L. Wernstedt and J. E. Spencer, *The Philippine Island World* (Berkeley and Los Angeles: The University of California Press, 1967), p. 189.

[6]Same, pp. 189, 373.

[7]Same, p. 373.

[8]Renze Hoeksema in his cited work attributes the cause of unrest specifically to economically undersized farming lots: "The cause of rural poverty and consequent unrest is due to the small area cultivated by the Philippine peasants with consequent low income, high tenancy rates, oppressive land rentals and exhorbitant interest rates."

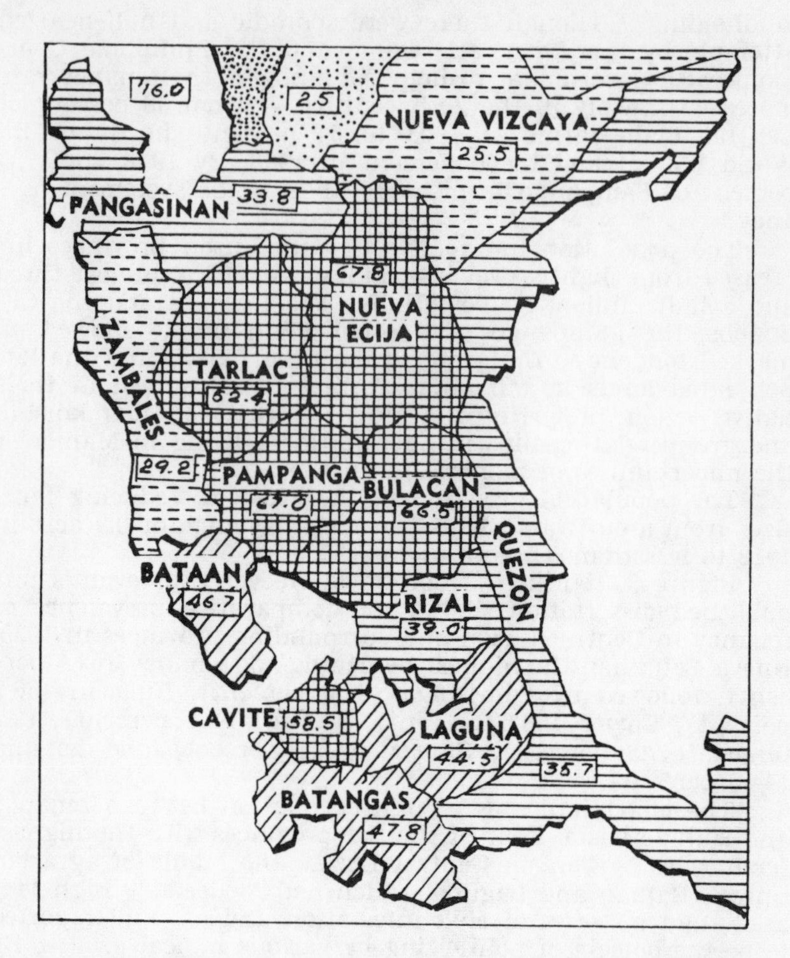

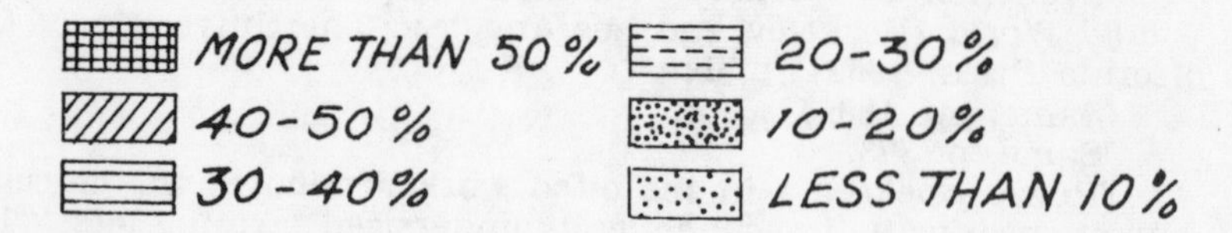

Figure 3: Percentage of Cultivated Land Farmed by Tenants in Central and Southern Luzon, 1939.
From Sturtevant's "Philippine Social Structure and Its Relation to Agrarian Unrest."

Widespread tenancy, however, is not an exclusive feature of Central Luzon. In 1960, the nationwide tenancy average was 50 percent. Serious tenancy problems were also reported in the Batangas peninsula, the Manila hinterland, the Ilocos coast and western Negros island. Even in the "promised land" of Mindanao, Filipino pioneer settlers tended to lapse back into renting small holdings despite the proximity or large tracts of uncultivated lands.[9]

Within the Central Luzon region itself, tenancy alone does not completely explain the relative intensity of dissident activities. For instance, Nueva Ecija has experienced serious landlord-tenant rifts since the thirties, and until mid-1970 was still effectively outside the land reform program. Yet, its dissidence problem is minor compared to the Pampango heartland.

Cavite is a notable variant from the tenancy-Huk correlation. It was No. 4 on Reeves' Luzon scale, yet it has never been endangered by Huk penetration. (Instead of Huks, however, Cavite has its notorious cattle-rustlers and outlaws. A Cavite official told the author that Huks cannot infiltrate his province because the cattle-rustlers would kill them if they did.)[10]

It is doubtful, historically speaking, if "land hunger" had been a truly significant cause of popular rebellions before the turn of the century. The rare uprisings in Spanish-time Pampanga were due to heavy exactions of labor and other infringements on liberties. Some of the bloodiest rebellions elsewhere in the Philippines were the result of religious frenzy. Indeed, Pampanga did not show any real agrarian unrest until the 1910's or 1920's and land ownership was even more concentrated then than now.

Rural poverty is possibly a contributing factor to social unrest, but it is not convincingly the dominant one. Pampanga's towns and countryside do not show widespread and abject poverty.

Pampanga sugar planters claim that their workers are better paid than the *sacadas* (migrant workers) of Negros. Any motorist passing the towns on the MacArthur Highway would see forests of TV antennas in the *poblaciones*. Nobody is obviously starving. If anything, the Central Luzon towns do better trade than a lot of communities in the Ilocos and Cagayan Valley.

Poverty does exist in large areas of Leyte and Samar, but since the 1910's these provinces have not experienced organized dissidence.

---

[9]Wernstedt and Spencer, pp. 190-192.

[10]Interview with Governor Delfin Montano of Cavite, October, 1969.

Philippine census data suggest that Pampanga residents are on the average slightly better off than the average *provinciano.* If urbanization can be considered an indicator of progress, Pampanga is ahead with 35.3 percent of its population in urban areas compared to the national average of 29.9 percent. Bulacan is only 15.9 percent urbanized but this is due to the fact that "a large percentage of the population finds it more profitable to live in the rural areas, preferring to live on their agricultural produce than on wages which they must fiercely compete for in suburban communities." Tarlac is below-average in urbanization, 24.1 percent, which could perhaps predispose it more than Pampanga to rural radicalization.[11]

Rev. Jose Sunga, a Catholic priest born in Masantol, and at various times a minister in Guagua, Angeles and San Fernando, rejected rural poverty as a primary cause of Huk dissidence in his testimony before a congressional committee. "I. . .agree that there is poverty in Pampanga but I have been in many other parts of the Philippines and I believe that the poor Pampangueños are better off than the other poor people in other provinces. It is a common belief that Pampangueños, including the peasants, dress better and eat better than many other people."[12]

The belief that Central Luzon unrest is due to the "ignorance" of the masses is not statistically supportable. According to the 1960 census, Central Luzon has higher literacy rates than the national average. Pampanga is 78.8 percent literate (83.7 percent have had some formal education) compared to the national average of 72 percent. Bulacan has an even higher literacy, 85.6 percent; Bataan has 82.9 percent; and Nueva Ecija 80 percent. Zambales has the fourth highest literacy (86.5 percent) among the 56 provinces of the Philippines, while Tarlac has the lowest among the Central Luzon provinces, 75 percent, though even that is still three percent above the national average.[13]

Pampangos are not only better educated than the average Filipino, but are probably more aware of political developments because of the relative proximity of Manila and the accessibility of mass media. The converse of the mass igno-

[11]Socio-economic provincial profiles of Pampanga and Tarlac prepared by the Presidential Economic Staff, Office of the President, Republic of the Philippines, 1969. Subsequently cited as PES profiles.

[12]Hearings of the Committee on Social Amelioration, Congress of the Philippines, presided over by Rep. Emilio Espinosa, committee chairman, Feb. 26, 1970. Subsequently cited as the Espinosa committee hearings.

[13]PES profiles.

rance theory may be more applicable. The above-average literacy of the Pampangos heightens their social and political awareness, and consequently makes them more receptive to Huk agitation.

A Revolutionary Tradition?

Jose Lava, Luis Taruc and other advocates have often harked back to the "revolutionary tradition" of Pampanga. There is some validity to this claim. A few leading families of Pampanga and Tarlac — the Alejandrinos of Arayat, the Hizons of Mexico, Pampanga, the Aquinos of Concepcion, the Hilarios and Abad Santoses of San Fernando — they all contributed leadership to the Philippine Revolution that inflamed the Tagalog region in 1896. The towns of eastern Pampanga were in close communication with the Bulacan communities affected by the nationalist movement. Their menfolk filled the ranks of General Aguinaldo's army during the Philippine-American war. Luis Taruc sees a straight line of "revolutionary development" from Andres Bonifacio's Katipunan of 1896 to the prewar *Aguman ding Maldang Talapagobra* (AMT) to the Huk armies of the 1940's and 1950's.

But the point can be overdrawn. There is nothing in Pampanga's recorded past beyond the turn of the century that specially qualified the province to be a hotbed of revolution. Before 1896, Pampanga was relatively stable compared to other provinces. There were more violent uprisings against the Spanish authority in the Ilocos, Pangasinan, Leyte and Bohol than anything ever recorded in Pampanga. And, of course, the most notorious anti-Establishmentarians of that time were the Moros of Mindanao and Sulu, who never considered themselves conquered by the sword and the cross of Spain.

The Tagalog-speaking provinces — Bulacan, Cavite and Laguna — are far more deserving to be called the cradle of revolutionary nationalism than Pampanga. The Philippine revolution of 1896 was essentially a Tagalog insurrection.

While there were some Pampangos in *rayodillo,* it was largely a Tagalog army that fought with General Aguinaldo against the Americans. The most celebrated actors of that era — Jose Rizal, Apolinario Mabini, General Aguinaldo, Andres Bonifacio — were all Tagalogs. This Tagalog nationalistic tradition has been carried into contemporary times by a succession of politicians including Manuel L. Quezon, Claro M. Recto, Jose Laurel, Jose W. Diokno, Manuel Enverga and Rogaciano Mercado.

But remarkably, since 1896-1904, the fiery nationalism of the Tagalogs has never been translated into protracted agrarian revolt despite the fact that the Tagalog region is coterminous in many respects — in geography, rice cultivation, tenancy conditions — with Central Luzon. Except for brief and spasmic uprisings like those of the Colorums and Sakdalistas which did not enjoy the support of any responsible Tagalog leader, and the Huk forays into Quezon and Laguna in 1950, the region has been relatively peaceful in recent years. The Tagalog *rebelde* streak has tended to be elitist rather than populist in character and expressed in terms of parliamentary nationalism. It may be said in passing that since Quezon's time national leadership has passed from the Tagalogs, the true heirs of the nationalist-revolutionary tradition, to the more numerous Ilocanos and Visayans.

John Alan Larkin, in his history of the Pampango society, called the Pampangos the Johnny-come-latelys of the Philippine revolution. The Alejandrinos and the Aquinos represented a small minority of the Pampango elites. As a class, the Pampango elites tended to react conservatively to each new political development, joining the bandwagon only when it was clearly in their own interests to do so. They behaved this way during the Tagalog-led revolution of 1896 and during the Philippine-American war.

Far from being fiscalizers of the central establishment, the majority of Pampangos have consistently supported it. They contributed supplies and manpower to the Spanish regime. For many decades, the Pampango regiments were in the service of the Crown. It was a Pampanga mercenary unit, the Macabebe Scouts, that helped Gen. Frederick Funston capture the Filipino rebel leader Aguinaldo in 1901.

The Macabebes' steadfast loyalty to the Spaniards and the Americans obtrudes in Pampanga's "nationalistic" past. The town of Macabebe, located on the north bank of the Pampanga river and flood-prone, is poor and depressed. Its menfolk for a long time have taken to soldiering as a means of livelihood. Bearing arms was an honored tradition and the important thing was to serve loyally whichever regime had the clear mandate.

Rafaelita Hilario Soriano, who traces her ancestry to Pampanga's revolutionary leaders, was told an anecdote by her father which might well explain the loyalist streak of the Macabebes. Col. Eugenio Blanco, commander of the Macabebe regiment, promised the Spanish army chief of staff, General Ricardo Monet, that he would protect the Monet family from the retribution of his fellow Pampangos if ever the general was captured. Colonel Blanco lived up to his word of honor and incurred the enmity of his fellow provincianos as a result.[14] This, too, was reflective of the Pampango character — a quixotic sense of moral obligation that tends to prevail over other external compulsions.

Rice and Sugar Cultivation

There is some correlation between Pampanga's sugar-and-rice economy and its dissident problem. What makes the cultivation of rice and sugar to some degree a determinant of agrarian unrest is not so much its physical hardships as the kind of "life style" it commends to the farmers. Fishing is another traditional occupation, equally demanding of time and effort and entails occasional risks to life, but few of the seafaring areas in the Philippines have been rebellious.

Traditional low-land rice-farming is one of the most laborious of agricultural activities—but only in short periods. The crush is felt twice in the year, once during the planting of the rice seedlings and in the harvesting of the grain. Each time the farmers are heavily occupied for only a few weeks. Unless the area has irrigation facilities, it has only one rice crop instead of the two or three possible with year-round irrigation.

Between heavy working periods, there is a long wait of several months when the farmer has little to do. His income comes from his share of the harvest and from the little extra income he and his family can get from fishing, handicrafts and other side crops. He has to support his family from the harvest shares which come once or perhaps twice a year and that has to last him the whole year round.

The long income cycle and the protracted periods of idleness affect the way the farmer lives. He is extremely dependent on credit for survival, and credit is available mainly from his landlord, and to a lesser degree, from his relatives. If he falls from grace with his landlord, the farmer would be in dire financial straits. Rural idleness breeds a fondness for gambling—the Sunday *pintakasi* and the village monte tables are part of the countryside scene. If Lady Fortune fails the farmer, he may soon be in need of cash. And in his distress, he is sometimes compelled to cheat on his landlord. These are some of the ingredients of trouble in the Central Luzon barrios.[15]

---

[14]Interview, July, 1970.

[15]Sturtevant quotes a pre-war writer, his identity undetermined, whose memorable description of the rice farmer's lot is deserving of an encore: "From the time the plowing and planting are finished in early August, up to harvest time, which comes in February, the farmer has practically nothing to do but

Sugar plantation labor is also conducive to landowner-worker friction. Less physical work is required of sugar workers and there are also long months of enforced idleness between the planting and the cane-cutting. The tall sugarcane fields also make ideal cover for the Huks. Many PC officers believe that Huk activism tends to rise from May to November when the sugarcane is tall and the plantation workers are unoccupied.

However, rice and sugar are crops grown in other regions. Rice is the major produce of Bulacan, Rizal, Laguna, and large parts of Quezon and the Bicol provinces, and these areas are relatively free from organized dissidence. Sugar is the primary crop of Negros and Iloilo. By most accounts, Negros should be teeming with social unrest. Its social classes are even more starkly divided. The Negros sugar barons live in handsome style in Bacolod and Silay; they drive the latest Mercedes-Benzes and Mustangs, and play golf the year round in their country clubs. Many of the plantation workers and the *sacadas* live more poorly than the Central Luzon peasants.

Despite a few attempts by radical elements to import Huk-style dissidence to Negros, the sugar-rich province has not followed the Pampango example.[16] One reason offered for this is that the Visayan aristocracy, while as conspicuously rich as the Pampango landowners, is probably more benign and humanistic in its relations with farm workers. Absentee landlordism is not yet the common case as it was in Pampanga shortly before its agrarian disputes reached a critical

---

see that his fields are well-supplied with water. He rests at home most of the day, giving his fingers and toe-nails — lost in the mud during the plowing and harvest season — a chance to re-grow, or patch his tumble-down house.

"Sometimes when the farmer has no more rice to eat, he will himself thresh a small part of the still undivided harvest, but this is prohibited by the Hacendero who sends out his *katiwala* (private guards) at night to detect violators. If the farmer is caught he either forfeits the whole harvest to the landowner or is haled to court, whence he goes straight to jail for theft though he may plead (honestly) that he intended to report to the Hacendero the exact amount he had threshed to save his family from starvation."

[16]In 1969, Huk propagandizing was reported in Cadiz City in northwestern Negros island. Two suspected Huk agitators were arrested and subsequently killed by the Cadiz police and the Philippine Constabulary, putting an end to that threat. Huk activism failed because of poor response on the part of the Negros workers.

level. Most Negros hacenderos still live in their farms.[17]

Tenancy, poverty, lack of education, radical tradition, agricultural "life styles" — all contribute to the making of agrarian unrest in Central Luzon. But they are not exclusive characteristics of the region, nor can each factor be placed on a scale of relative importance without experimental data to support these claims. There is only one factor exclusive to the Huk-infested areas and that is the nature of the Pampango society itself. Pampangos are a unique tribe indeed with a unique history.[18]

The life of a people is influenced by geography — land and water or the lack thereof — by weather and climate, by pressures of social competition, by the need to survive. What must be looked into now is the life-support system of the region and how it determines the behavior of its people.

The Physical Environs

The Central Plain of Luzon, stretching over a 100 miles from Manila to Lingayen Gulf and averaging 40 miles in

---

[17]Negros planters should find little comfort in the recent findings of an Institute of Philippine Culture research team which polled attitudes of permanent workers, *sacadas*, *encargados* and *cabos* (foremen) and the planters themselves. Rev. Frank Lynch, S.J., who authored the preliminary report warned the Negros hacendero that "his position is considerably more dangerous than he himself realizes." Among his findings:

1. Workers living on his farm greatly outnumber him and his household — "in cases there are as many as 50-100 times more workers than hacendero-tied people such as the planter and his family and the *encargado.*
2. Average workers are a full generation younger than hacenderos and encargados, a fact which widens the social distance between the two groups, adding age-group conflicts to whatever ill feelings may already exist due to economic differences.
3. Instead of acting in the deferential manner expected of them, Negros workers "reject planters openly" and to strangers at that, suggesting to Father Lynch that they are "fighting unsuccessfully to control a powerful resentment that has built up within them against the planters discourtesy and injustice."
4. Hacenderos living on the farm tend to be alone, "isolated from the mass of workers," diminishing even further the chances of conflict-resolving dialogue.

[18]Though there are some Tagalogs and a few Ilocanos in this specially-defined "Pampango" area, the population is heavily representative of the indigenous Pampango-speaking people.

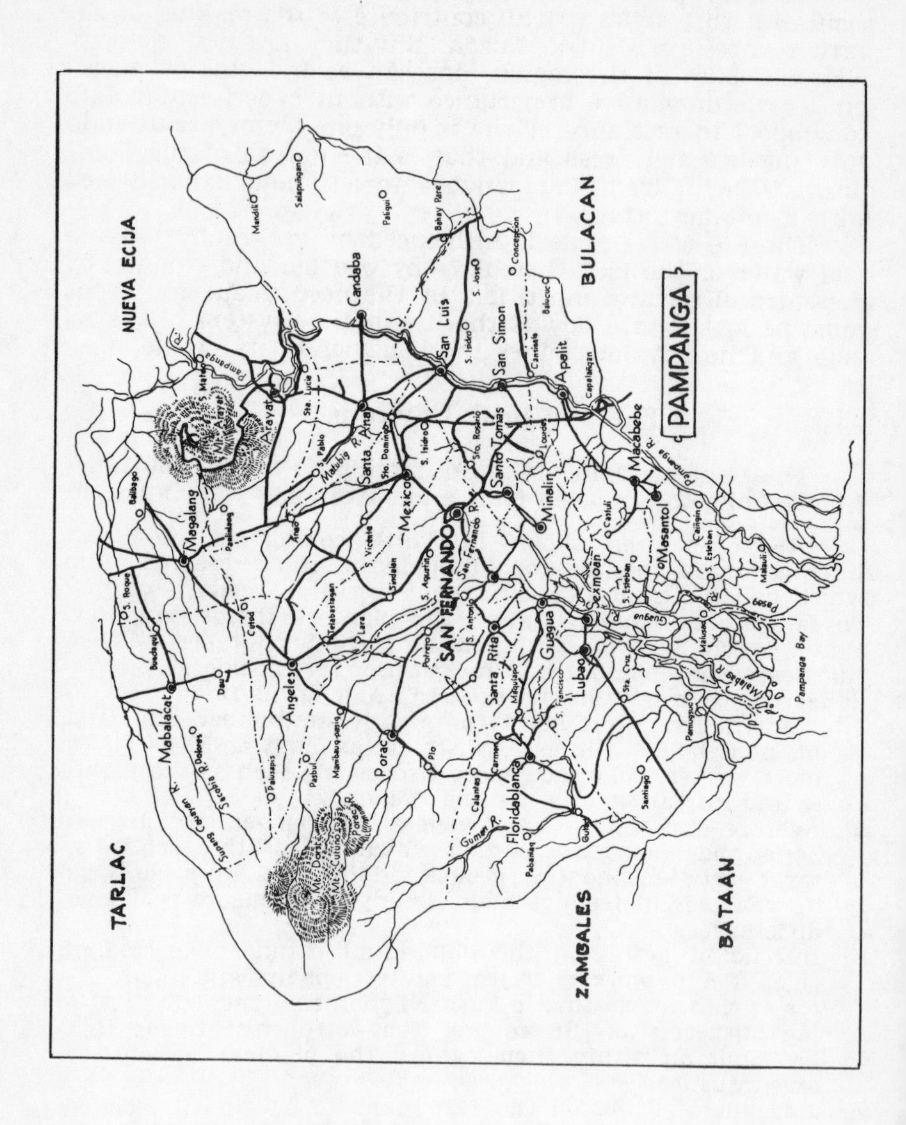

Map of Pampanga

Courtesy of *Atlas of the Philippines*, Phil-Asian Publishers, Manila.

width, is the largest continguous lowland area in the Philippines. Almost all of Pampanga and Southern Tarlac, the southwestern corner of Bataan — the geographical territory that we have designated as the Pampango-speaking area — are all inside this fertile plain.

The lowland is flanked on the west by the jagged Zambales range and on the east by the Central Cordillera. Only a few isolated peaks jut out of this plain. The highest of these is the 3,378-foot Mt. Arayat whose conic symmetry is all the more striking because of the alluvial flatness of the Pampanga and Tarlac farmlands for miles around. For many years, that mountain with its nearly Biblical name was the physical symbol of Huk defiance. The volcano-like peak was bombed and strafed by government planes when dissidents sought the cover of its forested slopes. But the Huks no longer use Arayat as a base. They have, since the late fifties, intermingled with the life of the lowlands.

The second most important feature of Pampanga geography is the Rio Grande de Pampanga which snakes through Nueva Ecija, flows below the southern slopes of Arayat and follows the Pampanga-Bulacan boundary before emptying through dozens of separate outlets into Manila Bay. The physical presence of the Pampanga river is relevant to the history and growth of the province.

An average of 60 inches of rainfall pours into the Central Plain each year and Pampanga's river system floods almost a fourth of the province periodically with crop-enriching waters. The province was indeed named after the fertilizing properties of the river — *pampangan*, the fertile lands by the river banks. But while the Pampanga river is an ecologically benign presence on the long term, it is occasionally destructive. Sometimes it floods whole municipalities, destroys rice crops and wreaks great privations on the people.

Candaba, though one of the oldest towns in Pampanga, is one of the least prosperous. It is good only for fish-ponds in the monsoon season and for growing watermelons when the great Candaba swamp dries in the summer. The other swamp and delta towns are the least populated and the poorest. In 1958, San Luis, Sta. Ana and Sta. Rita had incomes of ₱36,757.46, ₱36,501.22 and ₱23,986.86 compared to the ₱572,303.91 and ₱518,795.75 earned by Angeles City and San Fernando.[19]

It is on the eastern banks of Pampanga — in the depressed towns of Candaba, San Luis, San Simon and Arayat—where Pampanga dissidence first bred. It was here where the first tenant-landlord disputes broke out in the 1920's

[19]Mariano A. Henson, *The Province of Pampanga and Its Towns,* (privately printed, Angeles, 1965), pp. 60-61.

Framingham State College
Framingham, Massachusetts

and where the first socialist politicians came to power. This is not too surprising for the people of eastern Pampanga are perhaps the farthest removed from the central authority. They feel the most deprived. The Candaba swamp, a potentially lush garden that can feed all of Luzon, has never been developed by the government though such has been promised for years. This is the "true" Huk country.

West of the Pampanga river is the rice belt of Pampanga, low enough to be naturally irrigated by the rivers but not as swampy as the eastern banks. The environment is perhaps less harsh and the economy is more mixed. Sexmoan, Guagua, Lubao, Masantol, Macabebe and Santo Tomas have fishpond culture. Sexmoan and Masantol tend towards the middle range in income because they also serve as Pampanga's municipal ports. Bacolor and Guagua were the original settlements of the entrepreneurial Chinese and it is also from these towns that many of Pampanga's elites have sprung.

Northern Pampanga is generally the most prosperous. Its prosperity derives from the sugar belt which runs above the rice region through the communities of Angeles, Floridablanca, Porac, Mabalacat and Magalang. Angeles enjoys a spinoff of millions of pesos from Clark Air Base alone. It is here where the "Mafia" wing of the Huk organization has found a rich base.

A Fantastic Breed

Though no different ethnically from other Christian lowlanders in the Philippines except perhaps for a slightly more perceptible Chinese strain, the Pampangos have a distinct mini-culture of their own. The *Capangangan* dialect forms a tribal bond among the Pampangos whether they live in the mother province or elsewhere. There are, however, subtle variations in the dialect which indicate the specific origin of natives within the province. A central Pampango would say "*Kasingting ning sampaga*" (How beautiful is the flower) while an eastern Pampango would say "*Kalagu na ning bulaklak.*" These lingual differences are a significant factor in the territorial assignments of the Huk organizers, as we had noted.

A Pampango lady born in Bacolor and now established as a successful professional in Manila describes her people and her town in this manner:

> We are so clannish that when two Bacolor natives meet each other they find instant rapport upon discovering their mutual origin.
>
> The life in Bacolor shows strong Spanish influence and some Chinese influence to a lesser degree. The peo-

ple are hospitable and fun-loving to a fault. Pampanga fiestas are very elaborate. The people are also extremely religious. In Holy Week, the *pasion* is still fervently read and tourists from Manila still come to Guagua to watch the *flagelantes*.

The women are very industrious and the men by contrast tend to be spoiled and lazy. There is a town in Pampanga where at 6 a.m. you would see the menfolk fondling their roosters while their womenfolk are lugging foods and produce to market. The Pampanga men are like the Visayans in that they love to gamble. I know of quite a few genteel Pampango families whose fortunes were lost over the *monte* tables.

The wealthy Pampangos go in for flashy cars and loud horns. I imagine their profligacy has a very demoralizing effect on the tenants and the farmers. But most Pampangueños love good food and they will spend their money for that. Pampango cooking is so celebrated that even men become excellent cooks.

I think there is some truth to the belief that Pampangueños are rebellious by nature but what this probably means is that they are inclined to stick by their convictions, whether these are objectively right or wrong. And they are willing to die for these convictions. Many Filipino soldiers were saved from the Death March when Pampango women pulled them out from the road at the risk of brutal retaliation from the Japanese guards.

These observations have been confirmed by others. They provide some revealing insights into the Pampango character — the prodigality of the Pampango elites, the tendency of the male species to default economic activity to the female, the determination to avenge a slight, the valor of the men when they find a cause to fight for.

This ethnic-regional profile could be helpful in understanding why Pampango society has produced men willing to commit themselves to a lifetime of revolt. The poor are embittered by the profligacy of the rich and their apparent indifference to their welfare. The elites have a tendency to respond to grievances not with understanding but with repression.

"That much you can say of the Pampango," said Luis Taruc. "They refuse to be brutalized. If you get on the wrong side of them, they become implacable foes."[20]

---

[20]The Pampangueño's reputation for "treachery' may be largely undeserved. The Macabebe's complicity in the treacherous capture of Aguinaldo—the Pampangueño soldiers walked into the Filipino general's camp in the guise of rebel troops with

Senator Aquino calls his fellow *Capangpangans* a "fantastic breed." "They are one of the smallest of the Filipino tribes but they have produced some of our greatest artists, poets, musicians, politicians, priests and soldiers." Rufino Cardinal Santos, the highest prince of the Catholic church, is a Pampangueño; so is Luis Taruc, once the greatest foe of the Establishment. What Senator Aquino called *dugo adventurero* (adventurer's blood) flows in the veins of the Pampangos and this is why they have produced rascals and criminals like Asiong Salonga and notorious Huk chieftains like Sumulong and Fonting. Their "agricultural psychology" make gamblers out of most of them. "They do not worry about tomorrow," Senator Aquino said. "Why should they when the next crop, the next turn of cards at *monte,* or the next business deal can make them rich men." [21]

Above all, the Pampangos are romantics to a fault. The breed is represented too by matinee idols like Rogelio de la Rosa and Jess Lapid. The Pampango culture is perhaps the only other besides the Tagalog that has produced a substantial literature of its own. Pampanga had its own poet laureate in Aurelio Tolentino who wrote both in Tagalog and Pampango, and later in Zoilo Hilario and Amado Yuzon.

To complete Senator Aquino's ethnic portrait, the Pampangos are "fast-minded" and "glib-tongued." They have innate capacities for leadership. In any motley group of people, it is not infrequently the Pampango who takes charge.

The Spanish Era

For 200 years, the Spanish province of La Pampanga extended well beyond its present boundaries, to as far south as Hagonoy, Calumpit and the neighboring towns of the Baliuag river except Quingua and as far north as the missions of Cagayan and its mountains. The towns of Caranglan, Pantabangan and Puncan in Nueva Ecija where the Pampanga river originates, the mountains of Baler (now part of Quezon province) and the whole of Bataan, were within its ancient bounds.

Pampanga was the nearly exclusive supplier of rice and foodstuffs to the Spanish colonial capital of Manila "so that

"captured" American officers in tow and the ruse succeeded brilliantly — helped form that unfortunate image.

My personal experience with Pampangueños do not lead me to endorse so harsh a judgment. The Pampangueños are well represented in the Manila newspapers and other mass media. They make excellent editors, reporters and photographers. I can say that in all my professional dealings with them they have never let me down.

[21]Interview, July, 1970.

if the rice harvest should fail here, there would be no place where it could be obtained." In 1591 the province had 18,680 "tributes" and 84,820 "souls," with 28 "ministers in instructions" tending to their spiritual and other needs.[22]

There were already well-developed communities on the river banks even before the arrival of the Spanish in the mid-16th century. From the scant prehistoric evidence on hand, anthropologists believe the early Pampangos originated from either Sumatra (H. Otley Beyer's theory) or from South China or North Vietnam (based on findings in Porac of late Tang, Sung, Yunan and Ming pottery.)[23]

The prehispanic community had three established social orders. The *datus* were the recognized authority figures; the *timaguas* were freemen owing allegiance to the *datus*, and in a privileged position in relation with the slaves, who made up the third and lowest of the classes. This slavery took the form of a "severe debt peonage" rather than chattel slavery and it was not a permanent condition.

John Larkin ascribes great significance to the debt relationship traditionally existing in the Pampango society.

> ...the long wait between rice crops and the heavy demands of seed and cuttings for planting built a debt relationship between tenants and landlords that was particularly strong in Pampanga. The debt system and the landowning system combined to create a two-class society that was to have severe repercussion in the middle of the twentieth century.

Larkin suggests that the traditional native society was continued into Spanish times. The *datus* generally became the authorities recognized by the Crown. The two bottom classes became one. Once the natives fulfilled their obligations to Manila in the form of rice, lumber and soldiers, they were generally left alone.

There were only two or three major uprisings in Pampanga that merited recounting by the Spanish.

In 1645, a native rabble-rouser stirred up the villages of Gapang, Santos, Caranglan and Pantabangan to protest the collection of tribute. He urged them to rebel and restore their liberties by slaying the Spaniards and the religious. The uprisings occurred shortly after a series of severe earthquakes lasting several days. The rebel leader assured the natives that there were no more Spaniards left in Manila because the

---

[22]John Alan Larkin, *The Evolution of Pampanga Society. A Case Study of Social and Economic Change in the Rural Philippines*, an unpublished doctoral dissertion submitted to the Graduate School of Arts and Sciences, New York University, 1966.

[23]Same.

earthquake had swallowed the whole of Manila. The Galang natives summoned the aid of the Sambal Negritoes and burned the churches in Santos and Pantabangan. There was much perturbation in Manila after the numerous insurgents badly wounded an encomendero and slew many loyal natives. The rebels were eventually pacified by Fray Juan de Abarca, an Agustinian missionary whom the natives trusted.[24]

The economic burden on the Pampango was exacerbated by the corruption of government agents and the tardiness of the authorities in paying for the purchases. Pampanga was assessed 24,000 *fanegas* of rice at the price of 2 or 2½ *reals* per *fanega* and, according to Domingo Fernandez Navarette, it was "placed on credit until such time as God pleases." The rice quotas were "collected with great vigor and with many deceits" by the Spanish *arraezes*, (captains of Moorish vessels used to transport grain to Manila). The Pampango gave three *fanegas* to the Crown plus "at least one-half *fanega* "more" or a 15 percent "surtax" to the officials.[25]

Rather than revolt against the system, the Indians left their homes or refused to work their fields.

In 1660, the impress of Pampangos for the cutting of timber at Malasinglo and Bocoboco for Spain's undertakings against the Dutch led to one of the rare open revolts against the Crown in the province. The rebel leaders were Francisco Maniago of Mexico, Pampanga and Agustin Pamintuan of Apalit. The uprising was finally put down in 1661; Maniago and his brother were executed without benefit of trial.[26]

The Spanish reaction to the Pampango revolt was apparently one of hurt pride. At least one Spanish religious looked upon the rebelling Pampangos more as ingrates and disloyal subjects than as a people with legitimate grievances. The rebellion, wrote Casimiro Diaz, O.P. in his *Conquistas,* was

> All the worse because these people had been trained in the military art in our own schools, in the fortified parts of Ternate, Zamboanga, Jolo, Caraga and other places, where their valor was known but it needed the shelter of ours. . . They did not realize that the Spaniards had freed them from the harsh captivity of their barbarous tyranny, transferring them to an honorable subjection which made them more the masters of their liberty, because these rebels had not induced that tyranny. They came to know our lack of strength, and from that passed

[24]Father Casimiro Diaz, O.P., "Conquistas de Filipinas," Madrid 1968.

[25]*Tratados Historicas,* about 1656, Blair and Robertson, Vol. 37, p. 290.

[26]Henson, p. 28.

to despising it; they presumed more on their own strength than they ought, and rashly went on, without consideration, looking only at the end and forgetting the means (to attain it).

These rebellions were few and far between. The prevailing attitude of the Pampangos was acceptance of their lot and peaceful compliance with their obligations.

Larkin suggests some reasons for Pampanga's loyalty to Spain. The Catholic Church had a particularly strong hold on the people. The parish priest was almost a petty dictator who could influence the election of *gobernadorcillos*. A letter of reference from the parish priest was often needed to obtain an appointment from Manila. The *datus* personally benefited from their accomodation to the new regime; they were exempted from corvees and their social and political prerogatives were preserved.

The Pampanga society, however, gradually changed under the impact of economic forces. The traditional and new elements in the society "coexisted side by side" for a long time before the modernizing elements became dominant. The opening of the port in Manila increased the demand for Pampanga's produce of sugar as well as rice. The period from 1765 to 1820 also saw the rise of the entrepreneurial class of Chinese mestizos.

Early in the 17th century, a small group of Chinese traders fled to Pampanga to escape persecution in Manila. Most of them resettled in Guagua engaging in trade. The Chinese intermarried with the natives and by 1738, from 4,000 to 5,000 mestizos had settled in pueblos neighboring Guagua and Bacolor.[27]

The Chinese served as a revolutionary force in Pampanga trade. They loaned out capital for sugar production and collected high interest rates and profits. Soon they were taking over the sugar plantations of the native *principalia* in default of payments for loans. Some of the traditional elite survived the economic revolution brought about by sugar. They turned to professional careers like law and medicine, and managed to retain their status. Other native families fell by the wayside.

The Chinese entrepreneurs intermarried with the natives and gave rise to an economically dominant mestizo elite with Christianized names like Henson, Dizon, and Quiason.[28] According to Larkin, the ascendance of the mestizos was "not an invasion of outsiders into a native class but an infusion of a group of people, adapted to the new economic conditions of

[27]Larkin.
[28]Same.

society into the already existing niche of provincial leadership."

The mestizo-indio elite formed "an interlocking directorate that controlled all the municipalities and barrios of the province... Under their collective leadership Pampango society remained stable and free from unrest. In 1960 the Tagalog provinces to the south were on the verge of revolution; Pampanga was not."[29]

Sugar production was the major economic force which realigned Pampango society. Around 1820, Pampanga and Pangasinan altogether produced 7,000 tons. In one year during the 1890's Pampanga alone marketed 50,000 to 60,000 tons. By the 19th century, Pampanga was thoroughly committed to sugar. Rice had ceased being an export crop before 1800.

The agricultural revolution caused far-reaching changes in the demography of the province. The low-lying south and east, good only for growing rice and fish, stagnated. The northern towns grew and prospered as new sugar lands were cultivated. Today the poorest Pampango towns are in the second district. The richest towns are in the sugar belt — Angeles, San Fernando, Guagua, Lubao, Floridablanca, Mabalacat, and Arayat in that order.

Pampango participation in the Philippine revolution was half-hearted. Six days after the declaration of a state of war in eight provinces including Pampanga, there was a brief outburst of fighting in Betis. But after Sept. 10, 1896, there were almost no hostilities in the province whatsoever. In November, a contingent of Pampangos joined the rebel forces in a battle in Orani, Bataan.

For the most part, most Pampangos remained loyal to Spain, Larkin wrote. "The caciques not only continued to hold office under the Spanish government but gave profuse assurances of support as well."

Pampanga was firmly in the Aguinaldo camp when the U.S.-Philippine War broke out in February 1899. The Pampangos cooperated with the revolutionary government until May when it began to waver as American troops advanced on the province. Some towns offered resistance, but for the most part civilians fled in the onslaught of the victorious Americans. Bacolor had the dubious distinction of being the first Luzon town to take on civil government on Feb. 13, 1901.[30]

Such behavior smacked of opportunism but Larkin thought it would be unfair to judge the Pampangos so.

> The landlords belong to a conservative tradition that looked to stable government for the preservation of their

---

[29]Same.
[30]Same.

property. Politically they were committed to no ideology and none of the three powers in the struggle — Spain, the Philippine republic or the United States — threatened the sanctity of private property.

Pampangos... cooperated with the government that provided them the most peace and order. The choice was not always an easy one and many were killed for their commitment.

Debt-Patronage System

The two-class, debt-patronage system was onerous for the tenants. The sugar planter merely supplied the land and sold the pilones of sugar to the merchants. The tenant provided labor, tools, draft animals and was charged with the planting, harvesting and feeding of hired hands. Yet, the proceeds were shared equally.

In a typical contract, the landowner provided only rice for planting and consumption besides the use of the farm. Usually, he paid three *cavanes* for every two borrowed from the proprietor or a heavy 50 percent interest.

The landlord could also demand personal service such as bringing firewood or working with the family. Sometimes these services were volunteered by the tenants. They might want to show their gratitude to the landlord for past favors, or create an *utang na loob* (moral debt) for future requests for credit.

But the system worked. Pampango society operated under that one-sided arrangement for centuries.

What made this semi-feudal relationship tolerable was the element of personalism. The landlord traditionally served as the authority figure for his whole community of tenants. He stood sponsor to baptisms and weddings and offered contributions for education of children and deaths in tenant families.

Most importantly, he was there on the farm or lived close to it. He was the father figure of all his charges and he lived up to that responsibility.

The landlord class began its drift away from the farms close to the end of the 19th century. Sons and later daughters were sent to Manila schools. A few fortunate ones went to Europe to study and enjoy the *haute monde.* The rural "brain drain" increased in the American era. Pampangos went in increasing numbers into the professions and politics.

The plantations and farms were left in the hands of overseers who did not have the paternalistic attitudes of the propietors; they soon tried to drive a harder bargain with the tenants.

This led to the breakdown of the traditional system that had served Pampango society for centuries. With the old personalistic relations gone, the tenants now began to see the inequities. They remonstrated at first and when refused, they started cheating. The landlords or their overseers rode the tenants harder. What used to be a relationship built on trust became a battle of wits, a desire of one to get the better of the other.

Henson listed the ways a tenant could cheat or abuse his landlord and how the landlord could do the same to his tenant.

The tenant could:

—Impoverish the landlord by continued cribbing and soon become the landowner himself.

—Build his house on the farm and not on the homelot prescribed by law not to exceed 1,000 square meters. Raise vegetables and fruits and grow poultry, hogs and goats strictly for his own account.

—Let his animals loose on the fields, when hay or grass is scarce.

—Cut canetops for his carabao or to sweeten his coffee.

—Cut the palay early to make *pinipig* to eat or sell for profit.

—Fish in the dams and cut bamboo in the property and sell the stuff for his own profit.

—Borrow money from the landlord on the pretext of having family expenses and use it for gambling or on his cocks.

The landlord could:

—Make the tenant sign for a lump sum of principal and interest to conceal the usurious transaction.

—Fail to show the tenant or laborer the cane weights or sugar and molasses statements from the sugar central and delay liquidation of accounts.

—Eject tenants en masse to give way for "mechanization."

—Appropriate all the ratoon crop in the belief that it is an improvement on his estate and should accrue exclusively to him.[31]

Social Breakdown

It is obvious from this listing that the Pampango landlord was as likely to be abused as he was to defraud his ten-

[31]Henson, pp. 76-77.

ants. Many landlords were quite bitter about the treatment they received from their workers and tenants. It is not the usual form for landlords to organize themselves in unions and impeach the tenantry as a class. But that is how some of them honestly felt. It is difficult to convince the Pampango elites with such a frame of mind of the need for "social justice."

The crumbling of these traditional ties could not have had a more destructive effect on the tenants. The master of the hacienda could take leave of his angry tenants and enjoy his ease in Manila. The tenant had nowhere to go. Unlike his Ilocano and Cebuano brothers, he was reluctant to leave the familiar soil of his birthplace and the protection of his kin. The small plot he cultivated was his world.[32]

He no longer had an authority-figure to rely on. The political government the Americans instituted was largely coopted by the same landlord class that he had now come to distrust. He had only one recourse left to insure his survival and it was to join other tenants in protective and mutual benefit associations. The small farmers of Bulacan and Nueva Ecija were the first to organize themselves in this way.

This then was Pampanga before the outbreak of agrarian revolt — a pronounced two-class society that had become prosperous but had finally broken down under the pressures of modernization. It was a society torn from its moorings, its traditional leadership drained away by the metropolis, and the peasants left to the mercy of the power claimants trying to fill the void.

[32]Sturtevant, whose work is cited in the next chapter, describes the process of social breakdown as follows:

"As absentee landlords the caciques were no longer familiar with the problems and needs of their tenants. Many of the landlords hired managers to operate the haciendas. The new overseers had no interest in familial responsibilities and tended to run the estates according to strict business principles. Tenants were pressed for repayment of loans, charged for services rendered, and forced to perform extra labor without the compensation of a carefree fiesta. Impersonal efficiency had replaced the old easy going paternalism. As a consequence, the tenants ceased to look upon the cacique as a friend and a benefactor. The hacendero now lived in a fine house in the city, travelled from place to place in a luxurious American automobile, and sent his children abroad to be educated; but the peasant continued to live in a nipa hut, to drive a carabao to market, and was fortunate indeed if his children completed grammar school. The term cacique became an opprobium, and 'caciquism' became the expression for exploitation without a corresponding responsibility for assistance."

Chapter Four

ORIGINS OF SOCIAL PROTEST

The origins of the Huk movement are many and diverse. As American scholar David Reeves Sturtevant puts it, the Huks are "but the latest manifestations of deep-rooted peasant dissatisfaction." The Huks had numerous precursors in the peasant organizations during the twenties and thirties. Their intellectual forbears were of varying backgrounds and persuasions. In investigating their ancestry, one must come upon two distinct histories — that of agrarian protest at its very roots and that of the intellectual dissenters whose genius and philosophies overlaid the simple desire of the peasants to wreak their vengeance on the forces threatening their existence.

There were major rebellions at least once every generation under the Spanish rule. In all cases, except for the 1896 Revolution, they were localized in specific towns and provinces. Sturtevant wrote that in between these upheavals, "The archipelago was far from peaceful; individual attacks on Spanish priests and officials, messianic religious movements, and independent banditry interrupted the tranquility of the countryside." The Islands "manifested all the symptoms of cultural dislocation that have characterized frontier situations the world over."

Sturtevant identified several distinct "protest patterns" in the history of agrarian radicalism. Many of the rural disturbances were outlaw-led. The Philippines has a "well-developed Robin Hood tradition." Heavy exactions, crop failures, and intemperate priestly rule caused many peasants to fall into careers of banditry. *Ladrones* or *tulisanes* were particularly thick around Manila. Palawan had its *remontados* — natives who fled to the mountains in defiance of Spanish authority.

"As in China, the rural outlaw tended to be a discontented peasant rather than an inveterate criminal," Sturtevant wrote. "The slightest amelioration of the conditions which gave birth to armed resistance has generally been enough to restore peace to the rebellious district."[1]

---

[1]David Reeves Sturtevant, *Philippine Social Structure and Its Relation to Agrarian Unrest,* an unpublished doctoral dissertation submitted to the Department of History and Committee of Graduate Studies, Stanford University, March, 1958.

Other recorded rebellions took on characteristics fitting Ralph Linton's description of "magical nativistic movements." Linton defined nativism as "any conscious organized attempts on the part of a society's members to revive or perpetuate selected aspects of its culture." These movements are "shot through with messianic qualities," usually originating "with some individual who assumes the role of prophet and is accepted by the people because they wish to believe." The movements "always lean heavily on the supernatural and usually embody apocalyptic and millenial aspects."[2]

When the lowland Filipinos were brought "under the bell" by Spanish missionaries, they acquired only the nominal and ritualistic aspects of the imported religion. The Latin incantations and the colorful robes of the priests appealed to their senses; the vast company of saints, many of them enfranchised to alleviate specific mortal needs, fitted happily into the universe of the impressionable and constantly needy *indios*. But the native animistic traditions persisted, and perhaps even exist to this day. They survived in the form of superstitions, the demons and dwarfs peopling the imagination of the village folk, and in the *anting-anting* (amulets) worn by bandits and soldiers. "Immunity to death was a standard claim of *tulisan* leaders," Sturtevant noted. The amulets they wore ranged from small vials of fluid to elaborate breastplates.

The peasants were inclined to fanatical faith; they believed that saints could rematerialize in human form and offer instant redress. Hence, Philippine history is full of deviant religious or quasi-religious movements led by inspired visionaries and egomaniacs imagining themselves to be reincarnations of Christ and the Holy Virgin. During the administration of Governor General W. Cameron Forbes, there were one "God Almighty," three "Jesus Christs" and several women claiming to be "Virgin Mary" in provincial jails.[3]

The Native Messiahs

One of the largest of this home-bred religious-political movements is the *Iglesia Watawat ng Lahi* (Church of the Flag of Tears). It has a claimed membership of 50,000 scattered in 15 provinces of Luzon. This "flock" is ruled by

[2]"Nativistic Movements," *American Anthropologist,* XLV, 1943.

[3]Sturtevant.

an ecclesiastical body made up of a supreme bishop, two lesser bishops and 30 priests.[4]

Foremost in the Watawat's pantheon of divinities is the Filipino patriot Jose Rizal who was revealed to the founding fathers as the "reincarnation of Christ." Dr. Rizal, according to this revelation, will one day lead the believers to the New Jerusalem on top of Mt. Makiling facing the town of Calamba (the hero's birthplace). A divine parallel is seen in the lives of Rizal and Christ (Christ died at 33, Rizal was shot by the Spaniards at 36).

The Watawat's hagiocracy includes other historic figures. Mabini, Fathers Gomez, Burgos and Zamora. Bonifacio, Jacinto, the Luna brothers, Jaena. The founders gave witness that in 1914 in the island of Masbate these heroes appeared to them physically but, because of the unbelieving hearts of some of the brethren, Rizal and the rest of the "board of heroes" suspended their earthly visits. However, they still communicate with the elect through the *Banag na Tinig* (Holy Voice) heard in the inner chamber of a building beside the Watawat chapel.

The Calamba sect attracts many of the gullible, the impressionable and the despairing to the fold.

The various Colorum movements were among the most notorious of these outlawed sects. The original Colorum was founded by Apolinario de la Cruz, a native of Lucban, Tayabas (now Quezon province). Denied entrance into a monastic order after 18 months of dedicated service at the Hospicio de San Jose, De la Cruz set up his own pious cause, the Confradia de San Jose. He used his own funds to buy a mass on the 18th of every month and a monthly fiesta for his followers. Spanish and meztizos were forbidden admission to the fold.[5]

The religious establishment soon reacted to this unsanctioned competition and caused the ouster of De la Cruz and his followers from Lucban. Undeterred, he set up once more in a barrio of Isabang. The Governor of Tayabas led an expedition of *cabezas de barangay* to stamp out the sect; the sortie failed and the Governor was killed. The next time, on October 29, 1841, troops were dispatched to deal with the Colorums. A "bloody bayonet charge with drawn sabers" killed 800 members of the sect within a few minutes. De la Cruz himself escaped the carnage but he was captured a few

---

[4]Prospero R. Covar, *The Iglesia Watawat ng Lahi: A Sociological Study of a Social Movement,* an unpublished thesis submitted to the University of the Philippines Graduate School, October, 1961.

[5]Sturtevant.

days later, executed after a quick trial and his remains paraded as a warning to the faithful of the consequences of heresy.

The Colorums, Sturtevant related, were defeated in the field but not stamped out. The survivors took refuge in the mountains between Tayabas and Laguna and stories drifting back to the lowlands told how they had reestablished their "New Jerusalem" on the slopes of an extinct volcano.

Colorum became a generic name in the Philippines for many religious movements with lunatic leaders and fanatic peasant followings. A new Colorum movement was set up in Cavite and Manila by a female spellbinder who claimed to possess herbs and stones stained with the blood of Christ in New Jerusalem. Three men calling themselves "Favorites of the Nazarene" were also active in the sect. The coterie was soon broken up by the American government.

The movement went across the inland seas and found hospitable soil in the Visayas and Northern Mindanao in 1923. A Cebuano named Laureano Salome installed himself as the supremo of the Visayan Colorums and recruited villagers from Bohol, Samar, Leyte and Mindanao. The town of Socorro on Bucas Grande island was the spiritual center of the revived sect. He promised his flock immunity from government bullets through immersion in tanks filled with vials of oil and pulverized human bones. He proclaimed doomsday to be close at hand since the earth was tilting dangerously and about to plunge into the ocean.[6]

In December, 1923, five PC agents sent to investigate the goings-on in Bucas Grande did not come back. The police chief and a constable of Socorro town investigated the disappearance of the troopers and were killed in the attempt. The PC commander of Surigao led 18 troopers to the island to effect the surrender of the fanatics. Five hundred bolo men charged the detachment, leaving only three survivors.

Now fully alarmed, the Manila government sent 500 PC men and the *U.S.S. Sacramento* with a crew of 600 to destroy the Colorum outpost once and for all. The warship shelled the outskirts of the settlement and shortly afterwards Salome and his family surrendered. Remnants of Salome's rabble fought last-ditch battles with the PC in the Mindanao mainland. A PC patrol was ambushed by 200 Colorums near the town of Placer and in the bloodbath 54 of their number were killed and 22 wounded. Some of the fanatics were convinced the uprising was ordered by Jose Rizal. A week later another PC force was attacked by *Colorums,* resulting in the death of 11 government soldiers and 35 dissidents.

[6]Same.

In 1927, another mystic named Florencio Intrenchera-do, set up his own independent "kingdom" in parts of Iloilo and Negros. An uncannily accurate prediction of the erup-tion of Mt. Kanlaon on Negros island won many converts. The Iloilo-born "emperor" sought the lowering of the cedula tax from two pesos to 20 centavos, though he charged a three-peso fee for the privilege of membership in his kingdom. In 1926, he had 20,000 dues-paying "subjects."

His "Highness" held fort in a thatched palace in Jaro, conducted affairs of state in an ornate uniform complete with golden sword and gem-encrusted scabbard and a crown of gold reputed to cost ₱6,000. The authorities were un-moved by Intrencherado's royal pretensions. They charged him with rebellion, declared him insane and sentenced him to a rest cure in San Lazaro hospital in Manila. Intrenche-rado declined to be banished and his followers took to arms. The Intrencheradistas captured the Victoria town hall and disarmed the police. Within hours, Silay, La Carlota and Bago fell to the ragtag army The PC rallied and put the invaders to rout, killing two Intrencheradistas. The cap-tured followers said they were instructed to capture the public buildings, burn documents, and confiscate Chinese and Japanese goods. The proceeds were to be shared three ways — one third to the "Emperor," and the two other por-tions to the leaders and the followers[7]

Gov. Leonard Wood sent Maj. Burton Y. Read to arrest the demented Emperor with a minimum of violence. Accom-panied only by Attorney General Hill and Rep. Tomas Con-fessor, Major Read walked into the Emperor's fortified camp where 400 of the faithful, armed with clubs, bolos, axes and knives, awaited the bidding of their lord. Intrencherado finally yielded and was shipped off to Manila.

Early Uprisings in Central Luzon

Central Luzon's peasant troubles early in this century had some religious overtones but more pronouncedly than elsewhere; they arose from class antagonism between the tenants and the landowners. The *Guardia de Honor* (Guards of Honor) was founded by the Dominican priests in Panga-sinan on the eve of the Philippine Revolution to preserve the loyalty of the peasants and counteract the anti-clerical pro-paganda of the Katipunan. The Guardia acquired large fol-lowings in Pangasinan, La Union and Zambales and, accord-ing to James Leroy, had as many as 20,000 members in a new town called Kabaruan. After the friars were deposed, the

[7]Same.

brotherhood quarrelled with the landlords marking some of them for liquidation.

The *Santa Iglesia* (Holy Church) turned up in Nueva Ecija during the early American occupation. It was led by Felipe Salvador, an officer under Aguinaldo, who turned bandit chieftain after the defeat of the Filipino revolutionary army. Salvador was a thorn on the side of the American government for 10 years. Acquiring a grassroots reputation for divinity and invulnerability, Salvador posed a major problem in the pacification of the province for 10 years before he was killed.

Nueva Ecija was again the scene of major peasant unrest a decade later when Pedro Kabola, an Ilocano who migrated to the province in 1918, made himself general-in-chief of his poor people's army. He promised immunity from death to all of his followers. The Kabolan movement was more aggressively committed to class warfare than previous manifestations in the region. The "generalissimo" set March 5 and 6, 1925 as the dates for the attack and capture of San Jose town, certain that this would be the cue for the entire peasantry in Central Luzon to rise in revolt.

The PC, however, learned of the plot on December 19, 1924. While Kabola was delivering his address to the troops on the eve of the revolt, the PC agents dispersed the crowd by firing shots into the air. The master conspirator was killed in the fracas.[8]

There were "hysterical" reports of the uprising in Manila and the PC diligently searched far corners of Central Luzon for other evidences of insurrection before normalcy was restored a week later. Of the 85 Kabolans tried in the Cabanatuan Court of First Instance, 76 were jailed and six were acquitted.

Even more shocking to the local Establishment was the brief fling at glory of Pedro Calosa and his Colorum band in Tayug, Pangasinan. Calosa, a native of Bauang, La Union, had a "mystical nature." He was in one of the first waves of Ilocano plantation workers in Hawaii. He first tried Aglipayanism and then the "Filipino Federation of America" founded by that great egocentrist, Hilario Camino Moncado. Since Calosa could not afford the membership dues of Moncado's brotherhood, he formed his own.

The Pangasinan Colorums in 1931 had the seizure of Tayug as their first objective. Unlike in the Kabolan uprising in Pangasinan seven years before, the authorities were completely surprised. On a Sunday, the Colorums attacked the undermanned PC detachment in Tayug, killed 13 cons-

---

[8]Same.

tables including the commanding officer when he tried to escape. Though many of the townsfolk fled, the Colorums captured the treasurer. He was forced to unlock the filing cabinets containing documents. Land records and tax receipts were set afire. Then Calosa led the raiders to the *convento* to await the expected PC counterattack.

PC reenforcements gave battle for eight hours starting at 10 a.m. In the course of the siege a woman left the *convento* waving a Filipino flag. She was cut down by PC bullets. Four other Colorums were killed and 20 wounded before the rest of the defenders surrendered.

Calosa, escaping the PC encirclement, sallied with 24 of his men to the El Porvenir hacienda. He put the hacienda buildings to the torch but private guards foiled his attempt to capture the residence of the Lichauco family. The PC, spotting the smoke of the burning hacienda, rushed to the scene. By Monday Calosa and many of his cohorts were in custody.

Filipino officials, representing to a great degree the interests of the ilustrados and landed gentry, were slow to realize or admit the serious implications of the peasant risings. It attributed the Kabola revolt, according to Sturtevant, to the "agitation of criminal elements and the irresponsibility and ignorance of the masses." Secretary of Interior Honorio Ventura, a Pampanga politician otherwise unselfishly dedicated to public service, wrote off the Tayug rebels as having "no definite purpose in what they did." The movement was "a hash of religion, politics, fanaticism and a little of everything else . . . If the government could afford it there would be no problem. It is just a matter of adding some 10,000 men to the Constabulary and distributing the force in all the municipalities."[9]

Some American observers, unencumbered by the prejudices and the personal interests of Filipino landlords, had a grimmer and more perceptive view of the agrarian unrest. Governor-General Wood quickly saw the root of the problem in the early twenties. "Behind the (Kabola) revolt were homesteaders who lost the reforms and tenants with grievances against landlords."[10]

Harold E. Fey, covering the Tayug incident for the *Christian Century*, diagnosed the malady as caused by unhealthy landlord-tenant relations. He quoted a peasant's complaints:

> We are poor and work very hard. And yet we work on land that is not our own. We want an equal

[9]Quoted by Sturtevant in cited work.
[10]Same.

> division of the lands in our country. That is what we think is the meaning of equality before the law.[11]

A. V. H. Hartendorp, editor of the American Chamber of Commerce, puts the onus squarely on the indifference of the landlord-dominated Filipino officialdom:

> Our legislators should think more about the common people at other times than just before elections. We should be on our guard in this country against the government becoming an *ilustrado* government out of touch with the people and unsympathetic to their needs, leaving them ready to turn to men of the type of Pedro Calosa for leadership.[12]

The Sakdal Revolt

The Sakdal revolt, coming only four years after Tayug, finally brought the Filipino establishment to a full realization of the social problems that had long remained festering in the countryside. Sturtevant described the "bloodshed and death of May 2 and 3, 1935" as a transition between the agrarian movement of the twenties characterized by "inadequate organizations, unsophisticated leadership and unobtainable objectives" to the intelligently-led, professionally-organized peasant movement of the late thirties and early forties.

Benigno Ramos, the leader of the Sakdalistas, was a class apart from the Calosas and Kabolas who stirred up the blind, irrational peasant outbursts earlier in the century. The Bulacan-born Ramos was educated in public schools, clerked briefly for the Malolos provincial office, and, after getting a teaching certificate taught in the Bulacan barrio of Puli until 1912. Then he started a promising journalistic career in Manila, translating Spanish and English verse into Tagalog for a dialect newspaper. He finally landed a staff position in the nationalistic Spanish-language journal *El Ideal*. His by-line in the influential newspaper helped him get a job as fulltime translator in the Philippine Senate. He acquired civil service rank in 1921 and went up the bureaucratic ladder until he became director of the Senate clipping service in 1929. By that time Ramos had become respectably middle-class; he even boasted of an inside track to the Nacionalista party leadership. His poetic touch and platform eloquence made him in great demand as a campaign orator, and

[11]Same
[12]Same

he loyally helped the Quezonian cause in this fashion in minor rallies in Manila and Bulacan.[13]

But something happened that turned Ramos from a complacent creature of the ruling clique to a vehement anti-Quezonista and an unrestrained critic of the entire pre-Commonwealth establishment

In 1930, the Manila High School faculty staged a strike against an American instructor for his alleged "imperialist" views. Ramos, thinking he was following the official Nacionalista line, rallied to the side of the strikers. But to his great distress, the NP leadership, fearing a precipitate and premature granting of independence by the U.S., supported the American teacher. Ramos turned against those he believed responsible for this traitorous concession and vented his anger at Quezon, Osmeña and other NP leaders. Ramos soon got a letter from Quezon requesting his resignation from the Senate. The ousted bureaucrat thenceforth made it the "main purpose of his life to embarrass or undermine the Nacionalista leaders."[14]

Ramos founded the anti-Nacionalista sheet, *Sakdal* (meaning, to strike or accuse) whose first issue carried an attack on his former political allies. The *Sakdal* carried the portraits of Rizal and Marcelo H. del Pilar under its masthead to emphasize its nationalistic mission, and adopted the slogan, "Independent with no master but the people."

The alienated Bulakeño started flirting with the prospect of popular revolt when he met the leaders of the Tangulan society. The Tangulan was a nationalistic organization with a membership of 40,000. Its leader was Patricio Dionisio, a known Communist high up in the party councils. Ramos, however, was too smart to be associated with the suspect Tangulans, according to Sturtevant, and he officially disclaimed any alliance with the society in a special editorial in *Sakdal* on December 2, 1931. This did not deter the PC from compiling a massive dossier on Ramos; by 1935, when the Sakdalista rebellion broke out, the Ramos files in PC Headquarters were "bulging."

Ramos sought initially to catapult himself into power with the help of his own party. Its platform was a "hastily constructed pastiche of Sakdal issues." The NP's were charged with failing to gain independence in 26 years of administration and for being "insincere and inattentive to the demands of the poor."

---

[13]See also Ray Manning Stubbs, *Philippine Radicalism; The Central Luzon Uprisings, 1925-1935*, an unpublished dissertation submitted to the University of California, Berkeley, Calif., 1951.

[14]Sturtevant.

Taking advantage of a split between the Quezon and Osmeña factions over the Hare-Hawes-Cutting bill, the Sakdalista party secured the victory of three of their candidates in the elections for the House of Representatives. Mariano Untivero and Aurelio C. Almazan were elected to seats in Laguna, an acknowledged Sakdal stronghold, and Antonio Argosino captured the third seat in Tayabas. In addition, Marinduque elected a Sakdal governor and the Ramos party won more than 20 minor posts in Laguna, Bulacan, Nueva Ecija, Rizal and Cavite.[15]

The Sakdal performance amazed the politicians and the public. Actually, most of the Sakdalista winners won pluralities as a result of the splitting of the normally solid conservative vote between the Quezonistas and the Osmeñistas. As long as the Nacionalistas remained divided, Ramos had a fair chance of wielding the balance of power with his third party. But the NPs soon realized the threat to their mutual interests and closed ranks anew. The reunited NPs furthermore recaptured the initiative in the independence crusade, disarming what had been the Sakdals most potent campaign weapon.

Recognizing the futility of assaulting the NP frontally, the Sakdals boycotted the July 1934 elections of delegates for the constitutional convention. Ramos called the delegates "half-breeds and betrayers" and condemned the convention itself as a sinister ploy to perpetuate "oligarchic controls with American bayonets."[16]

Ramos shifted his attention to personal diplomacy with Japanese extremists, looking forward to a time when the Japanese would help the Filipinos win their independence from the Americans. He left the Philippines on November 25, 1934, ostensibly to fight the Tydings-McDuffie bill in Washington. Instead, he occupied himself in Japan seeking help from "Pan Asia" radicals.

Meanwhile, in Manila, the authorities were becoming increasingly alarmed over Sakdalista agitation in the nearby provinces. Acting Governor General Joseph Ralston Hayden estimated the Sakdal membership to be between 60,000 to 300,000; this was proportionally larger than the claimed mass base of the Huk movement at its peak. Government agents reported that Sakdal orators were getting more unbridled in their denunciations of the government. Rumors of an imminent uprising drifted in from the outskirts of the city.

On May 1, 1935, Labor Day, government officials braced themselves for a possible blow. Nothing unusual happened.

---

[15]Same.
[16]Same.

The traditional May Day parade in Manila was "a model of civil solidarity and obedience." Brig. Gen. Basilio Valdes, overconfidently took a steamer for an inspection trip in the south. But towards evening, PC headquarters in Manila received a report that the RCA transmitter in San Jose del Monte, Bulacan was about to be dynamited. By 8:30 p.m., the PC reported that all power lines north of Marilao, Bulacan and south of Biñan, Laguna, Rizal and Bulacan were cut off.

That panicky night it seemed to the PC that Sakdalista insurgents were everywhere ready to strike. They were reported massing in Calamba, Cabuyao and Sta. Rosa. At 6:30 p.m., the Laguna PC ordered two officers and 14 constables to check the troubled areas and flush out any possible dissidents. The patrols left in two trucks. It stopped in Calamba to find that the situation there was peaceful. The PC split into two parties, one holding position in Calamba and the other bound for Sta. Rosa in response to the advice of local officials that the town was swarming with Sakdalistas.

When the PC lieutenant and his seven men reached the *poblacion* it was dark, the power lines having been cut off. They saw shadowy figures moving in the plaza and the officer drove on to the spot when firing broke out. The patrol was caught in the sudden burst of gunfire. Though wounded, the soldiers valiantly fought their way to the *municipio*. In the 15-minute skirmish, three PC soldiers and four Sakdalistas were killed. Five other PC men, including their officer, and four Sakdalistas were wounded.[17]

North of Manila, in San Ildefonso, Bulacan, another PC-Sakdal clash occurred. The troopers advanced on the municipal building occupied by the rebels and, after a firefight lasting a half-hour, 88 of the beseiged peasants surrendered. There were no PC casualties, but two Sakdalistas lay dead and one was wounded.

The bloodiest battle took place in Cabuyao, Laguna. A large PC force of four officers and 32 enlisted men, bent on avenging the bloodying of their comrades in Sta. Rosa, trapped the Sakdalistas behind the waist-high stone fence around the convento. Governor Cailles of Laguna stepped up on a bench to beseech his provincemates to surrender peacefully. His plea was cut short by a murderous blast which felled three PC men including an officer standing behind him. The PC instantly returned fire.

The PC force was divided into three groups; two flanking the Sakdal line prepared to deliver a withering crossfire, and a third positioned to attack frontally. The peasants hud-

---

[17]Same.

huddled behind the stone fence. The flankers opened up with accurate and concentrated rifle fire, and the third squad with fixed bayonets charged the wall. The Sakdalistas had not a ghost of a chance. It was all over in minutes. Of the 79 Sakdalista die-hards only seven remained alive and uninjured. Fifty were dead and 22 seriously wounded. The PC casualties were an officer and three enlisted men wounded.[18]

The carnage in Cabuyao ended the Sakdal rebellion. The followers of Ramos had been led to believe that a token show of force would be enough to frighten the government into giving concessions to the farmers. They thought that the PC, composed largely of provincianos with backgrounds similar to theirs, would desert their commanders and join their popular cause.

The initial reaction of Quezon — then in the U.S. — to the Cabuyao Massacre was highly critical of his Sakdalista opponents who masterminded the ill-fated rebellion. He condemned Ramos as an "irresponsible demagogue" and his movement for operating on a "purely racketeering basis." Sturtevant observed, however, that in only two hours, the politically astute Quezon sensed a change in the wind from half a world away and reversed his position. He now admitted that the economic depression and dipping copra prices had preconditioned the Laguna farmers to violence.

The Philippine government had finally shaken itself loose from its reactionary isolation and began to attend with greater sympathy to the needs of the peasants. Unfortunately, the "social justice program" began too late.

The Intellectual Protest

Until the thirties peasant protest expressed itself characteristically in a half-blind and irrational fashion. Its leaders tended to be of rustic origin, and in these demagogues and charlatans were personified the peasants' wish-fulfilments of power, glory and vengeance — and perhaps escape from the unbearable realities of their own meagre existence.

But "peasant power" did not really become an effective social lever until it acquired more sophisticated leadership, either by adoption from the upper classes, or by producing it from within its own ranks. Throughout the modern history of agrarian reforms, that competent leadership tended to come from higher levels in the vertically structured Philippine society. "Outside" leadership was provided by

[18]Same.

enlightened politicians and some of the more benign landlords, by Communists, Socialists and ideologues of other stripes, by labor unionists who came from equally poor circumstances but were at least better skilled in organization, and from the university students.

The peasant class was also to develop its own leaders capable of matching wit and valor with the class enemies, but this did not come until later.

Elitist leadership took over the peasant movement in Central Luzon in the 1920's and 1930's, and when that happened it was ready for a serious confrontation with the central government. That leadership descended in an almost unbroken line from a minority of the Pampanga-Tarlac elites who made common cause with Tagalog nationalists during the Revolution. "Revolutionary tradition" is the neat catchphrase of propagandists like Luis Taruc and Alfredo Saulo and it has to be broken down into more comprehensible components.

At its roots was the liberal intellectualism which many of the upper-class Pampangos educated in Manila and Europe affected in the 1880's and 1890's. The Filipino liberals were engaged in a struggle with the Spanish colonial regime for the future governance of the Philippines.

Part of that tradition can be explained simply as the friendship of like-minded souls. Jose Rizal shared quarters for a time with Jose Alejandrino in Brussels and Ghent; it is not surprising that Alejandrino later became one of the staunchest supporters of the Revolution.[19] Tiburcio and Cecilio Hilario were the law partners and relatives as well of the great revolutionary propagandist Marcelo H. del Pilar.[20] Some of the Pampango elites were drawn into the revolutionary struggle by ties of blood and friendship, and once danger threatened them all they became a closely-knit force against the established order.

Pampanga's intellectual dissent took the form of anti-clericalism, for the propertied priestly orders were closely identified with the conservative forces stubbornly resisting reform.[21] It is noteworthy that many of the province's "revolutionary" elite were also associated with Masonry. Seven of the founders of the first Philippine lodge Nilad in Manila

---

[19]Larkin.

[20]Rafaelita Hilario Soriano, *Tiburcio Hilario of Pampanga*. A Historical Bulletin, the Philippine Historical Society, Vol. VIII, No. 4, Dec., 1964.

[21]These Pampango elites were anti-clerical but not necessarily anti-religious. The Catholic faith continued to be strong in Pampanga.

(in 1891) were Pampangos, including Ceferino Joven, later governor of his province.[22] The first Pampanga triangle was put up by Ruperto Laxamana, *gobernadorcillo* of Mexico, Mariano Alejandrino (father of Jose) of Arayat, and Eugenio Blanco of Macabebe. Laxamana and Alejandrino cast their lot with the Revolution and Blanco with the Spaniards. Two other Masonic lodges were founded in the province, one in San Fernando by Cecilio Hilario, and another in Bacolor by Francisco Joven.[23]

The Pampango revolutionaries were lawyers, writers, poets and soldiers. The "triumvirate" of the movement in Pampanga were Gen. Maximino Hizon, (its organizer), Aurelio Tolentino (its coordinator) and Tiburcio Hilario (its chief architect)[24] Tolentino, who wrote fiery epistles in both Pampango and Tagalog, and Hilario, who served heroically as revolutionary governor of the province after many months of suffering as a political exile, helped the cause as much as the generals who fought the battles.

The careers of two revolutionary leaders — a propagandist in Pampanga and a soldier in Tarlac — provide some of the more memorable episodes of that time.

The Hilarios of Pampanga

Tiburcio Hilario was born on August 11, 1863, in barrio San Juan, San Fernando, Pampanga. His father, Anastacio Hilario, practiced law in Quiapo, Manila, and when he settled in Pampanga he became the first lawyer of that province. Tiburcio followed his father's profession and became, along with his brother Cecilio, one of Pampanga's ablest lawyers.[25] He soon acquired a reputation for being a protector of the oppressed with a great capacity for righteous indignation. A Spanish judge of the Court of First Instance in Bacolor was so patently biased against Tiburcio that the latter could scarcely hope for a fair judgement of any case he was handling in the Bacolor sala. Things got to a point that Tiburcio's good friend, Colonel Eugenio Blanco, challenged the judge to a duel. After that, the judge was more careful and impartial in his decisions.[26]

Tiburcio had two brothers, Cecilio and Procopio, who both figured in the libertarian movement in the region. Cecilio, the oldest of the three, was a tall, ascetic-looking man, who

---

[22]Larkin.
[23]Same.
[24]Soriano, as cited
[25]Same.
[26]Soriano interview, July, 1970.

later held important positions in the revolutionary government including a seat in the Malolos Congress in 1898.[27] Procopio, who settled in Tarlac, was killed with his brother-in-law, Francisco Tañedo, as a result of Spanish persecution.

Tiburcio's first contact with the propaganda movement came when he and Cecilio were visited in their San Fernando home by one of the movement's organizers. Their surprise guest was none other than Jose Rizal. He had heard of the Hilario brothers' reputation for integrity and patriotism and sought their cooperation for his plan to form the *Liga Filipina* (Philippine League). He told his hosts that many of the Bulacan intellectuals were enthusiastic about the idea. Rizal left pamphlets and other literature with the Hilarios after coming from Tarlac where he looked for the third brother, Procopio.[28]

The Hilario brothers were quick to pay the price for their patriotic commitment. Barely a month after Rizal's visit the Spanish regime imposed a ban on the distribution of literature opposing the Catholic church or "national unity." The Guardia Civil was ordered to watch the movements of suspected liberals in Batangas, Bulacan, Cavite, Pampanga and Laguna. Cecilio's house in Palawi, a short distance from the ancestral home in San Juan, was searched and the incriminating pamphlets were found.

Tiburcio was placed under arrest, and though he tried to warn his brother. Cecilio preferred to share Tiburcio's fate rather than flee. Both were imprisoned in Bacolor and exiled, Tiburcio to Siasi, Jolo, and Cecilio to Balabac island in Palawan. Among the first Filipino liberals to suffer deportation for their convictions were Maximino Hizon, Mamerto Lacsamana, and Mariano and Felix David. Though Tiburcio failed to save himself from arrest, he succeeded in forewarning two friends — Don Leandro Ibarra, a lawyer of Lubao, Pampanga who later became Secretary of Interior under General Aguinaldo and his cousin, Marcelo H. del Pilar. Hilario sent his swiftest horses to warn del Pilar of his imminent arrest. Thus, del Pilar was able to escape Spanish vengeance and became the propagandist of the Philippine Revolution abroad.

Tiburcio's mother and wife had to sell the family lands in Bacolor, Santo Tomas and Minalin to keep their menfolk alive in their places of exile. After two years the brothers were returned to Manila by the authorities in the hope that they would testify against Rizal. They refused. Later, Tiburcio was allowed to live with his family at a rented floor

---

[27]Soriano, as cited.

[28]Same.

of the three-storey house of Don Francisco Reyes at 1414 Azcarraga. The house became a center of revolutionary activity. Modesto Joaquin, later to become Director of Labor, Felix Galura, Pedro Liongson, Andres Serrano and Aurelio Tolentino, all Pampango liberals, frequented the house. Ambrosio Rianzares Bautista, later a political adviser of Aguinaldo, kept an office in the Reyes house. He and Gregorio Aglipay, who later founded the Philippine Independent Church, took turns masterminding anti-Spanish activities. The Guardia Civil kept vigil on the suspicious activities in the house but never caught on. When they surprised the occupants in possession of incriminating documents, Tiburcio sent his only daughter Filomena and her cousin, Florencia Halili, to burn the evidence in the bathroom.[29]

Three months after the arrival of the American forces, Tiburcio and Hilario escaped Spanish surveillance and returned to Pampanga. The province was in a fever of war preparation. In Bacolor, they saw smoke in the distance. It was Tiburcio's house which the Guardia Civil had put to the torch.

Tiburcio returned to Bacolor a proclaimed hero. In his absence, the town *presidentes* elected him revolutionary Governor. Without a home of his own, Tiburcio used the *convento* as his office and residence. He appealed to his compatriots to donate food and provisions for the revolution. Dorotea Rodriguez Sioco, Manuel Escaler, Florentino Hizon, and Joaquin Gonzales were among those who responded generously.

The Governor sent out rations for the Revolution's soldiers from the rice and palay stocks he kept at the *convento*. He tempered his patriotism with humanitarian consideration. Seeing an accused spy hanging dead from a tree and learning that he was given capital punishment after a summary trial, Hilario rebuked a Pampango General for the "indiscriminate execution." He told the General that the life of every Filipino was worth saving and that the revolution was intended to guarantee the individual liberties of the people.[30]

With the advent of the Filipino-American war, Tiburcio Hilario was forced to move once again. This time his travel was more perilous because he had to bring with him the entire *emprestito* (wartime treasury) of the province amounting to about a million pesos. The treasury which included all the voluntary contributions and war bonds subscribed to by the Pampangos was packed into a stout iron and wood trunk four feet long, four feet high and more than a meter

---

[29]Same.
[30]Same.

wide. Four carabaos were needed to pull the cart bearing the trunk — working alternately in teams of two animals. Four armed men escorted the precious cargo.[31]

Hilario followed the precipitous retreat of General Aguinaldo just ahead of the advancing Americans. He went to San Fernando and when the poblacion was captured by the enemy he moved to Apunan Awak where he was in frequent liaison with General Aguinaldo. From Apunan Awak, the Governor fell back to Concepcion. On June 21, 1899, Aguinaldo moved into Tarlac town and made it the provisional capital of the Republic. It was here that Hilario turned over to Aguinaldo the entire *emprestito* of Pampanga.

Hilario found himself a virtual exile in Pangasinan unable to follow General Aguinaldo farther. After Aguinaldo's capture, he returned to Bacolor to build up his old law practice. Here in 1903, he took ill and died, the only known victim of scarlet fever in Philippine medical history up to then. He was barely 40 years old; he had spent more than 10 of his last years in the faithful service of his country. He served as Vice President of the Philippine Congress in Tarlac, representative of Iloilo, and a member of the Philippine Supreme Court in Tarlac before his untimely death. The rich and the great of Pampanga came to his funeral in Bacolor but most of those who came to mourn were the common people whom he had helped and loved.

General Aquino of Tarlac

Servillano Aquino, squire of Concepcion and the son of the founder of Tarlac province Braulio Aquino, might have sat out the Revolution with most of the conservative landlords were it not for his pride and loyalty to his friends. He had gone years before to the University of Santo Tomas to learn the science of surveying. Now his old classmates were in the forefront of the revolution and came to Tarlac to urge Aquino to join the fight against the Spanish. They had read the Tarlaqueño's character well. Don Servillano offered his services. He organized his own unit, which he later called *Fusileros de Tarlac*. Francisco Macabulos organized the landowners on the La Paz side, and Tarlac province was ready to be counted on the side of the Revolution.[32]

Aquino's *fusileros* attacked the railroad station in Capas and captured the *guardia civil* defenders and all their arms. Breveted a lieutenant colonel, Aquino brought his regiment to Manila in response to the summons of General Aguinaldo.

[31]Same.

[32]Senator Benigno Aquino Jr., interview, July, 1970.

He took up battle positions in Caloocan and was wounded in action. He helped hold the Revolutionary Army's line in Angeles. After the Pact of Biak-na-Bato, he joined Aguinaldo in exile in Hongkong. He was back for war, this time against the Americans. Once again, he suffered exile. A portrait which has stood for many years in the family residence in Murcia, Tarlac, is amusingly revealing of the undaunted spirit of the General. It shows him attired in a prisoner's uniform but standing cockily and stiffly like a General reviewing his troops.[33]

Unlike his comrade-at-arms Gen. Maximino Hizon, who died in exile in Guam, General Aquino lived to an old age. He was still strong enough during the Japanese occupation to do an important errand for his son, Benigno Aquino, Sr. It was to make contact with a distant relative, Eusebio Aquino, and persuade him to give up his association with the Huks. During the confrontation, Tandang Bio looked over the old man coolly and said: "How many arms did you have when you decided to fight the Spaniards?"

"Four Mausers and two cavalry pistols," the General replied.

"Well, I have thirty rifles, three Browning automatic rifles, one machine gun, and any number of smaller arms. We have more guns than your revolutionary army when you started out. Do you expect me to surrender?"

To the General's credit, he quickly saw his nephew's logic and did not pursue his mission any further.[34]

Tandang or Apong Bio was a blacksmith in Magalang. He was not as well off as the heirs of Don Servillano, but he made it his mission to carry on the "revolutionary tradition" of the clan. He was one of the first Huk commanders under Luis Taruc in 1942, and he eventually became his second-in-command. One of his four sons, Felix (Flax) Aquino, married the daughter of Faustino del Mundo (Commander Sumulong) and his daughter Gloria became the wife of Peregrino Taruc, the younger brother of Luis who was once chief of the Huks' National Education Department. The revolutionary spirit even extended to a third generation. The daughter of Peregrino and Gloria Taruc, Erlinda, married Leoncio Co who was recently arrested by the PC and charged with being the chief of the Maoist party's educational department.

---

[33]This was the recollection of Nina Estrada Puyat, a grandniece of the late General Aquino.

[34]The meeting between General Aquino and Tandang Bio is one of the favorite anecdotes of Luis Taruc. Tandang Bio was his second-in-command during the Occupation.

A Revolutionary Inheritance

The Hilario family of revolutionary days also passed on its commitment to public service to the succeeding generation. Tiburcio Hilario's two sons, Ceferino and Zoilo, each represented the second district of Pampanga for one term. Zoilo founded what was probably Pampanga's first agrarian reform organization with a peasant-based membership, the *Katipunan Mipananpun* (Self-Help Brotherhood). In existence in 1925-30, the Katipunan preceded Pedro Abad Santos' Socialist party by three to four years.

Patriotism and a highly emotional kind of populism were virtually family inheritances of the Hilario family. Zoilo was tutored by Hilario Cañiza and Modesto Joaquin (the latter was one of Don Tiburcio's fellow-conspirators against the Spanish regime). Zoilo's daughter, Rafaelita, recalls how her brothers and sisters were "politicized" in their tender years with Sunday-school lessons in Philippine history. The Hilario children were taught to kiss the Filipino flag as a token of reverence.

The reformist "ideology" of the Pampango elites was an offshoot of Pampanga romanticism—more a thing of the heart than of the mind. This particular genius was crystallized in Zoilo more than any other Pampango of his generation, with the possible exception of Pedro Abad Santos.

Don Zoilo was a born leader and organizer. He was among the foremost celebrators of cultural, historical and social events in Pampanga and Tarlac. He loved parades and enjoyed crowning barrio queens.[35] He founded many organizations including the *Boni Cives, Labrantes Civicos*, Academia Pampanga and the Pampanga Historical Society. He was an unabashed romantic, a political leader who was at the same time poet laureate of his province. He inherited the laurel from Juan Crisostomo Soto, and Don Zoilo in turn crowned his successor Amado Yuzon, who was later the Democratic Alliance ticketmate of Luis Taruc. Poetry was almost synonymous with political propagandism in those good old days.

The most socially significant of Hilario's organizations was the *Katipunan Mipananpun.* It was Pampanga's first elite-led popular organization seeking agrarian reforms through peaceful means. It was Masonry-like in the secrecy and esotericism of its rituals. Initiates had to sign a blood compact and their rites lasted three days.

At its peak the Katipunan had 20,000 members, includ-

[35]One of the local queens he crowned was Doña Aurora Aquino, mother of Senator Aquino Jr.

ing Methodist ministers and intellectuals from Pampanga and Tarlac. It had headquarters in San Fernando and a branch in Manila. Many rich Pampangos including Don Gonzalo Puyat contributed to the finances of the movement. But it was short-lived, collapsing with the political defeat of its founder (though a Tarlac chapter was said to have persisted up to the 1950's). After the Katipunan's demise some of its peasant elements were incorporated into Abad Santos' Socialist Party and the Huks. One outstanding ex-Katipunero was Eusebio Aquino, the "Tandang Bio" who led one of Taruc's guerrilla columns.

In Congress, Rep. Hilario was known as a "champion of the peasants" and a "laborite." In his last year, he shared second place for most number of bills passed (four) with Rep. Guillermo Z. Villanueva and Majority Floor Leader Francisco Varona. The Hilario bills were distinctly authored in the spirit of agrarian reformism, labor upliftment, and unabashed patriotism. House Bill No. 1458 created rural libraries to increase the functional literacy of barrio residents. House Bill 1558 declared the last Sunday of May as National Flag Day; H.B. 1761 gave preferential credits to unpaid wages and salaries of laborers.

In an era when congressional performance was measured in the number of speeches made as well as bills introduced and passed, Zoilo Hilario was close to the top of the class with four brilliant speeches on the subjects of "National Heroes," "Public Works Contracts," "Woman Suffrage" and "In Defense of Aguinaldo's Pension."[36]

Hilario's non-violent, Christian creed is pithily expressed in a poem he wrote in the 1920's, *Dalit ning Musa ning Sinukwan* (Song of the Muse of Sinukwan*).

The Muse of Sinukwan
sings thus: "It is meet that
all men bow to what is right,
Peace will prevail
through the full cognizance and respect
by Pampangos of what is right.

Men of wisdom and the unschooled,
the rich, the poor
should all help one another.
Love of humanity should burn eternally
within their breasts
and shield one another.

They are all the children

[36]*Graphic,* February, 2, 1932.

of only one God
and must, therefore, obey
His Ten Commandments
and these will save them
from danger or a turbulent life.

They will defend
with all their might
the oppressed, those whose rights
have been trampled,
but will ask, no more or less,
what is their right, without violence."

(Translated from the Capampangan by Rosalina Icban Castro)

*another name for Mt. Arayat

Such are the peculiarities of Philippine politics that the best legislative record does not guarantee longevity in office. Hilario was a one-term wonder. He took all honors in that term only to lose in his reelection campaign in 1932. Hilario was conscientious in attending to his districts problems, bringing home in one session ₱80,000 in pork barrel funds. But he was too straight; he got jobs only for his constituents who qualified for them and politely told the rest that they had to accept something less. Most fatal of all was the Pampanga landlords' increasing distrust of his pleadings for the tenants. On the eve of the elections, the landlords feted their tenants, slipped favors to their leaders, and told their captive audiences to vote for Hilario's opponent.

From the start, Hilario had sought justice through legal means. Reform advocacy was only one plank of his personal crusade; his Katipunan also preached love of country and love of God. His defeat at the polls signified the refusal of the landlords to concede a fair share to the tenants. This was a turning point in the history of Pampanga. The peasants lost hope in their peaceful demonstrations and began to be attracted in greater numbers to more militant and radical organizations.

Abad Santos and the Socialist Party

The Socialist Party of the Philippines was largely the personal creation of Pedro Abad Santos, a well-born native of San Fernando whose single obsession in life was to give the poor farmers a large share of the wealth of the country.

His ancestral house in the provincial capital overflowed with unshod, impoverished farmers seeking his legal help. He had a staff of five lawyers shutting to and from the Pampanga courts in behalf of hundreds of indigent litigants. A steel safe stood near Abad Santos' desk from which he drew out peso bills to give his needy visitors Law was and still is one of the most highly rewarding professions in the Philippines, but Abad Santos was one of the few lawyers known to give more money to his clients than he ever received from them.

Judging from the Marxist literature mailed to him from Russia and China in the twenties, Zoilo Hilario was seriously considered as a transmission belt for communist indoctrination in Central Luzon. Ambassador Rafaelita Hilario Soriano believes that her father was on the Moscow mailing list earlier than Abad Santos. But Hilario rejected communism altogether. "Communism is not the answer," he often told his children. Eventually, the propaganda pamphlets stopped coming from overseas.[37]

The *Katipunan Mipananpun* was consequently more moderate in its tactical commitments than Abad Santos' Socialist Party. Zoilo, following his father's legalistic thinking, was convinced that the poor man in the barrio could better his welfare through peaceful and lawful means. This policy was as much an expression of Hilario's warm and generous nature as the Socialists' radicalism was an extension of the hot-blooded, highly combative character of their *guru*, Pedro Abad Santos.

Abad Santos was not physically an inspiring figure. He was tall, thin and ascetic, and his clothes were stained and mildewed. He was no platform orator; he left the speechfying to his young dapper assistant, Luis Taruc. His eyes were the most striking thing about him, Taruc recalled, the whiteness of the irises flashing like searchlights.[38]

Abad Santos was something of a maverick as far as the Pampango gentry was concerned. They feared his socialistic preaching as an evil thing that could bring the whole economic structure crashing down on them. Zoilo Hilario, who was his political rival despite the near-identity of their long-term goals, was better liked by the people because of his warmth, gallantry and eloquence. But Don Perico, as Abad Santos was commonly called, was highly respected for his intelligence and commitment. His Gandhi-like manner inspired awe rather than love. The fact that his younger brother, Jose Abad Santos, was a cabinet officer of President

[37]Soriano, interview.
[38]Taruc, interview.

Quezon and that he himself was a schoolmate of both Quezon and Osmeña in the Colegio de San Juan de Letran deterred the more reactionary elements from resorting to more direct ways to silence him.

Don Perico was a much older man than Zoilo Hilario, closer to the generation of Toribio Hilario than to Toribio's son. He was a youth during the Propaganda Movement and a mature man at the height of the Revolution. In the long span of his career, he personally transmitted the spirit of the revolution to the political climate of the thirties; he was his own revolutionary heritage.

He was the eldest of ten children — a large brood even by Filipino standards — of Vicente Abad Santos of San Fernando and the former Toribia Basco of Guagua. In the order of their birth, the Abad Santoses were Pedro, Emilia, Irineo, Escolastica, Antonio, Josefa, Jose, Quirino, Salvador and Catalino. Alvin Scaff, one of the earliest commentators of the Huk movement, described the Abad Santos family as belonging to the "landed aristocracy of Pampanga."[39] Ramon C. Aquino, the official biographer of the late Chief Justice Jose Abad Santos, disclaimed that. Pedro's brother Quirino told Aquino that the family did not own agricultural lands.

> His father owned only a residential house and lot and two other town lots. But the family was not poor either. It had three, and sometimes four, servants. The father left a substantial amount of cash when he died.[40]

It was no grand country villa where Pedro was born but a fairly modest house with nipa roofing, bamboo floor and three bedrooms standing on a 700-square meter lot. The house was on Blanco (now Capitan Mendoza) street, some 200 meters away from the church. In 1910 the family bought a larger house, of strong material, on Consunji street. This was the house where Don Perico lived in and used as the headquarters for his political movement in the thirties.

These circumstances suggest that the Abad Santos family belonged to the emerging middle class of Pampanga. Vicente Abad Santos attained the third year of the law course and at one point in his career became *Juez de ganados* (cadastral judge).[41]

Like his Letran College schoolmate Manuel Quezon, Pe-

---

[39]Alvin Scaff, *The Philippine Answer to Communism* (California: Stanford University Press, 1955).

[40]Ramon C. Aquino, *A Chance to Die, A Biography of Jose Abad Santos* (Quezon City: Alemar-Phoenix Publishing House, 1967), p. 9.

[41]Same.

dro Abad Santos put in for military service in the revolution. He was the aide of General Hizon with the rank of major during the Filipino-American war. Major Abad Santos was captured by the Americans and charged with "guerrilla activities and allied crimes." He was imprisoned in the Old Bilibid while awaiting trial.

John Haussermann, one of the brightest young American lawyers of his time and later to become the father of the Philippine gold mining industry, was retained to defend Abad Santos to no avail. The prisoner was convicted and sentenced to 25 years in prison.[42] He was later pardoned by President Theodore Roosevelt, after a period of incarceration longer than that suffered by Quezon who by 1907 was already delegate of the First Philippine Assembly.

Don Perico's ordeal only hardened his resolve to serve his people in some far-reaching, significant way. How he crossed the intellectual boundary between the blood-and-guts patriotism and romantic liberalism of his revolutionary youth and peasant activism is not firmly established. He is believed to have indoctrinated himself simply by reading — avidly and enormously. In time he accumulated what was believed at the time to be the largest collection of Marxist and socialist literature in Asia.[43]

Luis Taruc described his mentor as a "Marxist but not a Bolshevik." It is doubtful if Don Perico was even a Marxist. His favorites were Norman Thomas and Leon Blum, both non-Marxists, and he greatly admired the socialism of President Cardeñas of Mexico. He was also admirably non-dogmatic, never forcing his personal philosophies down the throats of his followers, but allowing them to think for themselves.[44] This suggests a highly discerning political mind, constantly searching for truth rather than entrenched behind absolutes. There was a catholicity in his socialist readings that made him almost intellectually incompatible with the Leninists and Stalinists who soon came to dominate the councils of the merged Communist and Socialist parties.

Don Perico and his younger brother Jose often had "heated arguments" over the former's political philosophy.[45] Jose, many years younger and spiritually unscathed by the trauma of the Revolution, remained a moderate and an honest and sincere liberal. Jose, also a lawyer by training, rose steadily in the ranks of the central government. He became Secretary of Justice, and shortly before the outbreak of the war achieved the highest position in his profession as Chief

[42]Same, p. 13.
[43]Taruc, interview.
[44]Same.
[45]Ramon C. Aquino, as cited, p. 3.

Justice of the Philippine Supreme Court. He was martyred by the Japanese on May 7, 1942 for his refusal to take an oath of allegiance to Japan.

In Pedro Abad Santos, the anti-clericalism of the revolutionary elites lived on. He was an agnostic, though tolerant of the church-going among his kin and associates. He founded Pampanga Lodge No. 48, a confirmed Mason like many of the Pampanga revolutionaries.

The difference between the reformism of Abad Santos and that of other Pampango liberals was in the former's willingness to use measured violence. To Abad Santos, it was like fighting fire with fire. The peasants were oppressed, their rights violated, and the poverty inflicted upon them was a greater form of violence than any number of ricestalks the peasants could burn or animals they could destroy.

Don Perico once advised a carpenter to hit a man who cheated him out of his due wages. Luis Taruc related how Abad Santos would test the resolve of an aggrieved peasant by asking him if he were willing to kill his landlord. When the tenant clearly showed no stomach for such an act, Abad Santos would mentally strike him out as a prospective member of the Socialist Party.

In the few cases the peasant had made his resolve to slaughter his tormentor, Abad Santos would stop the man just before he would leave his office and tell him, "You have proven to me your strong conviction and nerve. But you need not kill the landlord. I asked you that just to test you. If you kill him, you would become a fugitive and if ever you are caught you would be at the mercy of the judges — *they* are more partial to the rich men than to your kind. What you should do now is to *steal* the harvest. Most of it is yours by right of your labor anyhow. Let him sue you in court and I will defend you."[46] Abad Santos was an alien in his feudalistic environment but for many years he was pragmatically making whatever use he could have of its legal and parliamentary processes. He served two successive terms as representative of Pampanga's second district from 1916 to 1922 and he ran twice for Governor, losing both times. But where his own person was concerned, Abad Santos was beyond corruption. His daily diet of only two meals of the simplest food was the point of Quezon's personal tribute to Don Perico. "You hardly eat," he told the grand old man. "I cannot starve you, like other labor leaders who eat much and live luxuriously."[47]

---

[46]Taruc, interview.

[47]Ramon C. Aquino, as cited, p. 176.

The most dramatic confrontation between the two Filipino leaders, one the President of the Philippine Commonwealth and the other the Gandhi of the peasant masses, came in February, 1939. That year Central Luzon was rocking with class warfare. The Pampanga Sugar Mill (PASUMIL), the Bulacan Mill and the Rural Transit bus company were hit by massive strikes. Four hundred workers of the Hacienda Bahay Pare had taken 3,000 cavans of palay from the fields without the landowner's permission.[48] In an effort to restore peace to the troubled region, President Quezon accepted an invitation to speak at a massive rally organized by the Socialist party in San Fernando. Secretary Abad Santos took the precaution of advising his brother not to embarrass the President by greeting him with red flags, clenched-fist salutes or the singing of the Internationale.[49]

Before the biggest gathering of workers and peasants ever assembled, Pedro Abad Santos introduced the President as "a friend of the masses and of the poor." He told his workers, "Plant in your hearts what he will say." But as a preliminary to the speech of Quezon himself, Abad Santos ran down an inventory of peasant grievances. He accused the judges of being pawns of the landlords. He turned to his brother, sitting with the President, and challenged the Justice Secretary to clean up the courts. Showing impatience with his brother's "pacific temper and methods," Pedro sarcastically commented that, "the Secretary cannot help us if he just sits in his office."[50]

President Quezon, one of the greatest orators of his day, had the challenging task of reaching out to the hearts of the thousands of "sullen and skeptical" workers before him. He tried to establish an alliance with them by appealing to the sugar central owners to give the workers a larger share of the profits. He warned that if the millers were tardy in providing a more equitable sharing, he would get the National Assembly to tax sugar production higher and distribute the additional proceeds among the sugar workers.

However, he reminded his listeners that social justice was not for the proletariat alone but for all. He urged them to refrain from strikes and sabotage until he had time to reorder the system of government. He was completely opposed to Abad Santos' proposal to arm the peasants so that they could resist the abuses of the ruling class. "What will other countries say if the social justice program of Quezon is to

---

[48]Same, p. 94.
[49]Same, pp. 94-97.
[50]Same.

arm the people?" the President asked.

It was true, as Pedro Abad Santos said, that Secretary Abad Santos was chosen for his job because "he is with the masses." "But this does not mean that whatever you do, Secretary Abad Santos is with you, but merely that he will not permit abuses on you and will be with you as long as you are right."[51]

The meeting of the titans did not result in any perceivable lowering of the temper of the area. Two weeks after Quezon's speech, the PC and peasant strikers clashed and 15 were killed. The PC deployed 400 troopers in Central Luzon to prevent further violence. There were more reported cases of unsanctioned harvesting of palay by striking tenants. The situation in the region was clearly getting out of hand.

Luis Taruc

Until the mid-thirties, the Socialist party was little more than a personal cult of a few hundred men around Abad Santos. The party did not have any branches, nor did it even have a constitution. A good organizer was needed by the party, and Luis Taruc aptly filled that role.

Taruc was born in Santa Monica, a barrio of San Luis, Pampanga, close to the seasonally flooded Candaba swamps. His parents were peasants. The poverty of his youth, and possibly the fact that his father served in the Philippine Revolution, led Luis Taruc towards a reformer's career

What kept him from turning into a thoroughly ruthless revolutionary were his religious convictions. Today, pardoned from his prison sentence, he peacefully pursues his reformist mission as a spokesman of the Christian Social Movement.

He became a Communist not by deliberate choice but as a result of events that overtook him. The merger of his Socialist party and the CPP with the new organization bearing the Communist party's name made him a Communist nominally. But Taruc never accepted the atheism and "crude materialism" of Communist doctrine, and the "dictatorship of the proletariat" was repugnant to his peasant's sensibilities.

He had lingering qualms about needlessly shedding the blood of his followers and in 1954 he surrendered to the government rather than follow what he believed was a suicidal course for the present rebels.

Taruc's earliest links with Abad Santos was through a mutual associate, Lino Dizon, "a poet and a radical," as the former Huk supremo called him. When Taruc was still a senior in the San Miguel, Bulacan high school, Dizon asked

[51]Quoted by Ramon C. Aquino, as cited, p. 97.

him to join the Socialist party. Taruc declined because he was more interested in working his way through college.[52]

Unable to find a steady job in Manila, Taruc returned to San Miguel, listless and discouraged. One day Abad Santos and Dizon, who was one of his lieutenants, came by to see Taruc and the San Fernando socialist personally pressed the offer to Taruc. His own secretary, Marcos Manalang, was ailing; he needed somebody to help him. Taruc accepted. It was October, 1935. A great revolutionary career was on its way.

With Taruc as the General Secretary, the Socialist party took firmer roots in the countryside. He had already organized the *Aguman ding Maldang Talapaobra* (AMT) in 1932 and with that behind him it was an easy thing to establish socialist strongholds in Mexico, Angeles, Candaba, Arayat, Guagua, Floridablanca, Lubao, Apalit and Minalin. The AMT, the Socialist party chapters and the United Peasant Center set up by Communist leader Juan Feleo in Cabanatuan were later to provide the mass support and the militia for the Huks when the time came for them.

The political strength of the Socialist party was demonstrated in 1940 when eight of its candidates won electoral seats in Pampanga. Casto Alejandrino, later to become a ranking Huk chieftain, was the new mayor of Arayat. Abad Santos polled an impressive 33,000 votes against the 40,000 of his Nacionalista opponent, Sotero Baluyot. The Socialist party patriarch won the biggest towns — San Fernando, Angeles, Mexico, Guagua and Apalit — and Taruc believed that if the election had been more "honest" the contest would have been much closer.

The Socialist Party had succeeded in raising hell in Pampanga, stirring the conscience of the *ilustrado* politicians in Manila and placing the landlords on their guard. But victory was still far from sight. The Socialists needed a powerful ally to force the issue. Such an ally was available and it was the Communist Party of the Philippines.

---

[52]Taruc, interview.

Chapter Five

THE COMMUNIST CONSPIRACY

Communism came late to Central Luzon. Long before it manifested itself in Pampanga in the late thirties, modernization had worked its disruptive effects. Pampanga's peasant masses had become radicalized by their own elitist leaders and demagogues. By the time the first communist cadres came to Pampanga many of the workers and farmers were already organized into AMT chapters by Pedro Abad Santos and Luis Taruc.

This established the intellectual identity of the Huk movement. While Don Perico's socialism and the reformism of other Pampango liberals were products of the changes in the Pampango society, communism was a completely exported commodity. The communists took over at the propitious time when the peasant organizations were gearing for a showdown with their enemies. They got a free ride on an essentially indigenous protest movement.

It is therefore greatly misleading to regard the histories of Philippine communism and the Huk movement as identical. Philippine communism is more properly a part of the history of Philippine labor, since its roots spring from the power struggles among various laborite factions in the late twenties and early thirties and it gained strength in an urban milieu.

Comintern Contacts

The earliest communist contacts in the Philippines were made as a direct result of Comintern expansionism in Asia. In 1920, Grigor Zinoviev enlisted Turkish, African, Persian, Hindu and Chinese delegates to the cause of international communism in the Congress of the Peoples of the East in Baku. In the same year, the Chinese Communist party was born. In 1922 laborites from China, Japan, Korea, India and Indochina met in the First Congress at the Toilers of the Far East in Petrograd. A Far Eastern Bureau was set up in Shanghai in 1923. The Comintern was plotting to establish footholds in the European colonies in Asia; Communism had a dazzling intellectual appeal to nationalists all over the region and it had great worlds to conquer.

Alfredo Saulo, historian of Philippine communism, considers 1924 as one of the most important years in the growth of the movement. This was when William Janequette, alias Harrison George, came to Manila armed with a recommendation from Pedro Guevarra, former Philippine resident commissioner in the United States.[1] His official purpose was to observe labor conditions in the Philippines. Actually, Janequette was an active member of the Communist Party of the United States (CPUSA) and he was casting about for likely candidates to manage an apparat in Manila. Not suspecting Janequette's intentions, Secretary of the Interior Teodoro M. Kalaw introduced him to several Filipino labor leaders including Domingo Ponce, Joaquin Balmori, Jose C. Hilario, Potenciano G. Saliata and Jose Ernesto del Rosario.[2] Bognot was later cited as the authority for the belief that Crisanto Evangelista, Jacinto Manahan, Ponce, Francisco Varona and Bognot himself were picked by Janequette as "likely to be interested in Communism."[3]

Granting the truth of Bognot's statement, some of Janequette's choices were quite prophetic. Evangelista, leader of the extremist *Union de Impresores de Filipinas* (Philippine Printers' Union) was so well regarded that he was chosen labor delegate of the first Philippine Independence mission to the United States. There he fell under the spell of American leftists and returned a confirmed Marxist.[4] In 1924 Evangelista, Ponce and Bognot failed to win Nacionalista party nominations for the Manila council and in their dissappointment they quit the established party and formed their own *Partido Obrero*.[5] In six years Evangelista would become the "father" of Philippine communism. Jacinto Manahan, founder of the *Union de Aparceros de Filipinas*. (Philippine Farmers Union), also bcame a co-founder of the CPP and for many years its most important leadership link with the farm workers.

Another fruit of Janequette's visit was the participation of five Filipino delegates in the First Congress of the Oriental Transportation Workers in Canton in June, 1924. The delegates were Domingo Ponce, Jose C. Hilario, Eliseo Alampay, Jose Salazar and Eugenio Enorme. They were the first Fili-

---

[1]*Handbook on the Communist Party of the Philippines*, Armed Forces of the Philippines, 1961, p. 11. Subsequently cited as AFP Handbook.

[2]Saulo, as cited, p. 12.

[3]Same, p. 13.

[4]Same, p. 10.

[5]Same, p. 11.

pino labor representatives ever to attend a Communist-sponsored international meeting.

By 1924, international communism won a foothold in the Philippines. But there were great obstacles in its path — the rather chaotic state of unionism, the bitter rivalries among laborites and the conservative nature of the Filipino masses.

Early Labor Organizations

Saulo credits the printers and writers guilds with a seminal role in the development of the socialist and labor movements. Hermenegildo Cruz, organizer of the *Union de Litografos y Impresores de Filipinas* (Union of Lithographers and Printers), helped Isabelo de los Reyes found the first labor federation in the country, the *Union Obrera Democratica* (Democratic Labor Union) in 1902. According to Saulo, de los Reyes carried home from Europe the first batch of socialist and anarchist literature to reach the country in January, 1901.[6]

De los Reyes' federation lasted only three months. He was arrested and jailed after declaring his third strike, "not for his communist leanings," according to an AFP history, "but for denouncing the authorities." De los Reyes knew enough when to quit and he retired from unionism to enter politics.

Dominador Gomez, a colorful Spaniard, took over the union and renamed it *Union Obrera Democratica de Filipinas* (Democratic Labor Union). He personally led a battalion of unionists to Malacañang chanting anti-American slogans and demanding an eight-hour day. They were restrained from breaking into the Executive Office by the bayonets of American troops.[7] Gomez came to grief when American officers raided his home and printing press. The authorities threw the book at him including charges of labor racketeering and Gomez had to put in for a term on a prison gang on Corregidor island. Gomez was soon liberated from servitude and making more of a nuisance of himself to the American authorities by running for political office in Manila (and sometimes winning).[8]

Lope K. Santos, another active politician-writer, tried to reorganize the UODF but it broke up after four years due to "intramural troubles and mismanagement of funds." But from the debris of the strife-shattered UODF emerged Crisanto Evangelista. He was a man inspired by the socialism of Lope

[6]Same, pp. 5, 7 and 8.

[7]Same, p. 7.

[8]W. Cameron Forbes papers, Houghton Library, Harvard University.

K. Santos' novel *Banaag at Sikat*. On Labor Day, 1913, he helped organize the *Congreso Obrero de Filipinas* (COF) which Saulo called the "biggest and best organized labor federation in the country for nearly two decades until the big labor split of May 1929."

Parallel with urban unionism, though trailing by many years, came the organization of peasant groups. In 1917 the Bulacan peasants organized the *Pagkakaisa ng Magsasaka* (Farmer's Union), which, according to Hoeksema, later became the *Union ng Magsasaka* with Manuel Palomares as president and Jacinto Manahan as general secretary. Two years later, Manahan was the head of the *Union de Aparceros de Filipinas*. In 1922 it was expanded in the style of *Kalipunang Pambansa ng mga Magbubukid sa Pilipinas* (KPMP). Saulo described the KPMP as the forerunner of the postwar *Pambansang Kaisahan ng mga Magbubukid* (National Peasants' Union) which "supplied the foot soldiers of the Hukbalahap."

The labor scene exhibited many failings which persist up to this day. Labor opportunism was rife. Labor leaders enriched themselves on membership dues and often used their followings to catapult themselves into public office.[9] The unions never acquired a majority of the working force large enough to legislate substantive reforms. The Filipino-Spanish press — as opposed to the American-owned English-language newspapers — tended to be sympathetic to the laborites. But their influence was doubtful.

Labor and farmer's organizations acquired right from the start an unfortunate tendency to fragmentize or change organizational names and goals. At the root of this chaos was the personalistic nature of Filipino grievance groups. A union was formed only to be supplanted or rivaled by another and a successor leader often started his regime by adopting another organizational name. The members he won over stayed with him; the others strayed away and formed yet another organization.

The early unions were more often than not confined within a few industries or localities. The *Pagkakaisa ng Magsasaka* was almost exclusively made up of Bulacan farmers; they were altogether only a small minority of all the farmers in the province. In 1924 Teodoro Sandiko, a revolutionary general who had turned to politics, revived the *Union ng Magsasaka* for the announced purpose of obtaining better terms for contractual labor in the province. After some time, it became yet another political organization.[10]

There was not much of a labor movement for the com-

---

[9]Same.
[10]Hoeksema, as cited.

munists to capture in 1924. The industrial sector itself was kept small by the country's overdependence on agricultural exports. The communists had to build from the bottom to have any chance of becoming a major political force in the country. But they seemed to have neither the time nor the genius for that monumental project. They got along with what labor fragments and factions were there for the picking. They were never at any one time able to control more than 20 percent of organized labor. And their failure to obtain a consensus among labor proved their undoing.

Tan Malaka

In July, 1925, a dark, rather handsome young man of 32 stepped off the gangplank of the *SS Empress of Russia*, and presented himself to the Manila port authorities as Elias Fuentes, a Filipino musician back from a tour of the crown colony. Actually, he was a notorious Indonesian agent fleeing from the Dutch police. He was known to his pursuers as Tan Malaka.

Malaka was a "quiet, contemplative man" who spoke English but no Filipino dialect, and was a bit tubercular. But, judging from his recorded exploits, his activities in the next two years were nothing short of Herculean. He cut a great swath among Manila's intellectual elite and the political salons. Among his newly-found admirers were Senate President Quezon, Claro M. Recto, Jose Abad Santos, Francisco Varona, Gregorio Perfecto, Ramon Torres, Ramon Fernandez and Emilio Aguinaldo.[11] He was the house guest of National University president Apolinario de los Santos and went on an excursion to the southern islands with Varona, co-editor of *El Debate*, friend of the *cocheros* (horse-rig drivers) and soon to be a member of the House of Representatives.

He even found time to work in Malaya and Siam in between his sojourns to the Philippines. It was just after returning to Manila from Thailand where Dutch agents once again got on his trail that Malaka's cover was blown. Capt. Juan Quimbe, PC assistant intelligence officer, put the cuffs on him at the foot of Jones bridge on August 12, 1927. The government instituted proceedings to deport him to the Dutch East Indies where an easily imaginable fate awaited him.

The ensuing furor over Tan Malaka was unprecedented. His Filipino friends rushed to his defense, justifying his work as inspired by a "prevalent thirst for liberty and justice among subject peoples." The encomium came from Quezon who at that time was pushing a political bandwagon on the inde-

[11]Saulo, as cited, p. 14.

pendence issue. Claro M. Recto, already building a reputation for being a super-nationalist, launched a Tan Malaka fund. Jose Abad Santos, a former Secretary of Justice (he took the position twice), lent his considerable prestige in helping Mariano Nable obtain a petition of habeas corpus in behalf of Malaka.[12] Quezon declared himself of the opinion that under the American flag Malaka was entitled to full protection.[13]

The Manila liberals finally won out and Tan Malaka was shipped to Amoy on August 22 instead of being handed over to the mercies of the Dutch. Malaka was able to go scot-free because he had cleverly played to the biases and naivete of his Filipino friends.

Unknown to them, Tan Malaka had been meeting with leftist leaders including Evangelista, Guillermo Capadocia, Mariano Balgos and Juan Feleo.[14] He was able to arrange for the participaiton of Varona, Ponce and Alampay in the Canton labor conference, sponsored by the Pan Pacific Trade Union Secretariat (PPTUS). Malaka, however, failed to convert Pedro Abad Santos to communism, and thus Pampanga was saved for the duration from the encroachments of the Manila apparat.

In 1928 came another RILU invitation for the Philippines to be represented in the Shanghai labor conference. In the Chinese city the Filipino delegates Evangelista and Bognot met a certain Chou En-lai, of the fledgling Chinese Communist Party, and top American communist Earl Browder. Browder arranged a Moscow visit for the two Filipinos. They were joined in the Russian capital by Jacinto Manahan, his trip financed by the *Krestintern* or Peasant International.[15] When the Filipino labor leaders returned to Manila they formed a "secretariat," reportedly under Comintern direction, and started circulating a propaganda sheet called *Dawn*.

Just before the 1930's there was feverish activity by the few hardcore radicals. Manahan was credited with having made the first attempt to indoctrinate Central Luzon peasants with undiluted communism; the occasion was the National Confederation of Tenants and Farm Workers in Pitpitan, Bulacan on December 1, 1928. Upon his return from Moscow, Bognot organized the Philippine section of the Anti-Imperialist League with the purpose of rallying Filipino students and young intellectuals behind Comintern goals. The league lasted for only as long as Bognot remained in the CPP councils.[16]

[12] Ramon C. Aquino, as cited.
[13] AFP Handbook, p. 12.
[14] Saulo, p. 15.
[15] AFP Handbook, p. 13.
[16] Same, p. 14.

It would not be until four decades later that the Filipino studentry became a potent political force.

The CPP Organizers

The Communist Party of the Philippines was organized in an atmosphere of coup and countercoup, in the inimitable style of Bolsheviks all over the world. The precipitating event was the ouster of Evangelista and his comrades from their positions of influence in the COF by a conservative majority led by Ruperto Cristobal, Isabelo Tejada and Antonio D. Paguia. Evangelista and his hardcore were in Moscow on Profintern business and when his rivals called a national convention in May, 1928, the few Evangelista loyalists left behind could not put up even a token opposition to the conservatives. Varona and Evangelista, the president and general secretary of the Congress, were replaced by a "caretaker" administration pending a final showdown with Evangelista.[17]

This was a blow to Evangelista who had planned to expand the COF as the "national center" of the Philippine labor movement, organize workers along industrial instead of craft lines and "carry the workers' struggle beyond trade unionism" and into something more decisive.[18]

Returning to the Philippines, Evangelista tried to regain lost ground by proposing a radical program for the approval of the executive committee, knowing that the conservatives did not have a majority in that body to defeat it. The conservatives accepted the Evangelista "thesis" in the committee, taking one step backward with the full intention of treading Evangelista and his cohorts under with the next two.

The showdown came in the next COF convention on May 1, 1929. The day was an unmitigated disaster for the Evangelista faction. They were so badly outnumbered by their rivals — Lava later charged that Cristobal and his "yellow leaders" produced "gangsters and dummy labor delegates without unions" to pack the roster — that Evangelista had no choice but to stalk out to avoid defeat.[19] Joining Evangelista in the schism were Antonino D. Ora, Manahan, Balgos, Capadocia, Urbano Arcega and Patricio Dionisio.

The Evangelista walkout created a deep cleavage in the ranks of Philippine labor. Polarized and broken up into special-interest groups, the labor front would never again be able to act as a single advocate for the rights of the working man.

---

[17]Saulo, as cited, pp. 18-19.

[18]Same, p. 19.

[19]Jose Lava, *Milestones in the History of the Communist Party*, an unpublished manuscript.

Philippine radicalism was also thenceforth doomed to permanent minority status.

Still staggered by their defeats, Evangelista and his followers formed a new labor federation, *Katipunan ng mga Anakpawis sa Pilipinas* (Association of the Sons of Sweat) while they figured out their next move. Retreat was out of the question. A more militant revolutionary party was what was needed to capture the initiative from the conservative laborites.

On August 26, 1930, the 34th anniversary of the Cry of Balintawak, a convention was held at the Templo del Trabajo, Tondo, to organize the new party. There were 60 participants representing various pro-Evangelista unions. Among the various names suggested for the party were Proletarian Labor Party, Socialist Party, Bolshevik Party and — Evangelista's proposal — the Communist Party. Not surprisingly, Evangelista's wish prevailed.[20]

In forming the Central Committee, the organizers made sure that as many crafts and occupations were represented. It has five printers including Evangelista himself, four farmers led by Manahan and Feleo, Bognot and Patricio Dionisio as well as two writers, seven cigarmakers, two mariners, four woodcutters led by Antonio Ora (also the president of KAP), two cooks including Capadocia, two electricians, two slipper makers, one plumber, one railroad worker, one clerk and two Chinese.

The Politburo, formed out of the Central Committee membership was made up of Evangelista, Ora, Manahan, Feleo, Felix Caguin, Urbano Arcega, and a Chinese representative called Comrade "C." Evangelista was elected secretary-general.

The party had a little more than two months to whip up popular support for its proclamation on November 7. The date added historic significance to the occasion for it was the 13th anniversary of the Russian Revolution. A strong agitprop team led by Evangelista and Capadocia launched a membership drive in Laguna, Bulacan and Rizal. Manahan and Feleo led another drumbeating squad assigned to Nueva Ecija, Bataan, Batangas, Cavite and Tayabas. Ora and Arcega touched bases with the firewood dealers, marines, printers and other urban workers while Jose Ventura and two others were to work on the tobacco factories.

On the night of November 7, only a modest crowd of 5,000 turned up at Plaza Moriones, Tondo. Silvino Tablan acted as the master of ceremonies and Dominador J. Ambrosio of Laguna read the preamble of the Party constitution. Mana-

---

[20]AFP Handbook, p. 15.

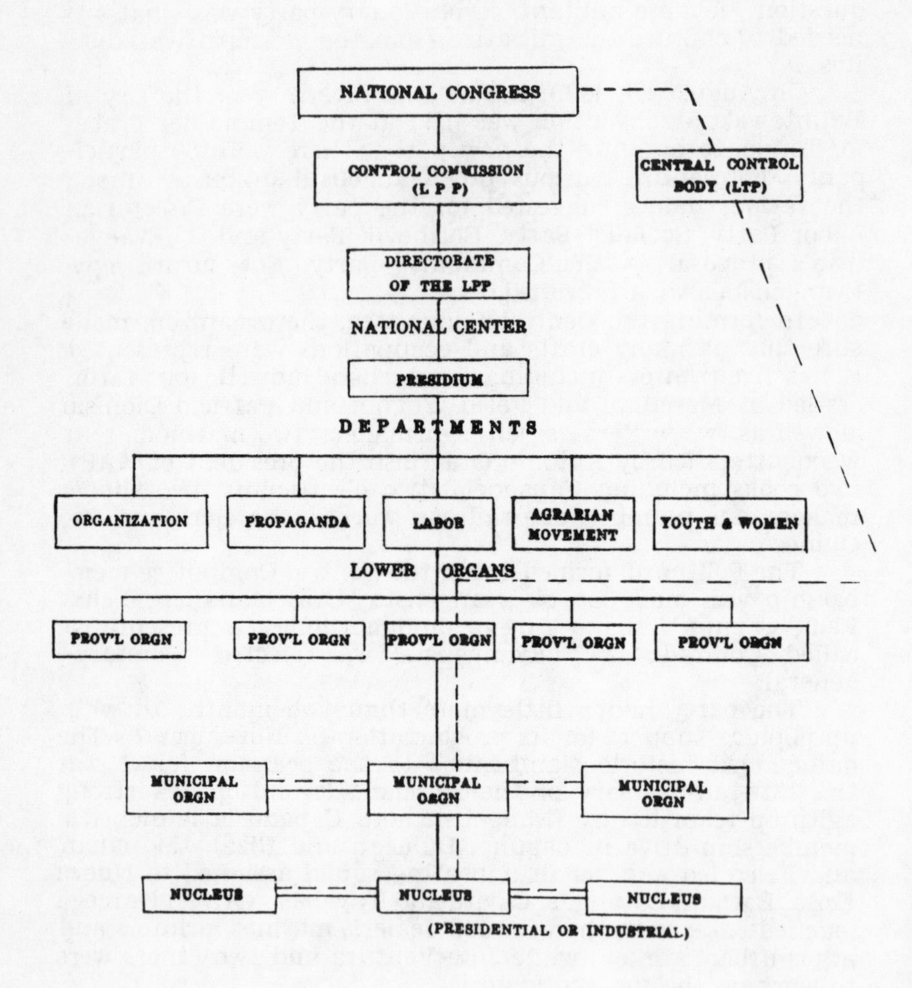

Figure 4: Organization Structure of the Communist Party of the Philippines according to the 1930 Party Constitution. From the Armed Forces of the Philippines.

han and Ora then recited the resolutions to which the crowd gave their *viva voce* approval.[21]

Agitation and Propaganda

The CPP set up headquarters at No. 8 Basa, Manila, ran a newspaper *Titis* (Spark) and supplemented this propaganda with broadsides and handbills (urging, among others, the proletariat to take to the barricades and form a communist government). The party received financial help from its old CPUSA adviser Janequette and Agnes Smedley.

Less than a year after its founding, the CPP was in trouble with the government. Its labor arm, KAP, planned a huge parade for its first May Day in 1931 but Mayor Tomas Earnshaw of Manila refused to grant a permit. The party succeeded in getting a permit to march from the Caloocan plaza to Bonifacio monument, but at the last minute Mayor Aquino changed his mind and cancelled the permit. The cancellation came too late. Thousands of CPP sympathizers were already at the designated places for the demonstration.[22]

A PC detail led by Captain Jalandoni was sent to disperse the crowd and a tense, hostile situation developed. The PC captain permitted Evangelista to speak to the crowd provided he would ask them to go home. But the secretary-general got carried away and his philliphic inspired a bystander, Abelardo Ramos, to cry, "Let us die fighting them." Evangelista and Ramos were promptly arrested, and it took hastily-summoned firetrucks from Manila to break up the threatening crowd with water hoses.

Evangelista and Ramos were charged with illegal association and sentenced to six months imprisonment and a fine of ₱400. The verdict was appealed while Evangelista remained on bail. Then came a bigger blow. Judge Mariano Alberto of the Manila Court of First Instance found Evangelista, Manahan, Capadocia and three other CPP members guilty of sedition and sentenced them to a year of imprisonment and a ₱1,000 fine. In addition, Evangelista, Manahan, Capadocia and many of the party's key men were declared banished *(confinamento)* for eight years and one day to different provinces. The Supreme Court affirmed this judgment. Thus was the CPP outlawed for the first time — by a judicial act.

The party was hurt considerably. Bognot, Dionisio and many other invaluable workers resigned earlier due to the government pressure. The loss of Manahan followed shortly. He confessed that the CPP was not the proper vehicle for

---

[21]Same, p. 16.
[22]Saulo, as cited, p. 22.

advancing the peasants' cause. He formed a new (but short-lived) peasant organization, the *Kalipunang Pambansa ng mga Magbubukid sa Pilipinas* (KPMP), and was promptly declared a renegade by the party.

In explaining the ideological differences between the two party titans, Saulo called Manahan "more of a nationalist than an internationalist" and a "tioist," and Evangelista a "rabid pro-Comintern internationalist of the Leninist school."

There also was undoubtedly an element of personal rivalry between the two. So long as the party councils assigned the vanguard role to the urban proletariat, Evangelista would be permanently entrenched in his doctrines and leadership while Manahan would have to remain in a secondary role.[23]

The Communist party thus failed its first test. It could not shake the foundations of the bourgeois state; it was even alienated from the majority of the urban labor. Many years later Mao Tse-tung's monumental contribution to revolutionary theory — placing the numerically superior peasantry in the forefront of the armed struggle — would be better appreciated by Asian communists. But this simple strategem with its obvious applicability to the Philippines escaped Evangelista and his colleagues for many years.

All throughout the party's formative years the peasant specialists were in the minority compared to the printers, writers and unionists in the Central Committee and Politburo. The party did not even have a strong Pampanga contact; Manahan had his base in Bulacan and Feleo in Nueva Ecija.

Now it sought to strengthen that weak flank with a coalition with the strongest of the peasant organizations, the Socialist AMT complex run by Pedro Abad Santos and Luis Taruc.

The Communist-Socialist Merger

Happily, such a union was what best fitted the new ukase laid down by the Comintern in its seventh world congress in Moscow. The 1935 directive placed ultimate importance on united front tactics in combatting world fascism. A spirit of cooperation with socialistic elements was the prescription for all parties, the CPP included.

The principal sponsor of this unlikely union was an emissary from the American Communist Party named James S. Allen. It was Allen, posing as Dr. Sol Auerbach, who conveyed the new Comintern ruling to his Philippine comrades in 1936. He convinced Evangelista and his comrades to accept con-

---

[23] AFP Handbook, pp. 23-24.

ditional pardon so that they could revive the moribund party in league with other anti-fascist elements. Allen then worked on President Quezon and persuaded him that Evangelista would be of better service preparing the country against imminent Japanese invasion if he were out of jail.[24] Shortly afterwards, on December 31, 1936 Evangelista and his fellows were released from prison.

Two years later, Allen returned to the Philippines to complete his plan. He had breakfast with President Quezon and presumably used the occasion to plead for Evangelista again. On Christmas Eve of 1938 Evangelista, Capadocia, Balgos, and eight other communists were granted absolute pardon.

Capadocia soon afterwards brought Allen to San Fernando to meet Pedro Abad Santos and propose a merger between the two parties. Abad Santos was amenable; it was up to his leaders to speak their minds about the proposal. Socialist party opinion was initially split. Taruc and Casto Alejandrino were willing to abide by whatever the Grand Old Man would say but among those who opposed the merger were Agapito del Rosario, Lino Dizon and Bernabe Poblete. They reasoned that the "godlessness" of the Communists antagonized the church-going Pampango peasants. Appealing to Don Perico's vanity, they foresaw that he would have to accept a subsidiary position in the combined leadership. But Abad Santos was already beyond such apprehensions; he stuck to his original decision, convinced that the common threat demanded unity among Filipinos.[25]

The merger was approved by the CPP at its third national congress on October 29-31, 1938 and formalized by a joint convention between the two parties on November 7, 1938.

"Merger" was perhaps not the best word for the settlement. Despite the apparent equitability in the distribution of positions, the Communist Party with its more compact and militant leadership simply absorbed a potential Pampanga subsidiary, retaining corporate control of its own original operations. The Communists would not once yield top command to their new "comrades."

Under the terms of the merger, the name of the Communist Party of the Philippines would be retained except for an added phrase "Merger of the CP and SP." The KPMP and the AMT would maintain separate identities but under the supervision of the Peasant Department. The socialist party had one major concession; it would have supervision over party organs and mass organizations in Pampanga and some towns of Tarlac and Bataan.

---

[24]Same.
[25]Same.

The new CPP leadership was headed by Evangelista, chairman; Abad Santos, vice chairman; and Capadocia, general secretary. The new Central Committee included Evangelista, Abad Santos, Balgos, Taruc, Primitivo Arrogante, Lazaro Cruz, Felipe Sevilla, Pedro Castro, Mateo del Castillo, Feleo del Rosario, Godofredo Mallari, Antonio Pablo, Mamerto Carlos, Vicente Lava and a Chinese member.

There was little prospect of a happy union from the start. Though Abad Santos took no offense at being relegated to No. 2 status, his Socialist colleagues showed marked indifference to jointly called projects. They dismissed summonses to conferences with an "I-agree-with-whatever-you-take-up" attitude.[26] The Socialists were also prone to act unilaterally on concerns involving their Pampanga territory. They resisted CPP directives to hook up their AMT units with the Communist party machinery.

As Taruc recalled the CPP-SP liaison, "We were not accustomed to the iron discipline of the Communist Party but what we lacked in discipline and doctrine we made up in idealism and enthusiasm. When we were troubled by the things our comrades did, we consoled ourselves with the thought that dedication to a good cause would produce good men."[27]

---

[26]AFP Handbook, p. 26.
[27]Taruc, as cited, p. 17.

Chapter Six

THE WARTIME HUKS: 1942-1945

The military arm of the merged Communist-Socialist party was conceived as early as October, 1941, two months before Japanese bombs fell on Pearl Harbor and Clark airfield. Probably through their Comintern contacts, the party chiefs were more sensitized to the imminent Axis assault on democratic countries and they busied themselves preparing for the inevitable Japanese occupation just as General MacArthur's headquarters and the Quezon government tried without completely succeeding to place the country on a war footing.

It proposed "national unity for an anti-Japanese United Front" and preparations now — instead of waiting for eventualities — for massive guerrilla resistance against the expected Japanese invasion. All anti-Fascist organizations, including the AMT, KPMP and labor unions, were urged to organize fighting units and train for guerrilla operations. All able-bodied citizens were on call for patriotic services. All resistance groups should learn how to commandeer enemy property; all traitors and backsliders must pay with their lives.[1]

Then came the catch. The people were urged to form Yenan-style governments in areas liberated from the enemy. The memorial strongly implied centralized control of the underground movement, without hinting that the Communists — the original United Front promoters — were best capable of leading the entire effort. To assure President Quezon and U.S. High Commissioner Francis Sayre of their patriotic motives, the party pledged loyalty to the cause of democracy and to the governments of the Philippines and the United States.

Quezon and Sayre ignored the memorial. They apparently distrusted the intentions of the Communists. There was fear that a communist-led national resistance would lead to a communist takeover after the war. Chin Peng, for a fact, allied the Malayan Communist Party with the British shortly

[1]AFP Handbook, p. 29.

before the fall of the Malay peninsula and unknown to his benefactors armed some formations in the Malayan jungles. After the war, the MCP launched a vicious and long-lasting guerrilla war against the British.[2] According to Taruc, the CPP offered its help "in all sincerity." He knew of no such treacherous plan. The idea of massive aid for guerrilla forces was academic anyway because the Philippine Commonwealth did not even have enough arms to supply its newly mustered-in regiments.

The party executed its plans even without the Commonwealth's blessing. Hundreds of arms and other material left behind by the retreating USAFFE forces were salvaged by Pampango partisans. According to Pampanga's unofficial historian, Mariano A. Henson, the arsenals and warehouses of Fort Stotsenburg (now Clark air base) were opened to anybody who wanted to help himself to guns and provisions. This windfall in hardware led to "the indiscriminate use of military weapons... in Pampanga and elsewhere."[3]

Arrest of Evangelista and Abad Santos

The CPP suffered a major blow even before it had dug in for protracted resistance. The party leaders had been warned to leave Manila before the Japanese flying columns reached the city. But, Saulo writes, they "tarried too long, relying on the Communist maxim that 'the safest place for communists to hide is right next to the enemy — where the enemy is least likely to look.' It turned out, however, that this communist tactic merely saved the Japanese much time and effort in trying to capture them."[4]

On January 25, 1942, the Japanese *Kempeitai* (Military Police) arrested Pedro Abad Santos in his own residence in Ermita, Manila. Unaware that anything was amiss, Evangelista and Capadocia walked into the Abad Santos home that same evening and right into the hands of the Japanese. The efficient Japanese net snared Agapito del Rosario and several non-CPP members including Quirino Abad Santos and Manuel Abad Santos (Pedro's brother and nephew) and Dr. Angel Ancajas.

The captives were taken to the Manila Hotel and separately interrogated. A desperate del Rosario jumped out of the hotel's fourth floor window. He survived long enough to be executed in Fort Santiago. Evangelista and Pedro Abad

---

[2]Kennedy, as cited.
[3]As cited, p. 81.
[4]As cited, p. 37.

Santos, both aging and sick, were valuable to the Japanese only if they could persuade their younger comrades to surrender to the Imperial Army.

The Japanese tried to make the two party patriarchs agree to a set of conditions for their release. Negotiations should be held between March 15 to April 15, 1942 for the surrender of all CPP units in Central Luzon. The CPP should not only sever relations with the Central Luzon bandits but use force to effect their surrender. All arms were to be turned in to the nearest Japanese Military Police stations. Pedro Abad Santos had to place his signature on a document, to be published in all newspapers, declaring the abolition of both the CPP and the Socialist party. As a further concession to the CPP, its unarmed functionaries would be free from arrest. All communists surrendering to the Military Police would be allowed to return peacefully to their homes.[5]

Evangelista refused to sign the agreement, while Abad Santos was too ill even to read it. Col. Kodama of the *Kempeitai* had to try the alternate scheme of sending Capadocia to Central Luzon to personally negotiate with the guerrillas. In the company of Quirino Abad Santos and Dr. Ancajas — also released by the Japanese for the same purpose — Capadocia was guided to the barrio of Balite where an unexpectedly hostile reception awaited them. The Huks disarmed the party and arrested Capadocia. The party suspected the secretary-general of collaboration with the Japanese and though Capadocia explained the extenuating circumstances of his capture and incarceration he was sentenced to a year's imprisonment in the Huk stockade.[6]

The Huk defiance doomed two of the party leaders still confined in Fort Santiago. Evangelista and del Rosario were executed by the Japanese. But the Japanese decided to be more merciful with the Socialist party founder. He was too ill to pose any more trouble for the Japanese regime; he was possibly even dying. Abad Santos was allowed to go back to his native Pampanga to spend his last days with his kin. He died of his lingering illness in a barrio of Minalin in 1945.

The party was organized to survive such a contingency as the loss of top leaders. It had a "first," "second" and even a "third front" in its formal hierarchy and right after the fall of Evangelista, Abad Santos and Capadocia, the second front took over.[7] Dr. Vicente Lava, (Comrade VY) the first of three Lava brothers to successively direct the fortunes of

---

[5]AFP Handbook, pp. 30-31.
[6]Same.
[7]Same, p. 32.

the party, moved up as secretary-general. Taruc was besieged by his old Socialist partymates to take over the chairmanship of the captured Evangelista. After all, he had been the No. 3 man in the CPP-SP hierarchy after Evangelista and Abad Santos. But his old qualms about conspicuously identifying with Communism emerged again and he gave way to Dr. Lava.[8]

Vicente Lava was now the No. 1 party executive since the positions of national chairman and vice chairman were abolished. The other party hierarchs were Mateo del Castillo, chairman of the organization department; Juan Feleo, chairman of the United Front department; Primitivo Arrogante, chairman of the educational department; Emeterio Timban, chairman of the finance department; and Luis Taruc and Casto Alejandrino, chairman and vice chairman of the military department. The ever-present Comrade "C" liaised between the CPP and the Chinese Bureau.[9]

The reorganized party leadership held a "struggle conference" on February 16, 1942, in Sitio Bawit, San Lorenzo, Cabiao, Nueva Ecija, as Saulo describes it, "a forested area linking the three provinces of Nueva Ecija, Pampanga and Tarlac."[10] The party agreed to continue its united front tactics, placing long-term party objectives in the background and attracting as many sectors as it could to the anti-Japanese cause.

The Huk Army

It was in the *Pampangan* where agrarian radicalism first found roots that the Huks became a guerrilla army. The towns of Arayat, Mexico, San Simon, Apalit and Candaba were strongly loyal to the movement. And across the Candaba swamp were barrios like Mandili and Bahay Pare which communicated by roads and trails with the Bulacan towns of San Miguel, San Ildefonso and San Rafael.

These were Tagalog towns but they were bilingual because of their close contacts with the Pampangos. The northern Bulacan towns had a "revolutionary tradition." San Miguel was the birthplace of General Tecson; San Ildefonso was one of the communities overtaken by the Sakdal revolt. San Rafael had one of the biggest tracts of friar lands and its farmers were solidly behind Taruc's advocacy for land reform.[11]

---

[8]Interview, July, 1970.
[9]Saulo, as cited, p. 38.
[10]As cited, p. 39.
[11]Taruc, interview, July, 1970.

Taruc had complete access to virtually all of Pampanga, the "Pampanganized" Bulacan towns and Nueva Ecija. He moved about freely with only a few escorts and had the protection of barrio people. Only when he had to enter the large poblaciones where there were puppet Constabulary and police did he have to take extra precautions.[12]

The time soon came for the Pampango guerrillas to be tested. Early in 1942, the guerrilla band operating in the Candaba area was under the command of a woman, Felipa Culala or "Dayang Dayang" as she was called. Eight of her men were captured and imprisoned in the town jail by the puppet mayor, William Arroyo. On March 8, Dayang Dayang marched into town with several of her followers and freed her comrades. This brazen act provoked a counterattack by the Japanese.

On March 14, the Japanese set out from San Miguel with a company of puppet police. Guerrilla intelligence alerted Dayang Dayang. Together with Bernardo Poblete, alias Banal, she laid a perfect ambush behind the irrigation ditches in barrio Mandili. In the ensuing battle the 130 guerrillas under Dayang Dayang and Banal slew 30 to 40 Japanese soldiers and 68 puppet police and captured 38 enemy arms. The proud Japanese troops made themselves easier targets by refusing to lie flat on the rice paddies, firing back at their ambushers from a kneeling position. "Despite our bad marksmanship, we got a lot of them that way," Taruc recalled.[13]

The Mandili victory electrified the countryside. The guerrillas had proven a match man for man with the Japanese Imperial Forces. In less than a month, the various guerrilla bands in the Central Plain formally organized the *Hukbo ng Bayan Laban sa Hapon*. The peasant militia was mustered into service in the same Cabiao forest where the party had held its struggle meeting.[14] Taruc, who as military department chairman was also the Huk commander-in-chief, wanted to call the force "People's Liberation Army" but a Chinese adviser persuaded the committee that *Hukbo ng Bayan Laban sa Hapon* would be more in keeping with the united front tactics. So it was. The military committee functioned also as Huk headquarters and Casto Alejandrino was second in command.

It was a ragtag army at best. Culala headed a squadron of 100 men from Candaba, Banal about 20 to 40 from San Luis and Minalin, Lope de la Rosa a unit from San Miguel,

[12]Same.

[13]This description of the Mandili battle is based on Luis Taruc's personal recollections and Hoeksema's cited work.

[14]Saulo, as cited, p. 40.

Bulacan, Eusebio Aquino 30 to 40 men from Magalang and Mariano Franco about 50 from Cabiao.

Poblete, or Tandang Banal as he was called, was probably the only professional soldier in the group. He was a Philippine Scout and a veteran of World War I. Culala, though a woman, had the respect of the guerrillas because of her stunning victory in Mandili. Tandang Bio had little more than "revolutionary tradition" behind him. Taruc by his own admission was no soldier. He justified his top command on the grounds that the Huks were a "political force more than a real army."[15]

The Huk commanders were responsible generally for their native territory — a pattern that continues to the present. Eventually, the Huk command was divided into five military districts. Poblete was in charge of the 1st military district (southern Pampanga), Culala, the 2nd MD (Baliuag, Apalit, San Ildefonso, San Simon, San Luis, Candaba, and Sta. Ana and a part of Arayat), Aquino, the 3rd MD (area north of Arayat and all of Nueva Ecija), and Abelardo Dabu the 5th MD (western Pampanga from Mexico through Bacolor to Lubao and Floridablanca).[16]

The basic Huk formation was the squadron, equivalent to a company in a conventional army, or about 100 men. By September, 1942, the Huks had 30 squadrons deployed in the field or about 3,000 men.[17]

Huk resourcefulness made up for the initial lack of firearms. Aside from the recovered USAFFE material, village blacksmiths made crude, single-firing *paltiks* or handguns. Licensed firearms were confiscated from civilians. Ambuscades of Japanese patrols and the capture of puppet constabularymen also added to the stockpile. By the end of the war, the Huk command had accumulated some 7,000 weapons of all types.[18]

The Communist character of the Hukbalahap was no-

---

[15]Taruc, interview, July, 1970.

[16]Hoeksema, as cited. Of the original Hukbalahap Military Committee, only Taruc and Alejandrino stayed on through the postwar rebellion. Culala, the Huk amazon, was later executed by her comrades for being "leftist" asd an "opportunist," according to Simbulan in his cited work. Banal, with two USAFFE officers, Pacifico Briones and Major Angelo Fajardo, broke away from the organization when they discovered it was Communist-directed. The "Banal Regiment" was the only original Huk unit recognized by the U.S. Army and awarded backpay.

[17]Hoeksema believes that the Huks never had more than 2,000 regulars during the Japanese occupation.

[18]Hoeksema, as cited.

where apparent in its charter.

> The object of this army is to drive out the Japanese fascist aggressors from the Philippines; to safeguard the lives, properties and democratic rights of the people and for the people. But before this government is in proper function, it is under the Command of the People's Anti-Japanese Military Committee which is organized by the anti-Japanese people of the Philippines.
>
> The Army cooperates with the United States Armed Forces in the Far East (USAFFE), for the resistance against the common enemy — the Japanese fascist aggressors.[19]

A Political and Military Training school was established in May, 1942, on the slopes of Mt. Arayat. Part of Huk legend is the entry of "competent Chinese officers smuggled in from the Chinese mainland" to fill the shortage in training personnel. The AFP handbook records that the guerrilla warfare instructor was a "colonel in the Red Chinese Eighth Route Army." The "Fundamental Spirit of Guerrilla Tactics" by Mao Tse-tung and Chu-teh were translated for the edification of the peasant soldiers. Edgar Snow's classic "Red Star over China" also provided inspirational reading.[20]

The Huk command welcomed the proposal of their Chinese comrades to activate a Chinese squadron. Ong Kiat, "a Red Chinese officer," organized 80 men into the "Overseas Chinese 48th Detachment of the Philippine Anti-Japanese Forces," or the "48th Wa Chi" for short (the numbers were taken from the Chinese Communist 4th and 8th Route Armies). The "Wa Chi" was reported later to have six squadrons of 200 men each based in San Miguel, Bulacan and Paete, Laguna.[21]

The peasant organizations formed before the war — the AMT and the KPMP — provided the mass base for the guerilla army. Both prewar organizations were dissolved and reconstituted as the Barrio United Defense Corps (BUDC).

---

[19]By-laws of the Hukbo ng Bayan Laban sa Hapon, March 29, 1942, translated from the Tagalog.

[20]p. 33. The AFP handbook, however, did not state how Chinese Army officers were shipped across the South China Sea and sneaked into a Japanese-occupied country — a rather improbable feat.

[21]Same, p. 35.

A typical BUDC council — a microcosm of the party organization — was composed of a chairman, a vice chairman, a secretary-general and members responsible for recruiting intelligence, transportation, communications, education, sanitation and agriculture.

The BUDC council was virtually an underground "government," very much the precursor of the "invisible government" reported by Sen. Manuel Manahan in 1967. Its intelligence service was invaluable to the Huks. Nothing could stir without the Huk command knowing about it. The transportation chairman arranged carts, carabaos, bancas and an occasional motor vehicle for strike units and political commissars. The BUDC imposed "taxes" and "communized" the barrio economy so that provisions could be laid aside for Huk operations. The council solemnized marriages and adjudicated disputes.[22]

The BUDC had the "power of life and death over the barrio." This police power, plus the not infrequent occurences of grudge killings by undisciplined Huk members, gave the movement a mixed reputation in Central Luzon. The poor barrio people who were helped by the Huks and their barrio auxiliaries were naturally grateful. But there were many other Pampangos to whom the Huks were a menace. The Huks themselves admitted that only 5,000 of the 25,000 casualties inflicted on the "enemy" were Japanese soldiers. The rest were puppets, uncooperative politicians, spies, landlords, or simply personal enemies. Many of the barrio vendettas persisting to this day can be traced to the fraticide of the Japanese occupation.

The Guerrilla War in the Philippines

The USAFFE defeat in Bataan and Corregidor left thousands of officers and men, mostly Filipinos but some Americans as well, separated from their commands. Many of the Filipino stragglers simply returned to their homes, thankful to have escaped the ordeal of the Capas and O'Donnel concentration camps where many of their comrades-in-arms did not survive pestilence, hunger and the abuse of their captors. But the others elected to continue fighting the Japanese in loose guerrilla bands. Most of the Americans did not have any choice but to stay in the hills; the unappealing alternative was to become prisoners for the rest of the war.

The Huks were just one of a dozen major guerrilla com-

---

[22]Same, p. 34.

mands in Luzon; there were others almost as large in the Visayas and Mindanao. Northern Luzon was the undisputed territory of Maj. Russell W. Volckmann, an unsurrendered officer from the 31st Infantry, and there were many subcommands under him. Maj. Donald Blackburn held forth in the mountains of Ifugao, Bontoc and Kalinga; Major Parker was holed out in Benguet; and George Barnett ran herd over the volatile Ilocano guerrilleros in Ilocos Norte, Abra and La Union.[23]

Marking's Guerrillas, one of the largest of the Luzon commands, was staked out in Rizal. It was led by the colorful Marcos Villa Agustin whose fame was rivalled by that of his wife, Yay Panlilio. Eleuterio "Magtangol" Adevoso later to become Secretary of Labor under President Macapagal, formed Terry's Hunters with 300 former ROTC and PMT (high school reservists) cadets.

In the southern islands, Col. Ruperto Kangleon, who became Secretary of Defense under President Quirino, was appointed Leyte area commander with 3,200 men under arms. Lt. Col. Charles M. Smith, who was not an unsurrendered USAFFE officer but an advance man from General MacArthur's headquarters, smuggled into the country, consolidated three separate Samar units into a division-sized command of 8,000-9,000 men.[24]

Panay had a guerrilla operation which surpassed even the Huks in size, discipline and firepower. It was run by the inimitable Macario "Mac" Peralta, a cocky junior officer from Tarlac with such unsurpassed gall that he could hold on to a large guerrilla command in an island that was not even his birthplace. General Peralta had close to 25,000 military and civilian personnel in his payroll and kept voluminous clerical

---

[23]Some of these descriptions of wartime Filipino guerrilla organizations are based on *Guerrilla Resistance Movements in the Philippines,* a collection of monographs prepared by Philippine Subsection, G-2, General Headquarters, United States Southwest Pacific Command, and issued on a "confidential" basis by General MacArthur's headquarters in March, 1945. These documents are not entirely reliable since they were based largely on intelligence reports brought out of an enemy-occupied country under the difficult conditions of war. The monograph on the Huks, for instance, is largely conjectural, which is understandable since this communist-controlled organization operated outside the range of Southwespac direction. However, the other guerrilla outfits with which MacArthur's headquarters was in close contact are described with reasonable accuracy. Subsequently cited as Southwespac monographs.

[24]Same.

records as though operating well behind his own frontlines.[25] The Panay command had 6,800 rifles, eighteen 30 cal. machineguns, 576 45 cal. submachineguns, ten 81 mm. mortars and one 77 mm. cannon—an amazingly well-stocked arsenal for a unit operating 2,000 miles away from the nearest Allied command.[26]

The Huks had to share parts of Central Luzon with rival guerrilla outfits. To the north of them in Pangasinan and a portion of Nueva Ecija was Capt. Robert Lapham, late of the 26th Cavalry. Capt. Ralph McGuire, another ex-26th Cavalry holdout, defended the western sector of Lt. Col. Claude Thorp's Central Luzon force early in 1942 (both Thorp and McGuire were killed later that year.) A sizeable force of 1,000 guerrillas with 500 arms and 10,000 rounds of ammunition was commanded by Lt. Col. Gyles Merrill in the hills northeast of San Marcelino, Zambales. John Boone, a corporal in the 31st Infantry, organized five guerrilla regiments in Bataan — some of whom crossed over to Pampanga to fight the Huks. To the east of the Huk territories was Maj. Edwin Ramsey and on the east coast of Tayabas between Mauban and Infanta was the substantial Anderson's Guerrillas under Maj. Bernard Anderson, an escapee from Bataan[27]

The Communist party's ambition to lead the nation-wide anti-Japanese resistance was quite impossible under these circumstances. The guerrilla commands were fragmented not only by geography but by mutual distrust and suspicion. They were extremely jealous of their territorial rights and violently resisted poaching by neighboring outfits. There were frequent intra-guerrilla clashes involving the Huks, particularly in early 1944 when the Pampanga organization became envious of the comparative prosperity of neighboring commands in the way of smuggled arms and equipment. They felt discriminated against by Southwestern Pacific headquarters, and by most accounts they really were.

The Huks had Pampanga, "almost all" of Nueva Ecija, the southern half of Tarlac up to Victoria and Camiling and the Pampango speaking portions of Bulacan and Bataan.[28] But further territorial expansion was bloodily opposed. A Huk squadron under Col. Catindig and the San Isidro (Nue-

[25]Panay guerrilla collection in the possession of the Central Iloilo University, Iloilo City. These are a collection of 30,000 documents of General Peralta's Panay army and Tomas Confessor's "civic" government — a veritable treasure trove for scholars interested in the wartime history of Panay island.

[26]Southwespac monographs.

[27]Same.

[28]Taruc, interview, July, 1970.

va Ecija) unit of Anderson's guerrillas fought each other for three days until an intervening U.S. force broke up the fight.[29] Alejo Santos down in Bulacan brooked no trespassing by the Huks. Silvestre Liwanag recalled that 109 of his comrades were killed in an "accidental battle" between his force and USAFFE troops in that province.[30]

The Huks tried from the start to coordinate their activities with their guerrilla allies. Taruc sent Alejandrino, Fernando Sampang and Benedicto Sayco to contact Col. Thorp, who then assumed overall "command" of the entire region. On July 7, 1942, two of Thorp's officers, Capt. Joseph Barker and Maj. Bernard Anderson, sat down with the CPP military committee and they agreed on a joint guerrilla command in Central Luzon. It was understood that the Huks could act independently on organizational and political matters provided they cooperated in the overall military strategy for the region. The Huks also expected to assist and be assisted by other guerrilla units.[31]

Col. Thorp's scheme never really got off the ground. He was captured and executed by the Japanese and though his successor, Col. Gyles Merrill continued to keep in touch with Taruc, coordination was never fully effected.

General MacArthur's Southwestern Pacific Command had few illusions about the readiness of the Huks to cooperate with the American army. Its reading of Huk long-range objectives was as follows:

> The Americans were to be allowed to liberate the Philippines but were then to be attacked if immediate independence were not granted.
>
> Political figures of the Commonwealth Government were to be accepted only in so far as they could furnish a government not dominated by the U.S.A., Japan or any other foreign country, either politically or commercially. The Hukbalajap (sic) has said in its manifestos that the right of private property will be guaranteed in their postwar government, as well as freedom of speech, press, assembly, residence.
>
> Although the Hukbalajap has maintained this propaganda line to the present day, reports indicate that their policy is definitely communistic and that their plans include the establishment of a communistic government in the Philippines after the war, on the

---

[29]Major Kenneth M. Hammer, U.S. Air Force, *Military Review,* April, 1956.

[30]Espinosa Committee hearings.

[31]Hammer, as cited.

early Russian model. It is probable that there are also connections with communistic elements in China.[32]

A further deterioration of Huk-American relations was evidenced in Lt. Col. Roy Tuggle's letter to the Huk command a few days before the Leyte landing:

> Any organization which fails to cooperate will be regarded by incoming troops as unlawful armed bands... United States Army does not recognize any political aims of ambitions and it is the position that in time of war the only political activity which is legal is political activity aimed at the maintenance of the loyalty of the masses of the established, the legal government.[33]

The Huks bitterly resented this reading of the riot act by Col. Tuggles.

Huk Operations

Whatever devious political aims they might have had, the Huks soldiered with great credit. Even the AFP histories concede that. That Huks were at their fightingest in their first nine months, from March, 1942 to about December, 1943; they lapsed into passivity after absorbing their worst defeat at the hands of the Japanese, and retook the initiative in late 1944 when General MacArthur's liberation forces were already close at hand.

In those glorious first months, the Huks carried the fight to the Japanese. In May a squadron under Jose de Leon (Dimasalang) ambushed a Japanese patrol near Laur, Nueva Ecija, killing many of the enemy. Huk ambuscades were frequent on the roads between Magalang and La Paz and Angeles and San Fernando. A ranking Japanese officer was slain in a clash between San Luis and San Simon. The steady sniping at convoys and shipments jeopardized Japanese supply lines between Manila and the north.[34]

Not content with holding the countryside, the Huks boldly sallied in force into the *poblaciones.* A raiding party under Capule (Mateo del Castillo) and Pacifico Briones hit San Antonio, Nueva Ecija, raising the Filipino and American flags for

---

[32]Southwespac monographs.
[33]Quoted by Hammer, as cited.
[34]AFP Handbook, p. 36.

a spell. Another squadron surprised the puppet government in San Luis, snatching the mayor and many of his policemen. A soldiers barracks in Nueva Ecija was attacked. Dimasalang's men reported 150 Japanese casualties in two battles near Zaragoza, Nueva Ecija.[35]

What probably hurt the Japanese more was their being denied access to much of the rice harvest. The Huks prevented the Japanese-sponsored *Bigasan ng Bayan* (Rice Corporation) from collecting the grain by enforcing a strict licensing system of their own. Those engaging in blackmarketing rice were summarily executed.

The Huks had various organizations working for them in Manila, most notably the Free Philippines which collected intelligence and funds for the guerrillas. The party even found time to run an underground newspaper, the *Patnubay* (Guide).

Stung by the succession of Huk raids, the Japanese struck back on September 6 and December 5, 1942. The second counter-attack was a major effort with 22 Japanese planes called in from Clark and Manila fields to soften up Huk positions in Masantol and Minalin, followed by infantry closing in by motor launches from the river. The Huks were finally trapped in Macabebe. They fled, leaving behind their weapons and their dead.[36]

In March 5, 1943, an even bigger Japanese offensive was launched against an overconfident Huk force trapped in the Cabiao forest in Nueva Ecija, close to the site of the founding of the organization. A Japanese command of 5,000 men and an equal number of puppet constabulary and police forces overran the Huk lairs and captured a large number of Huk cadres and soldiers. They took off for the underbrush but were starved out by the Japanese after 10 days of continuous action.

Among those who escaped the encirclement were Vicente Lava and Luis Taruc. Crushed by their defeat, the party leaders abandoned the initial strategy of continuous harassment of the enemy and adopted one of "retreat for defense." The new strategy was put into effect, resulting in diminished Huk contacts with the Japanese.

The Japanese had the thankless opportunity of experimenting with anti-Huk strategems many years before the Philippine government's turn came. They recognized quickly enough that the Huks' strength lay in their mass base. To minimize the Huks' access to the towns and barrios, they re-

---

[35]Same.
[36]Same.

quired every citizen to possess a residence certificate. The Huks prohibited their followers from carrying these *cedulas*, a somewhat thoughtless reprisal since that placed many a citizen in a fatal predicament whatever he did.[37]

After their March, 1943 victory over the Huks, the Japanese also tried a policy of attraction. They promised kinder treatment to surrenderees, particularly Bataan veterans, hoping to weed out the genuine patriots from the outright bandits.[38]

The "retreat for defense" policy did not enjoy favor with the party for long. Taruc objected to its defeatism; the policy was obviously patterned after the strategic retreat of the Chinese Red armies to conserve their strength for their postwar showdown with the Kuomintang. Vicente Lava, who was responsible for the policy, was removed from the post of general secretary in favor of a three-man secretariat composed of Pedro Castro, Primitivo Arrogante and Comrade "C". Among the new blood added to the Central Committee were Felipe Sevilla, Peregrino Taruc, Eusebio Aquino, Bernardo Poblete, Teofista Valerio, Federico Maclang and Ramon Espiritu.

The Party tried to prepare the way for the liberating American army by setting up provisional governments in their areas. Casto Alejandrino was proclaimed governor of the liberated Pampanga province and Jesus Lava, of Bulacan. Feleo was already running an interim provincial government in Nueva Ecija.[39]

Then came the shock: the American military, distrusting the Huks to the last, ordered the disarming of the Pampanga squadrons and the arrest of their leaders. Silvestre Liwanag had joined forces with the Americans and USAFFE guerrillas in mopping up western Pampanga and Bataan. He helped liberate the Pasumil central and Floridablanca airfield and pitched into the fighting in Orani and Samal. Liwanag returned to Guagua only to be disarmed by an American colonel. He and his men were taken into custody for being "communists."[40]

On February 22, 1945, Taruc, Alejandrino, de Leon, and Sergio Cayanan were thrown into jail in San Fernando, Pampanga. After a mass demonstration protesting this cavalier treatment of the Huk commanders, Taruc and his comrades were rearrested by the Counter-Intelligence Corps on April

[37]Same.
[38]Rep. Jose B. Lingad, interview, July, 1970.
[39]AFP Handbook, p. 40.
[40]Espinosa committee hearings.

8, 1945. They were transferred to an army stockade in Calasiao, Pangasinan to prevent more pro-Huk demonstrations They were later moved to Bilibid for eventual transfer to the Iwahig penal colony.[41]

Of the Huk guerrillas, only Banal, the ex-Philippine Scout, and his regiment were recognized by the U.S. Army, and inducted into the service with pay.

Thus, Taruc's guerrillas, who were first to offer their services to the Comomnwealth and who probably suffered most, ended the war unrewarded and in disgrace.

---

[41]AFP Handbook, pp. 40-41.

Chapter Seven

POSTWAR POLITICS AND THE REBELLION: 1946-1954

The peasant guerrillas of Luis Taruc were embittered by their shabby treatment at the hands of their allies, but the professional revolutionaries in the CPP took encouragement from the growing economic chaos of the post-Liberation years. There was a giddy spell of apparent plentitude when the black market overflowed with surplus war equipment and goods. Fortunes were being made overnight by opportunistic politicians.

The guerrilla generation — the future Philippine leaders whose mores and social values were shaped by the predatory rules of underground life — began changing the style of Philippine politics from the arrogant paternalism of Manuel Quezon and the aristocratic detachment of Sergio Osmeña, Sr. to a backroom facsimile of their wartime struggle for survival. Opportunism and spoilsmanship were the rule. There were a few postwar politicians who clung to the old-school norms of public service, but the new "morality" prevailed.[1]

This was all part of the script to the Filipino communists who viewed the drama not as one shaped by historical circumstances and the pressures of modernization but as a confirmation of the familiar Marxist thesis: the bourgeois society was rotting within and a violent class struggle was in the offing. But revolution had to wait. The only revolutionary army at

---

[1]Most successful of the Filipino "guerrilla generation" were Ferdinand Marcos, an intelligence officer who served with Colonel Volckmann in northern Luzon. He was elected President of the Philippines in 1965 and re-elected for an unprecedented second full term in 1969. Other notable wartime guerrilleros who later made good in postwar public life were Sen. Alejandro Almendras, Raul Manglapus, Macario Peralta, Eleuterio Adevoso and Alejo Santos. Negros' three guerrilla leaders had successful postwar careers, Salvador Abecede later became lieutenant colonel commanding a Huk-fighting battalion combat team; Ernesto Mata rose to become AFP chief of staff and Secretary of National Defense under President Marcos; Alfredo Montelibano became chairman of the National Economic Council, acting chairman of the Rice and Corn Administration, and an outspoken member of the Negros "sugar bloc."

the party's disposal, the armed peasants of Pampanga, were weary of strife and wished to return to a peaceful existence. An urban insurrectionary force just did not exist in Manila. The CPP operatives, it must be recalled, were writers, printers, labor leaders, and academicians who would not know how to handle a gun if they had to. The likeliest course for the duration was a "legal struggle" with the objective of winning footholds in the political establishment.

While a good part of Manila was still in rubble as a result of a month-long battle for its liberation, the party set up headquarters in the city. Still believing that their organization was legally tolerated (as a result of the executive clemency given Evangelista and others in 1938), the communists opened the New Builders' Bookshop and published the *Katubusan* (Redemption), the successor of the wartime *Patnubay* (Guide).

A labor front was organized in the form of the Committee of Labor Organizations (CLO) with Capadocia (now restored to active party status), Balgos and Felixberto Olalia in the forefront. The CLO succeeded in raising the wages of their worker-members through skillful strike tactics and in time it had 76 unions under its wing with a combined membership of 100,000.[2]

On the agrarian front, Mateo del Castillo and Juan Feleo combined the KPMP and AMT units into the *Pambansang Kaisahan ng mga Magbubukid* (PKM). Neither front organizations represented the majority of the public they were intended to represent. The CLO at its peak had close to one-fifth of the total urban workers, sizeable as Philippine labor organizations go, but still far from being able to control labor as a whole. The party's minority status continued to be an impediment to its long-range goals.

The Democratic Alliance

With both labor and agrarian flanks well covered, the party launched a major political offensive with the help of sympathetic liberals and fellow-travelers. The Democratic Alliance was formed on July 15, 1945 with an uncompromisingly anti-collaborationist platform. Its national executive committee was made up of Judge Jesus Barrera, president; J. Antonio Araneta, vice president; Rafael Ledesma, secretary; Judge J. B. L. Reyes, Dr. Vicente Lava, Manuel Crudo and Jose Hilario. The DA leadership was a mixture of liberal-progressive Filipino intellectuals, old hands from the Civil Li-

---

[2]AFP Handbook, p. 44.

berties Union and hardcore communists from the CLO and PKM.[3]

Dr. Jesus Lava, back in the driver's seat after being relieved of major wartime duties in 1943, declared the NP of Osmeña a more worthwhile political ally since the Liberal party which had splintered off from the NP was identified with "collaborators" like Manuel Roxas, and worse, a likely tool of American imperialism. On September 23, the Democratic Alliance staged a large rally attended by 30,000 at Plaza Guipit. Orators denounced the conspiracy between U.S. capitalism and the Filipino feudalists and the rally then marched to Malacañang to present a manifesto, "moderately worded" for President Osmeña's benefit. Osmeña was gradually responsive to the DA demands, and this was enough for the Alliance to hit the campaign trail with some assurance of support from the NP. Taruc, along with Alejandrino, was released from prison and was now the DA's star performer.[4]

The CPP was also emboldened to display its colors publicly on November 7, its 15th anniversary. A spate of pro-Russian propaganda issued four days before had prompted Superintendent of Schools Venancio Trinidad to deny the party use of the Gregorio del Pilar Elementary School, so the big show was held at Plaza Guipit with the hammer and sickle displayed. Despite the alarming ideological bias shown by some Democratic Alliance spokesmen, the Nacionalista party leadership agreed to share bed and board with the radicals since the former stood to profit from the DA attacks on Roxas and from the considerable DA following in labor and in Central Luzon.

Roxas won the presidential election on April 23, 1946 but the DA scored an impressive victory for a minority party. All six Democratic Alliance candidates in Central Luzon won congressional seats — Luis Taruc in the second district of Pampanga, Amado Yuzon in the first district, Jesus Lava in Bulacan, Jose Cando and Constancio Padilla in Nueva Ecija and Alejandro Simpauco in Tarlac. "For the first time in 15 years," the AFP observed, "the PKP had succeeded in having its candidates elected to Congress."[5]

The DA, however, won under highly doubtful circumstances. The Commission on Elections reported violence and terrorism in Pampanga, Tarlac, Bulacan and Nueva Ecija during the elections. Rep. Jose Topacio Nueño introduced a resolution unseating the DA candidates and the Liberal-controlled Congress upheld him. This event remains highly con-

---

[3]Same.
[4]Same.
[5]Same, p. 48.

troversial. It is hard to believe that the Huks would sit still while their wartime heroes stood for elections. Yet, Taruc swears to this day he was not guilty of electoral frauds. He won overwhelmingly by 39,000 to 10,000 votes without making a single speech in his district.[6]

The Supreme Court which heard the protest of the disenfranchised DA candidates observed that their ejection had not as much to do with electoral anomalies as with their common opposition to the Bell Trade Agreement and the parity amendments to the Constitution.

The ejection of the DA congressmen turned Central Luzon into a "seething cauldron." President Roxas sought to placate the peasants by commissioning their own spokesmen, Taruc, Mateo del Castillo and Juan Feleo, to intercede for them. On August 24, 1946, Feleo was returning to Manila from a pacification sortie in Cabiao when he and some peasant leaders were taken away from their Military Police escort by uniformed men and shot to death.

That was the final provocation. The Huks dug up their World War II arms and Central Luzon once again became a battleground.

The Mailed Fist

President Roxas pledged to put an end to Huk insurgency in 60 days but in doing so he betrayed a profound lack of understanding of the Central Luzon situation and even of the basic capabilities of his security forces. The Military Police had become undermanned as a result of demobilization and it was untrained in coping with Huk hit-and-run warfare. In frustration, some MP units shelled barrios suspected of harboring dissidents.[7] This patent "overkill" only succeeded in fanning anti-government sentiment.

Roxas also initiated some mildly reformistic actions such as creating an Agrarian Commission and signing a crop-sharing law alloting 70 percent of the harvest to the tenants. But the Huk leaders would not be appeased; they demanded near-impossible conditions for their surrender (such as general amnesty, disbandment of the armed forces, and seating of the Democratic Alliance candidates).

This left Roxas no other recourse but the "mailed fist." On March 6, 1948, he declared the Hukbalahap headed by Taruc and the PKM headed by del Castillo as subversive organizations bent on "overthrowing our present government... by wresting the reins of government from the lawfully elected

---

[6]Taruc, interview, July, 1970.
[7]AFP Handbook, p. 49.

representatives of the people and establishing a government of their own, through force and intimidation." This was the second time the Philippine government cracked down on a subversive organization, though this time the Communist Party escaped direct liability.

The objects of Roxas' condemnation could not fail to see some irony in the fact that five weeks later he succumbed to a heart attack delivering a fiery speech at Clark air base.[8]

His successor, Pres. Elpidio Quirino, offered the Huks "accommodation instead of confrontation." He sent his younger brother, Judge Antonio Quirino, to dicker with Taruc and though the Huk leader's terms were virtually dictatorial — outright pardon of all Huks and Communists prior to an amnesty, and guaranteed protection of Huk surrenderees—he agreed in principle for the sake of agrarian peace, hoping that "minor differences could be straightened out afterwards."[9]

On June 21, 1948 a Piper Cub picked up Taruc from an improvised airstrip in Pampanga and the famed Huk chieftain was given a "hero's welcome" upon arriving in Manila. Four days afterwards both houses of Congress approved the President's amnesty. The respite lasted only two months. Taruc made a round of public appearances and picked up two years of uncollected salary and allowances. Then he returned to the hills accusing the government of bad faith and declaring that the Huks would not surrender their firearms until actual reforms were undertaken.[10]

Fighting broke out in Central Luzon again. The inept Military Police was replaced by the Philippine Constabulary and Sotero Baluyot, a hard-bitten foe of the Pampango radicals from way back, took over the anti-dissident campaign. The Huks renamed themselves the *Hukbong Magpapalaya ng Bayan* (Peoples' Liberation Army).

There were some indications that the communists and Huks supported Jose P. Laurel, the wartime Philippine President and now Nacionalista candidate for the same office, in exchange for pledges of agrarian reform. This was quite a reversal of the party's rabidly anti-collaborationist stance just after the war. But the communists were willing to bend over backwards just to insure the downfall of President Quirino.[11]

---

[8]Taruc, interview, July, 1970.

[9]AFP Handbook, p. 55.

[10]Taruc said the money he collected — about ₱15,000 — was disposed of in three equal parts, one third given as a contribution to the Huk movement, one third in payment of "personal obligations" and the last third for his personal expenses.

[11]Jose Lava described the CPP's qualified endorsement of Laurel as "critical support." To the communists, Laurel was a somewhat better choice, than President Quirino since the latter

The November 1949 election, the bloodiest and most scandalous up to then, was seen by the party as a signal that the long-foretold revolution was finally on hand.

A 'Revolutionary Situation'

Earlier, an ideological struggle within the CPP cleared the way for Dr. Vicente Lava's younger brothers, Jose and Jesus, to dominate the party councils. With a masterful display of dialectical infighting, they dislodged their biggest rival, Pedro C. Castro, who, as party secretary-general, held a majority in the Politburo between 1944 and early 1947. The Lavas and the Castro group first clashed over party strategy during the Japanese Occupation and resumed their rivalry in 1945 when the latter wanted the Democratic Alliance to run independently of any major political party while the Lavas opted for the DA-NP coalition. The Lavas' minority view prevailed.[12]

In 1947 the rival blocs were in bitter dispute again. The pacifistic Castro took exception to the way the Huks were provoking an armed confrontation with the government. The Lavas read the riot act to Castro, charging him with opportunism and irresolution. Jose Lava was already chairman of the powerful Organization Department and he had the solid backing of Luis Taruc, Lazaro Cruz, Alejandrino and most of the Military Department leaders. In a showdown in May, 1948, Castro was outmanuevered by the Lavas and listened to a recitation of his "errors" in silence. He was later expelled from the party for "appeasement of the enemy," along with Geruncio Lacuesta and Olalia.[13]

The Politburo shakeup placed the Lavas firmly in control of the party machinery. Jose Lava was general secretary; Jesus Lava, political commissar; Federico Maclang, organizational chairman; Peregrino Taruc, educational chairman; Ramon Espiritu, finance chairman; Luis Taruc, military chairman; Casto Alejandrino, assistant military chairman: and Balgos, Sayco and Cruz, Politburo members.

Jose Lava was primarily responsible for the declaration

---

was the perceived "American candidate." However, party sympathizers were duly reminded that Laurel's wartime collaboration record made him less than the ideal leader. Lava, in an interview with the author in October, 1970, said the party's critical support of Laurel was transmitted largely through oral channels to its political front members during the 1949 campaign.

[12]Lava, as cited, and AFP Handbook, pp. 189-190.

[13]Same.

of a "revolutionary situation" and for the launching of preparations for an armed struggle with the government.

The remarkable Lava family were among the most important actors in the history of Philippine communism. Three brothers took turns serving in the all-important position of secretary-general. The Secretariat virtually ran the entire apparatus; the office of chairman had been abolished after the death of Crisanto Evangelista.

The Lavas descended from a moderately-rich land-owning family in Bulacan town, close to Manila. Their father, Adeodato Lava, served one term as town *presidente* (mayor) during the 1930's. The Lavas had a local reputation for being socially concerned and politically liberal. One ancestor, a *cabeza de barangay* (local headsman), paid taxes imposed on his people out of his own pocket. At one time he presented himself as bond for his delinquent tax-payers, bringing his bedding to jail and staying there until the obligations were settled.[14]

The family was not only known for non-conforming with the norms of its social class but for producing intellectuals of high calibre. The capacity of Dr. Vicente Lava, the oldest of this singular brood, bordered on genius. He was a distinguished chemist who studied at the University of the Philippines and Columbia University. He perfected the so-called "Lava process" in the refining of coconut oil which could have made him rich had he chosen to cash in on his achievement.

Jose Lava graduated cum laude from the University of the Philippines College of Law just before the war. His thesis entitled "Prostitution of the Due Process Clause" won him first prize in a collegiate contest. Jesus Lava, the youngest of the three brothers who turned communist, was a medical doctor who gave up his practice to join the prewar *Frente Popular* and the ill-fated Democratic Alliance.

Adeodato Lava had 13 children of whom four are alive today. Two other brothers, though they did not join the Communist Party, distinguished themselves in their own professional disciplines. Francisco Lava, a doctor of jurisprudence, was once the dean of the graduate school of the Lyceum of the Philippines. Horacio Lava, a Ph. D. in economics, teaches at the Manuel L. Quezon University in Manila. Jose described his two older brothers as being "nationalist" by persuasion but temperamentally disinclined to actively engage in political advocacy.[15]

But mental acuity is not the sole requirement for revolutionary leadership. What most of the breed lacks is a sense

---

[14]Jose Lava, interview.

[15]Same.

of detachment, even from their own most firmly held convictions, an internal check-and-balance which can save them from their own excesses. For all their brilliance, the Lavas were not spared from that one fatal blind spot.

Moreover, they were now the prevailing counsel in the CPP. There were few devil's advocates who could challenge their judgment. Jose Lava dominated the party leadership not by strong-arm tactics or bluster but by the sheer, irresistable power of his dialectical materialism. His extensive readings of Marx and Engels provided him with a scientific system of analyzing "everything from courting a woman to the political situation of the country." He carried an encyclopedic knowledge of communist philosophy and strategy in his head, argued tirelessly with dissenters and never compromised with what his Marxist conscience dictated. When he was released from prison early in 1970, he told reporters: "I entered prison a Communist and I am leaving prison a Communist."

In mid-January. 1950, Jose Lava handed down to the enlarged Politburo a brief entitled "Analysis of the Developing Situation and Our Tasks." It argued Lenin-like for the existence of revolutionary conditions in the Philippines.

Lava declared that the country was headed towards an "irreversible" monetary crisis for the folowing reasons:

1. Philippine currency had no backing except for assets of the Central Bank, mainly its international reserve of only around ₱400 million. This was only 63 percent of the money in circulation amounting to ₱600 million.

2. In 1949 there was an unfavorable balance of trade of around ₱600 million notwithstanding import controls.

3. To avoid draining international reserves, import, credit and exchange controls were necessary but the target of ₱400 million savings "could only be achieved at the expense of businesses closing down, widespread unemployment, lower wages, high prices which because of present political instability will only tend to sharpen opposition to the LP administration."

4. The U.S. government's financial and economic assistance could save the Quirino regime but its availability was dependent on the success of corrective policies. But in the meanwhile, the "present hysteria" and lack of confidence in the peso was forcing the flight of both local and foreign capital, keeping new foreign capital away and encouraging hoarding of local capital in real estate, jewelry, etc.[16]

Coincident with the worsening economic situation, in La-

---

[16]Jose Lava, *Analysis of the Developing Situation and Our Tasks,* a document entered in the records of the trial of Jose Lava, et al, Department of Justice, Republic of the Philippines.

va's view, was the popular revulsion over the "wholesale fraud and terror" characterizing the 1949 election. The masses of workers and peasants would "struggle to defend their living standards" when the government enforces its retrenchment measures, and "they can be made to rally around the armed struggle to overthrow the (Quirino) administration." Both the government employes and the armed forces were in a "state of demoralization." The "most honest political leaders" could be expected to "sympathize and help directly in the struggle of the HMB."

Lava only saw one major contingency and that was massive intervention by the U.S. "imperialists." But this possibility was brushed aside in one breathless sentence. Lava noted the "present reluctance of the U.S. imperialists to come to the aid of the QLP (sic) administration, because of the limitations of its ability to give aid which it wants to be sure will not be wasted by an administration which no longer enjoys political support, and therefore, is not the most effective instrument of imperialist domination and exploitation."[17]

What strongly influenced Lava's perception of an economic crisis was his readings of American communist commentaries on Eugene Varga, the Marxist economist who predicted the 1929 stock market crash in the United States and an even more severe collapse in the mid-fifties. Since Varga was right in 1929, Lava reasoned, there was every reason to believe his prophesy for the mid-fifties would also come true. From the vantage of post-election 1950, the Varga thesis seemed to be borne out by evidences of economic distress in the Philippines.[18] Reenforcing the CPP leadership's confidence in the prospects of accelerating the armed struggle were the success of communist arms in China and to a lesser degree of Soviet cold-war strategy in Europe.

History proved Jose Lava wrong — tragically so. Saulo who had an inside track on the 1950 rebellion as an education and propaganda operative, wrote that Lava mistook a "revolutionary mood" for a "revolutionary situation":

> A revolutionary situation is a transitory or passing affair, which does not necessarily mature into a revolutionary situation. A situation may be described as revo-

[17]Same.

[18]It was not until some years later, while in prison, that Jose Lava read up on Keynesian economics and realized his error in not accounting for the various ways a capitalist country could correct and adjust the cyclical movements of its economy. Lava is so thorough-going a Marxist dialectician that he can submit himself to "self-criticism" and admit freely of his errors.

> lutionary only when certain objective conditions have been reached, such as when the people, or at least the majority of them, can no longer live under prevailing conditions, and are demanding radical changes; and on the other hand, the ruling class (i.e., the bourgeoisie) can no longer rule in the usual way because of the growing insurgency of the people. The situation is thus so tense that the masses, in desperation, are tumbling into the streets to man the barricades.[19]

The Philippines was indeed in a monetary crisis — but it was not irreversible. The Rand Corporation took note of the tendency of Philippine observers to "overperceive" such economic difficulties as "unemployment," "stagnation" and "inflation." The post-election "crisis" Lava reported in 1950 could well have been explainable in terms of the effects of a "two-year fiscal cycle corresponding to the biennial elections."[20] A similar "crisis" was reported after the 1969 presidential elections but it failed to lead to any revolutionary situation.

An NPA tract captured by the AFP in 1969 puts the onus on the Lavas more brutally: "The Jose Lava leadership was criminally responsible for the almost total obliteration of the People's Army within the short period of two years and for the most wanton sacrifice of the lives of Party cadres and Red soldiers in the history of the Communist Party of the Philippines."[21]

An unmistakable proof of their overly sanguine thinking was a plan to increase HMB membership from 10,000 in July, 1950 to 172,000 in September, 1951. This "geometric expansion" would be made possible by each of the original 10,800 HMB members recruiting three new members in the first quarter of 1950, and each member, old and new, recruiting another set of three in the second quarter, and so on until the membership of 172,000 was achieved.[22]

If this remarkable schedule of expansion had been carried out the HMB's would have been too busy recruiting members to do any fighting. It was also somewhat overpresumptuous to have expected all this frantic mustering in of new HMB's without the government scenting what was going on.

The elaborate scenario prepared by Jesus Lava and his associates Casto Alejandrino and Mateo del Castillo also anticipated the establishment of "provisional revolutionary governments" in barrios and towns "liberated" from the govern-

---

[19]Saulo, as cited.
[20]Rand report, pp. 159-163.
[21]AFP documents.
[22]Saulo, as cited, p. 56.

ment and peasant committees for the distribution of lands *(Lupon sa Pamamahagi ng Lupa sa mga Mangbubukid)* in Huk-controlled areas. At an anticipated stage of the revolution, the HMB would be converted from a guerrilla to a regular army.

Luis Taruc and his brother, Peregrino, opposed this fateful decision. "For my part, I argued that there was no real revolutionary situation, except that in Central and Southern Luzon, and that even there it was not sufficiently sustained. The rest of the country, I maintained, was passive and apathetic."[23]

But Taruc, unversed in the glib jargon of the professional revolutionary, could not bring out any "statistics and figures" that could match the cold Marxist dialectic of Lava. Sensing the folly of the course set by the Politburo but unable to challenge it strongly enough, the Tarucs grudgingly assented.[24]

Alarums and Excursions

On March 29, 1950, the eighth anniversary of the founding of the Hukbalahap, the dissidents launched simultaneous raids in two towns and 15 barrios causing great havoc. A hundred Huks swooped down on San Pablo City, killed one army officer, looted stores and raised the hammer and sickle in the heart of town. Another band stripped a PC outpost in San Mateo, Rizal of weapons and other equipment. In San Rafael, Bulacan, four soldiers were killed, seven wounded and two civilians killed in the crossfire when the Huks attacked the PC detachment. Manila was strewn with propaganda leaflets describing the Philippines in a state of economic collapse. Some of the Huk broadsides were dropped from the third floor of the City Hall.[25]

While the AFP was still in the process of reorganizing itself for a counterattack, the Huks struck again and again in the next two months. They raided the towns of Aguilar in Pangasinan, Laur in Nueva Ecija and Pangil in Laguna. The Army was bled some more by successful Huk ambushes in Batangas, Nueva Ecija and Laguna.

On August 26, another anniversary date that has come to be feared by the AFP, came the second wave of massive

[23]Taruc, as cited, p. 71.

[24]Jose Lava has a different version of Taruc's reaction to the Politburo decision. He does not recall Taruc voicing his objections to the Lava thesis. The only Politburo member who expressed a dissenting opinion, to his recollection, was Casto Alejandrino. Alejandrino was unversed in Marxist argumentation but had a "commonsensical" way of sizing up the situation.

[25]Heoksema, as cited.

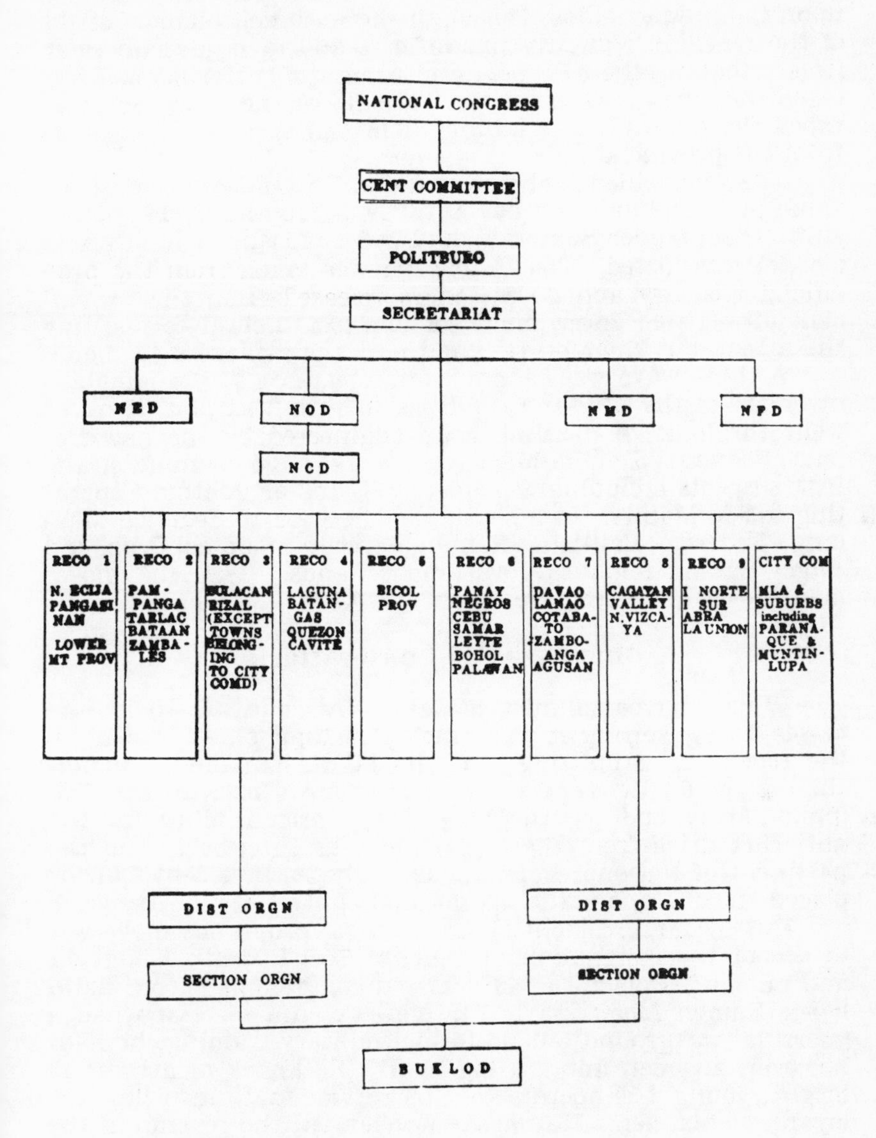

Figure 5: Organization Structure of the Communist Party of the Philippines as determined by the 1951 Central Committee Conference. From the Armed Forces of the Philippines.

raids. Two hundred partisans led by Silvestre Liwanag fell upon Camp Macabulos, Tarlac, in the most spectacular strike of the rebellion. Twenty-five officers and men gave up their lives defending the AFP post and when the garrison was overcome the Huks massacred the patients in the base hospital, raped the nurses before killing them and sprung 47 prisoners from the provincial jail.

The Macabulos raid was matched in audacity and shock value by the plundering of Santa Cruz, Laguna by Pedro Caguin (Commander Samonte) and 300 partisans. The business district was looted, ₱86,806 in cash was taken from the provincial treasury and 20 prisoners released from the provincial jail. Three government soldiers lost their lives resisting the attack but their brave stand cost the attackers 15 men.[26]

A third wave was planned for November 7, the joint anniversary of the CPP and the Russian revolution, but it never went through. A dazzling coup engineered by the new Defense Secretary Ramon Magsaysay bagged 105 communist and Huk suspects including the entire "PB In" or Politburo operating inside Manila. In a single day, Jose Lava, Federico Maclang, Federico Bautista, Ramon Espiritu, Salome Cruz and Angel Baking fell into government hands. The Huk movement never quite recovered from this blow.

Magsaysay's Counterattack

While the communist leaders were counting their successes, the government was quickly making plans to contain the rebellion. Admitting that the PC was unable to handle the emergency, it transferred 3,000 troopers back to the Phiippine Army and passed the primary responsibility for the anti-Huk drive from the Department of Interior to the Department of National Defense. On July 26, President Quirino placed the PC under the operational control of the Army.

But by far President Quirino's most propitious move was to accept the resignation of Defense Sec. Ruperto Kangleon and put in his place the 43-year-old congressman from Zambales, Ramon Magsaysay. The new defense secretary had a guerrilla background but no formal military training; he had, however, an open mind, a big heart, the knack of attracting bright, young technocrats to his service and inspiring the loyalty of his men. Magsaysay accelerated the revamp of the AFP establishment begun by the President; before the month was out 13 ranking PC officers whose performance was less than desirable were removed from their commands and replaced by more action-prone commanders. More sweeping changes were contemplated but Magsaysay had to buy time.

[26]AFP Handbook, pp. 61-62.

He badly needed a break and got it in less than two months.

A vital Huk informant, Tarciano Rizal, fell into his hands. He was willing to cooperate with the government by pinpointing the location of the communist apparatus in Manila. He told the secretary that if his agents would follow a woman courier, delivering Huk messages at the bottom of her grocery bag, they would know where the Politburo leaders were. This tip was verified and on October 18, 250 AFP intelligence personnel and 30 Manila police detectives spread out through the city and collected their suspects from 22 separate residences.[27]

Apart from the demoralizing effect of the movement, the loss of the entire urban apparatus deprived the movement of vital communications with its Manila supporters. From then on, the Huks were fighting half-blind. They were isolated in their mountain hideouts. To fight off discouragement, the Huk leaders told their men that "the Russians or the Chinese Communists were coming to help," but nobody really believed that they would.[28]

Mid-1950 marked the flood tide of the Huk rebellion. After the October 18th raid, events turned badly for the revolutionists. By 1951, the Philippine Army, better led and better equipped, was killing Huks at the rate of 40 to 50 a week. By the year's end the Defense Department claimed to have slain 2,000 dissidents in Luzon and captured another 2,000. This compared well with the AFP tally, in the nine-month period from April to December, 1950, of 1,268 Huks killed, 109 surrendered and 436 captured in 501 encounters.[29]

Within a year of Magsaysay's take-over, the AFP became a vastly more efficient Huk fighting force. With the help of American advisers, Magsaysay expanded the army from 10 to 20 battalion combat teams, each a mobile, self-sustained unit, with a total strength of 22,500 officers and men.[30] He blan-

---

[27]Jose Lava believed that Tarciano Rizal's role was just a cover story given out by Magsaysay to the press. He suspects that the PB In was betrayed by an expelled Politburo member. He said the PB In was ready to depart for the field when the Army intelligence closed in on them.

[28]The Kremlin did pay lip service to the Communist movement in the Philippines, praising the Huks for being part of the "global struggle against the U.S." but no material support was offered.

[29]Hoeksema, as cited.

[30]A BCT was a reenforced battalion with three rifle companies, supported by a heavy weapons company, a field artillery battery, a reconnaisance company, a service company, a headquarters company, an Intelligence section, psychological warfare section and medical and dental detachment.

keted Luzon with half of those battalions.

The Scout Rangers were Magsaysay's "strategic reserve." They were highly-conditioned, battle-toughened soldiers who could scale mountainsides in pursuit of Huks and sneak through the jungles as quietly as the guerrillas themselves.

The early "orthodox" warfare used by the AFP had little effect on the Huks. Taruc recalled how his comrades used to slip through the holes in the AFP encirclements and watch safely from a distance the Air Force waste their bombs and napalm on the hills they had just vacated.[31]

The AFP quickly expanded its book on "unorthodox" warfare. Every conceivable device was used. Dog patrols, sniping, surprise raids, infiltrators disguised as Huks. The "disguised Huk" gimmick became almost routine. On one occasion, two Huk units battled each other thinking the other was "phony."[32]

Returning veterans from the Korean War put their combat experience to good use. (The 10th and 20th BCT's, which saw service in Korea, are still on Central Luzon assignment today.)

Intensifying its anti-Huk campaign in 1952, the AFP launched "Operation Four Roses" which bagged William Pomeroy, the American communist serving as the Huk propaganda chief. The Taruc brothers barely escaped the AFP dragnet in the Sierra Madre mountains, but Luis' wife was killed in the fighting.

AFP intelligence scored one coup after another. Its biggest windfall, next to the October 18 haul of the Manila Politburo, was the successful penetration of the Huk Reco (Regional Command) 7 headquarters in Panay. With the aid of Commander Milan, a Huk defector, a Military Intelligence Service team posed as a gang of holduppers and robbers in the Iloilo City suburbs. The Iloilo press cooperated with the ploy by playing up the "exploits" of the gang.

In no time, Milan's group came in contact with Huk elements. Believing that Milan and his teammates could be recruited into the Reco service, the Huks pointed the way to the headquarters of the Reco commander, Guillermo Capadocia. A Panay Task Force detachment was sent to the spot and the elusive Capadocia was finally trapped and killed in barrio Pampanan, San Remegio, Antique.[33] Two more successive operations in Panay led to the capture of Commander Roland, one of Capadocia's top aides, and the killing of Commander Nery and 21 of his men. This put an end to the Huk expansion plans in Panay.

---

[31]Hammer, as cited.

[32]Valeriano and Buchanan, as cited.

[33]AFP Handbook, p. 215.

The Lavas not only grossly miscalculated the capability of the government to roll back the Huk offensive. They overestimated the willingness of the people to jump onto the Huk bandwagon. As Saulo noted in his history, there was a perceived revolutionary "mood" but only in Central Luzon where the Pampango masses had long identified with the social struggle. After the shocking frauds of the 1949 presidential elections, the chronically oppositionist Manilans expressed their profound disgust with the entire system and spoke darkly of an imminent "revolution." But what the communist leaders failed to account for was the fact that city folk often react with passion to political tomfooleries but are rarely known to back up their sentiments with organized violence.

When Huk terrorism escalated, thousands of citizens fled to the city for safety. There was no rush of able-bodied men into the ranks of the rebel army. The Huks lost whatever public sympathy they might have had as a result of needless violence. The brutal slaying of Mrs. Aurora Quezon, the widow of the late president, her daughter and son-in-law by a Huk band under Alexander Viernes (Commander Stalin) was a blunder the movement never quite lived down.

There have been some speculations about the American role in the breaking up of the 1950 rebellion. Col. Edward Lansdale, the celebrated *eminence gris* behind Magsaysay, gave most of the credit to the Filipinos themselves. Lansdale served as liaison between the Joint U.S. Military Assistance Group (JUSMAG) and the Department of National Defense and in that capacity was closely associated with Magsaysay for 18 months.[34]

Lansdale wrote that the tide began to turn when the Filipinos started helping themselves.

> The first was the so-called Peace Fund. About a million dollars worth of pesos were raised by a fund-colletcing drive, such as in a community chest or United Givers Fund drive, under the chairmanship of then Vice President Fernando Lopez. These became Magsaysay's contingency or confidence funds — used for rewards for action against Huk leaders, for purchasing firearms in the provinces to prevent them from falling into the hands of the Huks, and for operational intelligence. These Peace Funds put a weapon of great practicality into the hands of a man who knew how to use it well.

---

[34]Maj. Gen. Edward G. Landsdale, "The Story Ramon Magsaysay Did Not Tell," *Orient*, August, 1963, Vol. No. 7, p. 7.

The second example was a series of informational war councils, in which the real doers among the Filipino military participated. By doers, I mean commanders of all ranks and some staff officers, men who had been in thick of the fight, men of imagination and energy, men who wanted to win and who were not content to merely go through the motions just because the book said so. We, as American advisers, only used our "good offices," as interested friends to bring these men together in an informal atmosphere, provided plenty of coffee — and then let them alone to do a "re-think" on their campaign. These sessions sparked many of the ideas which were later developed into the winning tactics which became famous.[35]

Taruc Ousted from Party

Shaken by their recent reverses but still determined to continue the struggle, the party leaders convened the Central Committee — minus the captured Politburo In — in the vastnesses of the Sierra Madre in February, 1951. Jesus Lava succeeded to the secretary-generalship and a new Politburo was created out of the original PB "Out" and new personnel including Celia Pomeroy and Jose de Leon.

Significantly, Luis Taruc was relieved as commander-in-chief, a post he had held continuously since the activation of the Huks in 1942. Casto Alejandrino, who hewed closer to Lava's way of thinking, was Taruc's successor. By this time, a serious breach had developed between the Tarucs and the Lava-Alejandrino-del Castillo triumvirate. The Taruc brothers had consented with misgivings to the "revolutionary situation" pronunciamento of Jose Lava in 1951. Now they regretted not having opposed the document more strongly. Luis Taruc saw the ultimate defeat of his peasant army, even if the Lava group did not.[36]

In September, 1952, Taruc issued a "Call for Peace" seeking a non-violent settlement of the old quarrels that had brought strife to his region. According to Saulo, Lava initially showed some interest in the Taruc peace proposal but later reversed himself. Luis Taruc was suspended from the party and his brother Peregrino was expelled for writing a memorandum supporting Luis' peace call.[37]

Taruc took this second affront with admirable forbear-

---

[35]Same.

[36]Taruc, interview, July, 1970.

[37]Saulo, as cited, p. 65.

ance and tried hp to 1953 to call an enlarged Politburo conference to reconcile his views with the Secretariat. By then President Quirino had started negotiations with Huk commanders in Pampanga, virtually the only survivors left of the once formidable rebel army. Taruc at first had a hand in these talks, not for his account but merely to convey their substance to the Politburo. Unexpectedly, he was charged by the party with exceeding his authority and expelled in *absentia.* Later, Taruc was informed of a Secretariat plot to courtmartial him for alleged party "crimes." Taruc's "instinct for self-preservation" prompted him to give himself up to the government.[38] He was accompanied by Benigno Aquino, Jr., then a youthful and enterprising newspaperman, from his mountain hideout to Camp Murphy on May 17, 1954.

The Huk rebellion was for all practical purposes over. One by one, the Huk leaders were killed, captured or forced to give themselves up. Mariano Balgos, former CPP general secretary, was killed in Manito, Albay on October 17, 1954. Tomas Calma, alias Commander Soi, was killed in Candaba on December 19, 1955. Pedro Caguin, Central Committee member, surrendered in July 1957. Mateo del Castillo, the third member of the CPP secretariat, was killed by his own bodyguard on November 22, 1957.

After a long manhunt, the government finally caught Jesus Lava who had abandoned the field for a fugitive life in Manila with a ₱130,000 price on his head.

---

[38]According to Taruc's version of his surrender, he feared an attempt by Alejandrino to liquidate him for party insubordination and gave himself up to save his life. Jose Lava disputes such an intention on Alejandrino's part. "Peregrino presented himself to the Politburo to explain his actions and nothing untoward befell him," Lava said. "Assuming that Taruc's fears were justified, my brother Jesus would not have permitted Alejandrino to kill him. At most, Taruc's penalty, if he was found guilty of error, was expulsion, not death."

Chapter Eight

THE PAMPANGA ORGANIZATION: 1964-1970

The expulsion of Luis and Peregrino Taruc from the Communist Party ended the 16-year liaison between the Socialist party veterans and the urban communists. The break was complete. The Pampango Socialists had only known crushing suppression and copious bloodshed in their fellowship with the communists. They were "used" and they wanted no more of it. Only a small minority of the original Socialists — Casto Alejandrino most notably — had really professed communism, and even in Alejandrino's case it was as much a matter of personal loyalty to the Lavas as it was intellectual conviction. The rest of Pedro Abad Santos' apostles — the Tarucs, Eusebio Aquino, Jose de Leon, Silvestre Liwanag — remained agrarian reformers at heart and only communists by circumstances.

Luis Taruc's post-surrender career is already well known. When he came down from Arayat for the last time, he was whisked into an army stockade — no more hero's welcome for him — and made to stand trial on 26 charges. The prosecution tried to prove his culpability for the ambush-slaying of the Quezon family in Nueva Ecija, the killing of several soldiers and civilians in a Huk attack on an isolated army detachment in Guinayangan, Quezon, the killing of 14 civilians in a waylaid bus, and other acts of mayhem and rebellion.[1] Considering the gravity of these charges, Taruc got away lightly. He was sentenced to 12 years imprisonment and fined ₱20,000 by Judge Gregorio Narvasa.

Keenly disappointed by the verdict, President Magsaysay ordered fresh charges brought against the former Huk supremo, including the murder of Pampanga's occupation governor Feliciano Gardiner, his two sons and a driver. Taruc was convicted and sentenced to life imprisonment. In a book he wrote while in prison, Taruc confessed his error in making common cause with the communists.

> I came into the liberation movement with a fervent love of God; I nearly became a bitter atheist

[1]AFP Handbook, pp. 218-219.

> during my association with the Communists. I came with a burning love of my country, a traitor to my native land and nation... Any nationalist who makes an ally of the Communists is going for a ride on a tiger.[2]

What became of the Huk movement? It survived after a fashion. And in surviving it kept some of its old traits and acquired some new ones.

When Jesus Lava, the last of the Politburo holdouts, fell into government hands, the Huk organization was already in a decline. Table One in Chapter Two shows how Huk strength dropped sharply from its peak of 12,800 in 1950 to about 75 die-hards and a few hundred cadres and contact men in 1965. Their area of influence had shrunk from the six "regional commands" (Recos) to the places from where the Huks had originally sprung — the eastern half of Pampanga, with Angeles City as their new base The Huk survivors simply melted into the countryside and they were more intent on staying alive than on any second-wind effort.

Pedro Taruc and Sumulong

No clear mandate was left to the Huk remnants. Pedro Taruc, a distant cousin of the more famous Luis, was reported to have assumed the secretary-generalship of the CPP when Lava vacated the post six months before his capture. It is doubtful whether Taruc actually did so. We only have the word of the captured Lava that the changing-of-the-guard took place. Some Pampango sources claimed that Taruc was made the secretary-general of only one region, "Kalimihan One," covering what is roughly the Pampango-speaking areas. This version implies that there are other Kalimihans in the Philippines and other secretary-generals organizing them.

Pedro Taruc's own claim was that he was not a communist nor were his men, though the PC and the Manila press continued to call them Huks with all the previous associations the name evoked. He made this point emphatically clear in the two "audiences" he and Commander Sumulong granted in 1970, once to Rep. Emilio Espinosa's committee on social amelioration and the second time to the Senate ad hoc committee under Sen. Leonardo Perez.

What organization he represented was not made clear either. Sumulong, according to Sen. Eva Estrada Kalaw who was a member of Senator Perez's party, referred to a "Sama-

---

[2]As Cited.

han ng Bayan" (National Fellowship) as the precursors of the Huks before the 1950 rebellion. The organization became the armed HMB when the "para-military units" began to harass the peasants. When President Magsaysay removed these civilian militia the Huks faded away ("lumubog ang HMB") because "people mind their own security (sic)."[3]

In an earlier newspaper interview, Pedro Taruc said he had started the *Bayung Fuerza Democratica ding Memalen.* This was a non-communist, patriotic organization for "social justice and equality for all, rich and poor alike, before the law."[4]

Though Commander Sumulong deferred to Taruc as the "supremo," it was widely accepted that the latter merely wielded nominal power, a "front" for the Pampango organization run by the more aggressive Sumulong. There were persuasive reasons for this peculiar sharing of leadership.

Both Pedro Taruc and Sumulong were members of the Socialist party and in deference to the memory of Pedro Abad Santos the successor organization of the Socialist Party had to have an "intellectual" to lend legitimacy to the movement. Pedro Taruc quite likely served in that role. According to Representative Espinosa, he attained third year in commerce at the Jose Rizal College before the war. By contrast, Sumulong did not even finish his primary schooling.[5]

Pedro Taruc, on the other hand, did not have enough personal prestige to assume *de facto* leadership by himself. He was as obscure as Sumulong at the height of the rebellion. Neither his name nor that of Sumulong surfaced in the AFP order of battle until after Jesus Lava's capture in 1964. He was described as "old and ailing" but the ill-health factor might have been exaggerated. He appeared to his congressional interviewers as a tall, fair-complexioned, bespectacled man in his early sixties, but "relaxed" and in fairly good spirits.

In all probability, the Supremo's primary value to the organization was his family name. "Taruc" was still a byword throughout all of Pampanga and many Pampangos were still of the impression that Pedro was Luis' brother. A Taruc

---

[3]Sen. Eva Estrada Kalaw, "A Dialogue in Huklandia," a mimeographed transcript of a conversation between Pedro Taruc and Sumulong and members of Sen. Leonardo Perez's *ad hoc* committee for Central Luzon, July 10, 1970. Though the Huk commanders forbade the use of tape-recorders, they "allowed" Senator Kalaw to take notes by hand.

[4]Francis L. Starner, "Report from Arayat," *Far Eastern Economic Review,* Oct. 19, 1967. See also Saulo, as cited, p. 112.

[5]Interview, July, 1970.

leading the Pampango organization made it "legitimate" for all practical purposes.

There was one other reason why Taruc delegated the field command to Sumulong, and it was of such relevance that it overrode some personal faults of Sumulong that might have otherwise disqualified him from being the Huk chief-of-staff. To be that and chief of the finance department as well, a Huk leader must be of unsullied character and scrupulous in the handling of money. From many accounts, Sumulong was rather wanting on those scores. PC intelligence once got information that a Huk kangaroo court had sentenced Sumulong to die before a firing squad for various Huk crimes including "insubordination and accumulating wealth."[6]

What made Sumulong No. 2, if not No. 1 in Pampanga was the sheer accident of birth. In 1965, the Huk command divided Pampanga and the rest of Huklandia into subcommands each entrusted to half a dozen minor chiefs including Sumulong.[7] The area was like a pie cut into triangular slices with Angeles City at its center. The northeastern slice covering Magalang and part of Nueva Ecija was the territory of Commander Ely. Going in a clockwise direction, the other territorial slices were those belonging to Alibasbas (Magalang), Delio (Arayat and Cabiao, Nueva Ecija), Oscar (San Luis, San Simon, Apalit and the Bulacan towns of Baliuag, San Ildefonso and San Miguel), George Ocampo (Candaba, Sta. Ana, Mexico and San Fernando), and Freddie (Lubao, Floridablanca and parts of Bataan).[8]

The territorial assignments were largely made on the basis of the birthplace of Huk commanders — the Huks are strongest and most secure in the places of their birth. Sumulong hails from a western barrio near the boundary of Angeles and Porac. He grew up and gained personal influence in that area, and was the logical man to manage the organizational branch there.

Pedro Taruc came from San Simon, and he had some personal following in his native *pampangan* But San Simon was poor pickings as a logistical base. Since Angeles in time became the richest territory in all Pampanga in terms of revenue potential and political influence, his No. 2 man had to be the commander in charge of Angeles.

Angeles boomed in the sixties as a result of the enlarged U.S. military operations in Vietnam. Four air wings of the 13th U.S. air force operated out of Clark air base. It main-

---

[6]Philippines *Herald,* July 7, 1964.
[7]A confidential source whose identity cannot be revealed.
[8]Philippines *Herald*, August 1, 1966.

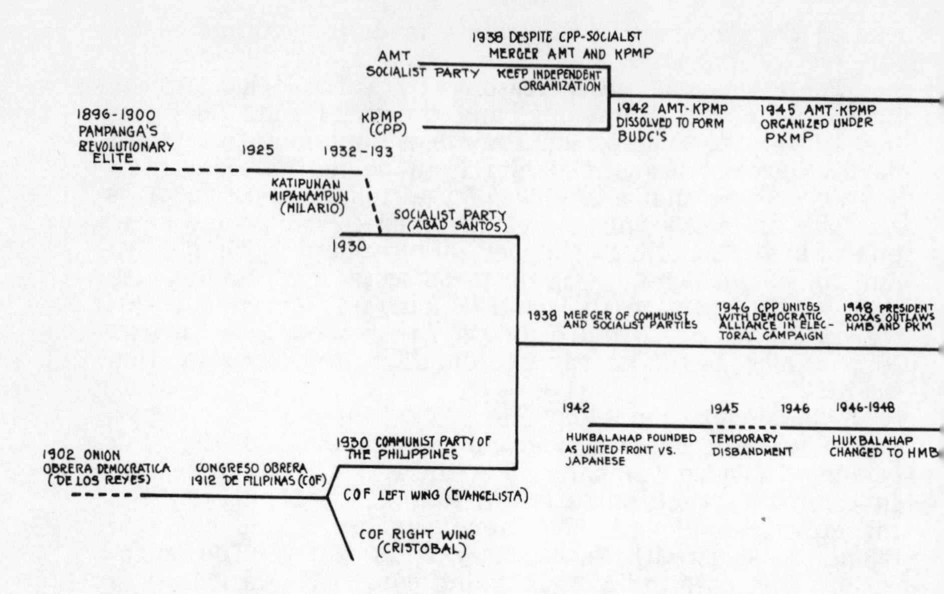

Figure 6 — Chronological chart of the development of the CPP, Socialist Party, the Huks and the peasant organizations. The middle chart represents the formation of the Communist Party, its merger with the Socialist and its travails through the fifties and early sixties. The lower figure represents the parallel development of the Huk organization, its 1968 split into the Tarlac and Pampanga wings and the reported reunification of these schismatic factions after the capture of Sumulong and the death

tained and supported "800 aircraft of 31 types, from the single-engine U-10 to the more complex F-4E's."[9] Clark became one of the largest American communities outside of the U.S. with close to 17,000 airmen and officers, 800 American civilians, and 17,000 military and civilian dependents. In addition, there were 14,000 Filipino contract workers and 7,500 Filipino "domestics" employed in 13th U.S. air force bases.[10]

Since Clark's facilities could not accommodate its population boom, as many as 12,500 American servicemen and dependents including 500 "illegal" families had to look for

[9]Symington subcommittee hearings, p. 49.

[10]These figures, submitted by Lt. Gen. Francis C. Gideon, Commander, U.S. 13th Air Force, to the Symington Subcommittee, referred to the "population of all Air Force organizations" in the Philippines. The great majority of these personnel are based at Clark. Colonel Holman, Clark air base commander, estimated the base population at 35,000 American military and dependents and 30,000 Filipinos.

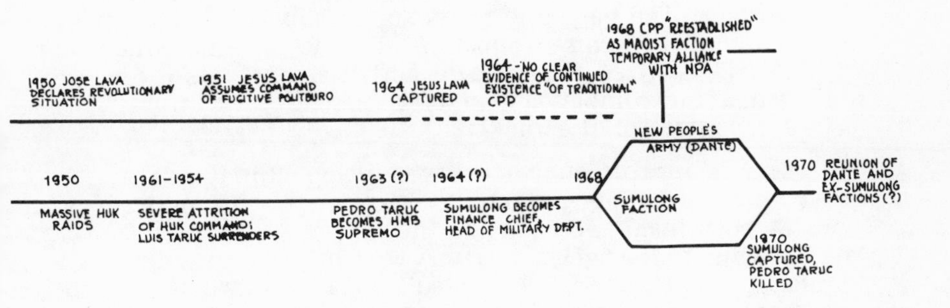

of Pedro Taruc in 1970. The upper figure traces the parallel history of the two peasant organizations, *Aguman ding Maldang Talapagobra* (AMT) and the *Kalipunang Pambansa ng mga Magbubukid* (KPMP). Unbroken lines represent full organizational continuity. Broken lines indicate either an informal successor organization or reported but unproven organizational existence.

housing in Angeles.[11] Real estate developments sprang up in Angeles — Clark View, L and S Subdivision, Trinidad Village, Diamond Subdivision among others.

Many Angeles property owners became rich overnight. In addition to the rapid appreciation of Angeles real estate, the entertainment district prospered from the business brought in by off-duty airmen. Two nightclub districts give Angeles its honkytonk atmosphere — "The Strip" running a kilometer on Balibago road from the Clark main gate and "The Block" located on the road leading to Pampang.

An unidentified American colonel described the "atmosphere of general lawlessness" in the Clark environs to the Symington subcommittee.

> There appears to be a general disrespect for law

[11]According to Clark authorities, an "illegal" family was that of an American serviceman who brings his dependents to live with him without authority from the Air Force.

> and order, a strong tendency towards violence as a way of settling personal and political disputes, easy availability of firearms, and inadequate law enforcement. Lawlessness has been particularly acute in the Angeles City area. . . where long-established criminal elements appear to operate with reckless abandon. The increased flow of personnel and equipment through the base due to its support of U.S. forces in Vietnam has raised substantially the revenue which can be realized from illegal activities and has intensified the competition among Angeles City interests for control of the rackets.[12]

It was in this enormously tempting climate of Angeles City that Sumulong quickly rose to power. Sumulong's critics — both inside and outside the movement — accused him of working the Angeles territory for his own account. Sumulong, it is claimed, "corrupted" the Huk movement. Since personalistic interpretations of history tend to be suspect, it may be fairer to say that Sumulong was a product of his times and his environment.

The end of the rebellion found the Huk survivors with the choice of plodding on to the last gasp in an unsupportable, futile struggle against a superior enemy, or simply quitting. A few Huks of sterner stuff were willing to do it the hard way if need be. Sumulong was smarter. He saw that the most important thing was for the organization to survive by strengthening and enlarging its logistical base. This was, from a strictly doctrinal point of view, the unspeakable error of "economism" but Sumulong and his kind were not communists. They were simple peasants trying to work out a better living for themselves.

"Ideology" was a thing of the past. It was quaint and anachronistic in the crassly commercial atmosphere of Angeles City. Neither did Sumulong nor his kind care to retire quietly to their villages and spend their remaining years in the same stark poverty they emerged from. They knew no other kind of existence; outlawry had become their life style.

This then was Sumulong's simple working philosophy. If they were to stay in the hills, constantly dependent on the farmers, the PC would catch up with them eventually. To maintain their corporate existence, the Huks had to go into business themselves. This was eminently safer and more comfortable and the organization would even pile up a surplus for a rainy day.

But first Sumulong had to get a firm hold on the entire organization. In 1965, it was split into two feuding camps

[12] Symington hearings, p. 185.

—the main force won over by Sumulong and a "rebel" faction beholden to Cesareo Manarang, better known as Alibasbas.

Power Struggles: Alibasbas, Oscar, Delio

His foremost rival, Alibasbas, was an equally senior Huk veteran; he would never cease to be a threat to Sumulong's authority as long as he lived. Alibasbas also had the loyalty of Commander Danilo's band. The two Huk chieftains were secure in their own bases, Sumulong in Angeles and Alibasbas in Concepcion, Tarlac, but they eyed each other with homicidal intent. On October 13, 1965, the two factions clashed in San Jose, Sta. Ana, Pampanga, resulting in the death of one Huk and the wounding of five others. The Huks were quarreling among themselves over which congressional candidate to support in the second district of Pampanga.[13]

Then fortuitously the Armed Forces stepped into the picture, hoping to exploit this cleavage between Sumulong and Alibasbas. Following orders from the Secretary of National Defense, Macario Peralta, Jr., the 10th Battalion Combat Team put into effect "Operation Homestretch" to win Alibasbas over to the government side and use his aid in defeating Sumulong's organization.

For months Alibasbas operated virtually as an "auxiliary" of the 10th BCT using arms and supplies "borrowed" from the Army.[14] Alibasbas later came to grief in February, 1966, under mysterious circumstances. The Huk chieftain, three of his sons, a daughter-in-law and five of his aides were killed in their sleep in a barrio of Concepcion, Tarlac. Two bodyguards who were supposed to be standing guard over the group confessed to the foul deed. Some 10th BCT troopers in the vicinity heard firing for 30 minutes — why they waited all of a half-hour before acting is another puzzling question —and when they rushed to the scene they saw Alibasbas and the rest of his murdered company lying amid a litter of empty bullet shells.[15]

The real motives for the ghastly massacre are still not known. The confessed killers claim they killed Alibasbas because they resented the promotion of his three sons who had only recently joined the Huks. Another theory is that Sumulong had bribed the bodyguards to liquidate their own commander. But just as likely was the possibility that the

[13]Philippines *Herald*, Oct. 14, 1965.

[14]Philippines *Herald*, Oct. 14, 1965.

[15]A fuller account of the Alibasbas episode is contained in Chapter 7.

Philippine Army officers responsible for "Homestretch" had Alibasbas liquidated to wipe out the last traces of their fraternization with the Huks and to make up to the incoming Marcos adminstration. Earlier, Danilo was killed under circumstances that made his AFP protectors the logical suspects.

Whoever was the perpetrator of the Concepcion massacre, its net result was that Sumulong became the undisputed leader of Huklandia. His leadership within the organization was challenged a few more times and Sumulong dealt with the non-cooperators with characteristic cunning.

When one harks back to the blood coups and countercoups that characterized Central Luzon in the late sixties. he is in a world of fact and apocrypha, where the official reportage is too pat or leaves many questions unanswered and where there are often two or more versions to every event. There were stories, part conjectural and part factual, that many of Sumulong's commanders were opposed to his methods and resentful of the commercialization of the Huk organization. Sumulong did not directly eliminate them; they met properly heroic Huk deaths, cornered by PC strike forces and resisting to the last. Several AFP officers were decorated and promoted for their part in tracking down the hunted commanders, not to mention sharing in the rich awards posted by the Department of National Defense. But was it just luck and good sleuthing which led the AFP teams to their quarry? Or were they tipped off by sources within the Huk organization?

Commander Oscar was the next of Sumulong's contemporaries to go. He met his end in San Pablo, San Simon, after he had conferred with 50 legal cadres. Col. Rafael Ileto (now Philippine Army commanding general) personally directed the encirclement of the house where Oscar was spending the night of December 11, 1966. When the first shots were exchanged, Oscar threw a hand grenade at Lt. Col. Wilfredo Encarnacion, the Pampanga PC commander, but it did not explode. Oscar survived the night but the next morning he was cut down in the backyard attempting to escape. Three of Oscar's bodyguards perished with him.[16]

The capture of Commander Ely (Dominador Garcia) by PC raiders in barrio Cacutud, Mabalacat on March 15, 1967 eliminated another of the pre-1965 territorial commanders. On November 9, 1967, Commander Delio was trapped by three PC Ranger teams in San Jose, Dinalupihan, Bataan. The No. 3 Huk, with a ₱40,000 prize on his head, was killed when he jumped out of a house. The successful Delio mis-

---

[16]Philippines *Herald,* December 13, 1966.

sion originated, according to the Manila press, from "intelligence reports."

There were rumors drifting in from Pampanga that Delio had been "fingered" by a ranking Huk who wanted the former out of the way. But there was almost no doubt that Commander Freddie (Efren Lopez) who had openly broken away from Sumulong over political matters had been betrayed by other Huks.

Commander Freddie

A month and a half before his death, Freddie met one of the Philippines *Herald* correspondents in a barrio in Bataan.[17] He was unhappy over Sumulong's decision to switch his support from one candidate to another in the election for the mayoralty of Tarlac town. His grief was shared by another young lieutenant of Sumulong's, Commander Dante, who hailed from Capas, Tarlac. On the strength of the Huk chieftain's word, both Freddie and Dante pledged to work for Dr. Jose Geronimo. But barely a week before the election, Sumulong had inexplicably changed his mind and now told his subalterns to campaign for Geronimo's opponent. "I cannot be bought by the highest bidder," Freddie said bitterly.

Freddie was one of an almost vanishing breed of idealist peasant reformers. He would have none of the bourgeois comforts enjoyed by his less-motivated comrades-at-arms. He was in the process of setting up the first "Mao Tse-tung University" in the Bataan wilds when his career was cut short. In his Bataan territory he had already organized a small corps of like-minded Huks hoping to reform the image of the movement.

Three weeks before his final battle with the PC, Freddie was engaged in a deadly hide-and-seek game in Laocpao, San Roque, Lubao, with Commander Fonting, the leader of Sumulong's killer squad. A clash was averted by the arrival of Lubao policemen riding in an armored car. This incident confirmed that Sumulong and his young subaltern had finally parted ways.

Two days before he was killed, Freddie was visited by Dante and 12 of his men in barrio Puli. Something was afoot, possibly they were joining forces and setting up a new movement against Sumulong. Already gathered in the vicinity were Commander Robert (Roberto Mandalla) and

[17]The correspondent was Andy Morales who covers Camp Olivas, the anti-Huk command headquarters in San Fernando. Morales got his interview with Freddie through the help of some relatives in Orani. Morales is also an important source in the recounting of the Huk commander's last days.

his own followers. Robert was no ordinary peasant but a small landowner in his own right with 54 hectares planted to rice.[18] Robert had fought under Linda Bie and now he was willing to be part of Freddie's undertaking.

A villager later told the PC that he had been asked to prepare food for 76 men while Freddie, Dante and his men were conferring in a thickly-forested hill in sitio Dumaon, barrio Sibul, Orani, Bataan. This was to be one of the biggest Huk caucuses in years.[19]

After getting definite word that Freddie and Dante were meeting in Orani, Brig. Gen. Emilio Zerrudo, PC zone chief, prepared his battle plans in the privacy of his bedroom to prevent any possible leakage. Camp Aguinaldo, the AFP heaquarters, very likely was not given advance warning for that same reason. On January 9, 1969 a task force rumbled out of Camp Olivas and other posts in Central Luzon and took up battle positions around Freddie's meeting place.

The initial contact took place that day at 4 p.m. A fierce battle and a 16-hour siege ensued. Freddie was among the first to fall. He broke with 10 of his men for cover at a nearby sugarcane field and was cut down by machinegun fire from an armored personnel carrier. Their bodies were strewn on the edge of the canefield. Commander Ligaya, the Huk amazon wife of Freddie, died in the arms of her husband [20]

As night fell, General Zerrudo ordered the PC Rangers to fix bayonets and tighten the cordon around the area to prevent any possible breakout by Huk survivors. But some Huks apparently escaped under cover of darkness. The suspected escape route was an improvised bridge over a ravine to the east of the encircled hill. It was left unguarded because of its precipitous terrain. The *Herald* was later informed that Commander Dante and his men did not take part in the firefight. He was lying low nearby outside of the PC encirclement, unable to come to Freddie's rescue without endangering the lives of his own command.[21]

The following morning the victorious Rangers counted the dead: besides Freddie and his wife, three other Huk commanders, Caviteño, Paras and Robert, were slain. The bodies of 17 Huks were lined up for the inspection of the PC chief, Brig. Gen. Vicente Raval, who had rushed from Camp Crame to catch the action. It was the biggest AFP victory over the Huks in nearly two decades.[22]

---

[18]Morales.

[19]Philippines *Herald*, January 10, 1969.

[20]Same, Jan. 10-11, 1969.

[21]Morales.

[22]Philippines *Herald*, as cited.

Freddie's death hit Commander Dante very hard. That same month Dante pulled out of Sumulong's organization and set up his own "army" with six of his subcommanders in his native Tarlac. Sumulong showed distress over the defection of his once loyal follower. "I knew Dante since he was a kid," he said. "I once picked him up when he was wounded, in the knee and in the stomach."[23]

Sumulong's possible complicity in the demise of his potential rivals is revealing of the character of the *de facto* leader of the Pampanga organization. Some may condemn his Machiavellian tactics. But from Sumulong's point of view he was merely acting in self-defense. Guile and deception are the necessary tools of the dissident trade. Without them, Sumulong would not have outlived his enemies. He held sway in Pampanga for six turbulent years and lived as a Huk for perhaps 28 years.

True Grit: Sumulong's History

Sumulong's most pronounced trait, according to a Pampango who knew him in his youth was his "animal instinct for survival."[24] He grew up in a harsh surrounding, near the foothills of Mt. Dorst and Mt. Catuno, where the sandy soil is inhospitable to farming. The landlords in that area were particularly oppressive. He had to scrabble to survive.

He was an extremely tough youth. As a Pampanga Sugar Mill striker, he used to be beaten up and mauled by company guards and thrown out bleeding onto the streets. But he always came back for more.

His previous guerrilla record is obscure. He was one of Linda Bie's minor functionaries, not distinguishing himself in any action or he would have been heard about earlier. But years of fugitive life have honed Sumulong's cunning and grit. He had been known to lie in mud for hours waiting for his pursuers to leave his lair.

He, too, is typical of the "guerrilla generation" — ruthless, opportunistic and skilled in the use of power. It is not altogether clear how he managed to be in line for the Pampango leadership, outside of having an inside track to Angeles commerce and politics. He probably just happened to be there when the opportunity offered itself — one of the few survivors of an army that had numbered in thousands.

Sumulong, whose real name is Faustino del Mundo, was 55 when he was finally captured in the house of his common-

---

[23]Senator Kalaw, as cited.

[24]Much of the description of Huk commanders and their operations in this and subsequent chapters was given by Pampanga town officials who naturally declined to be identified.

law wife in an Angeles City subdivision. He is a short, stocky man, almost barrel-chested, with a scar over his left eyebrow, a boxer's ears and a dazzling set of gold teeth. He was not at all put down by his capture. He traded jokes with reporters and seemed quite at ease in his televised conferences with Defense Sec. Juan Ponce Enrile and President Marcos.

Surprisingly for one running a local Mafia, Sumulong lived quite simply. His only known recreation was watching boxing matches on television. Following the usual precaution of much-wanted Huk leaders, he slept in different houses every night.

He showed some preference for Pampang, a barrio of Angeles City, where some of his political supporters have property. The barrio had to pay for its hospitality to the dreaded Huk commander. Its residents were sometimes harassed and shot at by Sumulong's enemies.

He moved about almost invisibly, his whereabouts known only to a few trusted associates. His commanders were his "eyes and ears." They reported directly to him and he gave orders on the basis of information given him. In the last year of his freedom, Sumulong had been increasingly accessible to "outsiders" who wished to get his ear (though they had to subject themselves to elaborate precautions to shake off any possible PC "tails"). Senator Kalaw related how her party was assembled at an undisclosed house in Pampanga at two o'clock in the morning and made to wait for almost an hour "to make sure that we were not followed along the way." At 3 a.m. they were brought to another house and made to wait another 15 minutes before the objects of their search — Pedro Taruc and Sumulong — materialized.[25]

Sumulong's 'Ideology'

Sumulong was not very educated, probably having completed only a few primary grades, but he had great native intelligence. He spoke only Pampango and a smattering of slangy Tagalog. He hated English and was not fond of Americans (though this apparently did not stop him from enjoying the prosperity brought about by the presence of the nearby American air force base).

The "dialogue" between Senator Perez's party and the two Huk leaders show some glimpses of Sumulong's political convictions. The Pampanga organization, Sumulong averred, was no longer bent on toppling the government. "We are helping the small (people). If feudal landlords abuse, we defend the farmer. It is not true that we take sides. We

[25]Senator Kalaw, as cited.

are for the right."[26]

He explained his falling out with Dante in this wise: "Our platform was not to topple the government. Dante did not like this. So we are now fighting each other. We believe in the right, not in communism. That is why Tarlac separated from us."

"Whoever it is that is not just, Dante or the Government, we fight. Justice for all, not just for the small (a verbal lapse, probably Sumulong meant "big"). Hacenderos before abused farmers. We resented this. Each one must be given his just share."[27]

During the interview, both Huk leaders were dubious about the efficacy of land reform. Taruc agreed with it in principle, "but not in practice." Sumulong foresaw that the heirs of the landowners would again acquire control of divided land. "It will be another vicious circle."

Sumulong had a poor judgment of the Marcos government, calling it "70 percent bad and 30 percent good."[28]

Contrasting with this picture of Sumulong as a benign *pater-familias* is the other picture of a "fat cat" who prefers the bourgeois life to the discomfort of the hills. His family, if not he himself, lived well. When his daughter married a member of a prominent Central Luzon family, the wedding was virtually a social event. It is, of course, characteristic of Filipino fathers to sacrifice everything for the welfare of their wives and children.

The most stinging rebuke of Sumulong came from the propaganda machine of the Maoist faction. In the NPA-CPP documents seized in Tarlac tunnels, Sumulong was vilified in the most scathing terms for "finance opportunism," "class betrayal," "luxurious and corrupt living," "petty warlord attitude," and other heterodox deviations from the true faith.

When the U.S. government purchased several hectares of land for the installation of a Voice of America transmitter, Sumulong was reported to have prevented Dante's men from resisting the "ejection" of farmers in that area. The Angeles "clique" was criticized for using the Huks to guard the landlords' rice fields and granaries "on the flimsy excuse of 'helping out the peasants to cheat the landlords'." The Taruc-Sumulong clique had also stood aside while labor and student strikers were pitched in unequal battle with the PC and armed strike-breakers. Indeed "for a paltry sum of money," the clique used its armed men to coerce strikers to submit to the capitalist owners.[29]

---

[26]Same.
[27]Same.
[28]Same.
[29]AFP documents.

> . . . There is no democratic centralism; there is only the centralism of one big shot, "Commander" Sumulong who has criminally made one-man decisions involving the execution of "erring" comrades and other people, the disposition of huge amount of funds and the like. Without due process and on the flimsiest grounds that usually have something to do with finance collections or some business enterprises, many comrades have been judged by him as deserving of the death penalty and mass murders have actually been committed on his orders. The Taruc-Sumulong clique has been directly responsible more for the killing of comrades and other people in connection with some shady business enterprise than in connection with revolutionary armed struggle. . .
>
> Since there is absolutely no democracy practised by the Taruc-Sumulong clique, since there is no committee system, no system of political commissars, no report system and no accounting of funds, the clique-masters have been in a position to make arbitrary decisions, abuse the mechanical discipline of some comrades and armed units and to commit finance opportunism on a grand scale as scandalously manifested by their luxurious and corrupt living, by their having several wives and spending party funds in such manner, by their lavish parties for their reactionary friends and "compadres" and also by having close relatives gain private titles over some sizeable property that properly belong to the Party and the people.
>
> "Commander" Sumulong appoints goons and police characters to high responsibilities on his staff, mixes them up with dedicated comrades and thereby endangers these comrades, personally administers beatings to them alike and orders their execution whenever they fail to satisfy his financial demands. "Commander" Sumulong has also made use of the name of the Party and Army in practising usury among comrades at the average rate of 50% a month, in forcing the sale of properties to him at the price he dictates. . .[30]

Some of the specific Maoist preachments against Sumulong were one-sided in the extreme. The VOA transmitter in Concepcion, Tarlac was later put to good use as a "sanctuary" for Dante's men. Some of the security guards hired by the U.S. agency could well have been Huks. (At one time, the PC encircled the VOA site in the suspicion that the chief of the New People's Army himself was hiding there.)

Sumulong had long reached an accommodation with the landlords — those unwilling to fight him openly — so he

[30]Same.

could now "supervise" harvests and prescribe their "equitable" sharing.

Sumulong was indifferent to labor unions and student groups because he did not want "competition." Up to the day of his capture, few labor organizations could penetrate his strongholds.

The Maoist attack on Sumulong has to be taken qualifiedly in the light of the power struggle between rival leftist factions in the late sixties.

Even allowing for the obvious bias of the Maoist diatribe, it adds to the evidence that Sumulong was a local strong man operating within rather than outside of the political system and not the classic Communist guerrilla leader.

Sumulong's collaborative associations with politicians were also borne out by countless witnesses. He campaigned for Tarlac congressional candidates (before the territory was preempted by Commander Dante), for a Pampanga governor and his politician wife, and for at least two presidential candidates. Before the 1969 elections, he was seen sporting a campaign cap with the names of a presidential team emblazoned on it. A cabinet officer of President Marcos was reported in contact with Sumulong at about this time.

When this cabinet member was asked why the Marcos government seemed to be tolerating the Sumulong organization, he replied, "We aren't worried about him. We can destroy his people at any time. But Sumulong serves the purpose of being a buffer against Commander Dante. If we eliminate Sumulong, Dante would surely extend his influence to Pampanga and that would be an extremely dangerous situation."[31]

This argument, incidentally, recalls the rationale made by the AFP for its "alliance" with Alibasbas against Sumulong. It is an inevitable conclusion that Sumulong's Huks — and possibly other dissident factions as well — are used by political factions for their own ends.

The popular conception that Sumulong "controlled" Angeles politics and trade was probably exaggerated. Governor Nepomuceno, who has a modest-sized army of bodyguards, controls a sizeable chunk of the air base-catering business in the city. He owns two or more of the largest residential subdivisions, the Oasis Hotel, the Nepo Mart and other facilities. His deadly confrontation with Sumulong probably accounted for the occasional outbreaks of "civil war" in the city.

---

[31]The information was given by an opposition senator but various independent sources confirmed it. In an interview with the cabinet officer referred to, he appeared extremely knowledgeable about the movements and actions of Sumulong.

Though Sumulong had fallen out with Nepomuceno, he had the support of the majority of Angeles barrio captains. The Angeles barrios were for a long time conspicuously indifferent to the AFP offer of self-defense units. Mayor Eugenio Suarez preferred to have the barrio captains decide in their own way whether to acquire BSDU's or not.[32]

Economic Base

Sumulong's economic base included some of the large nightclubs and bars, though he selected only those he trusted or were unquestionably sympathetic to the movement. An American oldtimer who headed the nightclub owners association in Angeles claimed he paid no protection money to the Huks. The proprietor of another popular catery in Balibago said he was never approached by any of Sumulong's men.

According to him, the ones who "demand" payment are not really Huks. There seemed to be another "syndicate" trying to muscle into Sumulong's territory and this could be one of the reasons for the occasional violence rocking the city.

Estimates of the size of Sumulong's income varied widely. James Wilson, deputy chief of mission of the U.S. Embassy, was asked by the Symington subcommittee his personal estimate of the Huk take from Clark air force base. He replied "as much as $1 million a year."[33]

If Sumulong earned that much from the Clark trade alone, his earnings from that source would have been 65 per cent more than the total revenue of Pampanga province including Angeles City.[34]

Frances Starner reported in 1967 a somewhat more modest Huk income of ₱1.5 million a year.[35] A young politician of Pampango descent believed many of these estimates were "exaggerated." His personal estimate was that Sumulong netted "in his best days" from ₱40,000 to ₱50,000 a month. He earned at least ₱3,000 a month from the sale of liquor. It was the "other group" that was starting a large-scale extortion racket in Angeles.

A Pampanga politician who had tried to buck the Sumulong system and hence could not be expected to be apo-

[32]Interview with Alfredo Pineda, secretary of Mayor Eugenio Suarez.

[33]Symington hearings, p. 230.

[34]The 21 municipalities of Pampanga and Angeles City reported a total income of ₱2,691,781.77 in the fiscal year ending June 30, 1962. At the time of Wilson's testimony, (1969) his $1 million would translate into about ₱3.9 million.

[35]As cited.

logetic about the HMB's gave an estimate of "₱50,000 (about $12,000) a month." This would amount to ₱600,000 ($180,-000) a year and well below the Wilson estimate.

Senate Pres. Gil Puyat described Sumulong's operations as a "shakedown racket." He charged that Sumulong's son-in-law controlled the security guard business in Angeles. Sumulong, according to the highly respected politician of Pampango descent, even had the "effrontery to ask Clark Field to give the security guard business to them."[36]

If we were to settle for an estimate somewhere in between the highs and lows — say, ₱1 million — Sumulong would still have been richer than the whole Huk organization ever was at the height of its power. If his payroll was estimated at an average of ₱200 for each of his 200 regulars (many captured Huks claim they received no more than food and a cigarette allowance of ₱30 a month), that would be ₱48,000 a year. Charge ₱100,000 for other sundry upkeep and another ₱100,000 for the purchase of arms and ammunition, and he should have some ₱600,000 to ₱700,000 left over. What Sumulong did with his surplus is an interesting question indeed.

To the AFP, Sumulong was no better than a common criminal except for having a high price of ₱150,000 on his head. He was charged with rebellion in the Pampanga court of first instance and with ten separate murder cases including complicity in the slaying of three mayors, Benedicto Dayrit of Magalang, Pampanga, on December 28, 1963, Eduardo Tiangco of Arayat, on December 23, 1964, and Anastacio Gallardo of Candaba on July 18, 1966.

Sumulong's Men

Sumulong depended on at least four sector commanders to do his bidding. Commander Tony (Gregorio Ocampo) was in charge of Porac, Floridablanca and Mabalacat, Commander Fonting (Florentino Salac) held down portions of Zambales and Bataan, Commander Pelaez (Felix Salac) covered northeastern Pampanga and Commander Zaragoza (Hermogenes Miranda) had the Candaba swamp for his territory.[37] All four commanders had impressive criminal records with at least a dozen murders each.

Tony seemed to have been the brightest of the lot since he held down concurrent positions of education department and finance chiefs. Fonting was the chief of Sumulong's liquidation squad. He was doing exceedingly well in that line, for he had no less than 15 murder charges to his credit. Tne

[36]Philippines *Herald,* Dec. 12, 1967.
[37]From an AFP intelligence briefing in February, 1970.

most prominent of his supposed victims was Mayor Levi Panlilio of San Fernando, who met his end in barrio Calulut of that town on December 28, 1968. Both Tony and Fonting were killed by AFP troopers in November, 1970.

Commander Pelaez was also complicated in the ambush slaying of Mayor Gallardo and five of his escorts and bodyguards on Kalinan road, Sta. Ana, Pampanga. He was charged with killing Angeles councilor Jose Roman, though it was rather doubtful whether Pelaez or any Huk for that matter killed Roman who was not only known to be a Huk "sympathizer" but an outspoken critic of the PC and its "Monkee" assassins.

These "criminal records" cannot tell much about the kind of men who ran Sumulong's "invisible government" in Pampanga outside of the fact that they killed when they had to.

It is doubtful whether many of the crimes attributed to them were indiscriminate killings. There is ample ground to believe that most of these "murders" were vengeance killings of politicians who "double-crossed" the organization, landlords and overseers who took a hard line against the Huks, and even Huk members themselves who misappropriated Huk collections.

Sumulong's commanders were a mixed variety. A few were extremely vicious men. Commander Tapang who was charged with killing 32 men before his homicidal career ended in a hail of PC bullets, was described by AFP officers as a "psychopath."[38] Yet some Huk leaders were well spoken of. "Commander Oscar didn't even ask the barrio people for cigarettes," a land reform official once said.

Under Sumulong's regime, the Huk movement formally returned to its original goal of peasant advocacy and added the new one of establishing a permanent and "legitimate" logistical base. It also retreated to its original jurisdiction of Pampanga and concerned itself with little else outside this area. "Revolution" was excluded from the organization's objectives; the central government only superficially impinged on the life of the Pampango tenant except in a negative way — poorly maintained irrigation ditches and barrio roads, abusive PC soldiers and self-serving public officials.

The Central Luzon conflict became more pronouncedly what Konrad Lorenz calls "intra-specific" — a fight of Pampangos against *other* Pampangos for the control of economic and political prerogatives

---

[38]Same.

Chapter Nine

THE TARLAC SCHISM: 1968-1970

Between Sumulong and Dante was a difference of 23 or more years. Though they shared the same covert existence they were of radically different molds. It was foreseeable that they would one day divide the Huk movement into two sharply antagonistic factions, and in 1968, the break became a reality.

In two years of independent operation in Tarlac, Commander Dante has become something of a legend, the object of one of the biggest manhunts in Philippine history, a wraith-like figure who has time and again given his helicopter-borne pursuers the slip. He has acquired a charismatic reputation extending far beyond his Central Luzon haunts without having been personally seen or heard by more than several score of his followers.

Part of the legend is grounded on fact. The possessor of such legerdemainist qualities — the fanatically followed leader of the largest Huk band in Central Luzon yet vaporous to the multitude of his enemies — is an unprepossessing young man of just over 30, a small, frail figure standing five feet and four inches, slightly stooped (he used to be called "Payat" or Thin Man) and reportedly consumptive. He is fair and not unattractive (some Huk sources said he is *pogi,* the fashionable Tagalog slang for "handsome"). But for the power at his command, he is of a singularly meek and unobstrusive disposition. He does not stand out in a crowd, which is certainly no liability for a man in his trade. He can ride a bicycle past a PC roadblock without the troopers suspecting he could be the much-wanted Commander Dante.

It is also part of the key to his leadership. A Huk leader must have life-or-death influence over his men; but he must also know how to handle them gallantly and humanely in the Pampango tradition of comradeship. Dante shared the simple food and provisions of his men; he took equal if not more risks. But he was nobody's patsy. No one had ever survived long in that occupation and Dante was the finished product of 16 years of professional outlawry under the wiliest master of them all, Commander Sumulong. Dante knew all the tricks. He could be as ruthless as the most cold-blooded killer in the ranks; his lengthy criminal dossier in the PC files attests to this.

On top of those qualifications, he was relatively well educated for a Huk, having attained two to three years of high school in Manila and in Angeles. He may be one of the few figures in the Huk movement who is really irreplaceable — a man of peasant stock with whom the Huk rank-and-file can identify — and sufficiently knowledgeable about modern organization and public policy to hold his own with the politicians and intellectuals.

"If he is killed, someone would take his place but it would take some time before anybody with his unique qualities can take over," a Tarlac official said.

Part of the legend was that Dante was pure-hearted. How could we be sure? "He was tried many times and was not found wanting," a reliable Tarlac source informed the *Herald*.

The student radicals in Manila romanticized Dante as the symbol of insurrection against a "feudalistic" and "fascistic" establishment. At the height of the student unrest early in 1970, his admirers stormed through the streets crying, "Dante for President." Neither the Lavas nor the Tarucs in their heydays ever got such an endorsement.

The legend was hauntingly reminiscent of Felipe Salvador of the Santa Iglesia, Pedro Calosa of Tayug, and many of the peasant-born spellbinders. Dante could have all those qualities but he would not have become the supremo of the Tarlac organization had he not possessed the all-important qualification — Pampango peasant birth.

The Apprenticeship of a Huk Leader

Dante was born in utter poverty, the son of a squatter on the property of the Ramos family in sitio Manga, barrio Talimundok, Capas, Tarlac. His real name is Bernabe Buscayno. Sitio Manga is like most hamlets in the Philippines, a cluster of flimsy shacks with a few trees, backyard poultry and a primitive, hand-dug well. Manga is a few kilometers off the North Road that connects Manila with the northern provinces, but it is fairly secluded since it can be approached only from Talaga and from a short turnoff from the Capas-Botolan road crossing Crow Valley and the rugged terrain of western Tarlac and Zambales. The PC Rangers tracking down Dante could not surprise their quarry in his own home because his lookouts at both ends of the dirt road passing Talimundok would always tip him off on any troop movements. The closest the government soldiers got to nabbing Dante in that neighborhood was during a helicopter raid.

Capas is on slightly rising ground and unsuitable for either rice or sugar cultivation. The Buscayno family had to live off the charity of the Ramoses who owned the mango orchard (hence, the name of the sitio) where their nipa shack stood. Jose Ramos, a retired school teacher, was one of the more benign landlords in Capas. Instead of evicting the Buscaynos, he allowed Bernabe's father to stay on the property with the understanding that he would help collect rent from the more solvent tenants. When Bernabe was old enough to begin his schooling, he and his brother Jose were sent to the landowner's house in Quezon City.[1]

Ramos also offered to take care of the education of the young Buscaynos. Bernabe reciprocated this kindness by helping in the housework. This was no imposition; many poor country folk stay with their better-off kin in the city and repay the hospitality by supplementing the domestic staff. They were *un poco parientes* — a part of the family rather than servants.

Ramos remembers Bernabe as a quiet, withdrawn youth. He was of "average" intelligence; his grades were not unusually high. He was well-behaved and was never known to have gotten into serious trouble. With the financial assistance of his patron, Bernabe completed grade school at Burgos Elementary School. He got up to second year at Roosevelt High School in Cubao, Quezon City before he and Jose left for Angeles City to live with an aunt.

The two Buscaynos worked as waiters in an Angeles restaurant; then they disappeared. Neither the Ramoses nor the friends of the Buscaynos in Manila have seen them since. What they did was to follow the previous calling of their father. The elder Buscayno was a Huk under Luis Taruc. The Buscayno boys joined the Huks for the same reason that many of their contemporaries did — it was part of the family tradition.

Bernabe and possibly Jose as well probably entered Sumulong's organization in their late teens. The older boy served as a runner. Dante, as he was known henceforth, later became one of Sumulong's most efficient killers. He had 25 separate murder charges before he went on his own. Some of these were spectacular. According to one charge,

---

[1]Most of the biographical information on Bernabe Buscayno was provided by Jose Ramos whom I interviewed at the home of Dr. Jose Geronimo in Tarlac town in September, 1969. Ramos' son, Rafael, was then running for the 2nd district congressional seat.

Dante was responsible for mowing down two PC corporals, Federico Correa and Romulo Gabriel, and wounding two other enlisted men in *front* of Camp Aquino, the Philippine Army supply depot and cantonment, on December 5, 1967. He was believed to have pulled off the killing of three municipal policemen and the wounding of two others in the Concepcion poblacion on October 12, 1968.

Dante's greatest asset probably was not his trigger finger but his "intellectual" capacity. He had one of the quickest minds in the Huk hierarchy. He had a territorial assignment in his native Capas but he concurrently held the post of chief of the Huk education department.

A new-comer though he was, Dante would not have climbed as rapidly up the Huk promotional ladder were it not for the extraordinary rate of attrition of the Huk leadership in the late sixties. From No. 13 in the AFP order of battle in July, 1967, Dante jumped to No. 4 in less than a year and a half.[2] His escalating career undoubtedly was something he could be proud of but it was not without some sorrow on his part. The ranking commanders who were being eliminated were comrades Dante liked and respected — Oscar, Delio and an earlier Commander Freddie (Domingo Yambao) who fought a gunbattle with the PC for more than six hours before he was killed.[3]

When the next DND awards were posted in December, Dante had arrived. The premium for his death or capture was upped nine-fold from ₱10,000 to ₱90,000—a token of increasing PC respect for the deadly Huk operative. In 1968—Dante's year of destiny—the youthful Tarlaqueño was just below the Top Huk leadership with only the second Commander Freddie (Efren Lopez) between himself and the two senior Huk leaders, Taruc and Sumulong.

The disenchantment the second Freddie (Efren Lopez) felt as a result of Sumulong's capricious maneuvering in the Tarlac mayoralty election in 1967 was more pronounced in the case of his friend and ally, Commander Dante. Doctor Geronimo, the candidate from whom the Huk boss withdrew

---

[2]By July, 1967, the top 13 in the AFP wanted list and the rewards offered were: 1. Pedro Taruc, ₱50,000; 2. Faustino del Mundo (Sumulong), ₱30,000; 3. Zacarias de la Cruz (Delio), ₱30,000; 4. Efren Lopez (Freddie), ₱20,000; 5. Dominador Garcia (Ely), ₱15,000; 6. Gregorio Ocampo (George, Tonie), ₱15,000; 7. Maximo Flores (Nestor, Taga and Max), ₱10,000; 8. Avelino Bagsik (Zaragoza), ₱5,000; 9. Felicisimo Bondoc (Felicing), ₱5,000; 10. Cristobal de la Cruz (Ubang), ₱5,000; 11. Hernando Subong (Sareno), ₱5,000; 12. Ricardo Ignacio (Oscar), ₱5,000; 13. Bernabe Buscayno (Dante), ₱5,000.

[3]Philippines *Herald*, Nov. 10, 1967.

his support, was a kin of the Ramoses, the same family that took care of young Bernabe Buscayno. Dante had pledged his all to the candidacy of Doctor Geronimo on the strength of Sumulong's commitment. Dante did work hard for Geronimo for many weeks. Now Sumulong inexplicably told both Dante and Freddie to junk Geronimo and campaign instead for Geronimo's rival.

This incident must have shaken Dante's faith in the old man. He had heretofore been a loyal, even a blind follower of Sumulong. Now he had some doubts. There was talk about some financial consideration in the switch of the Huk vote. When Dante got the word, he reportedly broke down and cried.[4]

But the final straw was the betrayal of Freddie. The two youngsters were so close they were known in the Tarlac underground as the "Katzenjamer Kids" (after the two hell-raising brats in a popular comic strip). Dante felt like he had lost a brother.

Shortly after Freddie's death on an Orani hillside, this column "Ideologue of the Rice Paddies," took note of Freddie's mission and was something of an augury of how the torch would be picked up by the bereaved Dante in the next few months.

> Commander Freddie was the late ideologue of the rice paddies. There may be more learned Marxists among us but they prefer the comparative safety of the university classroom, newspaper office and other havens of *embourgeoisement*.
>
> The vocal leftists — most of them I suspect — are nothing more than intellectual poseurs who prattle about revolution while enjoying the comforts of urban life and who spout anti-Americanisms because it is not in the least dangerous.
>
> Some of them have already gone over to the Establishment. One University of the Philippines firebrand is now respectably employed in the Senate. The luckier ones have been promoted to high office and now ride in Mercedes Benzes with low-numbered plates.
>
> But Freddie was at least an honest, practicing ideologue. He rendered the ultimate earnest of his beliefs by falling in unequal combat with General Zerrudo's crack troopers. A man less fanatical would have raised his hands in surrender and walked out of the cogon fields of Sibul alive.

---

[4]Confidential source.

Freddie's intellectual capacity has never been fully plumbed. All we know is that he was one of the brightest graduates of the defunct Stalin University. Unlike Che Guevara to whom one is tempted to compare him, Freddie was not known to have left any writings. There is no book like Che Guevara's "Guerrilla Warfare" to foster a living myth for other revolutionaries to emulate.[5]

Army intelligence described him as an ideological maverick who broke away from the other Huk hierarchs because they showed a distinct taste for fancy cars and air-conditioned hotel rooms and were bent on operating like a local branch of the Cosa Nostra rather than the armed tool of a proletariat movement.

There may be attempts to romanticize and mythicize Freddie's short-lived career as a true revolutionary who tried to subvert the Huks all over again and failed. But I doubt if such myth-making would prosper for long.

For Freddie was really not in the class of Che Guevara. He might indeed have been one of those really dangerous ones where "revolution began in the cerebrum and not in the stomach." But I doubt if Stalin University gave him philosophical understanding and a really perceptive world view aside from his rudimentary Marxism. He might have had the makings of an intellectual leader but he never had the opportunity to assert that leadership.

A wallet recovered from his blood-splattered body disclosed the names and photographs of many young students in Manila. Freddie obviously had been trying to spread the word on his own. He had a charisma of sorts. The people around Sibul thought he was "pogi." He was already starting to indoctrinate the countryside when the PC closed the trap on him.

After Che Guevara was killed by Bolivian soldiers in 1967, a whole cult sprang up in his honor. There were Guevarists who led the May revolt in Paris, Guevarists who stoned Chicago policemen during the hectic convention days, Guevarists in many campus donnybrooks on both sides of the Atlantic.

Will we soon have "Freddists" in our midst to

---

[5]I was later informed that Freddie did put some of his thoughts to paper in the form of mimeographer tracts — all in *Capangpangan.*

> carry on the creed of their late preceptor? I doubt it. There are too few Filipinos willing to practice revolution instead of merely talking about it.[6]

Dante now avoided Angeles and kept himself brooding in Tarlac. Sumulong sent many of his commanders — Madrigal, Tronco, Cruz and Zaragoza — after Dante to persuade him to come back. It can be safely assumed that early in 1969 Sumulong still hoped to win back the confidence of his sulking deputy.

Madrigal and others similarly commissioned worked on Dante all of March. Dante responded to the supplications by telling his comrades that they would be foolish to go back to so untrustworthy a liege as Sumulong. Dante did call on Sumulong once at that time, riding from Tarlac to Angeles on his Honda motorcycle. But Dante was just putting on appearances. Long before that time he had made up his mind to quit Sumulong's command and go on his own.[7]

He recalled that when Freddie was virtually banished to Bataan the young commander feigned illness and got leave to go to Manila for a rest cure. He rounded up some of the old-line Huks — Dabu, Robert and Caviteño among others. They had retired temporarily after Luis Taruc's fall and had not been contaminated by the corruption in Angeles. Together they planned to reorganize the Huk movement along its original lines. Freddie did not have a chance to rewrite Huk history, for his enemies — whoever they were — put him out of the way forever. But Dante who had formed his own NPA now believed he could complete that mission. He was young but already wise in the ways of dissidence. He had won over at least five or six of Sumulong's subcommanders and installed them in larger positions.

Fortuitously, there were important politicians to whom an independent Huk command in Tarlac would not be unwelcome. It could be used both as a buffer against the ambitious Sumulong and as a form of leverage in dealing with rival politicians. Late in 1968 there also were offers of an alliance with Manila students, all sworn Maoists and burning with a zeal to set the Tarlac countryside aflame with insurrection.

Initially, there was a rough identity of objectives in the peasant army and the students. The Tarlac Huks wanted

---

[6]Eduardo Lachica, Philippines *Herald,* Jan. 13, 1969.

[7]The circumstances of Dante's breakup with Sumulong were reconstructed from conversations with two of Buscayno's townmates and followers under confidential circumstances in July, 1970.

the legitimacy of a formal doctrine, while the Maoists, spurned by the majority of the student-intellectual front in Manila, wanted to acquire a miltary arm of their own.

And both had scores to settle against Sumulong. The student leaders had earlier been rebuffed in their attempts to reconvert the renegade Pampanga organization More compatibly, Dante and the student leaders were about the same age. On one plane, they spoke the same language of protest.

The day after Christmas in 1968 while the rest of the nation was still celebrating the holiday season in characteristically prodigal style, a group of young men gathered in sitio Manga, barrio Talimundok, for a "Congress of Reestablishment" that set the dissident movement on a new course.[8]

The date was the 75th birth anniversary of Mao Tse-tung. The Congress, which lasted until January 7 "reestablished" the Communist Party of the Philippines, drafted a new party constitution supplanting the 1938 charter of the merged CPP and the Socialist Party and created the New People's Army as the military arm of the new party. Both the new CPP and the NPA were founded "under the supreme guidance of Mao Tse-tung, the acme of Marxism and Leninism in the present era."[9]

A young student leader, who styled himself "Amado Guerrero," was proclaimed the Chairman of the new Maoist party, and the title of commander-in-chief of the NPA was conferred upon Commander Dante who was born in that very barrio 28 years ago.

The new CPP purged itself of two notorious deviants from the true faith — "Lavaism" and "Tarucism." It accused the Taruc-Sumulong faction of trying to "amass wealth privately and seek safety by making secret pacts with individual bourgeois politicians and by carrying out the line of mediation between landlords and peasantry."

The Lavaists, in their turn, were roundly condemned for "taking the road of peaceful and parliamentary supine attitude" supposedly taken by the followers of the Lavas in

---

[8]The site of the CPP-NPA Congress was reported as such in the original Philippines *Herald* series. The information was obtained through knowledgeable sources who declined to be identified. The official CPP-NPA Communique described the site as "in an area close to the border of Northern Luzon and Central Luzon" which is most ambiguous. That could place the site as far north as Pangasinan or Nueva Ecija. Capas, however, would be the most logical place for the clandestine meeting since it is Dante's native town and was at that time his most secure base.

[9]Captured CPP-NPA documents.

the "traditional" Communist Party — if it did indeed exist at all.

Both factions were reviled for their "helter-skelter-ideological pretensions." Their confusion, the new CPP articles of faith affirmed, would throw them into the "dustbin of history."

The NPA was organized not only to be a "fighting force," but also as a "propaganda force" and an "organizing force." Commander Dante brought into the fold several of the young commanders loyal to him, including Melody, Goody, Eddie, Juaning and Dante's younger brother, Joe.

The Radicalization of Tarlac

The locus of the agrarian conflict thus shifted from Pampanga, its historic hotbed, to Tarlac a province bordering to the north.

Tarlac is in a way more promising mission territory for a dissident movement. It has the stark and lonesome landscape suggestive of peasant cabals and the furtive movements of outlaw bands. As a motorist approaches the Tarlac boundary from the south, the thickly-populated Pampanga towns are left behind and he enters wide and open country. The brown, rambling hills of Capas are on the left, and beyond them the loftier peaks of the Zambales range. It was in Capas, an honored name in World War II history, that tens of thousands of Filipino soldiers captured in Bataan languished in a Japanese concentration camp, hundreds of them dying of hunger, dysentery and beri-beri. A modest monument stands in memory of World War II's heroes on the road to Capas. It is also in these same cogonal hills that Dante and his New People's Army prepared for the day of uprising.

On the right of the North Road are thousands of acres of sugarcane fields stretching all the way from Magalang in Pampanga to Paniqui in Tarlac. From these cane fields come most of the wealth of Tarlac. This wealth is collected by only a few of Tarlac's super-rich families. The Cojuangco clan is said to own "half of Tarlac." The rural population is even poorer than that of Pampanga. A middle class barely exists in Tarlac. The sugarcane itself, standing higher than a man's head, provides excellent cover for small columns of armed men, moving from barrio to barrio, spreading the gospel of Mao and hatred for the class enemies.

Tarlac was not always easy picking for Huk activation. In the time of Dante's grandfather, Tarlac was in a revolutionary ferment. Many of the Tarlac peasants were mus-

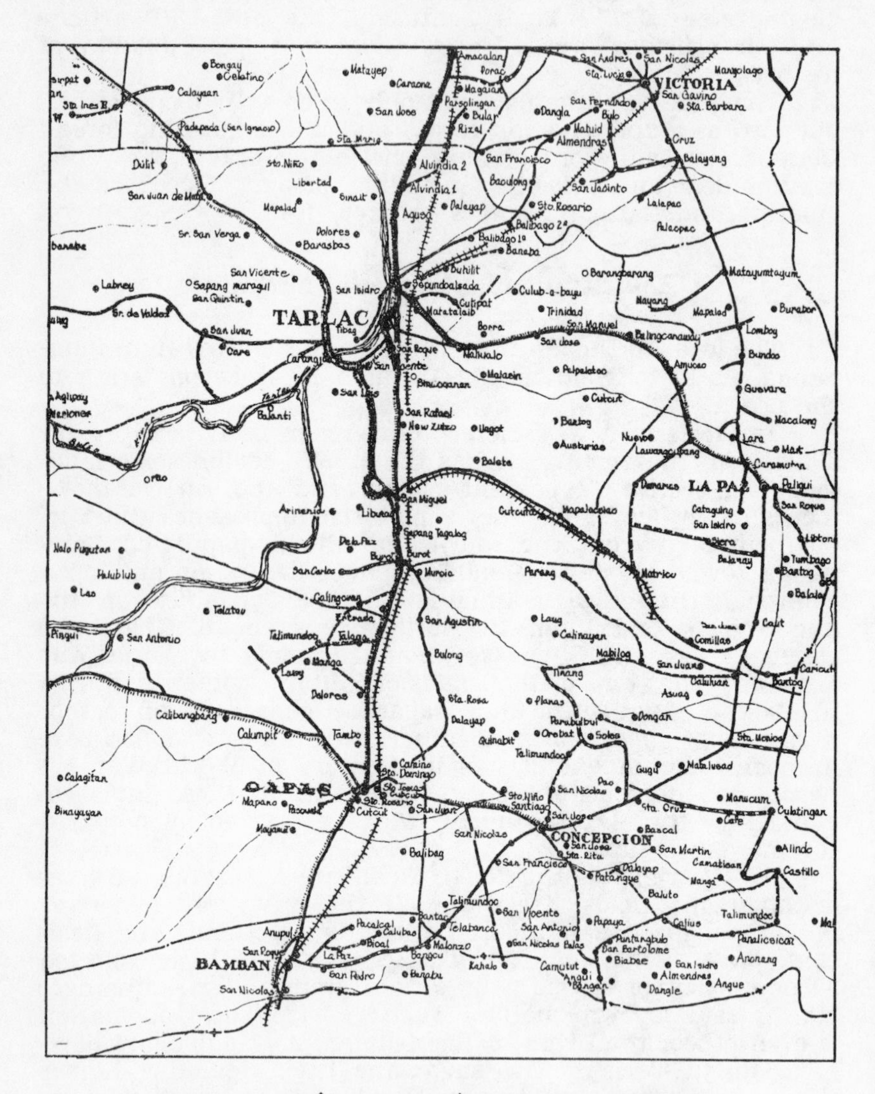

Map of Southern Tarlac

Courtesy of the Presidential Advisory Council on Public Works and Community Development, Camp Aguinaldo, Quezon City.

tered into Servillano Aquino's *Fusilleros de Tarlac*. Capas, Dante's hometown, was the scene of brief fighting. But for many decades later Tarlac was free from dissidence. Linda Bie's spectacular raid on Camp Macabulos shattered its bucolic peace at the height of the Huk rebellion, but for the rest of the 1950's up to the mid-1960's the Huks did not make much trouble.

What turned Tarlac into a second and bigger front of the Pampanga revolt was the well-meant but abortive "Operation Homestretch" in the last year of President Macapagal's administration. This was the beginning of the period of Huk-coddling, Senator Aquino claims. The Army unwittingly set up the Huk infrastructure in the southern part of the province. After Alibasbas' death, Sumulong recovered control of the territory and eventually placed his man, Dante, in charge. Dante did not have to start his new principality from scratch. Its foundations had been laid long ago and all he had to do was to reincorporate the business under new management.

Dante could not have built an army on ideology alone. He was getting material if not political support from somewhere. Commander Sumulong later denounced Dante's "voluntary exile" from the HMB and named two prominent Tarlac politicians among those who "poisoned" Dante's mind so that they could "use him and his men in intimidating voters in the elections."[10] It is likely that some support was extended Dante by some of the big landowning families and public officials in the province.

Unlike in Pampanga where Clark Air Base and its R-and-R satellite Angeles offer lush picking for crime syndicates, Mafia-style Huks and other *sub rosa* operators, Tarlac has little to support an extralegal organization outside of what the politically powerful Tarlac families can offer. Senator Aquino and his Cojuangco in-laws have been suspected by their political enemies of helping grubstake Dante for the reason that they are the only ones who can afford to do so.

Aquino's in-laws own Hacienda Luisita, one of the biggest sugar plantations in the Philippines. It sprawls over 6,443 hectares and has 12,000 people living in 11 barrios economically dependent on it. The hacienda has its own modern sugar central with the capacity to mill 7,000 tons of cane a day. There are 194 kilometers of railroad cars to transport cut cane to the mill.

The PC suspect that some of Dante's men use Luisita as

---

[10]From a mimeographed letter in the Pampango dialect addressed to *"Pakanalan ning kabalen at kayabe"* and signed "Sumulong." Its authenticity has not been verified.

some kind of sanctuary. This is not impossible for Luisita's vast hectares are too large to police effectively. But though the PC has "raided" the hacienda several times and posted PC detail in some of its barrios no proof of such a liaison has been presented.

The New People's Army

The AFP was admittedly caught flat-footed by this new development. On November 7, 1968, Central Luzon was "demilitarized" by an agreement signed by provincial and municipal officials and 1st PC zone brass and the primary responsibility for keeping the peace in the region was turned over to the local government. Task Force Lawin, the 2,000-man Huk-hunting force, suspended its patrols and for several crucial months the countryside was left unwatched while the NPA recruited soldiers, trained cadres, established camps and propagandized the barrios.

The military was not entirely unaware of the new activism. It was getting enough feedback from its barrio network to urge a resumption of suppressive operations. Ironically, while the CPP Congress of Reestablishment was going on in Capas, President Marcos rejected the AFP proposal for reassuming the peace-keeping responsibility in the area and insisted that the Huk situation was not serious.[11]

The AFP's increasing alarm was evident all through the first three months of 1969. On March 8, Defense Sec. Ernesto Mata announced to the press his favoring renewed military efforts. On March 31, the newly-designated acting Tarlac PC commander, Maj. Romeo Gatan, described the southern Tarlac towns of La Paz, Victoria, Concepcion, Capas, Bamban and Tarlac town as "Huk-infested." On April 2, Brig. Gen. Emilio Zerrudo, 1st PC zone commander, lost patience with civilian indifference to the situation and sent Task Force Lawin out after Dante. The AFP drive was held back momentarily when the PC Chief Brig. Gen. Vicente Raval countermanded Zerrudo's go-signal, but the AFP command got itself straightened out in a week's time. By April 10, the military was working in full force in Tarlac.[12]

In the three or four months the government had relaxed its vigilance, Dante was able to recruit over 300 regulars and hundreds of combat support and cadres. They built Vietcong-style tunnels in Talimundok, Capas, Comillas, La Paz and possibly in other places. A training camp was set up in the sparsely populated hills of western Tarlac

[11]Philippines *Herald,* Jan. 1, 1969.

[12]Same, March 8, April 1, 3, 10, 11, 1969.

— close to the U.S. military gunnery range where the sounds of American exercises would drown out the NPA's own shooting practice.

An elaborate political structure was laid out by the CPP-NPA commissars to strengthen the cooperation of the rural folk. For the first time in five or six years the dissidents were being reinvigorated by a link with Manila intellectuals.

At the outset, Dante had more guns than he could find men to carry them. The NPA armory was stocked with the latest Armalites — rapid-firing 5.56 M-16's which were yet to be issued to PC troopers.

The NPA got its recruits mainly through indoctrination but sometimes by coercion and kidnaping as well. One of the young men pressed into NPA service was a young ROTC trainee in Camp Aquino, Tarlac. He was snatched while walking on the highway. He was taken to the hills where the NPA had its best camp for cadres. The boy later escaped to tell his tale.[13]

The training site had no tents or other conspicuous evidence of encampment. The recruits slept either in the few huts in the area or under the trees. They practiced shooting with silencers to avoid attracting attention. Only small-unit tactics were taught, not too different from the company and platoon skirmishing taught by the AFP infantry.

Guerrilla techniques were emphasized. If a Huk is cornered by the enemy, he is to lie still wherever he seeks cover and stay there until he is certain of escape.

One thing was drummed into them — absolute discipline. They were to obey orders without question, though when not in action they could exercise the "democratic" privilege of "criticism and self-criticism."

They were given crash courses in Marxist-Leninist-Maoist ideology. They were taught the "Basic Rules of the NPA," copied verbatim from the rules instilled into Mao's own People's Liberation Army.

The NPA's "Three Main Rules of Discipline" were:

1. Obey orders in all your actions.
2. Do not take a single needle or thread from the masses.
3. Turn in everything captured.

The "Eight Points of Attention" were:

1. Speak politely.
2. Pay fairly for what you buy.

---

[13]The author interviewed the subject personally at Camp Olivas. He was apparently working for PC zone intelligence.

3. Return everything you borrow.
4. Pay for anything you damage.
5. Do not hit or swear at people.
6. Do not damage crops.
7. Do not take liberties with women.
8. Do not ill-treat captives.[14]

This kind of puritanical discipline must have been strictly enforced because the NPA was rarely known to kill, injure or rob civilians without cause. The death penalty was imposed upon NPA members for malversation of funds, abusing a barrio lass, running away with another man's wife, and settling personal grudges without the sanction of the commander-in-chief. Dante had to give his personal approval for any killings or executions.

According to a recently captured Huk commander, Amado Mariano, a ranking aide of Dante, Commander Melody was stripped of his command for alienating the barrio people of La Paz. The tainting of the NPA image in La Paz facilitated the setting up of an anti-Huk "barrio defense force."

NPA "justice" was also dispensed with prudence. When Dante showed his vengeance it was done with surgical neatness. Before a wrong-doer would be dispatched, there had to be at least 10 pieces of evidence brought against him. These so-called "proofs" were extracted from different persons — if possible not related to the intended victim — to minimize false or biased testimony.[15]

If the particular offense was not so grave, the culprit would be "invited" by the NPA for questioning. Sometimes the wrong-doer was given a chance to exile himself elsewhere.

The wanted man could sometimes plead his case to the Huks through a contact man and in their presence vow to reform his dealings with the barrio people. If the offender failed to mend his ways and the Huk warnings went unheeded, execution came with frightening swiftness.

The NPA's No. 1 enemies were the PC informers in the barrios. These were "traitors" to the movement and no mercy was spared them. When they fell into NPA hands, they were tortured and killed. Next in the NPA hate list were cattle rustlers, rapists, land overseers, abusive PC soldiers, usurers and robbers.[16]

The NPA had an amazing intelligence network. They had a way of ferreting out PC informers in the barrios and poblaciones. Even the PC was astonished at how the Huks

[14]Captured CPP-NPA documents.
[15]Amante Reyes, *Herald* correspondent in Tarlac.
[16]Same.

could manage to penetrate confidential files containing the names of PC operatives in the countryside.

A provincial official recently told a *Herald* reporter that the Huks knew the exact time he went to sleep and woke up in the morning. The Huks seemed to know every movement of their enemies and uncannily anticipated countermoves of civilian and military authorities.

The common characteristics of the NPA leaders were that they are generally young, fanatical in their cause, and scornful of the temptations that had sapped the revolutionary spirit of the older Huks.[17]

Dante's men were so newly-arrived that only few appeared until lately in the order of battle. The list of rewards posted by the Department of National Defense in July 23, 1969 identified only three NPA commanders in the first 30 wanted Huks. The rest were Sumulong's people. The NPA's in the list were Dante who had the same prize of ₱150,000 as Sumulong and Pedro Taruc, Madrigal (₱3,000) and Melody (₱2,000). Commander Goody was way down at No. 64 with a pittance of ₱200 offered for his scalp.

Commander Melody used to be sector commander of all La Paz barrios and some barrios of San Antonio, Nueva Ecija, until Dante broke him for bungling his job — he was just too trigger-happy.

Commander Joe, the younger brother of Dante, was a fast-rising leader whose sector included the San Miguel barrios of Tarlac town. He was reported killed early in March, 1970 in a clash with a home defense force unit in barrio Arengoreng.[18]

Commander Madrigal was in charge of the barrios of Concepcion and the neighboring barrios of Magalang and Arayat in Pampanga. Commander Ligaya's field of assignment covered all barrios along the national highway in southern Tarlac, plus the barrios west of Tarlac town in close coordination with Commander Pio Mallari, a newly-promoted sub-commander.

Commander Goody, whose real name was Ernesto Miranda, was temporarily assigned as Dante's bodyguard together with Commander Felman. Both Goody and Felman were wanted by the PC in connection with the shooting of Rep. Felix Amante in 1968.

Commander Rudy was assigned two barrios of Capas — Patling and Sta. Lucia — and the neighboring barrios of Botolan, Zambales. He was killed in May, 1970.

---

[17]One exception, age-wise, was Commander Layug who was in his fifties when he joined Dante.

[18]Philippines *Herald,* March 3, 4, 1970.

Commander Quinez used to be sector commander of the barrios of Victorias, Tarlac until he was sacked by Dante for falling down on his job. Quinez was reportedly absorbed into the group of Commander Madrigal.[19]

Some of these Huk commanders operated with the help of their political commissars — youths fresh out of the Manila universities. There was a rough division of labor. The Huks carried the guns and the students circulated the mimeographed Mao-think tracts.

In less than four months, Dante had not only become the first successful defector from the Sumulong camp, but he had also help create the first firm link between the Huks and Manila students. Nothing of the sort had been achieved either during the Japanese occupation or during the postwar rebellion.

---

[19]Amante Reyes.

Chapter Ten

THE IDEOLOGUES

Just as the difference in age between Sumulong and Dante was equivalent to a generation, there was a nearly identical time-span between the peak activity years of the masterminds of the 1950 rebellion and the student leaders who "reestablished" the Communist party in Tarlac. The two sets of actors were products of their own eras, the world-view and value systems of each shaped by the experiences and perceptions of its own generation.

Hoeksema was struck by the proximity in ages of a "great number" of leaders of the 1950 uprising. Jesus Lava was born on April 15, 1914; Casto Alejandrino on November 18, 1914; Luis Taruc on June 21, 1913. Saulo was also born at the beginning of World War I. These men shared the same experience of looking for their first jobs at the time of the Great Depression. The economic hardships they underwent, the prevailing mood of disillusionment with the entire social order, and the hopes of possible utopia were part of their spiritual equipment collected during their maturing years.[1] Allowing for some variations in personal background, it would not be unduly reductive to say that the depression years created the revolutionists of the post-liberation Philippines.

In like manner, the initiators of the Maoist cult of the late sixties were nearly identical in age. Jose Ma. Sison was 29 when the PC reported his retreat into the hills. Arthur Garcia and other Sison associates were just a few years younger.[2] The members of the entire conspiracy were within five college graduation classes from each other.

Generally from middle-class backgrounds, they did not experience economic deprivation comparable to what the Luis Taruc-Jesus Lava generation went through. They had better education than the students of the thirties and enjoyed stronger institutional support for their activism. They were

---

[1]As cited.

[2]Specific names cannot be mentioned because of the pendency of certain court cases at the time of writing.

not revolutionists of the stomach but of the cerebrum. The vehicle that transported them to the forefront of their revolution was the student movement.

The University of the Philippines: A Tradition of Intellectual Dissent

Their training ground was not the rice paddies of Commander Freddie or the labor unions of Evangelista but the campuses of the Manila universities, notably the University of the Philippines in Diliman, Quezon City. Since the thirties, the University of the Philippines has been the hotbed of dissent and ideological strife. So have been many of the major universities around the world — the Sorbonne, Tokyo and Kyoto, Berkeley and Harvard. But these doughty institutions do not have a monopoly of student rebellion in their own countries. The University of the Philippines for a whole decade almost had such a monopoly; only in the last few years did the contagion catch in other Greater Manila schools. The University of the Philippines radicals were the typhoid-carriers. The University of the Philippines stands far above most of the other educational institutions, public or private, in terms of faculty training, library resources (now over half a million volumes) and physical facilities. The next best quality schools are run by religious orders and hence traditionally conservative;[3] the rest of the educational establishments are a clutter of downtown "diploma mills" whose massive enrollments are strongly representative of the job-seeking working student class.

With its surfeit of faculty talent and honors students plus a long tradition of vigorous campus politics, the University of the Philippines shelters the most volatile student body in the Philippines. In the thirties, the University of the Philippines was already the jousting place of would-be politicians like Ferdinand Marcos and Wenceslao Vinzons. An "epidemic of nationalism" gripped the prewar University of the Philippines campus — then in its original site in Ermita, Manila. Marcos, later to become President of the Philippines, joined the Upsilon Sigma Phi "which specialized in political heckling." According to the President's official biographer, Hartzell Spence, the freshman Ferdinand launch-

---

[3]Until recently, anyway. The Jesuit-run Ateneo de Manila University produced in the late sixties leadership in the "moderate" National Union of Students of the Philippines, and the smaller but more activistic Lakasdiwa. De la Salle College, a Christian Brothers school favored by the Philippine elite, housed a student minority identified with the radical Movement for a Democratic Philippines and the *Kabataang Makabayan*.

ed his career in campus politics by ridiculing to death a proposal making folk-dancing compulsory for all male students. Marcos "cut classes to make fiery speeches criticizing the new Commonwealth government."[4] Ironically, Mr. Marcos found his role reversed in January, 1968 when he motored to the Diliman campus to try to appease a hostile, anti-Marcos student demonstration.

In their student days, Vicente and Jesus Lava savored radicalism in the University of the Philippines. Two other Politburo convicts, Angel Baking and Samuel Rodriguez, cut their ideological teeth in the campus newspaper, the *Collegian*. The thirties also produced the Political Science Club, a coterie of campus iconoclasts which included future progressive journalistis like Jose Lansang and future doyens in the University of the Philippines like President Salvador P. Lopez and philosophy professor Ricardo Pascual.

The intellectual *sturm und drang* is by no means university-wide. It is a passion convulsing only a small minority of the faculty and of the student body. By University of the Philippines President Salvador P. Lopez's estimate, only five percent of the Diliman students participate in radical politics, a proportion comparable to the politicized minorities in many western universities.[5] Just as Sorbonne activism tends to be dominated by the *sociologie* students, University of the Philippines radicalism is the stakeout of the Arts and Sciences teachers and students. The College of Law also contributes a few spear-bearers to the tribal wars, since many of the lawyers-in-making look forward to careers in politics anyway. Most of the students of the professional colleges — Engineering, Veterinary Science, Agricultural, the School of Economics — tend to look on with indifference, and sometimes annoyance at the *manifestations* of the intellectual minorities.[6] The radical leaders, however, make up in noise and combative spirit what they lack in numbers. Organized into professional *apparats* and more schooled in campus politicking than the indifferent majority, they tend to be exceptionally successful in getting themselves over-represented in the Student Council, the University of the Philippines Writers Club and other influential campus organs.

The University of the Philippines tradition of intellect-

---

[4]Hartzell Spence, *Marcos of the Philippines* (New York: The World Publishing Company, 1969), pp. 32-34.

[5]Interview, April, 1970.

[6]A notable exeception to the unpolitical nature of the professional schools is the College of Medicine which has often taken to the streets to protest the government neglect of the Philippine General Hospital.

ual dissent does not come down to the present in clearly defined stages. The University of the Philippines savants are individualists rather than schoolmen; they speak mainly for themselves and for their few minor disciples, usually of lesser tenure and hence obliged to defer to their seniors. Though no intellectual "mainstream" can be charted, there were discernible ideological fashions in certain periods. In the fifties, it was a species of anti-clericalism which inspired the University of the Philippines "liberals" to organize the Society for the Advancement of Academic Freedom (SAAF) to chop down the growing power of the university chaplain, John Delaney, S.J., who was the *eminence gris* behind the University of the Philippines Student Catholic Action.

The fighting issue was the introduction of religion courses in the University of the Philippines curriculum. "Father Delaney had a way of blacklisting dissenting professors," a University of the Philippines long-timer recalled. "He seemed to have backdoor access to President Vidal Tan."

Anti-clericalism was the intellectual heritage from Rizal, del Pilar, and other prominent Masons of revolutionary days and hence eminently respectable as a profession of faith in faculty lounges. But this protest was not so much directed at priestly rule, for there was no longer such a thing, as it was at the stultifying anti-intellectualism of the Philippine establishment. The professors were the *ilustrados* of the mind demonstrating against the barbarianism of the extramural world.

Identified with the SAAF were senior faculty members like Prof. Ricardo Pascual and Prof. Fred Lagmay (now chairman of the Department of Psychology). The younger liberals kept themselves aloof from the "academic freedom" debate (though political scientist and later "progressive" activist Francisco Nemenzo, Jr. did the maverick thing of joining the UPSCA because it was a "strong" student organization). Most of the University of the Philippines intellectuals were too leery of administrative suppression to speak up. The campus was silent on the Huk rebellion of the fifties. When the witch-hunting Committee on Un-Filipino Activities (CUFA) of the House of Representatives directed its scrutiny at the SAAF, it "died a natural death."

Second-Wind Nationalism

In the sixties faculty-student dissent had perceptively changed its character. The big thing was "nationalism." It was woven from such diverse threads as the respected liberalism of Cesar Majul, now Dean of Arts and Sciences, the "Bonifacism" of historian Teodoro Agoncillo,[7] the "partyless democracy" of Ricardo Pascual, the anti-Americanism of Hernan Abaya and the younger Nemenzo, and the oratorical classics of Claro M. Recto.

In 1960, the Philippines was 14 years an independent republic, so this "second-wind" nationalism seemed dreadfully like flogging a dead horse. But the nationalists of the sixties chose to disinter the moldering corpse and sing the dirges all over again. The torment felt by these belated nationalists harked as far back as the Spanish regime and they were prone to break out in stigmata for whiplashes inflicted by the colonial masters centuries ago.

A sample, from Hernan Abaya's "The Untold Philippine Story," would suffice:

> Under the Spanish rule the Filipino was kept in blind ignorance, exploited, denied all freedoms. But such domination was by no means tranquil or secure. Throughout the long night of Spanish occupation, the Filipinos rose in bloody revolt 260 times against what Rizal called the "holy ignorance" of a "brutalizing regime." At the root of these uprisings was the feudal economy of 16th century Spain which the *conquistadores* implanted on our soil. Through royal grants, known as encomiendas, the king awarded not parcels of land but parcels of people who were not better than slaves. They could be sold from one *encomendero* to another, or forced to work in mine and forest.
>
> . . . It is necessary to break the *indios'* pride and that in all places and on all occasions they should consider the Spaniards as their master and not their equal. There should be no noble blood but the Spaniards'. Whoever should raise his hand against a Spaniard, even in defense of his life, should be consigned to the public works for the rest of his life. A Spaniard should not seat an indio or a mestizo in his house, much less eat with him. Under no pretext should a Spaniard be permitted to contract marriage with any Filipina or mestiza. He could keep them as concubines, however. . .
>
> Because the Spaniards were a small minority, they needed natives they could trust to maintain

[7]Agoncillo, former chairman of the University of the Philippines history department, popularized the historical view that Andres Bonifacio, the plebeian founder of the Katipunan, is more deserving of being the "national hero" than the illustrado-born Jose Rizal.

> the status quo. They established monastic schools, often in *conventos,* for the sons of native chieftains. . . . It was the aim of those schools to train an elite class who could act as intermediaries between the Spaniards and the natives. It was from this principalia class which came to be popularly known as the *ilustrados* that the *gobernadorcillos* and *cabezas de barangay* were drawn. The aristocracy of money, rather than that of blood, was recognized. The native Bourbons identified their interests with those of their white masters and fought for these interests at the expense of the common good, in exchange for privileges for themselves.[8]

In such style, mortally aggrieved, hyperbolic and reductive to an astonishing degree did the nationalists recall the affronts and indignities of the past. It did not matter if the history was oversimplified and selectively perceived. The Spaniards had many faults but distaste for inter-racial unions was not one of them, at least compared to the Dutch, English and Americans. The Filipino race would be as creole as the Latin American today if there had been more Spanish studs to start with. As for the *encomienda* system, it was not half as bad as in South America. By the middle of the 17th century, according to Sturtevant, it "ceased to play an important role in the Philippine economy"; none of the original estates except for the friar lands survived the 18th century. Often the nationalist tracts would refer to the imposition by the Spanish of its feudal social system on the Filipinos. This argument ignores the fact that the pre-hispanic Filipino society was already feudalized, divided into three distinct castes of *datus, maharlikas* (freemen) and *namamahay* (commoners or slaves). The Spaniards merely preserved the social system they found already existing. Feudalism is as indigenously Filipino as the *barangay* which brought our forefathers to these islands.

Expressed rationally and with a minimum of emotionalism, balanced with the perspective of the Philippines in a rapidly modernizing world, and addressed to credible objectives (turning back the clock of time would not solve present problems), nationalism could have been a healthy exercise in self-appraisal and identity-seeking. But in the sixties, it became a wilful, runaway engine of great mischief. It had ceased being simply an academic conceit. It was now primarily the vehicle for the leadership mobility of a small radical faction out to usurp power in the student front.

---

[8]Hernan Abaya, the Untold Philippine Story (Quezon City; Malaya Books, 1967), pp. 5-6.

Jose Ma. Sison

After the SAAF was rent asunder by congressional witch-hunters, the younger campus liberals stepped into the breach and formed in 1959, a new front called the Student Cultural Association of the University of the Philippines (SCAUP). The SCAUP was the creation of Jose Ma. Sison, Heherson Alvarez, Jose David Lapuz and other liberals who were in campus politics in the second half of the fifties. The SCAUP played a key role in the transition in campus politics from anti-clericalism to nationalism. It also served as the foundation for a personality cult around Sison.

Sison was born of middle-class parents on February 8, 1939 in Cabugao, Ilocos Sur. He finished his high school at Letran College in 1956 and graduated cum laude with a Bachelor of Arts degree in political science at the University of the Philippines in 1960. He began his career in radical politics early in college, becoming a director of a campus publication, the *Diliman Observer,* and a member of the University of the Philippines Writers Club.[9]

He was a student leader of intense, uncompromising convictions; a scholarly-looking youth almost painfully shy in his personal contacts. But from his prolific pen spewed an unceasing flow of tracts, speeches and manifestoes—vitriolic, dogmatic and jargon-ridden. Pushy and ambitious, he brooked no opposition in his councils and his career in activism was frequently marked with bitter wranglings and fallings-out with those who differed even in the slightest with the Sison writ.[10]

The SCAUP was set up as a permanent nationalist youth organization to enable Sison and his disciples to continue their influence in the campus even after their own graduation. After college, Sison started to earn a living as an instructor in the University of the Philippines, but he was dropped from the faculty roster for allegedly imparting "leftist ideas" to his students.

He was always busy organizing and agitating in the early sixties. He first attempted to set up the Alliance of Socialist Advance (ALSA) as the SCAUP student-youth arm in 1963, but it failed to generate enough mass support outside of the University of the Philippines. In 1964 he founded the *Kabataang Makabayan* (Nationalist Youth) with the help of his colleagues at the Lyceum, Francisco Lava and

---

[9]Handbook of the *Kabataang Makabayan,* 1967

[10]This description of Sison and his personal history was obtained through interviews with his acquaintances and associates who requested anonymity.

Jose Lansang, and radical labor leader Ignacio Lacsina. Other founding members were Rodolfo Larracas, Prospero Palma, Ricardo Valmonte, Angelo de los Reyes, Nilo Tayag, Carlos del Rosario and Ernesto Macahiya.

The KM was founded on the 101st birthday anniversary of Andres Bonifacio, the "Great Plebeian" of the Philippine Revolution. The selection of Bonifacio as the patron saint of the youth organization was explained in Sison's founding speech:

> Thus Andres Bonifacio today stands as a guide of militant nationalism, of militant anti-imperialism, among the Filipino youth. His proletarian-revolutionary courage is a beacon to us all. If *Kabataang Makabayan* will ever succeed in its patriotic mission, one important requirement it shall have met is to be imbued with the proletarian-revolutionary courage of Andres Bonifacio, the only courage that gives life and force to the principles that we uphold in this epoch.[11]

The KM was initially created to be the rallying point of Filipino youth for "national democratic" programs, and the struggle against American imperialism and domestic feudalism. Sison and his colleagues were apparently still hopeful for a "united front" of socialist and progressive elements.

Though unmistakably Marxist in philosophy, the KM addressed itself to broadly reformist objectives and principles. Its charter makes no reference to the Communist Party.

Sison also worked in the labor front. He became vice-president for organization for the *Lapiang Manggagawa* (Workers Party) and first deputy chairman of the Socialist Party of the Philippines founded by Sison's like-minded ideologue, Ignacio Lacsina. As an LM member, Sison provided "theoretical guidance" to its Youth Group. Sison also found time to be executive secretary of the Philippine-Indonesian Friendship and Cultural Association.[12]

Under Sison's influence, the extreme left of the youth movement became stridently anti-American and revolution-conscious. The *evenements* of the sixties certainly strengthened the belief of Sison and his disciples that the socialist redemption was at hand. In 1960, the year Sison graduated from the University of the Philippines, Fidel Castro installed himself at the head of a communist government in Cuba.

---

[11]From AFP intelligence reports. In fairness to Sison, he was not available to rebut or explain these disclosures.

[12]Captured CPP-NPA documents.

In the mid-sixties, the Vietnam war polarized youth all over the world; intellectual cults grew around the teachings of Giap, Guevara and Mao Tse-tung.

The "Programme for a People's Democratic Revolution in the Philippines," an NPA-Maoist document suspectedly written by Sison, conveys the strong conviction that the bourgeois capitalist world was crumbling under the onslaught of the freedom-seeking peoples of the world.

> The objective conditions for the implementation (of revolution) are excellent. American imperialism, modern revisionism and all reactionary forces are in a state of disintegration. This is indeed the era when imperialism is heading towards total collapse and socialism is marching towards world victory.
>
> Increasingly, armed struggles in the countryside of the world, Asia, Africa and Latin America, are ever intensifying and expanding to tear apart and destroy the over-extended power of U.S. imperialism and all the reactionary allies. In the close vicinity of the Philippines, the tide of people's war is ever rising under the powerful inspiration of Mao Tse-tung's thoughts. The heroic peoples of Vietnam, Laos, Thailand, Indonesia, Burma, Malaysia and others are fighting U.S. imperialism and feudalism. The Filipino people and the Communist Party of the Philippines are fortunate to be within the storm center of the world proletarian revolutions.
>
> Because of its losses in the Vietnam war, because of its expensive but futile aid to its puppet governments and because of its failure to further expand its foreign trade, U.S. imperialism is rocked in its very heartland by a serious crisis that is now agitating the American workers and youth, both Afro-American and white, who refuse to be carried away into imperialist wars of expansion and to be abused economically and politically at home. The deepening internal and external crisis of U.S. imperialism is clearly depriving the Filipino reactionaries of a significantly great amount of imperialist protection and support.[13]

In the sixties, Sison became a staunch Maoist, as indicated in his published writings which often read like literal

[13]The profession of Maoism or any other Marxist cult is not illegal under Philippine jurisprudence. The penalties under the Anti-Subversion Law (RA 1700) are invoked only in proven cases of association with the Communist Party, the HMB or their successor organizations.

translations form the *Jenmin Jih-pao* and the *Red Flag* It is not altogether clear how much of his Maoism was professed for its own sake or used as the spearpoint of his relentless struggle to preempt power in the nationalist councils.

Maoism combined well with Sison's impetuous and highly combative nature. Maoism was militancy; it was "revolution now." Sison and his kind would have none of the flaccid "awaitism" of the older generation.[14]

Maoism seemed to provide a ready-made language to express his messianic compulsion to lead the nationalists and progressives to their foretold triumph. It offered a world view suitable to Sison's apocalyptic vision of the Philippines being destroyed by the greed and opportunism of its own economic elite. Sison either ignored or was blind to the fact that the pronounced Maoist gospel was essentially the product of China's historic circumstances; the profound humiliation felt by the Chinese for all the affronts of the white "barbarians" from the Opium War to the Russian intervention in Manchuria; the perceptions of Mao and his aging directorate which were heavily biased by their shared experiences of the 1920's and 1930's; the internal need for a continuous revolution to keep backsliders in line.

Sison's messianism seemed to echo the mystical visions of Apolinario de la Cruz and Florencio Intrencherado. They lived in different times and different places but they preached essentially the same instant salvation, whether it was a "New Jerusalem" or "democratic centralism."[15]

Maoism had only a superficial applicability to the Philippines where 70 percent of the population live in the barrios and tenancy has been a predominant condition in many areas for centuries. But this was good enough for Sison. He had his credo and his foreordained goal in life. His problem was to get the troops to accept his mandate. This took a terrible lot of doing.

Doctrinal Disptues

During Sison's chairmanship, the KM was rocked with doctrinal and policy disputes which led to the walkout of key members. A rebel group headed by Juan Tapales, who identified with the Nemenzo faction, pulled out of the KM and formed the *Malayang Pagkakaisa ng Kabataang Pilipino* (MPKP) on Nov. 30, 1967 — three years to the date of KM's founding.

[14]The "moderate" student leaders tended to take a patronizing attitude towards their radical allies in the MDP. They often irreverently referred to the Maoist as "those nuts."

[15]AFP documents.

Further dissensions inside the KM ranks led to more defections. Perfecto Tera, Jr., chairman of the Cultural Bureau, Vicencio Jose, chairman of the educational department, Ramon Sanchez and Sixto Carlos, Jr. broke from the KM and set up a rival organization called *Samahang Demokratikong Kabataan* (SDK).

Sison had such a divisive influence on the KM membership that he retained his chairmanship only a few votes over Ricardo Ferrer in the 1967 KM national congress. He gave up the chairmanship to one of his henchmen, Nilo Tayag, though he continued to wield power as head of the KM consultative committee.

The indefatigable Sison sought other vehicles for his propagandizing. He and his disciples tried to take over the broad-front Movement for the Advancement of Nationalism (MAN) in 1967. He ran again into opposition from the Nemenzo faction and the MAN "moderates."

MAN's internal trouble was one of politicizers and reformers never quite agreeing on what particular steps to take. Sison apparently wanted to impose his down-with-the-Establishment shibboleths on the MAN. Nemenzo, a well-schooled theoretician educated in England, was inclined towards continued parliamentary struggle. Sison was already then obsessively hung up on Maoism while Nemenzo thought Sison's waving of the "little red book" a little uncouth for the distinguished assembly.

The MAN moderates like Renato Constantino and Alejandro Lichauco tried to pacify the feuding doctrinaires. Constantino, who was chairman of the policy and planning committee, got them to put their quarrels aside temporarily while they contributed to the chastisement of the Philippine Establishment in a tract entitled "MAN's Goal" for the second National Congress on March 15-16, 1969.

Sison's group refused to be bound by the milder reformism of the majority and soon lost interest entirely in the MAN. By that time Sison was looking for the country's salvation in the hills of Tarlac.

The bamboo curtain was also parted for some chosen Filipinos. Filipino newsmen like Maximo Soliven and Nick Joaquin were invited to visit the Chinese Mainland. Sen. Maria Kalaw Katigbak led a group of university students on another jaunt to Peking. Sison, Arthur Garcia, Vicencio Jose and other progressives visited Communist China for periods as long as three months. It was believed that some of the mainland visitors undertook instruction in Maoist-style wars of national liberation.[16]

---

[16]Same.

The AFP believes that some of the young "pensionados" in China received training in sabotage techniques, guerrilla warfare, the techniques of mass action, and Vietcong-style terrorism in populated areas.

The only manifest proof of Communist China's interest in the Philippines at the time were the Radio Peking broadcasts in Tagalog beamed towards Luzon. According to the AFP, the programs were "clearly received in Northern Luzon and partly up to Bulacan and Greater Manila area." The broadcasts "seldom vary, and usually deal on local Philippine developments, Mao's thoughts, his economic accomplishments, U.S. imperialism and Soviet revisionism."[17]

Though it was broadly hinted at by government sources, there was no unchallengeable proof that Communist China was financing either the student unrest or the Huk Movement in the Philippines.

AFP intelligence sources saw some significance in the fact that the rift between Sison and his doctrinal rivals "coincided" with a growing schism in the Communist Party of the Philippines. The fight was between the upstart student leaders and the traditional leadership which claimed "noble lineage," (apparently a dig at the Lava family). It was obvious that the two factions were not reconciled.

Sison had failed to win over a sizeable number of the studentry, he was rebuffed by the more urbane socialists. He could make no headway either in the councils of the underground party. His one last hope was to win over the peasantry.

The government was not unaware of what was brewing. Many of these would-be insurrectionists had dossiers in P.C. intelligence files dating many years back. Their shipments of Maoist literature and propaganda were impounded at the airport and the piers. The postal authorities also kept a sharp check on all printed matter originating from Hongkong.

Despite the outlawing of the Communist Party, it was extremely difficult to get a prima facie case against the commuters to China. The military could only watch helplessly while the objects of their surveillance laid the groundwork for their revolution. Just when the PC had enough "goods" on the young radicals, they vanished from the city. They were not heard of again until First PC Zone agents reported them in the company of Commander Dante in the Tarlac hills

In October, 1968, one of the China scholars was invited to talk with a group of progressive Liberal congressmen calling themselves the "Young Turks." A Central Luzon congress-

[17]Captured CPP-NPA documents.

man invited the "professor" to the hills to meet Dante. The ideologues took over from there.

Arthur Garcia

The AFP claims that Sison was the "Amado Guerrero" who converted Dante's army into a *Capangpangan* version of Mao's People's Liberation Army. It is doubtful that Sison himself had much to do with the physical organization of the CPP-NPA infrastructure. He was an Ilocano and probably could not communicate effectively with the Pampango-speaking dissidents. But he had a fellow-ideologue who could: Arthur Garcia, a ranking member of the *Kabataang Makabayan.*

Garcia was a youth of middle-class means, his father having been the secretary of Mayor Arsenio Lacson of Manila. Garcia was a hardened activist. After graduating from the University of the Philippines, he got an instructor's job at the Mapa High School and indoctrinated many of his students until he was exposed by the Manila superintendent of schools.

Garcia held down a commissarship in the territory of Commander Joe in La Paz. A husky, athletic young man, Arthur seemed to thrive in the dissident life. He would accompany Joe on his jeep rounds of the territory as though on a lark. He did no fighting himself, though he carried a .45 cal. pistol.

According to a reliable Tarlac source, it was Arthur who built the tunnels in Sta. Rita and Comillas. He was the only one of the commissars who could actually lead the peasants; he was of Tarlaqueño descent and spoke Pampango. There is indeed a minority belief that Arthur Garcia *was* Amado Guerrero, the "proof" of that being their common initials "A. G."

The youths transferred the "second Propaganda Movement" to Tarlac.[18] Between January and around October, 1968, the CPP-NPA propagandists published *Ang Bayan*, an organ of the "Central Committee" of the reestablished Communist Party. This was not a publication for popular consumption but a theoretical journal for the edification of party members. *Ang Bayan* was published in English and Tagalog versions (the *Herald* team could not locate any Pampango edition). The May and July issues were printed on an electric typewriter.

---

[18]The first Propaganda Movement refers to the journalistic efforts of Marcelo H. del Pilar and his *Solidaridad* coterie in Madrid prior to the Philippine Revolution.

A few copies were reported floating around radical student circles in Manila but *Ang Bayan's* circulation could not have been more than a few thousands. Four editions came out before intensified AFP raids on CPP-NPA bases forced the underground paper out of circulation.

The Maoist Writ

The NPA-CPP, according to *Ang Bayan,* defined its primary mission as the destruction of feudal oppression and of the "forces of U.S. imperialism in the Philippines." This was virtually a lift-out from the "General Line of the International Communist Movement" promulgated by the Central Committee of the Chinese Communist Party on June 11, 1963. "In the capitalist countries which U.S. imperialism controls or is trying to control the working class and the people should direct their attacks mainly against U.S. imperialism, but also against their own monopoly capitalists and other reactionary forces who are betraying the national interests."[19]

Mao-directed internationalism, not the "narrow nationalism" that most Filipino progressives espoused in the past was the key to the whole movement. The CPP sought the "great unity of all nationalist people" under the "invincible thought of Mao Tse-tung."

The Maoists not only washed their hands of "Lavaismo" and "Tarucismo" but also chided the right wing of the *Malayang Samahang Magsasaka* (MASAKA) for being "committed to peaceful settlement" and "endlessly quarrelling" for funds and political patronage.

They were also contemptuous of "pseudo-leftists" and the "labor aristocrat circle." The "yellow trade union leaders" were dismissed as being without true revolutionary fervor.

When the CPP-NPA "program of people's democratic revolution" is examined in detail, it shows some accommodation with the more popular and not necessarily ideological wish to "provide every citizen with a decent livelihood." The program is definitely more liberal than a strictly Maoist regime would allow. This is obviously a concession to a "short-range" program appealing to liberals and progressives.

The economic and political rights of individuals will be respected. Small private enterprise will be "respected, encouraged and assisted." And most surprisingly, the constitutional freedoms of religion, speech and assembly will not be tampered with, though the unwritten proviso here is "so long as

---

[19]Quoted by Franz Marek in *Philosophy of World Revolution,* (New York: International Publishers, 1969).

it does not obstruct the revolution."

The Maoist concept of "democratic centralism" will be followed in the organization of government. There will be representative assemblies governing all levels of government, but all "subordinate to the People's Revolutionary Congress."

Only "heavy industries" will be appropriated by the state. The lighter industries will be run by cooperatives and private enterprise. Land will be given free to the peasants.

The proposed socialist regime will provide free education at all levels and protect the national minorities including "residents of Chinese ancestry, often the target of racist and chauvinist attacks." However, the "KMT Nationalist Chinese comprador bourgeoisie should be exposed and attacked for their class position."

In foreign affairs, the CPP-NPA program will seek to shuck off all "unjust treaties," support the "revolutionary struggle of oppressed peoples in Asia, Africa and Latin America," "resist Japanese exploitation, oppose regional arrangements, like the Seato and ASEAN," and the Maoist give-away — develop the "finest relations with the Peoples of Republic of China, Albania and all revolutionary governments."

The student linkage with the Tarlac Huk organization was apparently part of the grand design of revolution. The peasants had been assigned the vanguard role as prescribed by Maoist doctrine dating as far back as the late twenties. The germ of the idea appeared in Mao's "Report of an Investigation into the Peasant Movement in Hunan."

> In a very short time, in China's central, southern and northern provinces, several hundred million peasants will rise like a tornado or tempest, a force so extraordinarily swift and violent that no power, however great, will be able to suppress it . . . the peasant does not err.[20]

The doctrine of a peasant-led revolution was later obscured somewhat by Mao's difficulties in fitting the Chinese conditions into the traditional Marxist and Leninist constructs. But in his "On New Democracy" (January, 1940) Mao put out in Marek's view, "his most mature exposition of the new model."

> The struggle of the peasantry for land and soil constitutes the main content of the anti-imperialist and anti-feudal struggle in China is basically a peasant revolution.[21]

---

[20]As cited.

[21]Saulo, as cited, p. 30.

Though the suggestive model was there for any Communist to see as early as the prewar years, it did not sink into the inner workings of party strategy. Perhaps the Comintern bias of the CPP leaders prevented a fuller appreciation of the similarities in the peasant-support potential of China and the Philippines. The party had just suffered a serious rift between the peasant-oriented Jacinto Manahan and the classical Leninist Evangelista, and their Chinese comrades had to placate both sides by suggesting that the peasantry and urban proletariat should jointly lead the Philippine revolution.[22]

It had to take a new generation of ideologues to reintroduce the Maoist model to the Philippine setting. The new prescript was contained in the CPP-NPA "Programme."

> It is in the countryside where the enemy can become over-extended, where it is weakest, where the peasant main forces of the people's democratic revolutionary forces enjoy the widest grounds of maneuver and where they can take the offensive. It is here where the strategic majority of the enemy at the beginning of the people's war can become so dispersed as to allow the revolutionary forces to concentrate superior forces tactically. It is here where the enemy can be lured in deep territory and among the people with the greatest uncertainty for him.
>
> It is here where the fighting forces of the people's democratic revolution can retreat when the enemy advances, where they can harass the enemy when it is at rest, where they can advance when the enemy campaigns of encirclement and suppression can be smashed with counter-campaigns of encirclement and suppression by the Red Army.[23]

---

[22]Captured CPP-NPA documents.
[23]Same.

Chapter Eleven

THE FAILED REVOLUTION

Within four months of the joint inauguration of the New People's Army and the Maoist Communist party, Commander Dante was on the run. General Zerrudo, alarmed by the strange stirrings in the Tarlac countryside, sent Task Force Lawin into the bush in advance of authorization from Manila.[1] Lawin troopers chased some of Dante's men into Hacienda Luisita and nearly provoked a bloody battle with the Hacienda's uniformed security forces by attempting to frisk some of the plantation employes.[2] On May 29, 1969, a battalion strike force closed in on a secluded mountain base in Zambales, hoping to catch Dante, Layug, Madrigal and other ranking commanders. The Huk chiefs were not there but the troopers recovered eight long firearms and evidence of a training school for a hundred Huk recruits.[3]

For the first half of 1969, the Armed Forces thought they were just interdicting another Huk buildup, without knowing that they were facing a completely new formation. Even military intelligence was a little slow to catch on. The captured Zambales base was described to the Manila press as a "Stalin University," a name that would have been anathema to its Maoist sponsors. The first press speculation that all was not well between Sumulong and Dante came only in April.[4] The secret was finally out on June 9. A raiding party led by the First PC zone headquarters stumbled upon a Vietcong-style tunnel in Sta. Rita, Capas. What the intelligence officers found was enough to make their hair curl. The captured documents revealed virtually everything that had transpired in Tarlac since the "professor" joined Dante in the hills — the "reestablishment" of the Commu-

[1]Malacañang and the Defense Department were slow to react to the significance of the new Tarlac underground activity. But by mid-April, General Zerrudo proved his point and got authorization for Task Force Lawin to move in. This return of the AFP to the field virtually terminated the "memorandum of agreement" between the local Central Luzon officials and the President.

[2]Philippines *Herald,* April 11, 1969.

[3]Same, May 30, 1969.

[4]Same, April.

nist Party under Maoist auspices, the founding of the New People's Army, a blueprint for a "national war of liberation" after the Vietnam model, and "working alliances" among militant peasant, student and labor groups.[5]

Thoroughly alarmed, the government stepped up its operations in Tarlac. Pampanga, by contrast, was quiet except for the continuing duel between the killer squads of Sumulong and his enemies. Sumulong was sitting this out, hoping perhaps that the AFP would do him the favor of eliminating his renegade unit in Tarlac. In Camp Olivas, the battle plan was summarized into two words: Get Dante.

Task Force Lawin called into service a counter-insurgency technique borrowed from the Vietnam war — vertical envelopment. Three Huey helicopters were made available to Lawin headquarters to assist in patrol work. The choppers have been used several times to airlift strike forces to drop zones without giving any warning to the enemy.

Another Vietnam-proven stratagem employed by the AFP against Dante was the setting up of "barrio self-defense units" in the Tarlac barrios. The object was to deny Dante the use of his rural base. The strategy has been successful to some extent.

The AFP looked for people in the barrios willing to protect their homes and neighbors against the incursions of the Huks. Volunteers were not hard to find; in any barrio, there were a number of Huk-haters. They could be relatives of Huk victims, farmers no longer willing to pay "taxes" to the movement, or even former Huks themselves who might have deserted or fled their old units and were in fear for their own lives. The AFP provided the volunteers with arms and organized them into "barrio self-defense units" of 8 to 12 men. For added security, a detail of three AFP troopers headed by a non-commissioned officer was permanently posted in the barrio.

---

[5]From Gen. Manuel Yan's foreword to Vol. I of "So the People Would Know," AFP intelligence classified the contents of the captured Huk documents, releasing initially to the press only a general description. While researching the Dante story, the *Herald* reporting team was given permission to inspect one of the copies of *Ang Bayan* (Vol. I) confiscated in the Sta. Rita tunnel. This document was cited by the *Herald* to report the new political formation in Tarlac. The Sta. Rita documents were finally released in full on February 5, 1970 — five days after a bloody night-long clash between AFP units and radical students close to Malacañang Palace. AFP chief of staff Gen. Manuel Yan, who wrote a foreword to the documents, released them to "help bring about a more sober understanding of the threats that confront our people and provide a better insight to our national problems."

BSDU's were recently created in many of the barrios which Dante used to count on for support. In the most "critical" barrios and towns, full AFP detachments were stationed. At the same time, Task Force Lawin intensified its patrolling of Dante's known haunts.

With Tarlac barrios now too "hot" for him, Dante was forced deeper into the underbrush. His men fled as far as the Zambales mountains but even these remote hideouts were not beyond the reach of helicopter-borne Lawin troops. Since he could not operate in the barrios, Dante had to disband all but his elite guerrillas and scattered them in the *poblaciones* where they could inconspicuously mix with the people.

Breakup of Dante—CPP Alliance

With his army scattered, his infrastructure destroyed and his plans of expansion frustrated, Dante became disenchanted with his Maoist allies. When he first came in contact with the Manila-based intellectuals, he was carried away by their proselytizing. He unselfishly subordinated his command to the revolutionary junta dominated by Amado Guerrero. He fell in with the Maoist precept of "politics in command." For a while, the agrarian revolution took new life under the CPP-NPA banner. Those days were now over.

The Huks found themselves the losers; they suffered the brunt of the anti-dissident campaign. Before the "professor" came into Dante's life, he was just another Huk working his territory. But when the CPP-NPA launched its revolution with all propaganda trumpets blaring, the government rang the fire alarms and went after Dante with vengeance. Dante had become Public Enemy No. 1. His men were getting zapped not only from the ground but from the air. His own brother, Joe, braver and more reckless than Dante himself, was killed in a fire fight with civilian militia.

The initial source of friction was in the Maoist precept of "politics in command." The intellectuals had to be supreme; they dictated not only the political thoughts of the peasant recruits but also their mode of behavior. They preempted the major party roles including the chairmanship. That post went to "Amado Guerrero."

Sison, if indeed he was Amado Guerrero, was entitled more than anyone to the preeminent political power. But while the party headquarters was also sitting in Dante's backyard it created a discomfitting situation for the NPA commander. It was like an admiral flying his flag on the quarterdeck of a war vessel. Who commanded the ship, the admiral or the captain? Tarlac, after all, was Dante's territory claimed and won long before the "professor" came.

Dante and his peasant commanders were given positions in the Central Committee All told there were nine "cadres" from the New People's Army in this second leadership level — Dante, Melody, Goody, Eddie, Ruben, Elias, Juaning and Ben. It was not known whether a Politburo was chosen from among the Central Committee members after the fashion of the "traditional" Communist Party. The peasant "cadres" were outnumbered if the Central Committee had 22 positions as some accounts have it.

A conflict in tactics began tearing Dante away from the intellectuals. The Huks' strongest asset had always been their invisibility, their don't-make-waves caution This reduced their chances of capture. Dante's political advisers, in violation of this traditional guerrilla tactic, persuaded him to dig tunnels and use them as covert bases.

The outcome was disastrous. Informers tipped off the PC and the tunnels were promptly raided, their incriminating contents seized and the underground constructions destroyed.

There was one story relayed over the "bamboo telegraph" of angry disputes in the CPP-NPA leadership over the handling of union negotiations with Hacienda Luisita and other large Central Luzon establishments. The more radical Maoists wanted the haciendas broken up and given away free to the peasants. The Huks, knowing that their peasant followers would risk losing their livelihood if the hacienda operations were dismantled, balked at that "ultimate solution."

No details of the final breakup are known but Dante must have argued in vain with the dogmatic Maoists. In the end, he realized that with theoreticians running the revolution against the better judgment of professionals like himself, it had virtually no chance of success. Sison was reported to have fled Tarlac to escape Dante's wrath. The Huks-Maoist alliance did not last more than a year and a few months.

Other suspected political commissars have fallen into government hands. Leoncio Co, the husband of Peregrino Taruc's daughter and charged with being Dante's educational chief, was captured by the AFP in a raid in barrio Talaga, Capas on March 11. Nilo Tayag, to whom Sison entrusted the Kabataang Makabayan faced charges of subversion in the Tarlac court of first instance.[6]

---

[6]Tayag won the first round in September, 1970 when Judge Simeon Ferrer ruled that the anti-subversion law was a "bill of attainder," thus nullifying the AFP information brought against the KM chairman.

Arthur Garcia met his end in an exceptionally ironic way. He went one morning with two Huk members to swim in a creek near the poblacion of La Paz. He reportedly riled one of his companions by calling him "no-read-no-write" (referring to the man's illiteracy). In a fit of anger, the peasant shot Arthur. The body of the commissar was buried near the site and his death was not reported until several weeks later.[7]

The Tarlac episode demonstrated once again the unworkability of city-bred ideologues taking command over Pampango dissidents. The scholar's world is vastly different from that of the ill-educated peasant. Despite all the teach-ins for the edification of their rank-and-file guerrillas, the Maoists were never able to bring the latter around to a full appreciation of what their philosophy was about. It would indeed take a fairly high degree of political sophistication, not to mention a college degree, to begin to understand the nuances of dialectical materialism.

There was also something improper in the eyes of the Huks of non-Pampangos taking command of a Pampango movement. Even if the ideologues were physically present in the Tarlac hills, the lingual boundaries of the Huk movement were something they could not effectively cross.

Not the least source of Huk-ideologue friction was plain human relations. The Garcia tragedy was a case. Young Arthur tended to be arrogant and commanding when he dealt with his men. The Huks may be outlaws but they are basically Pampangos in temper. They lay much store in *galang* (grace), the simple barrio custom of respecting the dignity of their fellows. A young man must call an older one "Tatang," "Apo" or "Lolo." One just does not shout at a Pampango without expecting retribution.

The Student Riots

Foiled in their plans to capture the countryside, the student radicals attempted to lead an uprising in the streets of Manila.

Often in surly opposition to the party in power, Manila never lacks for armchair Bonifacios and cocktail-party Guevaras. The "revolution" is something that is constantly talked about but never put into effect. In late January,

[7]This version of Garcia's death was reported in similar details by the defense department reporter of the *Manila Times*. Subsequently, it was corroborated by Tarlac sources acquainted with Garcia's activities.

1970, it became a little more than a conversational ploy. It seemed a chilling possibility.

Two months earlier, President Marcos won reelection with an "overkill" that left the nation stunned and not a little shamed. Roughly 200 million pesos — more than is normally needed to elect an American President for a country five times as populous and a hundred times as rich — was lavished on the electorate. Hired gangsters in PC olive-green uniforms, if not PC troopers themselves, terrorized opposition workers and voters in many provinces. Scores were killed throughout the country in a record outbreak of electoral violence. The post-election malaise was worsened by a financial crisis caused by the fiscal excesses of the government.

A senior American embassy official was struck by the similarity of the events that overtook Manila with the student rebellion that unseated the South Korean patriarch Syngman Rhee in 1960. For weeks there was an ominous quiet. On December 28, radical students began an escalating sequence of street violence by cherry-bombing the motorcade bearing Vice President Spiro Agnew. By mid-January, students were massing in front of Malacañang Palace to demand the release of long-promised funds for state colleges.

On January 26, after the President had delivered his State-of-the-Nation message at the opening of Congress, demonstrating students heaved a papier mache replica of a crocodile at the President and his First Lady. The presidential couple escaped a hail of stones, placard handles and other improvised missiles, and minutes later baton-wielding policemen went after the youths. Scores of students were clubbed, kicked and beaten by the gendarmerie before horrified television watchers.

Four days later came the horrible climax. Holding aloft Maoist banners and crying "Dante for President," demonstrators, mostly students, broke through a gate of Malacañang Palace with the help of a commandeered firetruck, they set afire two cars on the Palace grounds before they were beaten back by teargas bombs. In a running battle on Mendiola street and deep into the heart of Manila's "university belt," four students and two other adults were killed by gunfire, presumably by the PC or the Manila police.

For several weeks, as protest rallies were held in Plaza Miranda and rampaging demonstrators stoned the U.S. Embassy, the Manila Hilton and other conspicuous symbols of "imperialism" and "feudalism," the Philippine democracy appeared to be skidding downhill very fast.

The student uprising quieted down in the summer

months. Actually, the sense of impending doom was largely the product of momentary public hysteria, inept overreaction on the part of the government, and clever symbol manipulation in the bourgeois mass media by the student radicals. The government was never really in danger at any time of being overcome by an armed uprising. By April, when most of Manila's students returned to the provinces for their vacation and the usual summertime torpor slowed the tempo of Manila life, things did not look as bad as they seemed.

Still the question is of more than academic interest to students of Philippine politics. Can prolonged student unrest in Manila combined with the Pampanga dissidence lead to a more generalized "people's war" against the regime? There is little evidence that this denouement will come about in the near future.

Though some disturbing echoes of the 1950 Huk insurrection are being heard now, the situation is not the same. The Philippine Left is uncompromisingly divided and unable to provide the strong doctrinal direction that any underground movement needs. Increasingly, the so-called student "moderates" committed to reform through non-violent means are taking the thunder away from the radicals. The Huks, as stated earlier, are a self-commissioned militia committed only to the protection of peasant interests and not significantly involved in national politics. Even if the Huk movement is preempted by a truly revolutionary leadership as it was in the fifties, it has no military capability to challenge the Armed Forces. In a speech before the University of the Philippines reserve officers alumni association in March, President Marcos assured his listeners that the AFP could put down an open Huk rebellion in a matter of days.[8]

The urban support a revolutionary party could draw from is limited to a few thousand student and youth front members — an insignificant minority compared to the nearly half-million students in Greater Manila — and an even smaller number of radical labor unionists.

There is considerable dissatisfaction with the Marcos administration among the politically-conscious Manilans. But much of this animus is directed at the personalities of those in power. The institutional reformists seek a change in the "system" only to the extent of making it more honest, efficient and beneficial.

There is little evidence of popular support for radical politics. A national poll taken from February to March, 1970 when student "demos" were at their height, revealed

[8]Philippines *Herald,* March 8, 1970.

that less than three percent of the population identified with the "radical" issues — foreign imperialism, inefficient government and lack of social justice — as the primary problem of the country. Only 5.61 percent opted for radical change of government as against 81.17 percent who still hoped to achieve meaningful reform through the existing political structure.[9]

Failure of Maoist Model

If it did anything, the Tarlac experience demonstrated the doubtful applicability of the Maoist model to other situations. The young communists hoped to establish a "fixed base of support" in the Central Luzon countryside—a Yenan-like sanctuary in which they could engage in "party-building" and "army-building." This was an intellectual conceit of immature and inexperienced revolutionaries overly influenced by their doctrinaire Maoism and blind to the facts of Philippine geography and demography.

As that perceptive student of revolution, Regis Debray pointed out, the reenactment of the Chinese experience requires a combination of favorable circumstances:

1. An extensive territory with a consequent lack of communications facilities in the hinterland.
2. A high density of rural population.
3. A common border with a country sympathetic to the revolution (e.g., Russia vis-a-vis China before 1949).
4. The absence of airborne troops which are the government's greatest counter-insurgent shock forces.
5. The numerical insufficiency of the government forces.[10]

---

[9]De Jesus and Benitez, as cited, pp. 51,98. In response to a question whether a "complete change" in the form of government was desired, 49.88 percent of the respondents replied favorably and 29.33 percent were against the proposition. In the absence of comparative data, the authors were cautious about assessing the magnitude of support for extra-constitutional change in the form of government. "In terms of absolute numbers, however, 27 percent of the population 16 years and above, based on 1960 census figures, would amount to about 3.8 million persons," they wrote. "Any radical movement that can count on the support of 3.8 million people could pose a serious threat to the stability of any political system."

[10]*Revolution in the Revolution*, translated from the author's French and Spanish by Bobbye Ortiz (New York: Grove Press, 1967), p. 61.

The Philippine situation only partly meets two of Debray's conditions and fails absolutely in the other three.

The "Programme" writer who described the Tarlac countryside to be "where the fighting forces of the people's democratic revolution can retreat when the enemy advances, where they can harass the enemy when it is at rest, where they can advance when the enemy retreats" just had no concept of geographical scale.

He must have imagined Central Luzon to be five or ten times as big as it is and envisioned Task Force Lawin overreaching itself deep in the mountains and being cut to pieces by the partisan army. How disillusioning the reality must have been to those who took this writ seriously.

In the early days of the Huk movement the relatively inaccessible Candaba swamps and the western hills of Pampanga and Tarlac provided safe havens for guerrilla warfare. The Japanese occupation army controlled the main highway and the *poblaciones*, but the rest of Central Luzon belonged to the Huks.

Since the last war, Central Luzon was shrunk by feeder roads to the remote barrios and by the expansion of the farm population. The "countryside" of the Mao-quoters is a tiny backyard compared to the broad reaches of north and central China where the Fourth and Eighth Route Armies successfully outmaneuvered the Kuomintang and the Japanese. The Central Plain is an extremely compact region. It was sheer folly to build "fixed bases" in the pocket-sized arena of Central Luzon. Capas and La Paz are less than a half hour's drive from the 51st BCT's Jefmin Village base. The battlefields of Central Luzon are so close to the Task Force Lawin headquarters that its commander can pull out of action for a coffee break in an air-conditioned Angeles restaurant and get back in time to catch the rest of it.

The classic "guerrilla zone" is a place remote from the national center like the hills of northeastern Burma, or the jungles of Malaya where a man can only see six feet ahead of him. Central Luzon is too close to the metropolis. From Manila, it is an hour and a half's drive to Angeles City and a two hours' drive to Tarlac town. A government force can blanket the area in a day.

The Maoist prescription for "fixed bases" is of doubtful applicability to geographically small countries in this age of sophisticated counter-insurgency techniques. Debray wrote from a profound knowledge of Latin American insurrectionary movements when he debunked the "guerrilla zone" stratagem.

> . . .for a guerrilla force to attempt to occupy

> a fixed base or to depend on a security zone, even one of several thousand square kilometers in area, is. . .to deprive itself of its best weapon, mobility, to permit itself to be contained within a zone of operations, and to allow the enemy to use its most effective weapons. The notion of the security zone raised to a fetish is the fixed encampment set up in reputedly inaccessible spots. This reliance on the characteristics of the terrain alone is always dangerous, after all, no place is inaccessible; if anyone has been able to reach it, then so can the enemy.[11]

The Philippines, being an archipelago of 7,000 islands, theoretically has ample room for other guerrilla movements. Macario Peralta commanded a guerrilla group of 25,000 in Panay island during the war and there was little the Japanese could do about it. The Bicol provinces, still relatively underdeveloped, the destitute and crime-prone islands of Leyte and Samar, and the sugar-rich Negros Occidental are physically ideal for bush fighting. If a highly-organized Communist Party were to set up bases in many separate areas of the Philippines, the government forces could be thinly and precariously spread out. While there is some belief that the Communists are precisely trying to spread out, there is no hard proof that they are succeeding.

Central Luzon has a high population density but it hardly qualifies for the third of Debray's conditions. If the Huks had set up in Mindanao in the southern Philippines in the fifties, they might have enjoyed something of a sanctuary in Indonesian Kalimantan which is only a few hours' cruise by vinta. Under the politically adventuristic Sukarno, Indonesia might not have minded sheltering a few rebel Filipinos at that time.

In Central Luzon the Huks are nowhere within friendly territory. The Chinese mainland is 600 miles across the South China Sea and up north is the Nationalist China bastion of Taiwan which could not conceivably be hospitable to communist-leaning fugitives from the Philippines

The Philippines, unhappily for revolutionists, is equipped with airborne troops. It is virtually impossible for an insurgent force to mass in any area without drawing immediate counteraction. The Philippine armed forces total more than 50,000 officers and men, sufficient to cope with a dissident force of any possible size.

G. S. Girling states somewhat differently the conditions for a "successful outcome of people's war, judging from the

---

[11]As cited, pp. 62-63.

Chinese experience."[12] They are peasant support, protracted war, breakdown of the opposing regime, leadership, organization, and national appeal. The Philippines partially satisfies two of Girling's conditions but it is markedly deficient in the other four.

In Central Luzon, the Huks enjoy some degree of peasant support. Its agrarian troubles have persisted for more than half a century, though in only brief periods did they escalate to the proportions of a "war."

The reading, using the Girling formula, is unfavorable the rest of the way. Despite its occasionally violent elections, the Philippines continues its long tradition of political stability. President Marcos looked a little wobbly shortly after the January, 1970 riots but he has recovered since and is in firm command of the government.

Failure of Revolutionary Leadership

In both the 1950 rebellion and the half-baked revolution of the late sixties, Communist Party leadership was greatly deficient. The Lavas were probably the best-equipped of them all but they had their limitations. And as Hoeksema pointed out, the Lavas and their contemporaries lacked the popular appeal to carry the Party plans out. "As long as the CPP remained purely a 'force party' it might get by with leaders like Jose and Jesus Lava and Jorge Frieneza, but who are really these men on the Philippine national scene? They know little of politics. They have had even less experience — a bank examiner, a medical doctor and an American-educated Filipino who had done nothing else except work amongst the Communist youth in the Philippines."[13]

The "revolutionaries" of the late sixties were even more naive and suicidally inflexible. If they were guilty of one tactical blunder, it was tipping off the security forces of their insurrectionary intentions — if indeed those were their intentions — by resorting to a printed propaganda campaign. A more experienced group of conspirators would have been more discreet about the communistic nature of their movement until a larger mass base was acquired.

This duality in Huk leadership has been a constant source of weakness. The Lavas, whose vision of a communized Philippines was shared by few of their followers, sounded the charge but after an initial rush the foot soldiers faltered

---

[12]G. S. Girling, *People's War: The Conditions and the Consequences in China and in South East Asia* (London: George Allen and Unwin, 1969), p. 50.

[13]As cited.

and retreated. Taruc's Huks were willing to die for Taruc but not for the committeemen who handed them their marching orders. The "ideologues" have *used* rather than *led* the Huk movement, commanding the troops but rarely risking their own hides.

It was the same thing all over in Tarlac. Dante and his peasant followers soon tired of being told what to do by their university-educated comrades. The NPA recruits were loyal to Dante and not to Amado Guerrero, and when the showdown came the "Professor" had to quit.

Perhaps there are better "models."

Debray pointed out, perhaps with great wisdom, the unwieldiness and unworkability of separate political and military leadership in an insurrectionary situation. The "staggering novelty" introduced by the Cuban revolution, the French theoretician wrote, was that the

> vanguard party can exist in the form of the guerrilla force itself. The guerrilla force is the party in embryo. Or as Che Guevara put it, the political and military leaders should be "united, if possible, in one person."[14]

An outsider, no matter how intellectually qualified, cannot go up the hills and take over the command of unlettered peasant guerrillas. The traditional distrust for the *dayuhan* —the stranger — is a wall between him and the peasants. His intellect is completely different from the peasant mind; he may be able to accommodate the peasants' short-range goals within his own vision, but when the going gets rough, personal survival dictates the actions of all. If the urban-bred leader cannot speak the dialect of the proposed guerrilla zone, he is doomed to failure.

Debray attributed much of the success of the Vietnamese liberation movement to the quality of its leadership. Its leaders were "not artificially appointed by a congress or coopted in traditional fashion, but tested, molded, and tempered by this terrible struggle which they led to victory."[15]

More than a group of ideologues, the dissident movement has to have political strategists who can perceive the situation in the most realistic manner, operate on the basis of "hard facts" rather than borrowed ideology and experiences, and plot moves accordingly. The ideological bias of the CPP-NPA leadership resulted in inflexibility in strategical thinking, and consequently in tactical errors.

At this stage of development of Philippine socialism, its leadership should be accumulative rather than divisive. The

---

[14]As cited, pp. 62-63.
[15]As cited, pp. 106-107.

"ideal" leader should be one who grows up with the movement, someone whom the peasants can readily identify with, but sufficiently educated to discern ways of manipulating the political mechanism of the country. Amado Guerrero tried to be an "instant Mao" without Mao's benefit of decades of wartime experience.

Lack of National Appeal

Both the 1950 Huks and the Maoists failed Girling's final test — that of national appeal.

The major weakness in the CPP-NPA gospel is that it is beyond a simple peasant's comprehension. The average farmer dosen't care about the Maoist "world view"; neither can he be stirred up against "U.S. imperialism." What moves him are things directly affecting his own welfare and that of his family and neighbors.

Shortly after the January-February 1970 riots in Manila, the Philippine Publishers Association commissioned a nation-wide poll to determine attitudes towards the government, demonstrators, and their perceived problem.[16]

The findings corroborated those of the Citizenship Research Foundation poll a few months earlier. The publishers' survey noted a tendency of Filipinos to identify their problems in terms of economic difficulties experienced individually or as members of family units.

Of the causes cited for "civilian unrest," 39 percent were of a particularistically economic nature — high cost of living, high prices of prime commodities, high transportation rates, high tuition fees and cost of books, etc. Thirty-one percent of the causes were what would be perceived by educated and reform-oriented people — graft and corruption, abusive officials, government overspending, election frauds, budgetary management, etc. Only nine percent of the perceived causes indicated awareness of social conflict — poverty, unemployment, exploitation of tenants, "the rich getting richer and the poor getting poorer," etc.

The "radical" issues — foreign control of business, American imperialism, etc. — were perceived by an insignificant 0.5 percent of respondents. In other words, the Maoists were getting their message across to only a tiny fraction of the body politic.

[16]Conducted by the Asia Research Organization, an independent Manila-based group, in June, 1970. The poll was based on 3,000 interviews — a statistically large sample — allocated among 10 regions of the Philippines in direct proportion to population. A total of 160 cities and municipalities were selected at random as well as respondents within those primary sampled areas.

No matter how the CPP builds up a Mao Tse-tung personality cult, Mao can never be a father-image to the barrio folks simply because he is an alien — and worse, Chinese.

The Maoists' symbol manipulation was doomed because of one elemental psychological fact — the profound mistrust and hostility of Filipinos towards the Chinese. This sinophobic tradition dates as far back as the 16th and 17th centuries when the Parian, the Chinese commercial settlement outside the Spanish walled city of Manila, was sacked several times and pillaged and thousands of its inhabitants massacred.

According to a University of the Philippines social scientist, Rodolfo A. Bulatao, the long-standing animus of the Filipino towards the Chinese is based on:

1. Economic competition;
2. Resentment of illegal activities such as arson and smuggling attributed to the Chinese;
3. Family difficulties such as the common Chinese practice of taking a Filipino spouse due to the shortage of Chinese women; and
4. Fear generated by the triumph of communism in China.[17]

In his University of the Philippines graduate thesis, Bulatao noted that anti-sinocism was reenforced by:

1. "Group self-hatred," the rejection of the Chinese as a symbol of the oriental elements in the Filipino culture and physique;
2. The portrayal of Chinese as dangerous aliens in control of two-thirds of the retail trade;
3. "City-hatred," the discontent of migrants to the city with the highly visible Chinese businessman, who symbolizes the difficulties of urban life;
4. The Chinese as a sex symbol, threatening to the Filipino women;
5. A self-fulfilling prophecy relating to Chinese business ethics leading Chinese businessmen to cheat in naturalization proceedings, to shady business deals, and to bribery;
6. The Chinese being the obvious representatives of an unsatisfactory economic system.[18]

---

[17]Rodolfo A. Bulatao, *A Test of the Belief Congruence Principle in Prejudice Against Chinese in the Philippines,* a thesis submitted to the University of the Philippines Graduate School, June, 1967. The thesis writer cited survey data from B.T. Catapusan, "Patterns of Social Relationship in the Philippines," ***Philippine Social Science and Humanities Review,*** **Manila, 1954.**

[18]Same.

There is little evidence that the "ideological" basis for the Huk revolt has any appeal outside of Central Luzon. Its most compelling shibboleth among its own mass base is "land for the landless." It is doubtful whether land reform is as strongly appealing to Manila's working class.[19]

The Huks, in sum, are the Pampango version of a continuing agrarian demonstration in various parts of the Philippines. History has brought out other agrarian movements differing from the Huks only in locality, degree of political sophistication, and longevity.

The Pulajanes of Samar which opposed the American army at the turn of the century have been described by Agoncillo as an insurrection against American occupation. This is another attempt by "nationalistic" historians to fit historical evidence into preconceived ideological frames.[20]

The Pulajanes are more accurately classified as a nativistic, messianic type of agrarian protest. They were led by their own Pope, "Papa" Bulan, who claimed divine inspiration and "the miraculous power of conferring invulnerability on (his) followers."[21]

The Pulajanes movement was a characteristic reaction of ignorant country people against their stark poverty. Samar was and continues to be one of the most neglected and undeveloped islands in the Philippines. Lying in the path of highly destructive seasonal typhoons, the island is unsuited

---

[19]The Rand Corporation summed up the Huk's mischief-making potential in these few lines:

"In our estimation, the HMB are likely to remain a major nuisance. They are not concurrently a great threat to the government. On the other hand, they have shown some resiliency and they do have access to a considerable flow of resources. Yet even if there were signals of widespread discontent that we have not picked up and this were a precondition of insurgency, the HMB do not now appear to be an organization that could mobilize and exploit that unrest."

[20]Teodoro A. Agoncillo and Milagros C. Guerrero, *History of the Filipino People* (Quezon City: Malaya Press, 1970), pp. 160-161, 285-288. The authors disregarded the quasi-religious nature of the turn-of-the-century protest movements such as "Papa" Rios' Leyte sect and the Santa Iglesia and gratuitously credited them with nationalistic motivation. "Guerrilla resistance was so widespread in the Philippines that while they were apparently unrelated to each other and seemingly lacking in direction due to a tragic lack of able and cohesive leadership, it could not be denied that all these uprisings during the early years of American rule were part and parcel of a national movement to overthrow American sovereignty." p. 186.

[21]Fifth Annual Report of the Philippine Commission, Bureau of Insular Affairs, War Department, Government Printing Office, Washington, 1905. Part 1, p. 3.

to either large-scale agriculture or industry. It is an out-migration area along with the neighboring Leyte island, where many of the womenfolk turn up as domestic servants of affluent Manila families.

Quasi-religious fanaticism involved only a small portion of the Samar population. The Pulajanes were a small band of about 200 hillmen from the headwaters of the Gandara river. Other Samar folk living near the coast were not at all associated with the movement. In fact, they were the primary victims of the fanatics who slaughtered their own provincemates.[22]

The Philippine Constabulary took several years to completely suppress the movement, long after the American army had yielded control to the civil government. Some captured members of the sect confessed that the cause of their insurgency was their oppression by "certain Filipinos prominent in the insurrection" who bought hemp from them at nominal prices and resold the produce at great profits.[23] There was little Spanish influence in the province. From this, the Samar troubles can be diagnosed as a breakdown of social relationships similar to what precipitated Pampango dissidence early in this century. The Pulajanes are gone but the fact that next to Manila, Samar and Leyte contribute proportionally the largest numbers of convicts to the penal institutions indicates that the agrarian protest continues in more muted and indiscernible forms

A more contemporary example of armed agrarian protest was the outlaw band of Tiruray tribesmen organized by an Ilocano migrant named Feliciano Lozes, alias "Toothpeck." Toothpeck was something of a Robin Hood who stole from the abusive Muslim datus to help the otherwise defenseless Tirurays. The PC tolerated the capers of Toothpeck's Merry Band because it could not singly discipline the politically powerful Muslims. Toothpeck gave up his colorful career by surrendering to President Marcos in October, 1970 but soon afterwards returned to his outlaw ways.

These types of organized lawlessness will continue indefinitely while large sections of the Philippines remain under "warlord" rule or under conditions of marginal security and economic development. But in all likelihood, these movements will continue to be largely localized and self-contained.

The Huk rebellion will continue to be confined in the Pampango-speaking areas, unable to spread further because the Tagalogs, the Ilocanos and the Visayans can only superficially identify with its objectives.

The Huk movement has taken a new turn since the

[22]Same.
[23]Same.

capture of Sumulong in September, 1970. A month afterwards, on October 17, the aging HMB supremo Pedro Taruc was killed in Angeles City under rather mysterious circumstances. The Philippine Army's version was that he was slain by two intelligence operatives when he resisted arrest. A Constabulary major whose command covered Angeles had the theory that Taruc surrendered peacefully and was executed by the Army. *Herald* correspondent Ben Maglague was told by local residents that the Huk chieftain was liquidated by his own bodyguard for the ₱150,000 bounty on his head.[24]

The elimination of the top two HMB leaders created a vacuum of leadership which Commander Dante quickly exploited. There are reports that the Pampanga and Tarlac Huk commands are now reunited under Dante, giving the AFP a tougher peace and order situation to deal with. Dante, reported to be ailing from tuberculosis and malnutrition, has passed on active field command to two subordinates, Felman and Panchito.

While the Huks cannot expand beyond the Pampanga areas, neither can they be easily stamped out. They will probably remain, in the words of one of the Rand authors, a "low-grade infection" coursing through the bloodstream of the Pampango society. Mere anti-biotics cannot knock it out. Only a gradual restoration of the health of the agrarian society itself can eliminate the contagion completely.

---

[24]Philippines *Herald*, October 17, 1970.

Chapter Twelve

THE POLITICS OF CENTRAL LUZON

Governors of Pampanga Since 1896
PHILIPPINE REVOLUTIONARY GOVERNMENT
AND FIRST PHILIPPINE REPUBLIC

Tiburcio Hilario .... from 1896 to June 26, 1898
General Tomas Mascardo (appointed by President
Emilio Aguinaldo) 1899
General Jose Alejandrino (—do—) 1900
US MILITARY GOVERNMENT
General Frederick Dent Grant ...... from August 1899
General Arthur MacArthur .. May 4, 1900 to July 3, 1901
AMERICAN REGIME
Ceferino Joven (appointed through Executive Order
No. 64) .... February 27, 1902 to July 3, 1901
Macario Arnedo (elected) .... March 7,1904 to 1912
Francisco Liongson (—do—) .... 1912 to 1916
Honorio Ventura (—do—) .... 1916 to 1922
Pablo Angeles David (acting) .... August 16, 1917
Olimpio Guanzon (elected) .... 1922 to 1925
Sotero Baluyut (—do—) .... 1925 to 1931
Eligio Lagman (appointed) June 15, 1931 to Oct. 15, 1931
Pablo Angeles David (elected) .... 1931 to 1937
Sotero Baluyot (elected) .... 1938 to 1941
JAPANESE REGIME, SECOND PHILIPPINE REPUBLIC
(All appointed)
Lazaro Yambao 1942
Eligio Lagman .... 1942 to 1944
Urbano Dizon 1944
Jose Y. David 1944
AMERICAN LIBERATION (All appointed)
Gerardo Limlingan 1945
Pablo Angeles David 1945
THIRD PHILIPPINE REPUBLIC
Pablo Angeles David (appointed) .... 1946 to 1947
Jose B. Lingad (elected) .... 1948 to 1951
Rafael Lazatin (—do—) .... 1952 to 1955
Rafael Lazatin (—do—) .... 1956 to 1959
Francisco G. Nepomuceno (elected) ..... 1960 to 1963

Francisco G. Nepomuceno (—do—) 1964
(incumbent, to seat until 1967)

From Mariano Henson
"The Province of Pampanga and
Its Towns."

Over the past 72 years, the official attitudes of Pampango politicians towards the Huks (and earlier to the "agrarian problem") have swung from liberalism to conservatism and back, depending on the prevailing political climate and the individual idiosyncracies of the men in power.

During the brief revolutionary period, Pampanga had a succession of liberal caretakers — Tiburcio Hilario, General Tomas Mascardo, and Gen. Jose Alejandrino — before two American military commanders, Gen. Frederick Dent Grant and Gen. Arthur MacArthur took over. After the American "pacification" campaign, there was relative peace in Pampanga and other rural areas in the Philippines. In the 1920's agrarian disputes erupted in Pampanga and Nueva Ecija without attracting attention from the national politicians in Manila who were then involved in the independence movement. But in the province, the landlord-descended officials reacted to the situation with expected conservatism. Honorio Ventura, who served as governor from 1916 to 1922, had a respectably "revolutionary" background — his family supported Hilario's wartime regime — but he showed a lack of understanding of the peasant turmoil outside the *capitolio*.

Sotero Baluyot, who served two gubernatorial terms (1925-1931 and 1938-1941), was a "hard-liner." He beat the *Frente Popular* (and Socialist Party) candidate Pedro Abad Santos by only a narrow margin in 1938 and that was a fair indication of the class split in the province. Pablo Angeles David, three times an appointive governor (the first in 1917), was an even more relentless scourge of the Huks. Appointed by President Roxas to restore peace at all cost, Governor David employed civilian guards to protect the haciendas and other private property, their salaries paid by the landlords but with virtual police powers authorized by the provincial government.[1]

Jose Lingad, who replaced David as Pampanga's first postwar elected governor in 1948, was compelled to pursue the hard-line policy because of the threat of a Huk uprising.

His most notable act as governor was to create Huk-fighting civilian guards serving as auxiliaries of AFP military units. These were probably the first "para-military

---

[1]Abaya, as cited, p. 32.

units" (PMU's) put into action in Central Luzon. Lingad started with one civilian guard detachment in his native barrio of Gumi, Lubao and built up this militia to about 200 men posted mainly in the anti-Huk towns of Floridablanca, Guagua, Bacolor and Macabebe.[2]

Lingad's anti-Huk stance was a direct consequence of his wartime experience. A Bataan veteran who fought with the 301st Field Artillery, he escaped from the Death March in his hometown of Lubao and joined Ramsey's Guerrillas, a unit competing with the Huks for control of parts of western Pampanga and Bataan. He was captured by the Japanese three times but each time managed either to escape or use political connections to secure his liberty.[3] In 1944, his brother, Jesus, and uncle, Marciano, were killed in Gumi by Huks under Silvestre Liwanag.

Many years later, Liwanag (Linda Bie) had a face-to-face meeting with Lingad who was now an elected congressman sitting with Rep. Espinosa's committee investigating the Huk problem. Liwanag explained the circumstances behind the slaying of Lingad's kin.

> *Noon pinatay sila nagkaroon ng* retaliation, *siempre gaganti at nagkaroon ng galitan ngayon.* But no personal *na pagkakagalitan o away, kundi ako'y nagtago ako dahil sa principio ko o* idea *kong lumalaban ako sa nagsasamantala, komo mahirap ako at sila naman ay karaniwan lamang na ipagtanggol nila yoon kanilang kapakanan komo mayaman.*
>
> (When they were killed, what naturally followed was a grudge. But there was nothing personal on my part since I was a fugitive for my own principles, since I was poor and they had to fight for their rights because they were rich.)[4]

Even among the Pampangos, blood runs thicker than ideology. Lingad swore to avenge his kin if it was the last thing he would do. He became uncompromisingly anti-Huk. In the post-Liberation election, he resisted Huk terrorism. The Democratic Alliance scored a landslide victory in Pampanga but one of the few places in the province where Roxas won was the barrio of Gumi. Roxas had the Huk-fighting Joe Lingad to thank for that.

When Lingad became governor, he built up the civilian guards, believing they were the best defense against the com-

---

[2]Lingad, interview, July, 1970.
[3]Same.
[4]Espinosa committee hearings.

munists. Many of the civilian guards were Lingad's own trusted men, Bataan veterans or fellow-guerrillas during the Occupation. But the civilian guards — and Lingad himself since he was identified with the hard-line policy — came to grief as the result of the "Maliwalu massacre."

Portrero, an anti-Huk barrio in Lubao, was attacked by Huks, resulting in the death of Maj. Numeriano Serrano. The asailants were believed to have come from the neighboring barrio of Maliwalu, which had a radical tradition dating back to prewar days and was notoriously sympathetic to the Huk movement. Two of Serrano's brothers were civilian guard leaders and a reprisal was planned against Maliwalu. One evening, the civilian guards raided Maliwalu; seven persons were killed outright and several others kidnaped.[5]

The Maliwalu massacre was a national scandal and Lingad fell out of power, not to surface again in politics until his townmate from Lubao, Diosdado Macapagal, made him a cabinet officer.

During the regime of Rafael Lazatin there was a moderation, at least unofficially, in official attitudes toward the Huks. In the late fifties, the Huks had ceased to be a genuine security threat; their members were rapidly depleted by old guerrilleros returning to normal life. Governor Lazatin kept the Huks at arms' length, almost in "neutralist" fashion. "I believe the Huk problem is not ours," he said. "It belongs to the national government."[6]

During the early gubernatorial years of Francisco Nepomuceno, many provincial officials had already arrived at a discreet accommodation of the "invisible government." The municipal officials who refused to accommodate formed the Pampanga Anti-Huk Mayors League. However, pro and anti-Huk sentiment was no longer decided on "ideology" but on political expediency. The Huks, in practical political terms, had become a "constituency" whose support was to be solicited along with other Pampango sectors.

Peaceful Coexistence

Half the credit for this post-rebellion accommodation should go to the Huks themselves. No longer interested in a violent seizure of power, the Huks have taken a "soft line" with the bourgeois government, not interfering with its functions so long as they are left well enough alone. "Look at all the things the government has in Pampanga — the Phil-

---

[5]Lingad, as cited.

[6]Rodolfo Tupas, "Fight for the Hearts and Minds of Huklandia," *The Sunday Times Magazine,* July 29, 1967, p. 13, quoted by Indiongco, as cited.

cag, the Land Reform People, the APC (Agricultural Productivity Commission), and the ACA (Agricultural Credit Administration)," Sumulong told two members of the House of Representatives who interviewed him recently, "Do we bother them at all? No. We let them conduct their business because what they are doing is for the good of the people."[7]

True enough, the brace of government agencies operating in Central Luzon to reduce peasant sympathy for the Huks has not been interfered with. The Philippine Civic Action Group, shipped over from Vietnam duty to help in the home front, worked on the Magalang-Concepcion road without incident.

Dante, farther to the left than the Pampanga leaders, did not burn his bridges behind either. He enjoyed (and probably continues to do so) the protection of some Tarlac politicians or his New People's Army would have withered on the vine long ago.

The Huks have shown their hand in Pampanga elections since the forties. They are naturally more concerned with local governments than with national offices since provincial governors, mayors, municipal councilors and barrio captains can more readily extend material or moral support to the movement. It is a safe bet that at least six of every ten town or barrio officials either sympathize with the Huks or tolerate their existence. This is an inference that has to be made backward for candidates for local office rarely make public pro or anti-Huk statements for the record.

A rule-of-thumb for gauging how local officials stand is whether they go around with bodyguards or not. Well-secured officials are likely to be anti-Huk, though there are a few cases of Huk-leaning politicians who arm themselves against the possibility of government or "Monkee" reprisals. Those who don't surround themselves with guards are probably tolerant of the Huk presence. They are in the majority.

The Huks' political interests seem to be particularistic and short-term. They are concerned primarily with their own protection and the continuance of their "invisible government." Though there is little evidence of their trading support for cash pay-offs, the Huks exercise some vested interests in the lower levels of municipal governments. For instance, some of their regulars or "combat support" are employed as members of municipal police forces or have key positions in municipal staffs. The Huks like to have the barrio captains cooperate with the movement. It is, however, not a one-sided relationship. The grassroots officialdom is

[7]Espinosa, interview, June, 1970.

compensated with specific favors or grants from the Huks. Until the barrio defense forces came into being, the Huks were *de facto* police forces in their areas.[8]

The Huks also participate in national elections, though in a less positive way. Sumulong campaigned for President Marcos in 1969. Dante supported Marcos' opponent, Sen. Sergio Osmeña, Jr.[9] A last-minute plea by one of Senate President Gil Puyat's kin for the support of Sumulong saved the Pampanga-born politician from losing in the province. (He eventually landed No. 4 in the senatorial contest in Pampanga).

Huk-Coddling: Crime or Necessity?

The prevailing conditions in Central Luzon have given rise to a kind of political behavior popularly referred to as "Huk-coddling." It is a pejorative term, suggesting softness on communism if not leftist sympathy or political opportunism. Nearly all the major contemporary political figures in Central Luzon have been charged with Huk-coddling. Is this behavior really so reprehensible and traitorous?

In most cases, Huk-coddling is simply an accommodation of the realities of Central Luzon. The Huks *are* there, whether a politician likes them or not. A politician antagonizes the Huks at the risk of losing his life and the high mortality of Pampanga mayors while in office shows just how perilous opposing the Huks can be. In a five-year period between 1961 and 1966, four mayors were assassinated by them.[10]

A few politicians are sincere reformers and openly identify with socialist creeds — Rep. Jose V. Yap of Tarlac is one of them. But the majority are just being "practical politicians." The most opportunistic ones swing from one end of the pendulum to another.

The zigzag tracks made by Governor Nepomuceno in nine years of Pampanga politics are illustrative of ephemeral political attitudes vis-a-vis the Huks. He became governor in 1959 without Huk support, thus proving that a politician can

---

[8]In confrontation with Mayor Eugenio Suarez and other Angeles officials, General Tanabe charged that 40 members of the 132-man Angeles police force were associated with the Huks. He claimed that 18 out of 30 Angeles police rookies were similarly involved.

[9]Kalaw, as cited.

[10]Mayor Marco Padilla of Mexico was killed on March 8, 1961; Mayor Benedicto Dayrit of Magalang on December 8, 1963; Mayor Eduardo Tiangco of Arayat on December 23, 1964; and Mayor Gallardo of Candaba in an ambush with five of his bodyguards on July 18, 1966.

buck the organization and still win. In 1967 he was openly sympathetic with the Huks. "What can you do?" he said. "That's politics here. I do not want to be a monument. I am practical." Testifying before a congressional committee under Rep. Felix Amante in 1966, the governor charitably described the Huks as "neither anti-American nor pro-Russian." They were "not the same as before."

Furthermore, Nepomuceno had become a "soft-liner."

> What is needed in Pampanga are not Rangers but Philcag troops who can build bridges and roads and provide medical care. What the Huks want are action and results. I told the President that if you give them justice and show them you are sincere, the Huk movement will disappear.[12]

In 1969, Nepomuceno reversed his opinions on the Huks once again. He broke openly with Sumulong when he refused a Huk demand for his wife's withdrawal from the congressional contest. Juanita Nepomuceno, then incumbent representative for the first district, reportedly aroused the ire of the movement when she failed to protest the shootup of Angeles City in May, 1969. Camp Olivas ingenuously claimed that the Huks were responsible for the raid though there were strong indications that persons posing as Huks were the real culprits.

Nepomuceno was sworn in as a Nacionalista (the President's party) and on July 19, the Manila press played up his "declaration of war" against the Huks.

Both Governor Nepomuceno of Pampanga and Gov. Eduardo Cojuangco of Tarlac (Cojuangco declared war on the Huks two days before Nepomuceno did) had to flee their provinces at the height of the terror killings. Today they still live in fear; Nepomuceno does his rounds in Pampanga inside an armored car, with two or three jeeps of security men trailing after him. His Angeles City hostelry is guarded by concrete pillboxes. Townspeople refer to the place as "Fortress Oasis."

"I'm marked for life," Cojuangco said with undisguised bitterness. "And all because I tried to do right by my province."[13] He ran for Congress in 1969 when it was no longer healthy for him to remain in the province. He campaigned by helicopter and travelled by road only with the protection of a motorcade of armed guards.

No less than President Marcos accused Sen. Benigno

---

[11]Tupas, "Pampanga: The Political H-Bomb," as cited.
[12]Tupas, "A Season of Content," as cited.
[13]Interview, September, 1969.

Aquino Jr. of "tolerance of the Huks" during the youthful Liberal's term as governor of Tarlac. Earlier, Senator Aquino had unveiled his own formula for ridding Central Luzon of its Huk problem once and for all. The President disposed of Aquino's peace-making offer in a few well-chosen and sarcastic words: "I would like to have him tell us who were those who committed the killings in Concepcion lately. This I think would determine then how talented he is and how quick he is in helping us out in the peace and order problem." While the Senator was the governor in Tarlac, the President charged that the province "became a rest and recreation area for the Huks."[14]

Three days later, the PC accused Senator Aquino of having given Commander Alibasbas a "carbine with a telescopic sight and flash holder" during his gubernatorial term. Aquino had allegedly helicoptered to a secret meeting with the Huks in barrio Almendras, Concepcion, sometime in 1965.[15] The PC disclosures were apparently made to embarrass Aquino for no charges were formally made in court.

The Huks are used by politicians as much as they use the latter. In 1965, Alibasbas, the third-ranking Huk left in the field, was virtually deputized by the 10th BCT to aid in the defeat of Sumulong. This was the "cover story" admitted by the 10th BCT commander, Lt. Col. Patricio Buyson, to an investigating congressional committee.

Since the scheme originated from Defense Secretary Macario Peralta, one of the key men in President Macapagal's reelection campaign in 1965, it was possible that Alibasbas' services were also being employed to insure the election of the President's younger brother, Angel "Star" Macapagal, for the second district seat.[16]

When some of the facts were later exposed in a hearing called by the House committee on national defense, they caused something of a scandal. The AFP sworn to fight Communism and other threats to national security was actually fraternizing with a ranking Huk commander and his followers. Colonel Buyson, who later had to face a court martial for this indiscretion, admitted having loaned Alibasbas firearms, transistorized walkie talkies, typewriters and other military equipment as part of an "integrated plan" to bust Sumulong.

Alibasbas, he testified, was accepted as an auxiliary force of the 10th BCT on the conditions that there would be "no

---

[14]Philippines *Herald,* Oct. 13, 1968. The PC had earlier charged Senator Aquino of "leading" a Huk raid in San Miguel, Tarlac.

[15]Philippines *Herald,* October 31, 1968.

[16]Philippines *Herald,* Aug. 3, 1966.

wanton killings of civilians," the Huks would refrain from asking for contributions except when necessary from the rich, and Buyson would direct his operations.

A corporal of the 28th PC company testified at the hearing that he had seen "Star" Macapagal, Alibasbas and two AFP men, Capt. Emilio Simbulan and Capt. Diosdado Peña, on the same platform at a political rally in barrio Balitukan, Arayat, Pampanga. Both Alibasbas and Captain Simbulan spoke at the rally. In another rally in Manalang town observed by the corporal, the Huk chieftain was introduced as Commander Alibasbas.[17]

Colonel Buyson and his fellow-accused were apparently victims of political circumstances. If President Macapagal had been reelected, he would not have had to go through this ordeal. "Operation Homestretch" would have been quietly buried in the capacious and often unfathomable AFP files. But Marcos became President and Colonel Buyson's neck was on the chopping block for his suspected complicity in the election of the defeated Liberal President's brother. More embarrassing for the colonel, Pampanga was one of the few provinces in Luzon which voted overwhelmingly for Macapagal. "Huk-coddling" was just the formal charge for the graver crime of playing politics — and not being on the winner's side.

The Ruling Elite

It is the supreme irony of Central Luzon politics that it continues to be dominated by wealthy landowners and millionaires after half a century of social upheaval. The agrarian revolution has barely gotten off the ground in its historic birthplace. The governor of Pampanga is also one of its wealthiest property owners. The mayor of Angeles, Eugenio Suarez, comes from a landed family and is a cousin of the governor, even if they occasionally quarrel over political advantage. Tarlac is the fiefdom of the Cojuangco clan. One branch represented by Eduardo (Danding) Cojuangco controls the Paniqui sugar mill and hacienda which spreads over a goodly portion of the first district. Jose (Peping) Cojuangco Jr.'s family "owns" another huge chunk of Tarlac including Hacienda Luisita, a 6,443-hectare domain worth about $25 million at current prices.

Danding and Peping are first cousins but outside of the common family interests, they go separate ways. The two Cojuangco families even own separate banks — The Philippine Bank of Commerce on Danding's side and the First United on Peping's.

[17]Same, Oct. 19 and 20, 1966.

The rivalry rose when Peping and Danding competed for Tarlac's first district seat in 1965. Tarlaqueños were simply deluged by largesse from the young millionaires. Peping outdid his cousin by spending a veritable fortune and won the election.

Danding bounced back by allying himself with President Marcos and capturing the governorship vacated by Ninoy Aquino.

In his year and eight months as governor, Danding lavished Malacañang-financed infrastructure on Tarlac, concreting highways, putting up a new drainage system for Tarlac town, and building feeder roads, public markets, a new concrete bridge linking Paniqui with Camiling and a new wing for the Tarlac general hospital. He was bent on fulfilling his congressional ambitions by spending more government funds in Tarlac than all previous governors. He succeeded in both, so the first district of Tarlac is represented in the House by another Cojuangco. The seat has been held by a member of the clan for three straight terms.

Ninoy Aquino is the most promising — and controversial — young politician to emerge from Central Luzon since the last war. His rise to national prominence has been meteoric, even in the Philippines where political dynasties abound and young heirs are rapidly moved up to positions of power. At 38, Ninoy is the likeliest successor to President Marcos in 1973. If he does reach that pinnacle, the Philippines would probably never be the same again.

The senator from Tarlac is the quintessence of the modern Pampango, quick-witted, combative, innovative and given to seizures of inspiration and enthusiasm. But his quicksilver temperament leaves many in doubt as to what really lies behind the political deftness. Is there substance behind the prodigality? Will Superboy grow up to be Superman?

Ninoy cannot be thoroughly explained without reference to his ancestry; the versatile Aquino clan has produced a revolutionary general and a chauvinist (the late Benigno Aquino, Sr.), leftists and rightists, landlords and Huks. Ninoy was fated to do something exceptionally well.

The young Aquino matched his father in one respect; he went up the political escalator in record time.[18]. They both married into wealth and used it to fight their political battles. But in other respects Benigno, Sr. and Benigno, Jr. are of two different molds. The first Senator Aquino was a gen-

[18]This account of the late Benigno Aquino, Sr.'s life and career was based on recollections by his daughter, Mila Aquino Albert, cousin Nina Estrada Puyat, and the young Senator Aquino himself.

tleman-politician of the old school, of clearly definable convictions and willing to pursue them to their logical and sometimes regrettable conclusions. His ultra-nationalism, more literal than what either Quezon or Osmeña dared profess, led to actions verging on collaboration with the Japanese. He collaborated not out of fear, cupidity or opportunity; he did so out of pride — he was no great lover of the colonizing whites — and out of conviction because he believed that history had passed the mandate to the Japanese.

The original model after which Ninoy planned his tightly calendared political ascent was his father's career. After finishing his A. B. in Letran and his law at U.S.T., Benigno, Sr. ran for Congress in 1919 at the age of 25, served for three terms and in the last six of those years (1922-1928) as Majority Floor Leader. In 1928 he ran for the Senate at the age of 34 and won by one of the biggest margins ever recorded by any candidate.

In trying to match his father's feat, Ninoy endangered his Senate victory by being just 13 days shy of the required 35 years of age. The Nacionalista party legal panel headed by J. Antonio Araneta hounded Ninoy with this legal technicality all the way to Election Day. The Supreme Court saved Aquino by affirming that he took office not on the day he was elected, November 14, 1967, but 30 days later when he was proclaimed. The furor probably did Aquino no serious injury for he came close to topping the Senate slate (he was No. 2) while the NP's were sweeping the boards elsewhere.

Benigno, Sr. joined the Osmeña-Roxas faction during the 1931 NP split — he was the Os-Rox team's only anchor in Luzon. After the Commonwealth was proclaimed he was back with Quezon as Secretary of Agriculture, Commerce and Industry, heading a huge bureaucracy that encompassed offices belonging to two separate departments today. He might have become President himself were it not for his unfortunate wartime affiliations and his untimely death just after the war.

Comparing father and son, some Aquino clansmen say, *"Malayo pa si Ninoy"* ("Ninoy has still far to go"). What Ninoy still has to attain is the *image* of statesmanship; he has much of the raw components already.

Ninoy, the son of Benigno, Sr.'s second wife, the former Doña Aurora Aquino, had three things going for him at the start. He had that quixotic clan history behind him; he married a Cojuangco; he was himself a youth of no mean talents, energetic, capable of being directed at a dozen separate enterprises all at once, a catholic mind that entertains with equal facility the most *avant-garde* political theories and the mindless trivia that usually fills up a politician's day.

Probably his strongest faculty is his prodigious capacity to absorb and retain information. He had that capacity when still a child. During the Japanese Occupation, Ninoy was the "messenger boy" of the large and far-flung Aquino clan. He would be fed a complex set of information and, without the benefit of notes, directed to convey it to other family members. Ninoy rarely garbled a message.

In 1950, Ninoy quit his Litt. B. studies at the Ateneo de Manila to join the Manila *Times*. He was no exceptional wordsmith but his enterprise was prodigious. He made a name for himself as a war correspondent covering the Philippine Expeditionary Force in Korea. He scored what was probably the journalistic coup of the decade by bringing Luis Taruc out of the hills in 1954.

In 1955, he bid for a government-auctioned property in the far end of Magao near the Chico river and found himself in politics with the mayorship of Concepcion as his first target. It was a three-cornered fight, with Gorgonio Narciso, the incumbent mayor and a former Huk, holding most of the barrios in thrall with a promise to give away land to the farmers; Nicolas Feliciano who controlled the *poblacion;* and Ninoy, the duly-proclaimed NP candidate, claiming the barrios of Murcia, San Francisco, Magao, Castillo, Tinang, Sta. Rita and Sta. Rosa where the family influence was still strong.[19]

Ninoy, barely 22, scored a remarkable victory, winning over most of the intelligent voters in the barrios while Feliciano was kept out of the bushes by Narciso's Huk friends.

In 1959 he aspired for the governorship. Warned that he would split the NP in Tarlac if he did so, he settled for the vice governor's slot to accommodate Gov. Arsenio Lugay's wish to be reelected. There was an understanding with President Garcia that in two years Lugay would be given an executive position in Manila and Ninoy appointed in his place. In 1961 Lugay was appointed Secretary of General Services and Ninoy moved into the governor's chair.

In 1963, Ninoy capitulated to the enticements of President Macapagal and was elected to the governorship as a Liberal. "I was promised the LP leadership in Tarlac and five million pesos for the province," Ninoy recalled. "That was a bargain nobody could resist. I flipped."[20]

Aquino had to live with the Huks for they were an ineradicable presence in his constituency. "They left me alone as long as I left them alone." The Huks respected the Aquino name. "They will never forget how his relatives served

[19]Senator Aquino, interview, July, 1970.

[20]As a Liberal governor, Aquino ran for reelection against his former party mate, Lugay, and won handily.

the cause," one Tarlac informant said.

Aquino subdivided his own personal farmlands among poor tenants and made his help available to any constituent in distress — Huk or otherwise.

How does Ninoy reconcile his "radical" politics with being part of the Tarlac aristocracy and married to a Cojuangco?

Ninoy met that issue in characteristic rapid-fire order in an interview with Quijano de Manila of the Philippines *Free Press:*[21]

> My grandfather was landed but between 1919 and 1945 our family lost 80 percent of those holdings because of my father's continuous political battles. When my father died he had no lands, they had been taken over by the Cojuangcos of Tarlac or the De Leons of Pampanga. What little land remains with us belongs to my mother.
>
> Also in 1955 I married into a family that's landed. I only married the daughter, I did not marry their property. This family, at my urging, has offered to unload their agricultural lands in exchange for shares in any government corporation. Or, better still, just buy them out. But the government has no money.

"Peping (Cojuangco) is willing to sell Luisita if he has to," Ninoy said. "*Our* side of the clan is not irrevocably committed to keeping its plantations in Tarlac." His wife's brothers and sisters have chosen other than agricultural pursuits. They are bankers, businessmen and professionals. Typical of the Pampango elites, Ninoy's Cojuangcos have elected to seek new careers and new fortunes outside the ancestral province.[22]

The thought that Ninoy Aquino may be president in 1973 alarms some Filipino conservatives. Ninoy himself concedes a modest possibility to this fulfillment. "In 1973, Gerry (Senator Roxas) and myself will agree on an independent research organization. We shall poll our popularity. Whoever wins will be the presidential candidate the other will be vice president. We are a *reversible* team, Gerry from the south, me from the north."

Another factor is the condition of the times. "If it's a time of prosperity and contentment, I imagine Gerry would be the best for President. But if it's a tumultuous time, I may be it."[23]

---

[21]Aug. 15, 1970.
[22]Interview, July, 1970.
[23]Same.

The 1969 Elections

The 1969 elections can serve as a case study of the political behavior of the various Central Luzon "actors" under the circumstances previously described.

Pampanga was one province Marcos wanted firmly in the Nacionalista column. It was bombarded with community development and social welfare funds. The First Lady, Mrs. Imelda R. Marcos, gave Pampanga her "whole attention," sending her own lieutenants to work on the doubtful towns. She visited the province twice to personally present ₱2,000 checks for barrio development to the barrio captains. Ernesto Maceda, the youthful Presidential Assistant for Community Development, helped Governor Nepomuceno coordinate the NP campaign.

Marcos, one of the shrewdest and most masterful political tacticians the Philippines has ever produced, probably realized the futility of beating Sumulong on his own homeground. According to many Pampanga informants, persons close to Malacañang struck a bargain with Sumulong, offering him protection in exchange for his political support. A cabinet officer served as "liaison" with Sumulong. If this story is true, it would have been almost a replay of the government's "fraternization" with Alibasbas in 1965.

In Sumulong's case, it might have been a matter of not having any other alternative. His organization was still reeling from the defection of Dante and his entire Tarlac organization. At the same time, he was engaged in a power struggle with Governor Nepomuceno for effective control over Pampanga politics. If he had to oppose Malacañang as well, he could well have had conceded defeat.

Sumulong placed his grassroots prestige on the line by supporting the Marcos ticket. He was seen riding a jeep around Pampanga with Marcos-Lopez propaganda while the PC, which showed equally partisan leanings, left him unmolested. As if to confirm the order of the day, the Angeles City government which was branded as pro-Sumulong endorsed the President as well.

Neither Marcos nor Osmeña found it expedient to campaign personally in Pampanga. Malacañang security officials claimed there were Huk and Muslim assassin bands out to liquidate the President. The Chief Executive prudently left out Pampanga and Sulu from his campaign itinerary. Osmeña tactfully kept his person out of Pampanga since former President Diosdado Macapagal, Pampanga's most prominent Liberal party leader, was distinctly cool towards him because of the cavalier treatment given him by the Osmeña partisans in the Liberal party convention.

The personal impact of the two candidates was consequently minimal. The outcome of the elections in Pampanga was a gut reaction to its own internal trials and agonies.

The Pampanga vote was the surprise of the entire 1969 election outside of the sheer magnitude of President Marcos' victory. He won an unprecedented second full term with an equally unprecedented margin of 5,013,817 votes to Osmeña's 3,042,093 — a majority of almost 62 percent. There was only one of 52 provinces of the Philippines where Marcos lost and it was in Pampanga. And in that dissident-prone province the President was beaten by an astonishing 34,801 votes to the 85,292 votes recorded for Osmeña. All Pampanga towns except Mexico voted against the President.[24]

Osmeña's running mate, Sen. Genaro Magsaysay, had an even bigger spread than Osmeña's — he beat Vice-President Fernando Lopez by 103,176 to 35,865 votes. (The extra votes of Magsaysay suggest that a good number of Pampanga voters saw no viable choice between the two presidential candidates and did not vote for the top national office.)

Why Pampanga's offbeat poll behavior? Political pundits believe that the Pampangos used their ballots to express their disgust and bitterness over the unleashing of "Monkee" terror and the lack of sincerity in the administration's Central Luzon policy. It was not that they liked Serging Osmeña better — Osmeña's crusty conservatism could scarcely be appealing to radical Pampangos — but that they loathed Marcos more. The fact that Pampanga managed to express this "negative" vote despite the obvious partiality of the PC was by itself a token of the ability of Pampango to defy the powers-that-be.

More surprising was the apparent ignoring of Sumulong's endorsement by those he claimed as his constituents. His popular hold might have slipped or this remarkable outcome might be explained by the fact that Filipino voters as a rule feel obliged to support the local candidates of their "liders'" but not necessarily the one they propose for national office.

In the congressional elections, there were no clearly drawn "pro-Huk" and "anti-Huk" lines. In fact, there was a veritable stampede of candidates — 14 in the second district and seven in the first district of Pampanga — which suggested that the Huks were not aggressively backing anyone in particular. A few of the aspirants were obviously emitting pro-Huk signals as if to invite Sumulong's support. One candidate, for instance, plastered his area with "Make Love, Not War" posters.

Sumulong's major interest in the congressional races

---

[24]Commission on Election, Dec. 1969.

seemed to be in working for the defeat of the first district's incumbent congresswoman, Juanita Nepomuceno, the wife of his arch foe. But his own candidate lost to Jose Lingad, the former anti-Huk governor of Pampanga. Sumulong was a little more successful in the second district. Cornelio Sanga of San Simon and Rogelio Tiglao of Magalang were said to be both acceptable to the Huks, and they topped the electoral free-for-all. Sanga won the seat after a recount of some protested returns.

Lingad's victory was a tribute in large part to his political acumen. He broke several "myths" about Pampanga politics. He did not have Iglesia ni Cristo backing, he did not have the endorsement of former President Macapagal, he had no fortune to spend, he declined to use terror methods — and he still won.

Lingad conceded Angeles, Mabalacat, Masantol and other areas of "Sumulong country" to the Huk-coddlers. Porac, a Nepomuceno stronghold, he gave up to the congresswoman. He zeroed his campaign on "middle" Pampanga — towns like Lubao, Guagua, Bacolor, Sexmoan and Floridablanca which were not only standing aloof from the Sumulong-Nepomuceno rivalry but had large voting populations in the bargain.

Since Dante was generally expected to boycott the presidential elections in 1969, it was something of a surprise when his commanders came out for Senator Osmeña in the last two or three weeks of the campaign. Osmeña won in Dante's territory, the second district of Tarlac, but not anywhere as overwhelmingly as in Pampanga. The Liberal candidate polled 31,072 votes to the President's 22,594. In the first district, controlled by former Tarlac governor Eduardo Cojuangco, Marcos won a resounding victory of 53,484 to 12,-415 votes to place the whole province in the NP column.

Again, Huk influence on the national elections was marginal. The decisive factor in the second district seemed to be the unpopularity of the government's "mailed fist" policy which hurt the well-being of the Tarlac communities more than it did its intended Huk targets. PC partisanship and outright acts of terrorism suspectedly encouraged by the government reduced Osmeña's potential gains in that district.

According to PC intelligence, a week before the election Dante summoned five of his top commanders — Melody, Madrigal, Joe, Quinez and Ligaya — for a conference in barrio Pitabunan, Concepcion, Tarlac to discuss the national and local candidates to be supported by the movement.[25]

In the hour-long meeting, the conferees were unanimously in favor of Osmeña but divided between Liberal reelectionist Jose V. Yap and independent candidate Max G. Llorente.

---

[25]Amante Reyes.

Yap got into office with the help of the "Huk vote" but towards the end of his term the Maoist elements in Dante's camp accused him of not being sufficiently cooperative in denouncing PC abuses. Though Yap was "progressive" in his convictions, there were certain limits beyond which he could not expose himself as a defender of the Huks. Thus, he entered the hustings uncertain about his standing with the movement.

Llorente, a well-known Tarlac lawyer, built up a large following among the Huks by interceding in behalf of persons brought to Camp Makabulos for suspected dissident activities. When nine private security guards were massacred by Monkees, Llorente volunteered his legal services for the survivors.

Dante's men apparently compromised by allowing certain areas for Yap and others for Llorente. According to *Herald* correspondent Amante Reyes, the barrio people "were at a loss whether to vote for Yap or Llorente because the Huk commanders themselves violated territorial limits in a mad attempt at making their respective choices win."

Political supporters of Llorente, however, suspected that his Huk support was "half-hearted." In all likelihood, Llorente was just made a "front" to draw votes away from the NP independent candidate Rafael Ramos and the NP official candidate Tomas Matic, Jr. The Llorente backers added that the areas given by the Huks to Yap were bigger in voting strength than those alloted to Llorente.

Yap was reelected by an unexpectedly large plurality of 19,748 votes. Matic polled the next highest, 11,809, and poor Llorente, who stuck his neck out a mile for Dante, came out third with 11,755. A more unfortunate aftermath for Llorente was his near-assassination by what could have been a band of vengeful Monkees in Tarlac town shortly after his defeat.

Hard and Soft Politics

In discussing Central Luzon politics, one has to make a distinction between "hard" politics and "soft" politics. A hard politician declares a program and executes it immediately. Soft politics tends to express itself in terms of affective, unspecified promises of reform and achievement usually without consequent performance.

Central Luzon politics tends to be largely of the latter type. The local officials, aware of the near-unsolvability of the Huk problem, tend to yield the initiative to the national government. The national government has blown hot and cold on the Huks, depending on the temperament and relative sincerity of whoever is in power. Various Central Luzon "programs" have been put into effect but these are of doubtful merit since whatever the government is doing is not enough. The crush-the-Huks school is equally unrealistic because it is based on the erroneous assumption that killing dissidents would solve the dissident problem.

The situation suggests that the Huks and the political establishment somehow complement each other and that few seriously want to change the *modus vivendi.*

Chapter Thirteen

TERROR AND COUNTERTERROR

Ambuscades, assassinations and kidnapings have been part of the Central Luzon scene since the agrarian troubles began. Many of these acts of violence can be attributed to the Huks. Both Sumulong and Dante had highly skilled liquidation squads which could track down and execute their victims for "crimes" against the movement. When a man is marked for death, his days are numbered unless he flees his home or surrounds himself with bodyguards. His pursuers are patient; they can wait for years until they find the opportunity. Village folk tell of men who mysteriously disappear and are presumably killed for offenses committed as far back as ten years previous.

For a long time, terror had been the exclusive weapon of the Huks. But in 1969, a new dimension was added to the climate of fear in Central Luzon. Other groups began to use precisely the same tactics of assassination and reprisal. Pampangos believed that these armed killers were in the hire of the government. Someone called them the "Monkees" (after the popular singing group) and the name stuck. Their Huk counterparts, naturally were known as the "Beatles." In 1969, the Monkees and the Beatles went on a rampage of terror and counterterror that left the whole of Pampanga in a state of fear.

Between the "demilitarization" of Central Luzon in late November, 1968 and October, 1969, 113 persons were killed in Pampanga and 147 in Tarlac.[1] It is not easy to determine which of the killings were perpetuated by the Monkees, which by the Huks and which by other agents. Some of the violence could have been due to personal motives, not at all related to the unrest.

But the fact that 95 percent of these killings are either unsolved or unsolvable strengthens the conviction that hired guns are indeed on the loose in Central Luzon and the authorities are almost powerless to stop their depredations.

Recent events have heightened the credibility of the Monkee scare. Many took the story lightly until Angeles City Councilor Benjamin Serrano was gunned down right inside the Angeles City Hall. His death was charged to pro-

[1]Briefing by 1st PC zone intelligence.

fessional assassins organized by the Constabulary.

There followed in stunning succession the killing of known Huk "coddlers" — Angeles Police Capt. Ben Cato, Lt. Ben Salas, Capt. Israel Lao and his brother Efraim. Still another victim was the popular Angeles Councilor, Jose Roman, just after he had criticized PC abuses on the radio and in the press.

The Angeles Raid

Something new was added to the repertory of the terrorists. It was called "spraying." At 10:15 p.m. on May 21, 1969, eight jeeploads of armed men, clad in black and with nylon hose over their heads, drove into downtown Angeles, passing through alleys to avoid detection. When they got to Bagumbayan, they fired at several loungers at a police outpost, killing one of them. They tore through the heart of the city, blasting away Wild West-style at the streets and houses on their way. The indiscriminate bursts hit a couple already asleep in their house, killing the husband.

From Bagumbayan, the motorized killers cruised down Francisco street peppering shanties on both sides. Another man and a hostess working in one of the Angeles dives were killed. Two others were injured. Coming out on Henson street, the raiders split up into two groups of four jeeps each, one turning towards the highway diversion road and the other heading towards Marisol village.

The group that went to the diversion road briefly traded bullets with a PC patrol headed by Maj. Teotimo Tangonan of the 172nd PC Company. The major's driver was hurt in the first exchange and three other PC troopers were injured but the raiders were forced to abandon a jeep.

By an odd coincidence, Brig. Gen. Emilio Zerrudo was just passing by Angeles in an armored car when the firing started. A *Herald* news story quoted him as saying that. He told the *Herald* that he proceeded to the 172nd Co. Headquarters to "direct" the PC reaction.

Neither the PC nor the Angeles police reacted fast enough to block the escape of the raiders. They escaped except for the driver of the disabled jeep whom the PC subsequently used as their source for the identities and motivations of the black-clad commandos.[2]

The following day, Lt. Col. Julito Lamayo, chief of PC zone intelligence, officially identified the attackers as members of Dante's command.[3] In his report to President Mar-

[2]Philippines *Herald,* May 23 and 24, 1968.

[3]Col. Lamayo was killed under strange circumstances on October 20, 1970. He was invited to the U.S. Navy communications

cos, General Zerrudo indirectly blamed the Angeles council for opposing an increase in the troop commitment in the city.

That could have closed the case except for a few bothersome inconsistencies in the PC's official version. It was a little too much of a coincidence for General Zerrudo to show up in Angeles in an armored car only minutes after the shooting started. The reason given for the escape of the entire band of raiders was the element of surprise. But at least one newspaper account described the raid as lasting an hour. Even if it had lasted just 30 minutes, the PC troopers on detail could have snapped out of their trance in time to block at least some of the escaping killers. It was also inconceivable that a motorcade of masked men with rifles could have escaped the notice of the pursuing PC patrols.

The "official report" submitted by Zerrudo to the President now looks on hindsight highly suspect. The general claimed that Commander Madrigal, one of Dante's trusted leaders, joined up with Commander Fonting, Sumulong's most feared trigger man, and undertook a joint operation against Angeles. By May 22, when the report was handed in, Dante had already formed his New People's Army and was fighting against Sumulong and his band. It was highly inconceivable even for Madrigal and Fonting to say hello to each other, much less team up in a suicidal stunt like the May 21st raid.

Angeles officials charged that the raid was pulled off by Monkees with the knowledge of the PC and their motive was to loosen Sumulong's grip on the city. This was just one of the many outbreaks of violence that may never be settled to the satisfaction of everyone.

While the PC authorities vehemently denied the presence of the Monkees, rumors persisted that they not only got arms and money directly from the military but were also backed by Malacañang.

Unconventional Warfare: The PMU's

Admitting the employment of professional killers would

---

station in Camp O'Donnel, Capas, Tarlac, by Mabalacat councilor Gerardo Perez who owns the security agency guarding the facility. Apparently without provocation, Perez's companion, Leonardo Concepcion, pulled out a pistol and shot to death Col. Lamayo, a Capas policeman and a U.S. Navy serviceman. Concepcion was killed by security men a few minutes after the incident. The PC charged Commander Dante with masterminding the assassination. Perez, however, offered the theory that Concepcion who had been drinking with the rest of the party simply went "berserk."

open the PC and the administration to charges of conducting a reign of terror in Central Luzon. Privately, Camp Olivas brass defended the usefulness and need of what they call "unconventional warfare."

"It's like a basketball game where we have to wear uniforms and follow all the rules while the other side dresses like spectators and commits all sorts of foul tactics," a high-ranking officer told a *Herald* team in Camp Olivas. "How can you expect the AFP to win when it's the other side breaking all the rules and we can't?"

Counter-insurgency justifies the use of terror tactics in retaliation for those of the enemy, the officer explained.

While Camp Olivas never officially admitted sending killers on specific assassination missions, it disclosed not long ago the existence of a large force of para-military units (PMU's) helping birddog critical areas.

According to the late intelligence officer Lt. Col. Julito Lamayo, the PC had 305 civilian agents on its intelligence payroll. Most of the PMU's were stationed in the two Huk-infested provinces of Tarlac and Pampanga.

Lamayo said the PMU's were civilians whose anti-Huk posture had made them the target of dissident vengeance. Given logistical support, the PMU's could protect themselves and at the same time feed the PC intelligence mill. The PMU's were always placed under the close supervision of a non-commissioned officer and never allowed to operate with their arms outside their jurisdiction.

When President Marcos witnessed the signing of the memorandum of agreement placing the responsibility of peace and order primarily in the hands of civil authorities, he ordered the termination of the services of these 305 civilian agents.

It is known that many PMU's were subsequently disbanded. The recall of some of these appointments had tragic consequences. Deprived of arms, known PC agents became vulnerable to Huk reprisals. Some of them had to leave their homes for safer domiciles.

But it is also known that the PC continues to maintain a network of informers in the barrios. This is quite obvious from the fact that Task Force Lawin has been getting good results in its surprise raids. Whether the PC covert operations include the use of the Monkees is something about which the civilian populace can only speculate.

The Monkees have become part of the everyday lives of the people. When children engage in their war games, one side inevitably calls itself the Monkees and the other the Beatles. The innocent play of the children only reflects a real fear harbored by their parents.

Town officials continue to denounce the deviltry of the Monkees. "I am not making any comment about the Monkees." said the spokesman of Angeles Mayor Eugenio Suarez, "but the fact remains that on May 21 our city was raided by armed men and innocent civilians fired upon. I condemn this act as the work of a mad man."

The spokesman, Atty. Alfredo Pineda, headed a committee created by then acting Mayor Ramon H. Arcilla to investigate the incident. The committee included City Fiscal Eller D. Torres and Chief of Police Democrito Lumanlan. The committee's findings were the grounds for the filing of criminal charges against 44 persons. Seven of them were identified. The case is docketed as CC No. C-69-158 in the Angeles City court.

The victims of terror — whether perpetrated by the Monkees, Beatles or Huks — are the hundreds of civilians in the critical areas.

When someone is killed people look at each other fearfully, shake their heads and wonder why and by whom the victim was executed. On the very day the *Herald* team visited Tarlac town, the body of Adolfo David, a landlord, was found in barrio Balincunaway. The killers took his jeep. Monkees or Huks? Or was it just plain robbery with murder?

Monkee terror now seems concentrated in southern Tarlac, which significantly is also the new zeroing-in point of the PC's counter-insurgency drive. Tarlac has never been the same since Vice-Gov. Nicolas Y. Feliciano was shot to death on the stairs of the capitol. His slaying remains unsolved up to now.

August 22, 1969 was a particularly harrowing day in barrio Caromatan, La Paz, Tarlac. At 8 p.m. seven armed men riding tricycles sprayed the house of Armando Rivera, a public works liaison officer for Tarlac. Rivera lay flat on the floor and escaped the fusillade, but his wife Visitacion and his son Audy were killed, along with a visitor, Teodoro Labanao. Another son, Dick, was wounded.

Thirty minutes later, armed men riding a jeep stopped two tricycles and shot to death one of the tricycle drivers and wounded a student riding in the other tricycle.

The following morning, two residents of barrio Comillas, La Paz, Gaudencio Buan and Francisco Bondoc, were mowed down by unknown men while waiting for a ride in front of a service station in Tarlac town.[4]

Monkees or Beatles? One could only guess.

Though all these killings were mystifying to the Manila

---

[4]Philippines *Herald,* Aug. 23, 1969.

press, the Tarlaqueños knew who were responsible for the carnage. In more cases than not, they pointed to the Monkees. The dead giveaway was the known sympathies of murder victims. If they were suspected to favor the Huks, the killers must have been none other than the Monkees. The Huks were the natural suspects if the victims were known to be PC informers.

The circumstances of execution also provided a clue to the authors. Huk victims invariably disappear and their deaths confirmed only when their corpses are dug up in some remote canefield. The Huks prefer to deal out justice quietly if only for their own protection. The Monkees, "licensed to kill" by either their political patrons or the PC, tend to perform in a more spectacular manner like "spraying" or streetside assassination.

Because they lead lives of extreme peril, Huks have to be a highly disciplined band of operatives. There were a few trigger-happy ones among them like Commander Tapang and Commander Melody. But more commonly, the Huks are discreet and quiet in carrying out their missions.

By contrast, the goon squads are recruited from the scum of society. They are ex-convicts, psychopaths, and even rejects from the Huk organization. They have no scruples about killing and they kill for the merest cause.

One of the hired guns of a prominent Pampanga politician was rescued by his patron from the Pampanga provincial jail. He reportedly landed there for impersonating a Huk commander. His aide is a similar type who was bailed from jail.[5]

Violence begets violence.

The shootup of Porac town on November 17, 1969 set off such a sequence of terrorism. Three jeeploads of men shot at a Porac police outpost, wounding three policemen including Chief Isabelo Limsin. Eight unintended victims including some attending a religious procession were killed by the surprise attack.

This was one of the rare instances of an indiscriminate "spray" job by the Huks. Its apparent motive was to get back at Governor Nepomuceno who was in control of the Porac police force. The incident apparently led to a "civil war" between the Porac and Angeles police forces. Two Angeles policemen were mowed down on the streets in a counter-raid. The Angeles-based Huks struck back by ambushing one of

---

[5]The source of this information was possibly biased since he belonged to the opposing political camp. But the unsavory reputation of the two bodyguards referred to was largely confirmed by other witnesses.

Nepomuceno's men, Samuel Lintag, near the U.S. air base. The waylayers fired a grenade-launcher into Lintag's jeep and blew it up, killing Lintag and two of his companions.

The vendetta affected even obvious non-participants. One day a group of men drove up to a road construction crew in Angeles, asked the workers where they came from and when one said he was from barrio Pampanga, he was shot dead.

The alarmed citizens of Angeles had to convene a "Peace and Order Council" to get the feuding principals to desist from further violence.

Each new incident sends tremors of apprehension through the civilian populace. Last January, Tarlac policemen reported the capture of Felicisimo Jayme, a suspected Monkee, in barrio Barut. In his possession was an identification card issued by the Camp Olivas intelligence chief, designating him as a civilian agent. He is reportedly still in the provincial jail, facing charges of murdering the barrio captain of Barut.

Tarlac Mayor Lino David, who is believed to have considerable Huk support, was the target of a hand grenade thrown over the wall of his house. David told the *Herald* that at least 50 Monkees were loose in his municipality. Even granting the understandable prejudices of Mayor David, Tarlac residents do not regard his fears as too far exaggerated.

After nightfall, few Tarlac residents venture out in the streets. They fear the mysterious men in plainclothes carrying long arms, sometimes riding in jeeps with government plates. Response to the last elections was without the usual zest. Few candidates went to the barrios unless accompanied by bodyguards. Up to late September, 1969 none of them were holding public rallies. "You could be an inviting target if you stand up on that stage," one congressional candidate commented.

Cutcut was a peaceful barrio before its *capitan* Angel Supan was killed. One night, he was dragged out of a *spiritista* chapel by three armed men and riddled with bullets some thirty yards from his home. The following morning the whole barrio folk packed up and evacuated to safer places.

It was unbelievable that a thing like this was happening. People had not evacuated from barrios since the last war. In September, 1969, the barrio of Motrico was abandoned by its residents after a PC raid uncovered an elaborate network of tunnels where many Huk documents and propaganda were hidden. The Motrico residents trickled back after a few days. But the exodus out of Cutcut lasted a whole week. When the *Herald* reporters came to the barrio accompanied by Hacienda Luisita manager Tom Henson, some of the residents were only beginning to return to their homes.

Such was the demoralization of the Cutcut residents that the first councilor declined to assume the job vacated by the slain captain. Asked why, Councilor Remigio Katigbak explained that he was "too young" for the responsibilities of the job. He was 27. The councilor next in line did not seem eager, either, to assume the position.

If barrio officials shirk their duties out of fear, something must be wrong. Terror may be keeping the Huks on the run but in the process the very innards of rural society are being destroyed.

Chapter Fourteen

THE MILITARY RESPONSE

The part played by the Armed Forces in Central Luzon entails much controversy. The AFP had its successes and its failures. Its greatest success was in rolling back the 1950 rebellion without intervention of American troops. But the Huk movement regenerated itself and in the late sixties the AFP was once again engaging the Huks in fratricidal blood-letting in Pampanga and Tarlac. It was in these last few years of the renewed conflict that the AFP came under sharp criticism for failing in its anti-Huk mission.

More precisely, it was the Philippine Constabulary and not the entire defense establishment whose performance came in doubt. The PC had taken over the responsibility for keeping the peace in Central Luzon since the mid-fifties. Other service branches, the Air Force, the Navy and the Marines are marginally involved if at all in the Central Luzon assignment; the Philippine Army combat units operate in the area under the tactical control of the First PC Zone headquarters in Camp Olivas. However, the Armed Forces of the Philippines command, and the civilian government that is supposed to supervise the military have to take the credit or blame for how these various units perform.

Search and Destroy

The government used two basic strategies to combat the Huks. The Philippine Constabulary, supplemented by crack Philippine Army units, were positioned in strength in critical towns and barrios to reduce the movements and mass base-organizing of the Huks. At the same time, the AFP commissioned Task Force Lawin made up of detachable units from these PC and PA commands to conduct mobile operations against the Huks in the classic search-and-destroy manner of the American forces in Vietnam.

Watching the most sensitive area of all, the southern towns of Tarlac, was the 51st PC Battalion made up of three battle-toughened PC Ranger companies. The 551st PC Co. was stationed in Concepcion, the 512th in Capas and the 513th in La Paz. Supplementing the Rangers was the Tarlac PC Command under Lt. Col. Romeo Gatan. It had the 181st PC Co. posted in Tarlac and the 183rd in Victoria.

They were engaging the wiliest Huk commander of all, Dante, and the remnants of his harassed New People's Army.[1]

The Pampanga PC command had four companies garrisoned in the most populous towns — the 172nd and the Service Company in San Fernando, the 173rd in Angeles and the 174th in Arayat.

The Philippine Army's contributions to the anti-Huk effort were two units which served nobly in the Korean War. The 10th Batallion Combat Team covered Angeles, Mabalacat, Magalang and Arayat. The 20th BCT had its headquarters in Bahay Pare, Candaba, and covered the southeastern reaches of the province.

Marine volunteers patrolled the rivers and swamps of Candaba while the Air Force conducted reconnaissance missions and lent helicopter support during field operations.

Task Force Lawin could call upon 1,000 to 2,000 officers and men for anti-Huk missions. The first PC Zone, based in San Fernando, Pampanga, was administratively responsible for keeping the peace not only in Central Luzon but in the whole of Northern Luzon as well. It had another 3,000 men in the geographical region of Central Luzon including Bulacan, Rizal, Nueva Ecija and Pangasinan. But for all practical purposes they could not be used in the Huk campaign. The units in non-critical areas were tied down by normal policing work.

This gave the AFP an effective manpower ratio of four soldiers to one dissident, if the combined Huk forces could be estimated at 500. This was far less than the minimum 10-to-1 ratio required for a successful counter-insurgency campaign.

The Central Luzon situation, of course, was not "insurgency" of the aggressive, widespread type in Vietnam. The AFP units were rarely attacked in force and most of the action occurred when the troopers went out into the field to seek out the enemy.

Lawin made up for its modest standing force by operating a wide intelligence network, creating "home defense forces" in the barrios willing to resist Huk encroachments and conducting psychological warfare.

Its most successful operations have resulted from good coordination between intelligence "tips" and swift troop deployments around areas where Huks are suspected to be present. The AFP got Tapang, Sumulong's most feared killer, in that manner, in June, 1969.

General Zerrudo, then 1st PC Zone commander, got strong signals from the bamboo telegraph that Dante and

---

[1]This deployment was as of mid-1970.

Sumulong were going into a huddle in sitio Dapa, barrio San Agustin, Magalang. A large force from the 10th BCT and PC units promptly moved into the small settlement not far from the Magalang agricultural school. Lawin Commander, Col. Roso Saballones, and both Col. Mario Kimseng, then 10th BCT commanding officer, and his executive officer and subsequent successor, Lieutenant Colonel Castro, were directing the operation — an indication that the AFP was after big game.[2]

The barrio captain at first denied there were Huks in the hamlet. The settlement seemed quiet and normal. Some of the troopers took a break and bought cigarettes and soft drinks from the village store.

But the alert officers and soon the troopers themselves noticed barrio people slipping out of their houses, looking frightened. *"May laman yata,"* ("There must be somebody in there"), they whispered among themselves.

While the 10th BCT stood on the village road, Commander Tapang and his men lay quietly in three or four houses, their guns trained on the troopers. Seven of them were in the house next to the *visita* (chapel) within spitting distance of the 10th BCT brass. "They could have killed at least 50 of us if they wanted to," Col. Castro recalled with a slight shiver.

Tapang of course, was not so much interested in the 10th BCT scalps as he was in escaping. He probably thought he was out of danger when he saw the soldiers moving away from the sitio.

Actually, the 10th BCT only pretended to withdraw. They deployed themselves in blocking position around the sitio. When Tapang saw through the ruse, he opened fire with his Armalite at the troopers near his hideout.

In a show of sheer bravado, the trapped Huk commander shouted at the soldiers to "surrender." When the AFP officers shouted back that he was surrounded and further resistance futile, Tapang delivered the parting line foı which he may be long remembered by his surviving colleagues: "Huks never surrender."

Tapang was felled in the first skirmish at 4 p.m. His body was identified by a spectacular tattoo of an eagle covering his chest where he received his mortal wound.

Five of Tapang's men were killed in sporadic firing that broke out during the night. When morning came, the troopers moved into the houses to recover the bodies of the slain Huks. A Huk amazon, Flor Gatchalian, and another

---

[2]This account of the Tapang operation was based on newspaper stories and an interview with Lt. Col. Bienvenido Castro, CO, 10th BCT.

Huk suspect were held captive.

General Zerrudo believed that Tapang met his end because he did not get out of the sitio in time. It was possible that he gave up his life to allow even more important Huk leaders time to flee the AFP trap. Dante and Sumulong? The full story is yet to be known.

The AFP's first frontal clash with Dante's men in Mabalacat in September, 1969, again demonstrated the quick reaction and combat skill of the Lawin troopers.

It came about when a "walk-in informant" notified the 10th BCT headquarters of the presence of Huk activity in barrio Baluarte. The tip came at about 10 a.m. on September 24. In a matter of hours elements from the 10th's three companies ringed the area. A PC company was called in for support and an armored personnel carrier (APC) from the 51st PC Battalion was rolled into battle position for extra firepower.

At four in the afternoon, a team from Charlie Company under Capt. Francisco Romboa trailed the Huks into a canefield and engaged them in the first firefight. One Huk was killed outright in the first action and possibly another. The second Huk's body was recovered the following day.

The only casualties sustained by the Army were three soldiers slightly injured in that first exchange. Since it was getting dark, the 10th BCT commander called off further action and ordered his men to keep an all night vigil in their positions of encirclement. Colonel Castro could have finished off the trapped Huks the same afternoon but he did not want to risk unnecessary casualties.

Just before daybreak, several of the trapped Huks made a dash for freedom. Two of them were mowed down by the soldiers who were waiting for such a move. Another Huk was accounted for when he launched a suicidal attack on an armored jeep. He was shredded by a burst from a .50 cal. machinegun mounted atop the army vehicle.

That made it five Huk fatalities against three soldiers injured. Not a bad score for the day. However, an undetermined number of Huks possibly including Commander Juaning, slipped out of the trap sometime during the night or early morning. There was a likelihood that the two Huks killed in the dawn action acted as decoys for the successful breakout of their commanders.

Given a chance to prove its mettle, the Army can perform creditably. Its officers and men are courageous, even daring. Colonel Sanson, the former 51st Battalion commander, was in the habit of driving on lonely barrio roads at night with only a jeepload of escorts. He deliberately exposed himself as a "bait" for a Huk ambush.

The AFP has vastly greater mobility than the enemy. In Mabalacat, the 10th BCT sprang a cordon of 300 men around the Huks before the latter knew what was happening.

As had been pointed out, the AFP does not have a decisive advantage in weaponry over the Huks man for man. There are only 200 Armalites (provided by the U.S.) issued among three Battalions. The PC and Army standard weapons are still the World War II Garand rifle and carbine.

Task Force Lawin can call upon the services of two armored personnel carriers. The Lawin APC's are nicknamed "Lapu Lapu" and "Lakandula." Lawin acquired extra mobility with the use of its helicopters.

The first helicopter raid was staged against a Huk encampment in Sapang Tagalog, San Miguel, Tarlac early in the morning of November 28, 1969. Three Huk suspects fell into the hands of the airborne raiders. The troopers also seized three Thompson submachineguns, two carbines and a load of propaganda material.[3]

It was only a matter of time before the Huks would start firing on pursuing helicopters and sure enough during a Lawin operation near Palpinto, Capas, a Huey carrying the 1st PC zone commander, General Tanabe, and the Task Force commander, Col. Felix Jazmin, was shot at by Dante's men. The helicopter's tail was slightly damaged but no one aboard was hurt.[4]

In terms of destroying Huks, the AFP did not do too badly. Under the previous PC zone commander Brig. Gen. Emilio Zerrudo, the AFP went at the Huks with a vengeance. General Zerrudo, by mid-1970, knocked off 30 of the top 35 Huk commanders in the 1968 order of battle. Only Pedro Taruc, Dante, Layug and Tony still survive of those top 35 dissident leaders in 1968.

The AFP reported fair success despite the clipping of military power last November. Since then the PC has netted 53 Huks killed, including seven ranking commanders, 33 captured, 8 surrendered and 405 firearms.

The Unreckoned Cost

All these are on the credit side. What does not readily show up in official statistics are the costs to the taxpayer of these purported exercises in counter-insurgency. To maintain for a year 2,000 officers and men in Central Luzon at the average cost of ₱5,000 per man, the entire anti-Huk operation eats up about ₱10 million of the AFP budget not in-

[3]Philippines *Herald,* Nov. 29, 1969.
[4]Same, May 25, 1970.

cluding its share of the intelligence fund and other undetermined expenses (these are just rough estimates for no cost-accounting of the military side of the government's Central Luzon activities is available).

Sen. Stuart Symington, obviously in a baiting mood, attempted to extract from his U.S. Senate subcommittee witness, James Wilson, a sense of proportion between AFP kill ratios and what they cost in terms of logistics. Wilson offered the information that in a 19-month period there were 46 confirmed Huk dead and two possible, 68 Huks captured and four surrendered as against 18 government soldiers killed. The U.S. embassy official declined to estimate the "total cost of each dead Huk," figuring that "it would be almost impossible to make that calculation."[5]

By the above reckoning, however, the cost of killing or capturing a Huk would be close to ₱160,000. Nobody on the government side has bothered to do a cost-benefit analysis showing what ₱10 million could return if invested in various non-combat, economically productive ventures in the same region.

What is even less calculable and possibly more injurious in the long run are failures of the Armed Forces in civilian relations. While the "mailed fist" resulted in an impressive bag of killed or captured Huks, it raised an outcry of "PC brutality" from people in Tarlac and Pampanga. Increased AFP pressure on the Huks has had the counter-productive result of stepping up incidents of homicidal violence. How many of the killings are attributable to the Huks and how many to the PC or their civilian instruments does not really matter; the point is that in its eager pursuit of the body count the AFP seems to have lost sight of its major mission of restoring peace to Central Luzon.

The cost in civilian morale is beyond reckoning but Senator Aquino, who keeps a finger on the public pulse in his native Tarlac, told his colleagues that the net effect of the "reign of terror" has been to numb barrio people into a state of no longer caring. "This is the thing that saddens me," the Senator said after delivering a privilege speech protesting the massacre of seven barrio officials on a busy section of the Tarlac highway. "I cannot detect anger in these people anymore. They are no longer shouting, they are no longer hysterical. They are just dumbstruck . . . as if a flood and a pestilence struck them."[6]

---

[5]Symington subcommittee hearings, pp. 246-247.

[6]In the Philippine Senate on June 25, 1970 in response to interpellation on his privilege speech protesting the assassination of eight Tarlac barrio officials.

False Concept of the Enemy

Perhaps the basic failing of the military engaged in Central Luzon is that it has no clear idea of its "enemy." The enemy is just a list of names in the order of battle; he is a suspect communist who must be stopped before he infects others with his ideology. It is rarely in the nature of military organizations to question situational assessments made by the superior command. The field units are given the target and they go after it with professional dispatch.

On July 22, 1970, four ranking officers of the Central Luzon command were made to testify before Sen. Salvador Laurel's *ad hoc* committee investigating the government's anti-dissident policies. The hearing was an eye-opener. The officers had no concept of who they were fighting except that they were dangerous "ideologues." Moreover, the officers had little sense of the social circumstances of the dissident problem. They suffered the indignity of being quizzed like schoolchildren. Senator Laurel and Senator Aquino used the Socratic method to get past the stolid defenses of their military minds.

Col. Cesar Jazmin, ranking officer of Task Force Lawin, placed the AFP on the defensive with the proposition that there is a peace and order problem in Central Luzon "purely because of the presence of the group of Dante, an ideological group wihch advocates the overthrow of the government for another type of government, that is, Mao-oriented communism." He conceded, however, that "the uneven distribution of wealth is also helping this ideological group to win. . . the support of these people who are poor."

The colonel stuck to his guns despite a storm of skeptical interrogation. He insisted that the main objective of the NPA was to "harass the Armed Forces," and that the only reason why it is not succeeding is the interdiction of their mass base by the barrio self-defense units (BSDU's).

Senator Aquino was unconvinced and proceeded to cut Colonel Jazmin's enemy down to more realistic proportions.

> SENATOR AQUINO: . . . When a group starts harassing, there must be a plan, there must be a direction. There are 6,000 PC in the area. They are killing, let's say at the rate of 20 a month, that's 240 a year, well it would take them a hundred years to knock off 6,000. . . You know if they do something there must be some logical sequence to this attack.
>
> COLONEL JAZMIN: Maybe, Your Honor, this harassment is to make the military more cautious, al-

so so that they will not be moving around, hunting them freely. I think that is their intention, Your Honor. To make us a little scared also so that we will not be openly running after them in groups of one team only. Instead of sending one jeep to go roaming around, we will have to send three jeeps. Actually, it will also restrict our movements.

SENATOR AQUINO: I see. Now, if that is the case, you think therefore it is not tactical, it's not military, it's more psychological?

COLONEL JAZMIN: I think so, your Honor.

SENATOR AQUINO: So all of these ambushes are psychological? Both to restrict the movement of the military and maybe at the same time, while you did not say it, to impress upon the people that they're still around?

COLONEL JAZMIN: Yes, Your Honor.[7]

By relentless interrogation, the Laurel committee was able to extract from the officers a rough picture of the people they were fighting. They seemed to fit into five "categories."

SENATOR AQUINO: First category are the jobless, looking for opportunity, their future and possibly small allowances, for want of a job, what also can they do. Second category are those outlaws, those who are running away from the law and the best protection that they can get is to join a bandit group or join the NPA and take their chances there. The third category are those relations of former Huks and present Huk commanders and because they are related they are easily recruited. The fourth category which we did not bring out here are those people with certain grievances against the authorities, either grievances against the PC, the local police because they feel that they were unduly harassed before or some (suffered) imagined harassment before they joined the Huk movement.... And then, we have also found out that there are Ilocanos and Tagalogs but (preponderantly) they are Pampangos.[8]

None of the descriptions suggested that the Huks were motivated by ideology. Colonel Jazmin desperately tried to recoup. "The hardcore men are these ideologically oriented people who are trying to utilize those people (the rank-and-

---

[7]Laurel *ad hoc* committee hearings, July 22, 1970.
[8]Same.

file) for these ideological movements." But again he was put to rout by Senator Aquino's curiosity about the "educational qualifications" of even these ranking Huk leaders. Aquino went down the list — Ligaya, who was recently captured, Felman, Panchito, Goodie, Villa, Juaning. These men, the senator later asserted, were not much different from the Huks just categorized. They were of doubtful qualifications as honest-to-goodness Maoist indoctrinators.

Colonel Jazmin put up a last stand around the top man in the order of batle. Dante was an ideological Huk who believed in Maoism. But it turned out that none of the officers had met Dante and could not personally vouch for their judgment. They just had it on "very reliable" authority.

Senator Aquino elicited the startling information that the AFP did not have a "psychological profile" of the enemy apart from the often-publicized quantification of armed troops and guns. There was nothing in the AFP's intellectual equipment remotely comparable to the depth-studies of surrendered Vietcong (the "Cho Hoy Program") undertaken by the Vietnamese government and the Rand Corporation.

"We talk of the NPA," the senator pursued. "Who is the NPA? What is it? What is his educational attainment? What is his outlook? What is his motivation? What is he fighting for, why did he become an NPA? Now, unless we can answer these we will not be able to . . . we can kill them, but I don't think killing them can solve the problem."[9]

Lt. Col. Ponciano Gonzales, PC provincial commander of Pampanga, denied there was a "modus vivendi" between the AFP and Sumulong. But he could give no reason why the brunt of the AFP effort was then directed in Tarlac rather than Pampanga other than the bromide that "Dante, being an ideological Huk is a more dangerous enemy."

The committee proceeded to break down this gratuitous assumption.

> SENATOR AQUINO: Did it ever occur to you that Sumulong has a tremendous staying power, that all of these dangerous commanders have come and gone but Sumulong has always remained? Has it ever occurred to you why that is so? All other Huk commanders live only for two years at the most, the most dangerous, name them, Delio, Zaragoza, Tronco, Cruz, all of them, their total life span is two years but Sumulong... has been around for 15 years.

---

[9]Same.

Second, has it occurred to you that everytime somebody fights Sumulong, the PC does the dirty job of killing his enemy for him? I will cite an example — Alibasbas for Sumulong, the Army killed Alibasbas; Freddie for Sumulong, the Army killed Frieddie; Dante for Sumulong, Dante is being chased by the PC.

I want to know whether the PC is the body-guard of Sumulong. Everytime he fights somebody, you are the one cleaning the mess for him When Alibasbas got killed, Sumulong became very big. It was only after Freddie and Dante left him that he became very small. So now, you are looking for the two, so he becomes big again. Then another guy, maybe Tony this time or maybe Fonting will leave, we forget Sumulong again, you would look for Tony and Fonting, but did it ever occur to you that maybe Sumulong is the father of all this?

SENATOR LAUREL: Or is there a deal between the military and Sumulong?

COLONEL GONZALEZ: I would like to assure you that there is on deal between the military and Sumulong.

SENATOR AQUINO: Colonel, I appreciate the estimate of General Headquarters because you all know that Dante was picked up by Sumulong. He was his bodyguard and Dante got his rudiments from Sumulong and of these, Madrigal came from Sumulong, Tronco came from Sumulong, Zaragoza came from Sumulong. All of them came from Sumulong so he is the well and these are only the springs (sic) so how can the spring rise higher than the well.

I am surprised at this estimate because empirical data will indicate that any Huk that fought Sumulong was killed by the PC and Sumulong has conveniently used the PC maybe unwittingly to purge the ranks like Stalin purged the Russian command... Sumulong keeps on purging people by lying low telling the government, *"Hindi naman ako kalaban, nationalist lang naman ako"* ("I'm not an enemy, just a nationalist"), so they don't run after him. When his enemies are killed, he again comes up. When there is a new enemy, he again lays low.

Now, did it occur to you that maybe the smartest Huk commander so far in that entire area is this guy, Sumulong whom we estimate as only a plain bandit?

COLONEL GONZALEZ: That is the assessment of our headquarters, but anyway, as far as we are concerned, we treat them all as outlaws and it has become our job to apprehend, to get them and to prosecute them if we have a chance to prosecute them.

SENATOR LAUREL: May I interject on that point, Your Honor. You said you treat them as outlaws, what is the price on the head of Dante, how much?

COLONEL GONZALEZ: ₱150,000.

SENATOR LAUREL: ₱150,000 is the reward that you are offering to anybody who can bring Dante dead or alive?

COLONEL GONZALEZ: Yes, Your Honor.

SENATOR LAUREL: How much is the price for the head of Sumulong?

COLONEL GONZALEZ: ₱150,000 also.

SENATOR LAUREL: ₱150,000 also dead or alive?

COLONEL GONZALEZ: Yes, Your Honor.

SENATOR LAUREL: In that respect, you can say that they are treated equally.

COLONEL GONZALEZ: Yes, Your Honor.

SENATOR LAUREL: Only you are exerting more effort to catch Dante because you consider him more dangerous than Sumulong.

COLONEL GONZALEZ: That was before the movement in Tarlac was at its highest. However, it seems that the pressure now on Sumulong and Dante will be just the same at this time.

SENATOR LAUREL: Beginning?

COLONEL GONZALEZ: At this time.

SENATOR LAUREL: Beginning now?

COLONEL GONZALEZ: Yes.

SENATOR LAUREL: When did this commence, now only?

COLONEL GONZALEZ: It was around yesterday.

SENATOR LAUREL: Yesterday only. That is very important. Before yesterday, you were more after Dante than Sumulong and that is perhaps the reason why Sumulong was free to roam around.[10]

Lt. Col. Tomas Diaz, formerly Tarlac provincial commander and now the zone intelligence chief, justified the trans-

[10]Same. After this exchange between the AFP and the Laurel committee, the AFP did make up its mind to go after Sumulong. The Pampanga Huk leader was "captured" in less than two months.

fer of the 51st PC Battalion from Pampanga to Tarlac because of "some ambushes in the national highway" requiring military presence to "keep the highway safe."

But in two places of Pampanga, Porac and Angeles, armed men "sprayed" innocent people with automatic fire, Senator Aquino countered. This had never happened in Tarlac. "At least, in Tarlac, if they kill, they kill you for a purpose, but in Pampanga, you die without a purpose."

The AFP's World-View

The AFP seems to have a monumental "hang-up" on the Huks as suspect communists.

In the official AFP world-view — as distinguished from the more critical and perceptive judgments privately made by AFP officers — the Huks are an instrument of the communist global conspiracy. The AFP chief of Staff Gen. Manuel T. Yan, described the subversive activities in Southeast Asia — the Philippines included — as "not accidents of history but . . . largely the result of Peking's grand design to establish dominance over the peoples of Asia." By process of guilt association, the Huks are linked to this massive Maoist plot.[11] Their every movement is given a conspiratorial meaning.

> Communist insurgent activities are generally confined to Central Luzon, principally in the provinces of Tarlac and Pampanga, and in the peripheral areas of Zambales, Bataan, Pangasinan and Nueva Ecija . . . . These activities generally include organization of insurgent units in rural areas; attraction of former insurgents back into the movement; recruitment and training of new members; procurement of equipment and supplies; terrorist activities such as kidnaping and liquidation of uncooperative persons; and other limited military operations including ambuscades, robberies, raids and intimidations.
>
> The *Communists* have an approximate insurgent strength of 700 armed regulars.[12] (*Underscoring supplied.*)

Since the number of "Communist" insurgents by General Yan's count tallies roughly with the number of known Huk regulars, the implication is that they are one and the same.

---

[11]Foreword to Vol. I of "So the People Would Know," AFP General Headquarters, February 5, 1970.

[12]Same, Vol. II. "So the People Would Know," AFP General Headquarters, March 10, 1970.

The AFP "hang-up" is partly the result of selective perception by field officers and braintrusters in the AFP general staff. The typical Army officer sees the Huk "threat" through heavy filters which tend to strain out all information except those operationally meaningful and useful. This could well be the result of his uncompromisingly anti-Communist biases, his deference to the judgments of superior officers, and the lack (until recently) of the humanities and political and social sciences components in his professional education.

The AFP has recently taken a propagandistic posture on the Huk movement. "Psy-war" enjoys great respectability as an operational tactic. Used in a limited way — e.g., countering Huk or Communist propaganda in the Central Luzon villages — the tactic is meritorious. But how far can the AFP stretch "national security" as the justification for deliberate misinformation? An overdose of psy-war can lead to something almost as destructive of the national security — an increasing AFP "credibility gap."

A column I wrote on July 1, 1970 appealed for an "AFP policy review" vis-a-vis the Central Luzon situation. It was one of the strongest statements I wrote on the subject. Several ranking AFP officers privately agreed that "there is some truth to that."

> The tradition of civilian review of military policy — the strongest safeguard of a democracy against rule-by-generals — seems to have quietly given up the ghost in the past few weeks. Defense Sec. Juan Ponce Enrile seems to have defaulted that all-important prerogative by caving in completely to the insistence of the Camp Olivas brass that the Tarlac massacre was the handiwork of the Huks.
>
> Instead of taking the fiscalizer's role, Enrile acted unblushingly as their defense counsel. "All indications point to the Huks as the killers," his press statement read. All indications? Apparently, the secretary whose lawyer's training should have made him warier about such dogmatic conclusions did not even entertain the slightest possibility that the information given him could be wrong.
>
> And in an admirable show of faith in the Tarlac PC commander and General Tanabe, he is sticking to that line despite the preponderance of contradictory evidence revealed by Sen. Benigno Aquino, Jr. and Gov. Jose Macapinlac.
>
> President Marcos backed the whole AFP policy to the hilt, proclaiming the absolute rightness of the

BSDU's and the twin offering of brass knuckles to the hardcore dissidents and "attraction" (???) to the rest of the Central Luzon populace.

The civilian government's pandering to the pet fetishes of the AFP brass raises the intriguing questions whether it's the dog wagging the tail or the other way around. The troubled circumstances in which the President is finding himself goes a long way to explaining this quixotic behavior. In a crisis it is the Armed Forces that will be his sword and his shield. It is his last-ditch defense against a leftist revolution or a liberal reformist takeover. Is this why, for the duration the AFP can't possibly do anything wrong?

It's the farthest thing from my purpose to denigrate the AFP. It has an officer corps of well-trained, disciplined men who will give up their lives defending the Republic from its enemies. But while most of these officers are unquestionably patriotic, their commissions do not automatically imbue them with infallibility.

The judgment of the Camp Olivas command could be strongly biased by the fact that the AFP has a vested interest in Central Luzon. It is their reason for being.

The AFP is institutionally biased not only in favor of a strong military presence. It is also biased for the basic strategy of the "mailed fist" and "counter-insurgency."

For the majority of the generals and colonels are line officers with infantry, Ranger, and artillery backgrounds. There is also a strong "Special Forces" cadre with Fort Bragg training. These line officers far outnumber the civic-action specialists, the engineers and the medical officers.

Their sheer number dictates the hawkish AFP policy and I strongly suspect to the prejudice of the minority branches whose services could be more productive in Central Luzon than those of the PC Rangers and the counter-insurgency specialists.

Since their career advancement depends to a large degree on their getting opportunities for heroics in Central Luzon, the AFP hawks are all for making Central Luzon their mock battlefield. This is fine for them. But what about the Pampanga and Tarlac farmers to whom the very sight of a PC uniform is odious And the barrio officials who are getting killed simply because the Special Forces people want to exercise the black art taught them in Fort Bragg?

The tragedy is that the exercise is not at all called for since Central Luzon is not the Mekong delta, the Karen hills of Burma, the Malaysian jungles, or the Thai Northeast. Dante's army is not the White Flag, the PKI, the Pathet Lao, Chen P'-ing's Malayan Communist Party, or the Viet Cong.

The AFP has blinded itself, willingly or not, to a crucial distinction between the peasant rebels with their peasant leadership (like Dante and Sumulong) and the urban Communist leadership that has twice tried — and failed — to co-opt the peasant movement which is "ideological" only after a fashion.

Just because *Ang Bayan*, a party organ, proclaims Dante's people as raving Maoists doesn't mean that they really are. But that is the picture the AFP seems to be trying to draw of the "NPA" and considering its institutional biases this picture is highly suspect.

The reassertion of civilian supremacy is needed to bring some common sense and balance into the Central Luzon policy. The last time the AFP's policies were sharply brought to question was when Sen. Genaro Magsaysay, as chairman of the National Defense committee, probed the Jabidah infamy. (Operation Jabidah was the code name for a secret mission reputedly to train Muslim volunteers to infiltrate Sabah, a part of the Malaysian Federation claimed by the heirs of the Sultan of Sulu. It became a national scandal in 1968 when several Muslim trainees were killed in Corregidor island under circumstances the AFP could not easily explain.) It is a pity that the Armed Forces committees of both Houses of Congress are seemingly unresponsive to their duty.

What is needed there more than BSDU's is a positive show of good will. Ramon Magsaysay licked the Huks in the fifties not so much with his reenforced BCT's and Ranger teams as with his EDCOR units, his Judge Advocate General Office (JAGO) officer-lawyer teams which adjudicated tenancy disputes, and his engineering battalions which built artesian wells for the barrio people.[13]

The AFP's ideological "overkill" has affected the con-

[13]Philippines *Herald*.

duct of its rank-and-file. A trooper keyed up to the chase can see Huks lurking in every rice paddy and canebrake. Mayor Rene Castro of Candaba protested the maltreatment of barrio folk by soldiers and informers during AFP sweeps through that area in 1967. He charged that fishermen were afraid to venture out to the swamp for fear of being picked up as Huk suspects. "It is regrettable that military authorities in their attempt to dramatize their success in the anti-Huk drive always use Candaba as a war playground and the Candaba swamp as a mock Mekong Delta," Mayor Castor told the press.[14]

Three members of an eight-man team of civilian surveyors were killed when army troopers jumped them in the mistaken notion they were members of Commander Ligaya's band.

One gets the impression too that the Army is just too professionally efficient. The Huk hunters in Baluarte used portable loudspeakers to ask their surrounded enemy to surrender. Failing to see a white flag, they virtually executed all Huks popping into sight.[15] Perhaps the Army could have tried harder to get some of the Huks alive. In a guerrilla war, a captured insurgent is certainly worth five dead ones. He could provide intelligence useful for future operations. And, of course, persons captured with guns in their hands are more likely to be Huks than the scores of unarmed suspects coralled during Ranger sweeps of the barrios.

Civic Action

In contrast with the adverse effects of the "mailed fist," the AFP's civic action phase in Central Luzon has been palpably successful. The Army Civic Action Force (ACAF) was created out of the Philippine Civic Action Group (Philcag) recalled from Vietnam duty, the 564th Engineer Construction Battalion, a medical-dental company and supporting units. The force was given the strictly non-combatant mission of the "social and economic environment" of local communities, promoting "civic consciousness" among the barrio people and in the process creating a more positive AFP image among them.

The army engineers got a release of ₱396,500 to build a steel bridge over the Bamban river on the Magalang-Concepcion road which cuts across Huk country. Establishing direct and easy communication between these border towns of Pampanga and Tarlac would go a long way to improve the economies of their barrios and undermine the Huk appeal to

---

[14]Same, Dec. 24, 1967.
[15]Same, April 11, 1969.

popular grievances. The 564th ECB was at work on the Baong Sikat-Ulanin feeder road improving lateral access between Tarlac and Nueva Ecija. Irrigation-flood control work was also in progress in Cuyapo. Southwards, the ACAF was building the San Luis-Baliuag and the Bahay Pare-Maasin roads transversing the Candaba swamps[16]

The army engineers put up Marcos-type schoolhouses, multi-purpose pavements (usable as basketball courts and palay drying), and poultry and piggery projects. Their work was supplementary to what civilian agencies were already doing and always on a self-help basis. As a matter of policy, an ACAF project started had to be completed. The army did not want to give the Huks more anti-government propaganda than they already had.

Using the same successful Vietnam formula, former Philcag doctors and dentists won over many of their barrio patients. The "medcap" program handled 153,542 cases in 153 days, working between January 19 to June 20, 1970 at the rate of almost 1,000 cases a day.

The ACAF soldiers, distinguished from the PC's by their jaunty bush hats with yellow braid, were among the best ambassadors the government ever had in Central Luzon. They went around unarmed (since carrying a weapon could have been an invitation for a Huk foraging attack). The ACAF operated in a thousand barrios, including some of the most critical ones, without incurring a single casualty due to a deliberate Huk attack.[17] The soldiers openly fraternized with the barrio people, attending their barrio fiestas and even marrying some of the local lasses. Tarlac officials were lavish in their praise of the ACAF program and asked for more of it.

Unhappily, civic action could not be maximized due to limited funding. The 564th ECB had enough construction equipment but the Philcag which left its gear behind in Vietnam was forced to borrow some from the reserves of the 51st Engineering Brigade and from the Bureau of Public Highways. The assistance it could provide for major constructions was limited to counterpart funds that the local governments could spare. The Tarlac provincial government, for instance, had only ₱51,000 to match the ACAF contribution.[18]

On September 14, 1970, there was discouraging news that the ACAF was being pulled out of Central Luzon. Governor Jose Macapinlac of Tarlac protested the move, saying that it would give rise to suspicions that civic action was lit-

[16]Briefing by Col. Andrinico Dumlao, Public Affairs Officer, ACAG, June, 1970.

[17]Same.

[18]Laurel committee hearings, July 28, 1970.

tle more than government propaganda. The governor regarded a reported plan to replace the ACAF with a combat unit as "highly suspicious, considering that the Constitutional Convention is nearing."[19]

Not the least, therefore, of the AFP's failures are its mistaken emphasis on "PC power" and its stinting of the phase that has proven most productive in terms of barrio relations and national image-building.

Institutional Rebuilding

Lest the impression be given that the Central Luzon command is saddled with incompetents or time-servers, it might be well to mention that many of its officers are highly-motivated professionals who would be a credit to any army. The Philippine Army commanding general, Rafael Ileto, was an intelligent, conscientious Huk-fighter. He was the creator of the PC Rangers, a tough, campaign-hardened elite corps that could lick twice its weight in Huks. Lt. Col. Bienvenido Castro, who commanded the 10th BCT in 1969, was another bright, innovative officer with fairly revolutionary ideas of dealing with the Huk problem. Unfortunately, he was not high enough in the chain of command to have his ideas sink in.

The AFP could be a good, efficient organization — if only the politicians leave it alone. It has a young officer corps benefitting from a greatly improved inservice educational system. The Philippine Military Academy used to have a strongly engineering-oriented curriculum that is now being liberalized with humanities subjects. There is increasing acceptability to the proposition that AFP officers should be broader, less inbred individuals. A recent National Defense College paper stressed the "need for our officers to include in their educational preparation knowledge of humanities and social sciences which will prepare them for another kind of war — the one which will ultimately win the hearts and the minds of the people."[20]

The National Defense College, founded in 1965, with Asia Foundation assistance, is the "graduate school for generals." It has an almost 80 percent social sciences and humanities component in its curriculum. The academic freedom enjoyed by the field-rank officers and senior civilian bureaucrats is a refreshing change from the typical conser-

[19]Philippines *Herald,* Sept. 14, 1970.

[20]Lt. Col. Geronimo G. Sabellano, *Armed Forces of the Philippines Educational System's Problems and Solutions,* an unpublished thesis submitted to the National Defense College of the Philippines, 1967.

vatism still found in the topmost staff levels. Unofficially, NDCP students rehash the Central Luzon problem and some of the students have been extremely critical of its handling by some operational commands.

The NDCP has generated new concepts for the improvement of the service. One of its papers by Lt. Col. Zorobabel F. Herrera, pointed out that "because of lack of legal basis, career management policies in our Armed Forces remain a near fiction." He proposed an enabling act to legalize these policies, including the creation of a Career Management Board comparable to what other national armies have.[21]

When he was an NDCP student, the AFP intelligence chief, Col. Fidel Ramos, proposed a revision of the Armed Forces act (and probably a constitutional amendment as well) raising the level of presidential confirmation of officers from colonel (or naval captain) to general. This would take away much of the political pressure on PC provincial commanders who usually are lieutenant colonels and often need political backing to go one grade higher.

Since the Philippine Constabulary has been the object of most of the criticism against the AFP, it is obvious that any reform should begin with this service branch. The PC has lost much of its pre-war glamor, partly because of its poor career management and partly because of political interference. "I don't want to knock a sister service," an Army officer said, "but it's hard to see why the PC continues to grow despite its sullied name." The PC is now the largest of the service branches, with 21,000 of the AFP's 50,000 officers and men.

Rep. Teodulo Natividad, a former PC criminal investigator, has drafted a plan detaching the PC from the AFP and converting it into a national police force. There are persuasive arguments for the proposed conversion. The PC used to be separate from the Department of National Defense before the war, and much of the security problems of the countryside require police rather than military expertise.

This observation applies especially to Central Luzon. The AFP, trained for warfare of both the conventional and unconventional kind, is too overpowering and punitive a weapon to be used against the non-ideological majority of the Huks. If in the balance the AFP mission in Central Luzon has been counterproductive, it is probably no fault of its own but rather that of politicians who have made them fight the wrong war in the wrong place and possibly even on the wrong people.

[21]*Military Career Management in the Philippine Army,* a thesis submitted to the National Defense College of the Philippines, Fort Bonifacio, Rizal (undated).

Chapter Fifteen

THE TRIALS OF REFORM

Revolution failed in the Philippines; it probably was not even possible in the first place. Can reform succeed in settling the grievances of Central Luzon and prevent Huk-style protests from occurring in other parts of the country?

In this sense, the Philippines has had similar experiences with other modernizing countries; the peaceful revolutionist has been almost as unsuccessful as the violent one. Prof. Samuel P. Huntington explains why this is so:

> The way of the reformer is hard. In three respects, his problems are more difficult than those of the revolutionary. First, he necessarily fights a two-front war against both conservative and revolutionary. Indeed, to be successful, he may well have to engage in a multi-front war with a multiplicity of participants, in which his enemies on one front are his allies in another. The aim of the revolutionary is to polarize politics, and hence he attempts to simplify, to dramatize, and to amalgamate political issues into a single clear-cut dichotomy between the forces of "progress" and those of "reaction." He tries to cumulate cleavages, while the reformer must try to diversify and to dissociate cleavages. The revolutionary promotes rigidity in politics, the reformer fluidity and adaptability. The revolutionary must be able to dichotomize social forces, to manipulate them. The reformer, consequently, requires a much higher order of *political skill* than does the revolutionary. Reform is rare if only because the political talents necessary to make it a reality are rare. A successful revolutionary need not be a master politician; a successful reformer always is.[1]

Huntington's thesis can be articulated in peculiarly Philippine terms. The distinction between "soft" and "hard"

---

[1]*Political Order in Changing Societies,* (New Haven and London: Yale University Press, 1968), pp. 344-345.

politics is called to mind once again. Reformism has been a recurring theme in Philippine politics since the days of Rizal and Mabini. It has tended to be rhetorical rather than actual. Reform is promised in the most sanguine manner but execution comes tardily. Worse, reformists are usually found in political opposition to promote themselves into favor by decrying governmental deficiencies or the common man's state and to offer themselves as the only ones who can make the necessary amends.

Once the reformists are in office, they realize the near-impossibility of their promises. The same pressures that have made captives of the outgoing officials entrap the incoming ones, and thus the situation remains until the next election comes around. Some positive changes, however, do take place. In Central Luzon, there is no question that the state of the farmer has improved since the 1950's, though perhaps not to the desirable extent. It is something of a miracle, considering the essential conservatism of the political elites, that some reforms are advanced at all. But having acquired so much, the farmer is frustrated in not acquiring more.

Brief History of Reformism

Ramon Magsaysay was comparatively the most successful Central Luzon reformer. He designed the winning formula of civic action which was his most effective weapon.

Special engineering battalions were put to work building artesian wells in the barrios. Judge Advocate General (JAGO) teams of law-trained officers adjudicated tenancy disputes in places where civilian public servants dared not venture. Medical-dental services were provided free of charge to the rural poor. Non-commissioned officers with agriculture and animal husbandry schooling accompanied surrendered Huks to the EDCOR farms to help set them up for a new life.

However, one must be careful about attributing too many wonder-working qualities to Magsaysay. He was the right man for the right time; he might well have been a disappointment in the sixties when political leadership required more sophistication and manipulative skills than he was capable of. Magsaysay had excellent advisers and technocrats around him, and he made full use of them.

But contributing as much to his success as his dedicated corps of braintrusters and the considerable American support behind him was his own personification of the common man, physically robust, active and big-hearted, and a complete departure from the *ilustrado* politicians who have traditionally supplied Philippine political leadership.

His populist qualities were believable. When he opened the doors of Malacañang to the common *tao,* they came in the thousands. People followed him in droves when he toured the barrios. Symbolically, Magsaysay was the *Kuya* (big brother) of the peasants, the authority figure that the Central Luzon countryside had long missed.

Succeeding administrations have attempted various "solutions" to the Central Luzon problem with not much success. President Macapagal, who was born in Lubao, Pampanga and recalls having been invited by Pedro Abad Santos to join the Socialist party (he declined),[2] sought a major breakthrough with his Agricultural Land Reform Code. But it fell far short of being the long-awaited panacea in his time because of niggardly outlays of less than a million pesos for a massive program that was intended to be financed by ₱200 million within a year of its enactment and ₱300 million in the next three years.[3]

The "poor boy" from Lubao, remembering his humble beginnings, was sincere in wanting reform, but he lacked the political skills to master his circumstances and the ruthlessness to insure his political survival. He withheld his "welfare program" for a second term which never materialized. The Negros "sugar bloc" and the Manila industrialists ganged up on President Macapagal and a new man — another campaign "reformist" — took over.

President Marcos has applied more "inputs" into Central Luzon than any one of his predecessors but there is yet to emerge a clear-cut "policy" or even a believable "program."

On December 31, 1968, he created the Central Luzon Study Commission to get a bipartisan consensus on the problems of the region. It had former Sen. Manuel Manahan as chairman and opposition Sen. Benigno Aquino Jr., Gov. Francisco Nepomuceno, Gov. Eduardo Cojuangco and *Manila Times* publisher Joaquin Roces as members. The very composition of the commission doomed it from the start.

Governor Nepomuceno and Governor Cojuangco were by then identified with a hard-line position vis-a-vis the Huks and moreover had vested interests in Pampanga and Tarlac politics. Neither could they have been expected to "study" Central Luzon with anything like an open mind. Senator Aquino, though already becoming an intractable critic of the Marcos administration, was still willing to help in a bipartisan capacity.

---

[2]Diosdado Macapagal, *A Stone for the Edifice, Memoirs of a President* (Quezon City: MAC Publishing House, 1968).

[3]The Land Reform Code, Republic Act No. 3844, Chapter IV, Section 81.

Aquino had hoped, in the event of a Liberal victory in 1969, to be made some kind of Central Luzon "czar" to solve the Huk problem once and for all. He would need ₱50 million outright and ₱25 million every year for 10 years plus all the infrastructure programs already in the works. Thus he would be able to wipe out tenancy, resettle the dissidents and their families, organize the farmers into productive communes, and make Central Luzon a region of prosperity.

This was a forthright approach, if a little too glib, but Aquino never got a chance to get started. His relations with President Marcos went from bad to worse. Old slights and new affronts accumulated. When the young Senator committed the ungallantry of calling Mrs. Imelda Marcos an "Evita Peron" and a colossal wastrel for building a ₱50 million Cultural Center at a time of widespread poverty, her outraged husband called Aquino a "congenital liar." Aquino promptly resigned from the commission.

The only man who undertook the CLSC work with any seriousness was Manahan. A chairman of the Senate Committee on National defense and security he released the now-famous "Manahan report" which disclosed the existence of an "invisible government" undermining the legitimate government in the area. Manahan, now in a private capacity as an executive of the Philippine Rural Reconstruction Movement, might have helped push an intelligent Central Luzon program had he been given decent support. He functioned virtually as a one-man commission for many months. He recommended a go-ahead on the construction of the Magalang-Concepcion road and urged the implementation of the Upper Pampanga multi-purpose project. But eventually, the study commission itself became another dead letter in the bureaucratic heap.

The Central Luzon Development Program was created by President Marcos in 1966 to coordinate both government and civic resources being pumped into the region. Ernesto Maceda, as presidential assistant for community development was its first chairman. He was replaced by Labor Secretary Blas Ople.

The CLDP probably came out on the plus side as far as facilitating the flow of government activity in the area. The number of participating agencies jumped from 21 to 47 in four years and if the CLDP has managed to keep most of these bureaucratic interests from getting in each other's way it would have done a fair job already.[4]

The CLDP can be credited with building some bridges,

---

[4]Rosendo R. Marquez, Undersecretary of Community Development, "Central Luzon Development Program," a report updated to 1969.

prefab schoolbuildings, feeder roads, irrigation systems artesian wells and rural hospitals in the seven provinces it covers. Central Luzon may have already received proportionally more benefits from the central government than it is entitled to on the basis of its revenues.

But even more than the Land Authority the CLDP continues to be strapped for funds. When Secretary Maceda was its chairman, the PACD virtually subsidized the CLDP with its own funds and personnel. Secretary Ople has no such reservoir to draw from and in its present situation the CLDP has "not a single centavo to its name" and depends "mainly on the hospitality of Gen. Felizardo Tanabe and Gen. Roso Sabalones."[5]

Despite the claimed increases in government spending in Central Luzon, Rep. Jose Lingad charged that a "retrogression" in the "socio-economic climate" had actually set in "due to the almost complete breakdown of government services."

National roads have been neglected, flood control and irrigation systems were not improved, commerce has declined, industries have folded up, many farms have been abandoned, unemployment has increased, health and sanitation services are inadequate and, worse of all, law and order has been supplemented by a reign of terror.[6]

For all their good intentions, government programs have had little effect on basic human relations without demonstrable good faith on the part of the national leaders. President Marcos' image of "insincerity" negates much of his intrinsically good works, and the bloody intramurals among the local faction leaders spoil whatever goodwill is left.

Though Pampanga has benefited economically from land reform, its "social impact" is still negligible, a ranking government official based at Camp Olivas said. "We have not mellowed the greed of people. Some cheat for profit and others cheat as an act of vengeance. It's the root of most of our troubles "

Civic and Religious Good Works

The civic conscience of enlightened Pampangos is beginning to be felt. The Angeles Peace and Order Council under Dr. Jose Pelayo successfully staved off a budding "civil war" between the Angeles police department and Governor

---

[5]Secretary Blas Ople's testimony to the House Committee on Social Amelioration, February, 1970.

[6]Privilege speech delivered to the House of Representatives, February 10, 1970.

Nepomuceno's private army. Dr. Romeo Taruc, the son of the former Huk supremo, ministers to the casualties on both the Sumulong and Nepomuceno camps in an admirable gesture of non-partisanship. Dr. Romeo Galang, the president of the Pampanga Rotary Club, offers his professional services to poor farmers and their dependents when he could conceivably make a better living elsewhere.

The Catholic church is not institutionally visible as an agent of social change in Central Luzon. This is rather disappointing since 93 percent — an overwhelming majority — of Pampangos are Catholics and a potentially large constituency for any Church-endorsed reforms.

What prevents the Church from taking a more active role is the stultifying conservation of its hierarchs. The first prince of the Church, Rufino Cardinal Santos, was born in Sto. Niño, Guagua, Pampanga, but he has rarely been heard to pronounce upon the morality of certain conditions existing in his home province. His attitude towards public affairs seems to be one of discreet non-involvement, as though fearful that one word of criticism on temporal matters would violate the constitutional separation of Church and State. He is maddeningly silent except when casting progressives and militants in his flock into hellfire.

Cardinal Santos has undertaken many good works, for which he is not given enough credit but he is better known for being the skillful comptroller of the vast diocesan holdings in banks, blue-chip stocks and real estate. The Cardinal was careered in the Church when it was still unquestionably authoritarian and disciplinarian. It is doubtful that the 62-year-old prelate could change his ways or that the more liberal churchmen and their followers would bide their time in seeking a more reform-oriented apostolate.

Since there are few sizeable tracts of friar lands in Pampanga outside of the 3,000-hectare Bahay Pare estate in Candaba, the Church is involved in few agrarian disputes. But the Pampanga diocese also tends to be circumspect in public affairs, possibly because it is a captive of the landowning families who are generous with endowments.

By contrast, many of the younger religious are of defiantly liberal persuasion. If the overlords of the Church continue to resist change, an "underground Church" similar to that which surfaced in Latin America may snatch the initiative from them.

A group of rural missionaries from Manila nave began working in Matatalahib, a barrio of Tarlac town notorious for breeding gangsters. They appear to be working on the sly, probably because the local diocese has not sanctioned such activities. This kind of grassroots evangelizing is what the

Huk areas need. One missionary sister has been so effective with Tarlac's rural youth that even Dante has been heard to complain about the "competition."

The Iglesia ni Cristo, a growing religious minority with demonstrated political strength, has a record of being violently anti-Huk. The INC draws its following from the poor and the lower middle class, and demands absolute fealty in both spiritual and temporal matters, brooking no competing loyalties. INC followers have been victims of Huk atrocities in the past for their non-ecumenical attiudes and they have shown a fair inclination to fight back.

Once in a long while, the Manila elites show a spark of inspired initiative and throw their support behind purely humanitarian missions in Central Luzon. One eminent example was the "health blitz" launched by Manuel Elizalde Jr. Young "Manda" Elizalde is an heir to one of the Philippines' oldest fortunes, Harvard-educated and consequently much more "radical" than the majority of the Forbes Park class and possessed with a burning enthusiasm to save the cultural minorities from neglect and exploitation.

With a license from President Marcos to do his good works in Pampanga, Elizalde led a 127-man Presidential Arm for the Cultural Minorities (Panamin) medical team into the heart of Huklandia and spread anti-biotics and good cheer among tens of thousands of indigents in Bahay Pare, Salapungan, San Luis, Santa Ana and Candaba. Scores of doctors, surgeons, dentists and medical assistants gave up their entire Christmas holidays to minister to their barrio patients.

The Panamin troupe traveled in five big trucks and an assortment of lorries and jeeps. Manda Elizalde's old limousine, converted into an ambulance, served to ferry the more serious cases to provincial or Manila hospitals. The Elizalde column would move into a town, set up its treatment rooms, usually in a schoolbuilding provided by the community, and take in close to 2,000 patients — all in one day.

The Panamin chief saw why the Central Luzon countryside was wide open for unrest. "The hospitals, the courts, the Army camps are all in the provincial capitals and major towns," he said. "Only those who live near the towns can benefit from the amenities of civilization. That means the rich and the middle class. Most of the poor peasants can't even afford the bus fare to see a doctor in town — if there are doctors willing to treat them for practically nothing."

Elizalde toyed with the idea of a Panamin floating clinic to go up and down the Pampanga river to attend to the have-not and dissidence-prone communities by the riverbanks. He had operated similar water-borne clinics in Cotabato and Palawan. But the scheme had to be scrapped when the river was found to be unnavigable for most of the year except for the smallest of boats.[7]

The Philippine Rural Reconstruction Movement (PRRM), a humanitarian organization backed by international and local funds, has fulltime rural workers in 11 barrios of Pampanga and Tarlac. Its philosophy is based on the interrelatedness of the "four basic problems of man" — poverty, disease, ignorance and civic indifference. According to the PRRM gospel:

> ...if a man is poor, it is not enough that he be given relief. He must be made healthy so that he can be educated on how to increase his production and income, and be aware of his being part of the whole. Similarly, if he is sick, it is not enough that he must be treated. He must be educated so that he will know how to keep himself healthy, so he can increase his production and income, and be made competent in self-rule. And so on down the line.[8]

With former Senator Manahan at its head, the PRRM has gained popular acceptance in the areas where it operates. Private-sector initiatives have been generally successful, though they are of a small scale compared to the need for their services.

Amnesty and Indemnification

Though the Huks in 1948 were offered a general amnesty and they refused it, Central Luzon problem-solvers have never given up hope in some kind of legal or judicial settlement with the armed elements. There is increasing support for "conditional" or "selective" amnesty as the starting point for negotiations with the Huks. While a general amnesty gives blanket relief to all surrenderees whatever crimes they may be charged for, a selective amnesty frees them only from the consequences of the anti-subversion law but not from liability for murder, homicide, arson and other crimes unassociated with rebellion.

Sen. Leonardo Perez drafted a bill recently for the creation of two special courts, one in Pampanga and another in Tarlac, with special jurisdiction over cases involving rebellion, sedition and similar crimes.

> In my bill I provided that within six months after the approval of the bill all members of dissident groups who surrender and lay down their arms will

[7]Philippines *Herald,* January 5, 1969.
[8]Jess Banguis, Philippines *Herald,* Sept. 16, 1970.

> not be prosecuted under RA 1700 (the anti-subversion law), that is, for mere membership in a subversive organization. But they will have to undergo trial for any (other) offense. However, if they . . . surrender within six months and they . . . (are) found guilty, they will be entitled to what they call the minimum sentence with a recommendation for executive clemency or pardon. This recommendation by the court is usually resorted to when the court believes that the (convict) is entitled to immediate release which the court cannot grant.[9]

What makes the proposition unacceptable to the Huks is the requirement to turn in all their weapons. They distrust the promises of government leaders. They fear that once disarmed they would be helpless against their enemies and unable to pressure the government to attend to neglected business.

President Marcos offered amnesty in 1969 but later reversed himself, presumably on the advice of the AFP. The arms question appears to be an area of non-concession on the part of the government. An Angeles-born professional volunteered the opinion that insisting on the surrender of Huk arms is meaningless because the Huks can give up an impressive pile of guns and still have enough leftover stock to start the revolution all over again.

Apart from amnesty, the Central Luzon problem-solvers feel very strongly about indemnifying the relatives of victims of Huk and Army slayings — and they are legion. Journalist and labor leader Mac Fabian, testifying before the Espinosa committee, said that the bereaved would "feel a little mollified if he receives even a token reparation . . . of his loss which is not of his own making. This (the loss) is the fault of society."

Indemnification, however, is a very expensive proposition. The AFP has recorded 494 victims of Huk killings from 1962 to 1969. This figure, obviously, does not necessarily include victims of PC, Monkee or civilian guard attacks. If the calculation extends to the entire period of Huk activism, the number of families to be ameliorated becomes impossibly large. Indemnifying, say 5,000 claimants at ₱1,000 each, would cost the government five million pesos.

Resettlement and Land Reform

Resettlement is not a feasible strategy to decongest the overcrowded farms of Central Luzon. Pampangos are not

[9]Laurel committee hearings, July 28, 1970.

particularly inclined to migrate outside their society, severing themselves thus from kin and credit. The record of government-sponsored resettlement projects is faulty at best. When the Calegian estate formerly owned by President Quezon's heirs was subdivided in three of four-hectare lots among poor farmers, the settlers struck out for themselves for only a few years before lapsing back into tenancy. Calegian is now reportedly owned by a few families.

That leaves land reform still a doubtful proposition up to now. The land reform code was barely wrung out of the landlord-controlled Congress in 1963 and even that was a Pyrrhic victory because the government never produced enough money to work the expected miracles.

Land reform succeeded in defeated Japan after World War II because Gen. Douglas MacArthur wanted it and, as supreme allied commander in an occupied country, wielded virtually dictatorial powers. Ironically, in the Philippines which shared the Allied victory, land reform came too late and with too little to alter the economic structure of the country.

President Macapagal had to resort to "surprise and secrecy" to spring the land reform bill on the conservative factions of Congress. That portion of his State of the Nation message containing the revolutionary measure was typeset in a private shop by the Director of Printing Serafin Lanot to prevent the reactionaries from getting wind of it ahead of time.[10]

When the issue was joined in Congress (Sen. Raul Manglapus led the parliamentary fight in the upper house and Rep. Juanita Nepomuceno sponsored the bill in the lower house), the proposal ran into stiff bipartisan opposition. The anti-land reform blocs used some 200 amendments to halt the passage of the bill or to reduce its sting if it were to pass. President Macapagal had to extend the congressional session *seven* times before he got out his pet measure and by then it was heavily scissored and amended, its most revolutionary provisions carefully excised, and its timetable so idealistically designed as to be almost impossible to meet. The law exempted sugar lands and fishponds and these loopholes alone placed a substantial chunk of Pampanga beyond the reach of land reform. It also spared coconut-producing land, properties smaller than 75 hectares, and land "to be converted into residential, commercial, industrial and similar non-agricultural purposes." Using the latter provision as an excuse, many Central Luzon landowners evaded expropriation by creating "ghost subdivisions" — large tracts of land declared

---

[10]Macapagal, as cited, p. 87.

for purposes of residential subdivision but with scarcely a road or house on them.

Eligio Tavanlar, the Land Tenure administrator during the Magsaysay regime, described the code as not "meaningful" because it can benefit only 10 percent of the Filipino tenants "even if it had all the money and resources it needed."[11] Actually, the Land Authority Administration never had sufficient resources to get a decent land reform program going. During Macapagal's administration, a mere pittance of ₱908,865 was released to serve 4,760 farmers cultivating a total of 12,711 hectares. Only 13 towns were covered by the program and only 11,600 farmers received any benefits from it.

These figures improved sharply in the first four-year term of President Marcos. In that period, 139 towns were proclaimed within the land reform areas. The number of leasehold agreements increased from 896 during Macapagal's time to 6,340 under Marcos's first four years. Oral agreements on lease rentals jumped from 2,205 to 15,028. There was an increase in requests for rent-fixing assistance from 5,114 as of December, 1965 to 20,734 between 1965 and 1969, indicating that "more and more landowners are becoming receptive to leasehold."

Though Land Authority Gov. Conrado Estrella is probably doing all he can, he is handicapped by limited resources. The percentage increases in land reform performance look good only because the starting bases were ridiculously small. As of 1969, only some ₱8 million worth of private agricultural lands totalling some 2,900 hectares have been acquired for distribution to tenants.[12]

It is also believed that an unduly large amount of government funds intended for agrarian uplift actually go into the overheads of government agencies. A responsible official told me that the Agricultural Credit Association should be "abolished" because it was spending more than the statutory five percent of capital for its own personnel.

Luis Taruc, though ideologically keen on land reform, was quite unhappy over the way it was put into effect. The Land Authority, he told the Espinosa committee, had been made a "dumping ground for many political proteges, casual workers interested only in their salaries."

A more professional critique came from John Montenegro, S.J., a rural sociologist commissioned by the U.S. AID

---

[11]Talk delivered during the CLDP executive seminar-workshop on "Perspectives in Regional Planning and Development," April 22, 1970, in Quezon City.

[12]Conrado Estrella, Governor, Land Authority, "The Philippine Land Reform Program, 1966-69."

to assess the land reform program in Pampanga's second district.[13] He observed the "frequent failure of the officials and technicians to be present and become directly involved with the farmers and workers in the rice fields and the infrastructure projects. Invariably one could find supervisors and technicians congregated in the land reform offices, but seldom could one come across them showing the farmers how to improve their farming practices and introducing them to better methods of increasing their production." These observations were borne out by Harold Koone, chief of the U.S. AID Agricultural Division, and recorded time and time again in his field trip reports covering most of the twelve municipalities.

It was not unusual for technicians to be recalled from field assignments for some "training or briefing session" at the main office. Often, poor inter-agency communication caused a "deplorable state of confusion and sometimes outright conflict of authority" between district project officials and the agency brass in Manila.[14]

To some Central Luzon farmers, land reform has been a boon. Governor Estrella likes to show visitors around the second district towns with newly-painted houses sprouting TV antennas — signs of new-found rural prosperity.

It has brought remarkable changes in the life of Gelacio Pangilinan, a 48-year-old farmer in Sto. Domingo, Minalin, pointed to as a "model recipient." A former share tenant, Pangilinan is now on the way to become the owner of his own six-hectare rice farm and orchard. The Land Authority bought the property from a Pampanga landowner who emigrated to Argentina. Pangilnan was given an easy 25-year repayment schedule to acquire full title.

Pangilinan borrowed a bulldozer from the Land Authority branch in San Fernando and built himself a small fishpond. With the proceeds from his rice harvest and fishpond, he saved enough for a down payment on an ₱8,000 water pump and the installation of a deep well. The pump now enables him to grow three crops of rice a year.

Pangilinan also learned how to plow his farm in straighter lines to get more use out of the land. Being something of a local show window, the Pangilinan farm has some farm animals from the Bureau of Animal Industry and they supply milk for home consumption. Pangilinan makes use of agriculture credit and is considered a good risk. A progressive

---

[13]Report on an Evaluation Study of Land Reform Related Operations in the Second District of Pampanga, submitted to US/AID Manila in early 1967.

[14]Father Montenegro believes that some of the defects reported in his 1967 AID study could since have been corrected.

farmer, he has invented some techniques not found in the book. For instance, he drives rats away from the rice fields by playing a tape recording of a rat in agony. The unorthodox method, his wife claims, has kept his fields reasonably rat-free.

Pangilinan's major advantage over other Pampanga tenants is the fact that he has finished high school. He is quick to learn new technology which he picks up from pamphlets and books. The less literate farmers have to be given personal demonstrations — a costlier method of farm education.

Pangilinan earns well above what a white-collar worker would in the city. He has a regular job as a mechanic at the Bureau of Public Highways and his wife is actually in charge of the farm. Three of his eight children are grown up and married. Pangilinan is a lot better off than many Filipinos can hope to be.

While Pangilinan and his famly may be thriving under land reform, there are reports of farmers relapsing into share tenancy after failing as independent producers or giving up their rights to others. Such cases do not appear in official land reform statistics but it is reasonable to expect an appreciable failure rate at this stage.

The second district, the birthplace of land reform, can use a lot more money than it has. According to the district branch manager Juanito Guzon, the agency disbursed ₱1.9 million in product loans last year. It needed at least ₱8 million.[15]

Guzon saw much room for improvement in the land reform program. He thought it was a mistake for the government to concentrate on expropriating private lands rather than developing public lands in less developed areas. "It would be cheaper in the long run to build new settlements in Mindanao and Palawan than to buy the highly-valued estates of the rich in Luzon," Guzon said. He also felt that the offer of 10 percent cash and the balance in government securities was not sufficient incentive for landowners to sell their property to the government. To get more cash, landowners tend to raise the prices of their properties and it is the tenants paying the amortization who eventually suffer.

Land for the Tillers

The proponents of land reform sincerely thought that, once enacted into law, it would extirpate all that was evil in the land tenure system and bring peace and prosperity to the farmers of Central Luzon. But after seven years of under-achievement and frustration, the reformists have become

[15]Interview, March, 1970.

acutely aware of the imperfections of the program and the need to rethink its philosophies.

One of the most important products of this re-appraisal is the replacement of the age-old shibboleth of "land for the landless" with the more practical "land for the tillers." Land for the landless generally means buying land from its original owners and reselling it to the former tenants. The new concept is to *lease* land only to those willing to work on it.

Until recently a mere idea promoted in seminars and conferences, it has won official acceptance among policy-makers and may indeed be the shape of things to come. The traditional concept of land redistribution is faulted on two scores. There is just not enough farmlands to go around, no matter how thinly they are sliced, and the population of the land reform areas is growing at least as fast as the national average of 3.1 percent. More important, it does not guarantee that once a farmer has title to land he would work it efficiently or even stay on it at all.

The Philippine value system places unduly large social importance on land ownership as distinguished from land utilization for it gives the titleholder not only social status but also an accumulative source of income far out of proportion to the real worth of the real estate. Fernando Santiago, one of the more thoughtful land tenure specialists, told a recent CLDP seminar that a person with a mere certificate of title could derive "seven kinds of income," including the basic rental, bank loans made on collateral provided by the land, and the returns on the investments made with bank credit. "By sheer contrast, a man who has no title to land has no income except from what he can earn from his labor," he said.[16]

The disproportionate attachment of Filipinos to land has bred many social evils — squatting, land-grabbing, speculation, and the now-familiar "feudalism" being denounced by the student radicals. Land ownership is the preserve of the rich (meaning the already landed), the politically influential or the plainly opportunistic and unscrupulous. The little man has usually neither the time nor the money to work out the bureaucratic requirements for obtaining Torrens titles, or to contest claims in court. He is consequently at the mercy of powerful neighbors. The courts are full of land-grabbing cases, some of the accused being those in high office. In Cadiz City, one of the henchmen of Negros strongman Rep. Armando Gustillo, was reported to have driven small farmers out of their holdings on the strength of a "pasture lease."

Student intercession in behalf of distressed small farmers has had nil results. The Federated Movement for Social Jus-

[16]Talk in the CLDP workshop, as cited.

tice and Reform broke off its Agrifina Circle "dialogue" when it realized the government was merely dragging its feet on about 160 farmers' complaints (including that of a Makiling, Laguna farmer who was ousted from his lot by a Philippine Air Force colonel using PAF personnel and equipment to enforce the eviction).[17]

Tavanlar proposed to curb these pernicious practices with a revolutionary change in land policy. "All public lands should no longer be given to private titled ownership but leased for indefinite periods to families and their successors who till the land," he declared at the CLDP seminar.

He pointed to an increasing global trend towards leasehold. "The American farmer, the most productive in the world, feeds not only himself but 47 other Americans. In most cases, he works on land leased to him by people who have gone into industry, or urban professions or the government service."

In Israel, under the Judaic law no single individual can own land, he said. It is leased for 49 years to families willing to work the soil. The Moslem lands still follow the Islamic belief that all land belongs to Allah. Tavanlar's prescript was supported by Judge Santiago who believed that man is entitled to land only if he uses it for socially constructive ends and not otherwise.[18]

"Land for the tillers" is now well on the way to becoming an operative policy. President Marcos has proclaimed 600 hectares of the Magalang agricultural college estate as the site of an Israel-style cooperative and specialists from Israel have been commissioned to oversee the project. House Bill No. 881, which "seeks to hasten agrarian reform through the medium of multi-purpose cooperatives," has been favorably reported out by the Espinosa committee.

The cooperative experiment began when the Filipinas Foundation, Inc., a philanthropical enterprise of the wealthy Ayala family, sent a study group to Israel in May, 1968 to find suitable community development models. The Ayala group favored the *moshav*, the more common kind of Israeli

---

[17]Philippines *Herald*, June 3, 1970. The Agrifina Circle committee was created in 1969 to bring government officials headed by Governor Estrella and representatives of the reformist Khi-Rho Movement together to facilitate action of tenant farmers' grievances.

[18]"Study-Tour of Israel and Rural Settlements Project," Report to the President and the Board of Trustees, Filipinas Foundation, Inc., 1970. According to the report of the 800 settlements in Israel, 260 are *kibbutzim* and 430 are *moshavim* and the rest an assortment of privately held farms with either private or cooperative productive and marketing schemes.

cooperative, as the most promising for adaptation in the Philippines.

As distinct from the *kibbutz*, a communal village where private and individual ownership is absent, a *moshav* is a village of small holders where each farmstead is individually leased to a family by the village cooperative association. Certain facilities are cooperatively owned and manged but the farm family "remains as the basic productive unit and private initiative is not limited."[19]

Thomas Gomez III, who led the Israel study tour, believes that the extremely communalistic life of the *kibbutz* would be too "sophisticated" for the typical Filipino farmer. In a *moshav*-type village, he would have the motivation of working on his "own" farm.

The Filipinas Foundation plan is to settle 60 families first, followed by two other batches of the same size, until a 180-family settlement can be established. Following the plan of Tasmach, one of the *moshavim* observed by the group, the settlers' houses will be clustered around a village center. This makes easier and more economical the laying of infrastructure like roads, waterpipes and power. Since the farm units are contiguous to one another, communal mechanization is possible.

The Magalang site is exceptionally attractive country, broad and fertile, nestling at the foot of Mt. Arayat. But because it lies smack on "Huk alley" — the unmarked communication route between Arayat and Angeles — it is sparsely peopled and unworked. This is where Central Luzon's "brave new world" can start, with courage, imagination and the will to work.

The Regional Solution

There are two ways of charting the future of Central Luzon. One view accepts Huntington's thesis that substantive reform demands more "inputs," more masterful management than the political system can supply. Judging from past performance and present capabilities, there is a good likelihood that the central government would continue to begrudge its purse and the good intentions of the reformers would go for naught.

In this event, the Pampango society would have to find its own destiny its own way. It has perhaps already found an implicit accommodation with its own internal conflicts for it does carry on after a fashion — growing and harvesting its rice and sugar, making a petty bourgeois living in its

---

[19]Same.

crowded *poblaciones,* coexisting both with the Huks and with the impact of Manila's secular culture.

Many schemes and designs have been proposed and attempted except for one that may be the most obvious of all — *letting Central Luzon alone.* The Huks have been shown to be no aggressive, expansionist threat to the rest of the Republic. They are content to stay within the confines of their native society. Huk "resurgence" is a fiction. If the military and the killer squads are pulled out, Pampanga and Tarlac would become more peaceful for there would no longer be any dispute over "control."

The Huks have been defeated in a military sense, but in a sense they have also won. They have pressured the central government into doling out precious resources. They have enforced their own "land reform," driving a good number of the landlord class out of Pampanga and authorizing farmers to divide their harvests on a 70-30 basis with the absent landowners.[20] They have captured a sizeable number of local political offices.

Even the grave injuries the Pampanga society has inflicted on itself can heal with time, in a generation perhaps, or two. When the conditions that have bred dissidence disappear, as indeed they are likely to in the process of "modernization," the Huks would simply die a natural death. As Pedro Taruc and Sumulong once put it, "we shall just fade away."

President Macapagal, in a rather undeliberate way, adopted this approach to his native Pampanga. His economic contribution to the province was not exceptionally large but his military policy was largely passive and tolerant. Between 1961 and 1965, the Huks were reduced to the smallest number in their entire history. They simply accommodated with the rest of their environment.

What brought about the post-1965 "resurgence" was increasing military pressure, the frustration of half-fulfilled reform and intensive political maneuvering by the Pampango leaders.

To extend this scenario to another region, a reform program in the Ilocos region would surely cause greater internal conflicts than it already has. The "feudal lords" would violently resist any attempt to reduce their power.

An accommodation of the regional identity of the Pampangos, however, is the farthest thing from the demonstrated policies of President Marcos. His politics are actually *consolidative* rather than reformistic . They are patently inten-

---

[20]In some portions of Nueva Ecija, the farmers were keeping 80 percent of the harvest and allowing the landowners 20 percent—a "New Deal" indeed under the auspices of the Huks.

ded to achieve not a "broadening of participation in society and polity" which is how Huntington described reform but a further concentration of political power at the center.

There is a long-term rationale for consolidation rather than reform. An inevitable consequence of modernization is the gradual diminution of regional differences and the emergence of a single national culture. Modernization will bring about increased social mobility; the traditional concentrations of lingual group will be deconcentrated as the native-born leave for the urban areas and their communities become more mixed.

The second option for Central Luzon, therefore, is to be gradually absorbed into the national maintream. The erosion of the Pampango identity has been taking place since the turn of the century — an inevitable casualty of modernization. Mariano Henson observed with obvious sorrow how the Pampango language, the strong bond uniting the members of this unique minority, is losing its hold among the modern Pampangos:

> In cosmopolitan areas of Pampanga at present, the (Capampangan you hear) more aptly resembles that of a newly articulating child than the once pure (language). And it is not infrequent to hear . . . a highbrow native (reply) in English when confronted with conversational Pampango!
>
> . . . a Pampango parent will be surprised to discover that his university graduate son or daughter cannot read nor write Pampango . . . (They tend to pronounce "Cezár," "parrece," and "apretada" as "César," "párrece," and "fritada.")[21]

Such are the indignities to which a language that once had such noble articulators as Luisa Gonzaga de Leon, Juan Crisostomo Soto (Crisot), and Aurelio Tolentino has to suffer as the ancestral traditions fade away.

A Strategy of Modernization

If we assume that the answer to the Central Luzon problem is to accelerate its modernization, many existing policies are due for thorough overhauling. For instance, land reform, the cherished goal of Pampanga's great reformers, may become obsolete even before it can effect substantive changes. From a cost-benefit viewpoint, the ₱50 million projected for the financing of land reform over 10 years can provide greatly more jobs, benefit greatly more people, and effect far wider economic changes invested elsewhere.

---

[21]As cited, pp. 170, 175.

The authors of the land reform code did not realize one fundamental weakness of land reform as an institutional policy. It would have the effect of continuing an agricultural economy which is far too inadequate to provide for the needs of the remaining decades of the 20th century.

Though the "green revolution" has made the Philippines self-sufficient in rice and promises other breakthroughs in food production, the contribution of agriculture to total national growth cannot exceed certain predictable limits.

Saburo Okita, president of the Japan Economic Research Society, told a conference on modernization that even with the most advanced agricultural techniques, the growth rate of agriculturally-based economies cannot exceed the optimum of four or five percent — "and this assumes good world prices, the prevalence of fair weather conditions and a minimum occurence of droughts, pests, and other contingencies."[22]

A four to five percent growth rate is not high considering that much of that growth would be eaten up by the expanding populations characterizing countries with a large proportion of rural dwellers. The Philippines with its predicted four to five percent growth will probably be outstripped in the next decades by its Asian neighbors like Taiwan, South Korea, Malaysia and Singapore. These countries have pushed their growth rate to eight to ten percent by wisely shifting from primary products to labor-intensive manufacturing for export.

The main thrust in Central Luzon then should not be agricultural reform but *industrialization*. A Central Luzon development plan should, as Senator Aquino suggested, provide strong incentives for new industries in Pampanga and Tarlac. "Any Manila-based industry wanting to transfer to, say, Tarlac would be guaranteed protection, loans, tax exemptions. In that way you disperse industry and decongest the Manila area. Admittedly, the government would be favoring one region over other regions, but if the cancer is in the region, it must be given more attention."[23]

The urban planners already see Greater Manila megapolis extending northwards, as far as Angeles City in the next two decades. With the new industries will come a more mixed economy and more pronounced urbanization.

Because of its proximity to Manila, Central Luzon may be the first primarily agricultural region to diversify its eco-

---

[22]"Modernization in Asia and Pacific, a Futuristic Perspective Based on Japan's Experience," a paper prepared for the Second International Conference on the Problems of Modernization in Asia and the Pacific, East-West Center, Honolulu, August 9-15, 1970.

[23]*Philippines Free Press,* as cited.

nomic activities. Many of its lowlands will remain agricultural but with the availability of cheap power and cheap labor the region will be just as naturally suited to industrial development.

The prerequisite to all this, of course, is the restoration of peace in the countryside. There may be a vicious circle in the fact that peace and order cannot be achieved without economic progress and progress cannot be attained without security. This is the implied reasoning behind the "twin-pronged" campaigns of Philippine presidents since Magsaysay.

Modernization may spell the end of the agrarian society of Central Luzon in some future time — and with it its tradition of protest and rebellion. The particular genius of the Pampango race, hopefully, will not die. It will continue to feed into the mainstream of the national society, turning out poets, politicians, innovators and even some useful non-conformists as it has always done.

Annex A

RANKING HUKS AND AWARDS FOR THEIR KILLING, CAPTURE OR SURRENDER

Sources: Department of National Defense, Philippines

July 31, 1959

	Name	Award
1.	Jesus Lava	₱130,000.00
2.	Casto Alejandrino	50,000.00
3.	Silvestre Liwanag	50,000.00

Awards ranging from ₱1,500 to ₱200 are also offered for 23 classes of Huks, their individual names not specified.

October 11, 1965

	Name	Award
1.	Pedro Taruc, alias Bayong, Junior, Fermin	₱ 45,000.00
2.	Faustino del Mundo, alias Sumulong, Fermin	20,000.00
3.	Cesareo Manarang, alias Alibasbas, Torio	20,000.00
4.	Efren Lopez, alias Freddie	15,000.00

February 3, 1967

	Name	Award
1.	Pedro Taruc, alias Bayong, Joaquin, Ruiz, Pilato, Junior, Fermin, Payat, Manuel, Perez, Tañada and "Supremo"*	₱100,000.00
2.	Faustino del Mundo, alias Sumulong, Fidel, Deluz, Manio, Mario, Delfin, Culet, Mulong, Ka Andres and Alba*	80,000.00
3.	Zacarias de la Cruz, alias Delio, Viray	40,000.00
4.	Efren Lopez, alias Freddie*	40,000.00
5.	Dominador Garcia, alias Ely	30,000.00
6.	Gregorio Ocampo, alias George, Tonie, Luna	20,000.00
7.	Maximo Flores, alias Nestor, Taga, Max	10,000.00
8.	Avelino Bagsik, alias Zaragoza	10,000.00
9.	Felicisimo Bondoc, alias Felicing	10,000.00
10.	Cristobal de la Cruz, alias Ubang	10,000.00
11.	Hernando Subong, alias Sareno	10,000.00
12.	Bernabe Buscayno, alias Dante	10,000.00
13.	Alberto Mercado, alias Trongco, Belo	5,000.00
14.	Diosdado Layug, alias Eddie Layug	3,500.00
15.	Nelson Vinuya, alias Ocar Tangkad, Nelson	4,000.00
16.	Salvador Macaspac, alias Ador, Badong	3,500.00
17.	Eliseo Salas, alias Cruz	2,500.00
18.	Anacleto Suba, alias Cleto, Bert	2,500.00
19.	Jesus Castro, alias Busok	2,000.00
20.	Pete Pineda	1,500.00

21.	Domingo Yambao, alias Fredy, Poling	1,000.00
22.	Fernando Guevarra, alias Pering, Bernie	1,000.00
23.	Paulino Rueda, alias Pauling, Binata	1,000.00
24.	Gregorio Garcia, alias Yoyong	1,000.00
25.	Guillermo de la Cruz, alias Imong	1,000.00
26.	Adriano Galang	1,000.00
27.	Felix Salac	1,000.00
28.	Paulino Galano	1,000.00
29.	Florentino Salac	1,000.00
30.	Junior Salac	1,000.00
31.	Florentino Medina, alias Forting	1,000.00
32.	Hermogenes Miranda, alias Buco, Mones	900.00
33.	Francisco Maniego, alias Koreano	900.00
34.	Manalastas Leon, alias Leon	900.00
35.	Eleno de la Peña, alias Leonon, Eleno	900.00
36.	Ernesto Punzalan, alias Esto	900.00

July 23, 1969

1.	Pedro Taruc, alias Commander Pedring*† Secretariat	₱150,000.00
2.	Faustino del Mundo, Alias Commander Sumulong, Chief, National Finance Department	150,000.00
3.	Bernabe Buscayno, alias Commander Dante*† Chief, Military Department	150,000.00
4.	Gregorio Ocampo, alias Commander Tonie Chief, Educational Dept.	80,000.00
5.	Diosdado Layug, alias Commander Eddie† Sector Commander	30,000.00
6.	Eleno de la Peña, alias Commander Roldan† Sector Commander	25,000.00
7.	Hernando Subong, alias Sareno† Political Director	25,000.00
8.	Hermogenes Miranda, alias Zaragosa, Buco† Group Commander	20,000.00
9.	Florentino Salac, alias Ponting Group Commander	20,000.00
10.	Felix Salac, alias Felix, Pelaez† Group Commander	20,000.00
11.	Adriano Galang, alias Ging† Group Commander	20,000.00
12.	Benjamin Laxamana, alias Ben, Liwanag Group Commander	15,000.00
13.	Jesus Sagun, alias Jessie, Beros Group Commander	15,000.00
14.	Hermogenes Parsolingan, alias Mone Group Liquidation Leader	10,000.00
15.	Rolando Manalo, alias Rolly Member, Ponting Liquidation Group	5,000.00
16.	Juanito de Leon, alias Rudy	5,000.00
17.	Gregorio Dimarucut, alias Gorio Group Commander under Sareno	5,000.00
18.	Ely Esguerra, alias Ely	

No.	Name	Amount
	Group Commander under Sareno	5,000.00
19.	Paulino Calanoc, alias Calanoc	3,000.00
20.	Mariano Mata, alias Mata	3,000.00
21.	Alias Roly, Vice Commander of Jessie	3,000.00
22.	Marcelo Tolentino, alias Madrigal	3,000.00
23.	Rogelio Balboa, alias Roger	2,000.00
24.	Abelardo Macaspac, alias Abel	2,000.00
25.	Berting Garison, alias Berting	2,000.00
26.	Alberto Macalino, alias Berting	2,000.00
27.	Canor Guzon, alias Canor	2,000.00
26.	Alberto Macalino, alias Berting	2,000.00
29.	Mariano de Guzman, alias Diwa	2,000.00
30.	Alias Melody, Ruben	2,000.00
31.	Alias Mike, Ner	1,000.00
32.	Felix Atienza, alias Magaling	1,000.00
33.	Vicente Samson, alias Limson	1,000.00
34.	Jose Rivera, alias Joe	1,000.00
35.	Maldo Sarmiento, alias Maldo, Waldo	1,000.00
36.	Alias Tagul	1,000.00
37.	Narding de Vera, alias Narding, Labuyo	1,000.00
38.	Romeo de Guzman, alias Romy, Romero, Castro	800.00
39.	Alias Ador	800.00
40.	Alias Mar, Tagalog, Darna	800.00
41.	Fidel Samia, alias Fidel, Fidel Castro	800.00
42.	Ricardo Dimalanta, alias Kulafu, Carding	800.00
43.	Pentong Santos, alias Pentong	800.00
44.	Felipe Simbulan, alias Salicsic	800.00
45.	Alias Pusti, Utul	600.00
46.	Alias Orling	600.00
47.	Rudy Balanditan, alias Rudy	600.00
48.	Jose Garcia, alias Joe	600.00
49.	Ricardo Balajadia, alias Al Capone	600.00
50.	Alias Rudy	600.00
51.	Manuel Icban Valero, alias Maning	400.00
52.	Marciano Manaloto, alias Marcing	400.00
53.	Alias Johnny	400.00
54.	Alias Navaroo	400.00
55.	Alias Baracosa	400.00
56.	Alias Lawin	400.00
57.	Alias Larry	400.00
58.	Alias Goido	400.00
59.	Alias Rodrigo	400.00
60.	Alias Erning	400.00
61.	Marcenlino Cayanana, alias Marcing	400.00
62.	Alias Dadoy	400.00
63.	Alias Inigo, Niggo	200.00
64.	Alias Goody, Goddie	200.00
65.	Claudio Madriago, alias Efen	200.00
66.	Florencio Mangino, alias Mangino	200.00
67.	Manuel Bantor, alias Bantor	200.00
68.	Pablo Canlas, alias Concejal	200.00
69.	Eduardo de Leon, alias Gestapo	200.00
70.	Apolinario David, alias Poling Jr., Payat	200.00

71.	Alias Polticus	200.00
72.	Alias Tiquio	200.00
73.	Alias Pepe, Peping	200.00
74.	Alias Marte	100.00
75.	Alias Manalili	100.00
76.	Estelita Manalini, alias Est	100.00
77.	Alias Seniong	100.00
78.	Erlinda Torres, alias Linda, Er	100.00
79.	Alias Pingas	100.00
80.	Teresita Flores	100.00
81.	Pedro (last name unknown), alias Iso	100.00
82.	Fernando Garcia, alias Bravo	100.00
83.	Alias Linda (wife of Eloy de la Peña)	100.00

March 16, 1970

1.	Bernabe Buscayno, alias Commander Dante*†+ Commander-in-Chief Member, Central Committee Member, Military Commission Member, Political Bureau Head Organizer of CPP/MA-MAO in Central Luzon	₱150,000.00
2.	Pedro Taruc, alias Commander Pedring*†+ Huk Supremo/Secretariat	150,000.00
3.	Faustino del Mundo, alias Commander Sumulong*†+ Assistant Secretariat Chairman, National Finance Dept.	150,000.00
4.	Gregorio Ocampo, alias Commander George, Tonie†+ Chief, Education Dept., HMB Expansion Force Supervisor Chief of Liquidation	100,000.00
5.	Florentino Salac, alias Commander Ponting†+ Sector Supervisor, Eastern Bataan Chief of Liquidation	40,000.00
6.	Benjamin Biet Jr., alias Jose Delgado, Fidel Garcia, Bie, Commander Melody+ MA-MAO Territorial Commander Member, Central Committee Director, Liquidation Group	40,000.00
7.	Diosdado Layug, Commander Eddie+ MA-MAO Territorial Commander Member, Central Committee MA-MAO Training Supervisor in Isabela	40,000.00
8.	Arthur Garcia, alias Commander Arthur MA-MAO Territorial Commander Educational Dept. Head	40,000.00
9.	Felix Salac, alias Commander Pelaez, Felix+ Sector Supervisor, Northern Pampanga Chief of Liquidation	40,000.00
10.	Marcelo Tolentino, alias Commander Madrigal+	30,000.00

11.	Hermogenes Miranda, alias Commander Zaragoza+ Group Supervisor Chief of Liquidation in Eastern Pampanga ..	30,000.00
12.	Hermogenes Parsolingan, alias Commander Quines, Monesa MA-MAO Asst. Territorial Commander Training Supervisor in Cagayan Province	30,000.00
13.	Hernando Subong, alias Commander Sareno†+ Group Commander Political Director in Isabela Province	30,000.00
14.	Adriano Galang, alias Commander Ging*†+ Group Supervisor in Western Bataan	30,000.00
15.	Juanito de Leon, alias Rudy, Bacbac+ MA-MAO Asst. Territorial Commander Training Supervisor in Zambales province	30,000.00
16.	Jaime Delgado, alias Commander Joe MA-MAO Teritorial Commander Member, Central Committee	25,000.00
17.	Alias Commander Goody+ MA-MAO Territorial Commander Member, Central Committee	25,000.00
18.	Alias Commander Ruben MA-MAO Territorial Commander Member, Central Committee	25,000.00
19.	Alias Elias or Commander Elias MA-MAO Territorial Commander Member, Central Committee	25,000.00
20.	Alias Juaning or Commander Juaning MA-MAO Teritorial Commander Member, Central Committee	25,000.00
21.	Alias Ben or Commander Ben MA-MAO Territorial Commander	25,000.00
22.	Manuel Dimatulac alias Commander Ligaya MA-MAO Territorial Commander Leader, Liquidation Group in Tarlac, Tarlac ..	25,000.00
23.	Jesus Sagum alias Commander Jessie/Beros Group Commander	20,000.00
24.	Juanito Rivera alias Commander Juaning MA-MAO Group Supervisor Liquidation Chief	20,000.00
25.	Telesforo Gatmaitan, alias Porong/Poring Chairman of CPP District Party Committee in Tarlac,Tarlac NPA Recruiting Officer	20,000.00
26.	Boy Batoc alias Boy Batoc MA-MAO Group Supervisor & Liquidation Chief	20,000.00
27.	Mariano de Guzman alias Commander Diwa Armed Group Commander of MASAKA Supervisor Liquidation Group	20,000.00
28.	Felino Manaluz alias Commander Sandoval Armed Group Commander of MASAKA	

	Supervisor Liquidation Group	20,000.00
29.	Policarpio Mallari, alias Comander Pio MA-MAO Group Supervisor Liquidation Chief	20,000.00
30.	Benjamin Laxamana & Commander Ben/Liwanag+ Group Commander	20,000.00
31.	Rolando Manalo alias Commander Rolly Leader of the Liquidation Group	20,000.00
32.	Ceferino Gamboa alias Commander Legaspi/Barredo Group Supervisor in Western Bulacan	20,000.00
33.	Berting Macalino alias Commander Berting Assistant Liquidation Group Leader of Pelaez	20,000.00
34.	Oscar Suarez alias Commander Suarez NPA Assistant Group Supervisor	10,000.00
35.	Narciso de Leon alias Commander Isong MA-MAO Assistant Group Supervisor	10,000.00
36.	Ernesto Bermudo alias Commander Freddie MA-MAO Assistant Group Supervisor	10,000.00
37.	Epifanio Manalili alias Commander Alipogpog MA-MAO Assistant Group Supervisor Security Officer of SARAFACA	10,000.00
38.	Ely Esguerra, alias Ely Group Leader Isabela Province	10,000.00
39.	Vicente Samson, alias Limson/Linda+ Assistant Group Leader of Zaragosa	10,000.00
40.	Benito Punzalan, alias Commander Bito+ In-charge of the Liquidation Group of Commander Pelaez	10,000.00
41.	Mariano Mata alias Mata In-charge of the Liquidation Group of Commander Zaragosa	10,000.00
42.	Rogelio Balboa alias Roger In-charge of Liquidation Group of Zaragosa in Southern Pampanga	10,000.00
43.	Fidel Samia, alias Fidel Castro+ In-charge of the Liquidation Group of Commander Pelaez in Northern Pampanga	10,000.00
44.	Natividad Bermudo alias Commander Liwayway MA-MAO Assistant Group Supervisor Intelligence Officer	10,000.00
45.	Merly Salas, alias Merly Salas/Merly Serrano MA-MAO Assistant Group Supervisor	10,000.00
46.	Maria Montenegra alias Comander Montenegra CPP/MA-MAO Organizer Assistant Group Supervisor	10,000.00
47.	Amado Mariano alias Commander Mado MA-MAO Assistant Group Supervisor	10,000.00
48.	Aurora Pagaling, alias Commander Auring CPP/MA-MAO Organizer in Gerona, Tarlac ..	10,000.00
49.	Julian Samson alias Commander Sampaguita	

	MA-MAO Logistics Officer Assistant Group Supervisor	10,000.00
50.	Abelardo Garcia, alias Billy/Junior/Rogelio Baluyot/Romeo Baluyot/Elvis In-charge of MA-MAO publication & Propaganda KM Ldr in Tarlac & MA-MAO Member CPP/MA-MAO Propagandist/Agitator/Activist	10,000.00
51.	Deogracias Dizon, alias Deog Assistant Group Supervisor Liquidation Chief of Dante	10,000.00
52.	Benigno Tolentino alias new Commander Cruz MA-MAO In-charge of Liquidation Squad	5,000.00
53.	Inocencio Pura alias unknown MA-MAO Assistant Unit Commander In-charge Liquidation Squad	5,000.00
54.	Ruben Castro alias Ben MA-MAO Assistant Unit Commander In-charge Liquidation Squad	5,000.00
55.	Rodolfo dela Peña, alias Commander Rudy MA-MAO In-charge Liquidation Squad	5,000.00
56.	Berting Cascon, alias Berting In-charge Liquidation Squad	5,000.00
57.	Roberto Santos alias Felman MA-MAO Member u/Ligaya	5,000.00
58.	Cipriano Bondoc, alias Supri/Opring MA-MAO In-charge Liquidation Squad	5,000.00
59.	Ernesto Miranda alias Panchito MA-MAO In-charge Liquidation Squad	5,000.00
60.	Billy Espique, alias Billy Bensut MA-MAO In-charge Liquidation Squad Assistant Group Leader u/Pio	5,000.00
61.	Boy Bildan alias Benjie MA-MAO In-charge Liquidation Squad	5,000.00
62.	Alias Rolly In-charge Liquidation Squad	5,000.00
63.	Osias Adona MA-MAO Fin O & Treasurer in Tarlac, Tarlac In-charge Liquidation Squad	5,000.00
64.	Jesus Borja In-charge Liquidation Squad	5,000.00
65.	Jose Reyes Personal Secretary of Dante	2,000.00
66.	Jose Rivera alias Joe Secretary of Commander Rudy	2,000.00
67.	Romeo de Guzman alias Romy MA-MAO Assistant Group Leader u/Juaning ..	2,000.00
68.	Domingo Bermudo Jr. Personal Security of Dante	2,000.00
69.	Roger Buscayno alias Roger MA-MAO Assistant Group Leader of Joe	2,000.00
70.	Lody Pineda Personal Secretary of Dante	2,000.00

71. Rogelio Tejada alias Rolly
Personal Secretary of Dante 2,000.00
72. Boyet Guevarra
Personal Secretary of Dante 2,000.00
73. Alias Dagul
Secretary of Madrigal 2,000.00
74. Alias Rudy
Personal Secretary of Dante 2,000.00
75. Antonio Buscayno alias Tony
Secretary of Dante in Capas, Tarlac 2,000.00
76. Ernesto Buscayno alias Erning/Boy
Secretary of Dante in Capas, Tarlac 2,000.00
77. Raymundo Arcilla alias Mundo
Secretary of Dante in Capas, Tarlac 2,000.00
78. Castro Arcilla alias Castro
Secretary of Dante in Capas, Tarlac 2,000.00
79. Danilo Galang
MA-MAO Member of Liquidation Squad under Ligaya 2,000.00
80. Totoy Galang
MA-MAO Member of Liquidation Squad under Ligaya 2,000.00
81. Roberto Pangilinan alias Soliman
MA-MAO Team Leader under Freddie 2,000.00
82. Felipe Simbulan alias Noly/Salicsic
MA-MAO Assistant Group Leader under Rudy . 2,000.00
83. Alias Darding
MA-MAO Assistant Group Leader of Quines .. 2,000.00
84. Armando Tolentino alias Mado
MA-MAO Assistant, Liquidation Squad Leader under Madrigal 2,000.00
85. Felix Atienza alias Magaling
MA-MAO Assistant Liquidation Squad Leader under Layug 2,000.00
86. Narding de Vera alias Labuyo/Narding
MA-MAO Assistant Group Leader under Rudy . 2,000.00
87. Maldo Sarmiento alias Maldo
MA-MAO Member, Liquidation Squad under Quines 2,000.00
88. Servando Lacson alias Bando
MA-MAO Member 1,000.00
89. Wilfredo Lacson alias Fred
MA-MAO Member under Joe
Personal Secretary of Dante 1,000.00
90. Alias Rolly of San Nicolas, Tarlac, Tarlac
MA-MAO Member under Joe 1,000.00
91. Zosimo Figueroa
MA-MAO Member 1,000.00
92. Robert Nixon (Mestiso Negro)
MA-MAO Member 1,000.00
93. Pat Benigno Castro alias Boy Castro
MA-MAO Member 1,000.00
94. Juanito Manalili

	MA-MAO Member	1,000.00
95.	Silvino Arcilla, alias Joe/Bino MA-MAO Member	1,000.00
96.	Mamerto Gatmaitan alias Mentong Secretary of Dante in Capas, Tarlac	1,000.00
97.	Tayong Leal Secretary of Dante in Capas, Tarlac	1,000.00
98.	Ramon Capis Secretary of Dante in Capas, Tarlac	1,000.00
99.	Aurelio Lacsa alias Jr. Mercado Secretary of Dante in Capas, Tarlac	1,000.00
100.	Rudy Balanditan MA-MAO Member Liquidation Squad under Eddie Layug	1,000.00
101.	Jose Salas Secretary of Dante in Tarlac, Tarlac	1,000.00
102.	Ricardo Polintan alias Carding Secretary of Dante in Tarlac, Tarlac	1,000.00
103.	Romulo Maglaque alias Romy Secretary of Dante in Tarlac, Tarlac	1,000.00
104.	Narciso Alfaro, alias Narcing Secretary of Dante in Tarlac, Tarlac	1,000.00
105.	Rene Reyes Secretary of Dante in Tarlac, Tarlac	1,000.00
106.	Reynaldo David Secretary of Dante in Tarlac, Tarlac	1,000.00
107.	Antonio Dayrit Secretary of Dante in Tarlac, Tarlac	1,000.00
108.	Antonio Bagsic, alias Tony Secretary of Dante in Tarlac, Tarlac	1,000.00
109.	Paterno Dayrit Secretary of Dante in Tarlac, Tarlac	1,000.00
110.	Rodolfo Taruc Secretary of Dante in Tarlac, Tarlac	1,000.00
111.	Alias Boy Personal Secretary of Dante at Tarlac, Tarlac	1,000.00
112.	Alias Jack Personal Secretary of Dante at Tarlac, Tarlac	1,000.00
113.	Alias Pabling Personal Secretary of Dante at Tarlac, Tarlac	1,000.00
114.	Benito Layug alias Benith/Benny MA-MAO Member Liquidation Squad under Ligaya	1,000.00
115.	Alias Joe Personal Secretary of Dante at Tarlac, Tarlac	1,000.00
116.	Patricio Dayrit MA-MAO Member under Dante	1,000.00
117.	Ricardo Balajadia, alias Al Capone MA-MAO Member Liquidation Squad under Rudy	1,000.00
118.	Maldo Magno MA-MAO Team Leader	1,000.00
119.	Orlando Mallari alias Orling	

	MA-MAO Br. Liquidation Squad Group under Madrigal	1,000.00
120.	Geronimo Garcia alias Imon MA-MAO Liquidation Squad under Madrigal	1,000.00
121.	Alias Peter/John/Martello MA-MAO, Member, Liquidation Squad under Commander Porong/Poring	1,000.00
122.	Anastacio Godo MA-MAO, Member, Liquidation Squad under Quines/Balbas	1,000.00
123.	Gaudencio de Dios MA-MAO, Member, Liquidation Squad under Commander Porong/Poring	1,000.00
124.	Ireneo Gatmaitan MA-MAO, Member, Liquidation Squad under Poring	1,000.00
125.	Reynaldo Galang, alias Ireng MA-MAO, Member, Liquidation Squad under Ligaya's group	1,000.00
126.	Fernando Borja alias Per Borja MA-MAO, Member Liquidation Squad under Ligaya's Group	1,000.00
127.	Gaudencio Maliwat alias Goding MA-MAO, Member, Liquidation Squad under Ligaya	1,000.00
128.	Lino Baun alias Lino MA-MAO, Member, Liquidation Squad under Pio	1,000.00
129.	Boy Culot MA-MAO, Member, Liquidation Squad under Ligaya	1,000.00
130.	Lito Policarpio MA-MAO, Member, Liquidation Squad under Pio	1,000.00
131.	Ben Pandan MA-MAO, Member, Liquidation Squad under Ligaya	1,000.00
132.	Tino Yalung alias Yongies MA-MAO, Member, Liquidation Squad under Pedring	1,000.00
133.	Marcelo alias Marcing MA-MAO, Member, Liquidation Squad under Pedring	1,000.00
134.	Alias Bingbing MA-MAO, Member, Liquidation Squad under Pedring	1,000.00
135.	Renato Bondoc alias Remy MA-MAO, Member, Liquidation Squad under Arthur	1,000.00
136.	Beck Beltran MA-MAO, Member, Liquidation Squad under Jose Buscayno	1,000.00
137.	Santiago Sacdalan	

MA-MAO, Member 500.00
138. Gregorio Bansangan
MA-MAO, Member 500.00
139. Peregrino Dizon alias Pere
MA-MAO, Member 500.00
140. Joaquin Lacsa
MA-MAO, Member, Pio's Group 500.00
141. Alberto Patawaran
MA-MAO, Member 500.00
142. Aurelio Salalila alias Eliong
MA-MAO, Member, Pio's Group 500.00
143. Conrado Pagco
MA-MAO, Member 500.00
144. Constancio Sudang alias Boy
MA-MAO, Member, Pio's Group 500.00
145. Rudy Tagubansa
MA-MAO, Member 500.00
146. Bocoy Dizon
MA-MAO, Member, Batoc's Group 500.00
147. Boy dela Peña MA-MAO, Member 500.00
148. Ireneo Galang MA-MAO, Member 500.00
149. Pedro Arceo
MA-MAO, Member, under Quines 500.00
150. Rudy Canlas
MA-MAO, Member of Melody's Group 500.00
151. Fortunato Bitagcol
MA-MAO, Member of Melody's Group 500.00
152. Jose Hernandez
MA-MAO, Member of Melody's Group 500.00
153. Juanito Ramos
MA-MAO, Member of Melody's Group 500.00
154. Alias Daniel alias Fighting
MA-MAO, Member, Pio's Group 500.00
155. Prudencio Inocencio
MA-MAO, Member of Melody's Group 500.00
156. Lamberto Pastural alias Beck
MA-MAO, Member, Pio's Group 500.00
157. Pedro Dayrit
MA-MAO, Member of Melody's Group 500.00
158. Eduardo de Leon alias Gestapo
MA-MAO, Member of Melody's Group 500.00
159. Claudio Madriaga alias Efren
MA-MAO, Member of Melody's Group 500.00
160. Bantor Manuel
MA-MAO, Member of Melody's Group 500.00
161. Inocencio Magino
MA-MAO, Member of Suarez' Group 500.00
162. Ireneo Bondoc
MA-MAO, Member, Batoc's Group
163. Florencio Mangino
MA-MAO, Member, Melody's Group 500.00
164. Fernando Garcia alias Bravo
MA-MAO, Member of Ben's Group 500.00
165. Celestino Vinuya

MA-MAO, Member, under Joe 500.00
166. Ising Garcia
MA-MAO, Member, under Joe 500.00
167. Simeon Garcia
MA-MAO, Member, under Joe 500.00
168. Primo Parsolingan
MA-MAO, Member, under Joe 500.00
169. Deo Garcia
MA-MAO, Member, under Joe 500.00
170. Felimon Parsolingan alias Felino
MA-MAO, Member, under Joe 500.00
171. Rodolfo Salvador alias Rudy
MA-MAO, Member, under Joe 500.00
172. Marciano Manaloto
MA-MAO, Member, under Joe 500.00
173. Angel Bermudo
MA-MAO, Member, under Joe 500.00
174. Alias Baracoso
MA-MAO, Member, under Rudy 500.00
175. Alias Navarro
MA-MAO, Member, under Rudy 500.00
176. Alias Johnny
MA-MAO, Member, under Rudy 500.00
177. Alias Erning
MA-MAO, Member, under Rudy 500.00
178. Alias Polticus+
MA-MAO, Member, under Dante 500.00
179. Alias Inigo/Nigo
MA-MAO, Member, under Dante 500.00
180. Alias Guido
MA-MAO, Member, under Dante 500.00
181. Alias Lawin
MA-MAO, Member, under Rudy 500.00
182. Alias Aman
MA-MAO, Member, under Rudy 500.00
183. Alias Rodrigo
MA-MAO, Member, under Rudy 500.00
184. Alias Erning
MA-MAO, Member, under Rudy 500.00
185. Alias Dadoy
MA-MAO, Member, under Rudy 500.00
186. Alias Pingas
MA-MAO, Member, under Rudy 500.00
187. Alias Iro/Pedro
MA-MAO, Member, under Rudy 500.00
188. Alias Delfin
MA-MAO, Member, under Rudy 500.00
189. Alberto Pamintuan alias Bert
MA-MAO, Member, under Rudy 500.00
190. Alias Daling
MA-MAO, Member, under Rudy 500.00
191. Alias Bernard
MA-MAO, Member, under Rudy 500.00

192. Manuel Valero Icban alias Maning
MA-MAO, Member, under Rudy 500.00
193. Ben Banag alias Ben
MA-MAO, Member, under Madrigal 500.00
194. Waldo Dayrit
MA-MAO, Member, under Madrigal 500.00
195. Alias Berting/Betty
MA-MAO, Member, under Madrigal 500.00
196. Alias Marcos
MA-MAO, Member, under Madrigal 500.00
197. Dading Quiambao alias Putot
MA-MAO, Member, under Madrigal's Group .. 500.00
198. Turing Malonzo
MA-MAO, Member, Madrigal's Group 500.00
199. Ciano Manalo
MA-MAO, Member, Madrigal's Group 500.00
200. Alias Peta
MA-MAO, ember, Madrigal's Group 500.00
201. Alias Dagul
MA-MAO, Member, Madrigal's Group 500.00
202. Roberto Pineda alias Berting
MA-MAO, Member, under Diwa 500.00
203. Cipriano Guias
MA-MAO, Member, under Diwa 500.00
204. Jose Mandani
MA-MAO, Member, under Diwa 500.00
205. Teodoro Mandani
MA-MAO, Member, under Diwa 500.00
206. Maximo Aquino alias Laya
MA-MAO, Member, under Diwa 500.00
207. Roman Manalastas
MA-MAO, Member, under Diwa 500.00
208. Cenon de Guzman alias Trench Mortar
MA-MAO, Member, under Diwa 500.00
209. Cornelio Lacsa
MA-MAO, Member, under Ligaya 500.00
210. Peping Gatmaitan
MA-MAO, Member, under Ligaya 500.00
211. Waldo Umali
MA-MAO, Member, under Ligaya 500.00
212. Leonardo Umali
MA-MAO, Member, under Ligaya 500.00
213. Federico Valdez
MA-MAO, Member, under Ligaya 500.00
214. Alias Laug
MA-MAO, Member, under Ligaya 500.00
215. Elong Reyes
MA-MAO, Member, under Suarez 500.00
216. Valerio Lapitan
MA-MAO, Member, under Suarez 500.00
217. Cesar Capindian
MA-MAO, Member, under Suarez 500.00
218. Pedro Santos

MA-MAO, Member, under Suarez 500.00
219. Zacarias Grande
MA-MAO, Member, under Suarez 500.00
220. Boy Cardinas
MA-MAO, Member, under Suarez 500.00
221. Andy Baking
MA-MAO, Member, under Suarez 500.00
222. Alias Bores
MA-MAO, Member, under Suarez 500.00
223. Alias Bagol
MA-MAO, Member, under Suarez 500.00
224. Alias Alberto Dimasupil
MA-MAO, Member, under Freddie 500.00
225. Alias Pacing
MA-MAO, Member, under Freddie 500.00
226. Alias Junior
MA-MAO, Member, under Freddie 500.00
227. Alias Beny/Ruben
MA-MAO, Member, under Freddie 500.00
228. Antonio Balingit
MA-MAO, Member, under De Leon/Isong 500.00
229. Erming Baluga
MA-MAO, Member, under De Leon/Isong 500.00
230. Alias Panground Force
MA-MAO, Member, under De Leon/Isong 500.00
231. Alias Cariño
MA-MAO, Member, under De Leon/Isong 500.00
232. Alias Tony
MA-MAO, Member, under De Leon/Isong 500.00
233. Mauro Bulacan
MA-MAO, Member, under De Leon/Isong 500.00
234. Nonong Garcia alias Liwayway
MA-MAO, Member, under De Leon/Isong 500.00
235. Berto Beltran
MA-MAO, Member, under De Leon/Isong 500.00
236. Feliciano Silvestre
MA-MAO, Member, under Sandoval 500.00
237. Jose Leodegario
MA-MAO, Member, under Sandoval 500.00
238. Alias Nestor
MA-MAO, Member, under Sandoval 500.00
239. Alias Ipe
MA-MAO, Member, under Sandoval 500.00
240. Alias Fred
MA-MAO, Member, under Sandoval 500.00
241. Estelita Manalili alias Est+
MA-MAO, Member 200.00
242. Erlinda Torres alias Linda+ 200.00
243. Teresita Flores 200.00

* Appears in the October 11, 1965 awards list
† Appears in the February 3, 1967 awards list
+ Appears in the July 23, 1969 awards list

Annex B

PROGRAMME FOR A PEOPLE'S DEMOCRATIC REVOLUTION

(A CPP-NPA document captured by the Armed Forces of the Philippines in Capas, Tarlac, on June 9, 1969)

I. THE BASIC CONDITION OF THE PHILIPPINES TODAY

The basic condition of the Philippines today is that of a semi-colonial and semi-feudal country, dominated by the U.S. imperialists, the comprador bourgeoisie, the landlords and the bureaucrat capitalists. These vested interests mercilessly exploit the broad masses of the people.

It is U.S. imperialism and domestic feudalism that are the main problems afflicting the whole nation and from which the masses of the people aspire to be liberated.

The Philippine Revolution against Spanish colonialism failed to achieve the goals of national liberation and the elimination of feudalism. The flabby leadership of the ilustrados (liberal bourgeoisie) failed to win the revolution and played into the hands of U.S. imperialism which brutally massacred the Filipino people and deprived them of their national independence and democratic rights in the course of the Filipino-American War and thereafter.

Since the beginning of this century, U.S. imperialism has made use of feudalism as its social base in the Philippines. With the defeat of the old type of national democratic revolution, which was imbued mainly with the ideas of liberalism, U.S. imperialism has succeeded in employing domestic puppet forces to frustrate the revolutionary aspirations of the Filipino people and deprive them of their national freedom, class freedom and individual rights.

U.S. imperialism has bred and made use of the comprador bourgeoisie as its principal agency in perpetuating a semi-colonial and semi-feudal type of economy, culture, and political system. The landlord class has persisted as the most important ally of U.S. imperialism and the comprador bourgeoisie in the perpetuation of feudal and semi-feudal relations in the vast countryside. The bureaucrat capitalists have also emerged under the imperialist tutelage for "self government and democracy" to perpetuate the dominance of U.S. imperialism, the local comprador bourgeoisie and the landlord class in the present puppet reactionary state.

The combined oppression of U.S. imperialism and feudalism involves the inequitable colonial exchange of cheap local raw materials (sugar, coconut, abaca, logs and mineral ore) and finished products imported chiefly from the United States and the investment of U.S. surplus capital in the Philippines chiefly to foster the semi-colonial and semi-feudal type of economy that exploits the toiling masses of workers and peasants.

During the direct and indirect rule of U.S. imperialism in the Philippines, the Filipino toiling masses have been exploited to serve the excessive hunger for profits of the U.S. monopoly capitalists and the local reactionaries. Acute exploitation of the masses of workers and peasants, a general state of backwardness in society and the corruption and brutality of the bourgeoisie reactionary state characterize the Philippines today.

The Filipino working class has significantly grown in number and experience since the later period of Spanish colonial rule. But its further growth has been stunted because of the limitations on local industrialization and emphasis on raw material production and, lately, on mere re-assembly plants, new plantations and businesses in the grip of foreign monopoly capitalism. The Filipino working class has suffered extremely low wages and the whole nation has suffered lack of opportunity and the remittance of super-profits from the Philippines by foreign monopolies and loan payments to imperialist banks.

Despite the emphasis on raw material production, there is the stagnation of Philippine agriculture and the exploitation of poor peasants and farm workers in areas where feudalism persists; and in areas where modern plantations are in operation both regular and seasonal agricultural workers also suffer low wages and sub-human levels of working and living conditions.

The rural poor, composed mainly of poor peasants, farm workers, and poor fishermen; and the urban poor composed mainly of workers, peddlers and poor handicraftsmen living in city slums, comprise together more than 90 per cent of the population. Though they are the overwhelming majority in the Philippines, they are now the most deprived and oppressed, politically, economically, socially and culturally. They are the vast source of revolutionary power against foreign and feudal exploitation.

The urban petty bourgeoisie also suffers from the state of foreign and feudal exploitation. Though they live in relatively better comfort than the urban and rural poor, their very limited and usually fixed income is subject to the pressures of foreign and feudal exploitation. They can easily be won to the side of the Revolution — because they are not free from the abuses of the state on their livelihood and democratic rights.

The national bourgeoisie is the most wealthy of the forces that may be won over to the side of the Revolution. It is restricted by foreign and feudal domination in its goal of nationalist industrialization. Though it wishes to lead the patriotic and progressive classes through its entrepreneurship and its political actions, its kind of class leadership is already surpassed historically by the revolutionary class leadership of the working class. The vacillating dual character of the national bourgeoisie should be recognized by the working class while working for a national united front of all patriotic and progressive classes, groups and individuals under the leadership of the working class.

At this stage of Philippine history, it no longer suffices to have the old type of national democratic revolution. The era of imperialism has long invalidated the leadership of the bourgeoisie. An exceedingly high stage of the world proletarian revolution has been achieved with the ascendance of Mao Tse-tung's thought, the acme of Marxism-Leninism in this era. The Communist Party of the Philippines itself can never hope to lead the Filipino people if it does not rid itself of modern revisionism or the black bourgeois line, particularly Lavaism and Taruc-ism that has marked its history.

The national bourgeoisie and the urban petty bourgeoisie, the latter especially, are allies of the working class within the national united front but they have long become inadequate at leading the Philippine Revolution in the era of imperialism as demonstrated as early as the start of the armed conquest of the Philippines by U.S. imperialism when the liberal bourgeois leadership capitulated.

The class leadership in the Philippine Revolution is now in the hands of the working class. A proletarian revolutionary leadership, guided by Marxism-Leninism, Mao Tse-tung's thought, is what makes the people's democratic revolution a new type of national democratic revolution. We are now in the world era in which U.S. imperialism is moving towards total collapse and socialism is marching towards world triumph. By adopting Mao Tse-tung's thought as the supreme guide for our revolutionary actions, we cleanse the vanguard party of its weaknesses (as presented by the document of rectification, "Rectify Errors and Rebuild the Party") and strengthen it to become the invincible weapon at the core of the revolutionary mass movement.

The Communist Party of the Philippines is now re-established and rebuilt as a party of Mao Tse-tung's thought. It is the most advanced detachment of the Filipino working class leading the Philippine Revolution forward. It strives to be a well-disciplined Party armed with the theory of Marxism-Leninism, Mao Tse-tung's thought, using the methods of criticism and self-criticism and linked with the masses of the people. It wields the two weapons of armed struggle and the national united front to deal death blows at U.S. imperialism and feudalism.

There is only one road which the working class under the leadership of the Communist Party of the Philippines must take. It is the road of armed revolution to smash the armed counter-revolution that preserves foreign and feudal oppression in the Philippines. In waging armed revolution, the working class must rely mainly on the mass support of its closest ally, the peasantry. The peasantry is the main force of the people's democratic revolution. Without the peasantry's struggle for land no genuine and formidable People's Army can be built and no revolutionary base area can be established. The peasant struggle for land is the main democratic content of the present stage of the Philippine Revolution.

From the countryside, the people's democratic forces encircle the cities. It is in the countryside that the enemy forces are first lured in and defeated before the capture of the cities from the hands of exploiting classes. It is in the countryside that the weakest links of the reactionary state are to be found and these can be surrounded by the people's democratic forces tactically before strategically defeating them. It is in the countryside that the People's Army can accumulate strength among the peasants by combining agrarian revolution, armed struggle and the building of revolutionary base areas. The Party and the People's Army must turn the backward villages into advanced military, political, economic and cultural bastions of the people's democratic revolution.

A true national united front exists only when it is founded on the alliance of the working class and the peasantry and such alliance has been strongly welded by armed struggle, by the creation of a People's Army mainly among the peasants, by the working class party, the Communist Party of the Philippines. A true united front is one for carrying out armed struggle. The urban petty bourgeoisie can join such a united front. The national bourgeoisie can also lend direct and indirect support to it although it always carries its dual character, its contradicting progressive and reactionary aspects. In a national united front of workers, peasants, urban petty bourgeoisie and the national bourgeoisie, the proletarian revolutionary party can best guarantee its leadership, independence and initiative only by having the People's Army firmly at its command.

In the countryside, a revolutionary anti-feudal united front must also be created. The working class must rely mainly on the poor peasants and farm workers, then win over and unite with the middle peasants and neutralize the rich peasants. In its close alliance with the masses of poor peasants and farm workers, the working class undertakes agrarian revolution, armed struggle and the building of revolutionary base areas to build the strong foundation of people's democracy.

While the old democratic leadership of the bourgeoisie no longer applies to the Philippine Revolution at this historical stage, the working class and the Communist Party of the Philippines cannot accomplish both democracy and socialism at one blow. While on a world scale socialism has already taken firm roots with the People's Republic of

China as its main bulwark, the Party must first achieve a new type of national democratic revolution, a people's democratic revolution in the concrete semi-feudal and semi-colonial conditions of the Philippines before reaching of stage of socialist revolution. Socialism cannot be immediately achieved when the Filipino people under the leadership of the working class still have to liberate themselves from foreign and feudal oppression.

The people's democratic revolution rejects the old liberal leadership of the bourgeoisie. U.S. imperialism has long made use of the jargon of liberal democracy to deceive the people. In upholding proletarian revolutionary leadership, it should not mean, however, that socialism shall be achieved without passing through the stage of national democracy. Neither should it mean that such progressive strata of the local bourgeoisie as the petty bourgeoisie and the national bourgeoisie have no more place in the revolution. They do have a role to play as national democratic allies of the working class. Indeed, people's democracy is a new type of democracy because of its proletarian, instead of bourgeois leadership. But this proletarian revolutionary leadership assumes the present democratic task of waging a protracted peasant war, an agrarian revolution, and organizing a national united front of workers in alliance with the peasantry, the urban petty bourgeoisie, the intelligentsia and the national bourgeoisie. The proletarian revolutionary leadership is the most important link between the stage of the people's democratic revolution and the stage of socialist revolution.

The immediate general programme of the Filipino people and the Communist Party of the Philippines is a people's democratic revolution and the long term maximum programme is socialism. It is dishonest, demagogic and utopian to insist that socialism is the immediate goal under conditions that the people are still dominated and exploited by U.S. imperialism and domestic feudalism.

In the political field, the Communist Party of the Philippines advances the revolutionary leadership of the working class, fights to overthrow the reactionary bourgeois regime and all reactionary classes supporting it and, in its stead, establishes a people's democratic state system, a coalition or united front government of the working class, peasantry, and urban petty bourgeoisie and national bourgeoisie. In the economic field, the Party fights for a self-reliant economy, a just and prosperous people's livelihood and a national industry and trade emancipated from foreign monopoly capitalism and feudalism which have restricted and exploited the productive efforts of the people and the patriotic businessmen, ranging from industrialists to petty producers. In the field of culture and education, the Party fights for the development of a national, scientific and mass culture and education. In the military field, the Party commands and builds up a People's Army that serves as the mainstay of the national and social liberation movement and, consequently, of the people's democratic state system.

II. PROGRAMME FOR A PEOPLE'S DEMOCRATIC REVOLUTION

The Communist Party of the Philippines is determined to implement its general programme for a people's democratic revolution. All Filiipno communists are ready to sacrifice their lives for the worthy cause of achieving the new type of democracy, of building a new Philippines that is genuinely and completely independent, democratic, united, just and prosperous. We are all keenly aware that the present bourgeoisie state and the reactionary classes that it serves will never surrender their political and economic power without a fight.

The Party is highly conscious that rebuilding itself as the principal instrument of the leading class and in building a united front of all patriotic and progressive forces, it must build a strong People's Army that can weld together the workers and peasants and destroy the local reactionary state and the interventionist forces of U.S. imperialism.

The Communist Party of the Philippines is the leading force at the core of the revolutionary mass movement against foreign and feudal oppression and for the establishment and consolidation of a people's democratic state. In the exercise of its leadership, the Party hereunder states ten guidelines for its general programme.

1. Destroy the Forces of U.S. Imperialist and Feudal Oppression in the Philippines:

National sovereignty and democracy can never be obtained without the destruction of the forces of U.S. imperialism and domestic feudalism whose basic interests lie in the continued national and class enslavement and exploitation of the Filipino people. The over-riding interest of the Filipino people now is to fight for national liberation and people's democracy. They must take the road of armed revolution to defeat the armed counter-revolution; and all patriotic and progressive classes, parties, groups and individuals must be aroused and mobilized to isolate and then destroy the power and influence of the U.S. imperialists, the comprador bourgeoisie, the evil gentry, the bureaucrat capitalists and all their political and armed agents. The political power and influence of these exploiters can be isolated, destroyed and replaced by both waging the armed struggle and building up the national united front. As a proletarian revolutionary party, the Communist Party of the Philippines should not be tied down by legalist and parliamentary struggle. The Party should concentrate on building up the people's democratic power in the countryside before seizing the cities and simultaneously on discrediting the monopolization of political power by the bourgeois political parties, like the Nacionalista Party, the Liberal Party and the like, which actually perpetuate the same single party of class interests.

2. Establish a People's Democratic State and a Coalition or United Front Government:

The ultimate goal of the people's democratic revolution is the establishment of a people's democratic state and a coalition or united front government The people's democratic state is under the leadership of the working class and it includes the participation of all democratic classes, i.e., the workers, peasants, petty bourgeoisie, and the national bourgeoisie. Its government is in the form of a coalition or united front of all democratic classes. In the course of the protracted people's war, a national liberation front may be created to combine all available forces and elements to isolate and destroy the enemy and prepare for a democratic coalition government. In the meantime, while a nationwide coalition government can not yet be established, the masses of workers and peasants under the proletarian revolutionary leadership can establish an armed independent regime in the countryside where they shall learn to govern themselves, defend and advance their independence and democratic gains and manage well their relations with all friends and sympathizers. The armed independent regime is the nucleus of the People's Democratic Republic of the Philippines.

3. Fight for National Unity and Democratic Rights:

The firmest national unity founded mainly on the basis of the class interests of the workers and peasants must be created. On this popular basis all patriotic and progressive classes, groups and individuals shall enjoy political and economic rights that U.S. imperialism and feudalism have deprived them of. Individual initiative and enterprise on the part of fishermen, handicraftsmen, intellectuals, the urban petty bourgeoisie and the national bourgeoisie shall be respected, encouraged and assisted.

All efforts shall be exerted by the state, cooperative and private sectors to provide every citizen a decent livelihood. All democratic classes, groups and their members shall enjoy all such democratic rights as freedom of domicile, person, thought, belief, religion, speech, assembly and the like in a democratic bill of rights. The interests and rights of overseas Filipinos shall be protected; they shall be allowed to have the amplest contact with their kith and kin in the Philippines or to return from the United States or elsewhere.

4. Follow the Principle of Democratic Centralism:

The national government shall have central authority over the local governments at various levels. The national government, however, shall base its decisions on the needs and aspirations of the broad masses of the people and the lower levels of government. This is centralized leadership based on democracy and democracy guided by centralized leadership. At every level of the government (barrio, municipality, city or district, provincial, regional), there shall be elected representative bodies where decisions are taken democratically for every corresponding area. A lower representative body shall be subordinate to a higher representative body. Any part of the government shall be subordinate to the People's Revolutionary Congress which represents nationally the sovereign Filipino people. In all elections or voting on any question, the rule of the majority shall be followed.

5. The People's Liberation Army:

There can be no people's democratic state without a People's Army whose principal and most essential function is to defend and secure it. The People's Army, composed mainly of soldiers from the peasantry, must be under the leadership of the working class and the Communist Patry of the Philippines. The most pressing task of the People's Army now is to defeat and destroy the reactionary imperialist-created and imperialist-supported Armed Forces of the Philippines and all other kinds of armed power in the hands of the exploiting classes and the reactionary state at all levels. The people's democratic government can be established only with the triumphant advance of the People's Army. The People's Army shall be a fighting force, a propaganda force and a productive force closely linked to the masses of the people. It constantly strengthens itself ideologically, politically and organizationally with Mao Tse-tung's thought. The armed strength of the People's Army includes its regular mobile troops, the guerrilla units, the militia, the self-defense corps and armed city partisans. The Party should see to it that troops are well-provisioned and the welfare of the families of fighters are well taken care of.

6. The Land Problem:

The main content of the people's democratic revolution is the struggle for land among the peasants. The people's democratic revolution must satisfy the basic demands of the poor peasants and farm workers for land. The agrarian revolution is the necessary requirement for the vigorous conduct of the armed struggle and the creation and consolidation of revolutionary base areas. Land shall be distributed free to the landless. Usury and all other feudal evils shall be wiped out. Plantations and estates already efficiently operated on a mechanized basis shall be converted into state farms where the agricultural workers shall establish proletarian power and provide themselves with better working and living conditions. In the whole countryside mutual labor exchange systems shall be created as the initial step towards higher forms of agricultural cooperation. Through agricultural cooperation, production shall be raised and well-planned, the sale of produce shall be assured at the best price possible and welfare services guaranteed. The higher purchasing power of the peasantry shall enable the ceaseless expansion of industrial production. The basis of the national economy shall be agriculture because it fulfills the food and raw materials requirements of expanding industrialization and mainly the peasantry absorbs the products of industrialization.

7. The Problem of Industry:

Foreign monopoly capitalism and feudalism which have hindered the growth of national industry are firmly opposed by the people's democratic revolution. All efforts towards the growth of national industry as the leading factor of the economy shall be mustered by the people's democratic government. There shall be three sectors in the national economy; the state sector, the cooperative sector and the private sector. All major sources of raw materials and energy, all heavy and basic industries and all nationalized enterprises, shall be run by the state sector. The private sector run by the patriotic entrepreneurs and merchants shall be given assistance and support by the people's democratic government. All peasants, fishermen and handicraftsmen shall be encouraged to organize themselves into cooperatives so as to increase their productivity and assure themselves of a ready market. While building up to the state and cooperative sectors of the economy as factors of proletarian leadership and socialism, the people's democratic government shall encourage and support all private initiative in industry so long as this does not monopolize or adversely affect the people's livelihood. The people's democratic government shall exercise regulation of capital only to protect the people's livelihood and guarantee a people's democracy.

8. The Problem of Culture, Education and the Intellectuals:

A people's democratic cultural revolution is necessary to rid the nation of the stultifying dominance of imperialist and feudal culture and education. It must advance instead a national scientific and mass culture truly serving the interests of the people. It shall see to it that the educational system and the mass media are securely in the hands of the people's democratic forces. Education at all levels shall be free, irrespective of class, religion, creed, sex or color. It shall promote the national language as the principal medium of communication in Philippine society. It shall give full encouragement and support to scientific experiment and technological progress. It shall see to it that the national language, art and literature shall be given revolutionary content and relate the revolutionary struggles of workers, peasants, soldiers and other participants of the revolution. Old forms as well as foreign forms of art and literature may be adopted so long as they shall be given revolutionary content. The working class assumes leadership in the field of culture and education in line with its leading revolutionary role. But it welcomes wholeheartedly the support of intellectuals for the revolution. All democratic intellectuals are given all the opportunity to serve the people and remould their own thinking. While freedom of thought and religion shall be accorded respect, it shall see to it that this freedom is not systematically employed to resist the people's democratic revolution or hurt the people's interests. In the course of the protracted people's war, the Party shall transform backward villages into cultural bastions cf the Philippine Revolution. Illiteracy and superstition among the masses shall be wiped out and the scientific spirit of Marxism-Leninism, Mao Tse-tung's thought shall prevail.

9. The Problem of National Minorities:

National minorities in the Philippines have been abused and grossly neglected. U.S. imperialism, the local reactionary government and the Christian churches have too long regarded the national minorities as mere objects of bourgeois charity and Christian proselytization. The four-million minorities, especially those of Mindanao and Mountain Province, can be powerful participants in the revolutionary overthrow of U.S. imperialism and feudalism. The bourgeois government, reactionary scholars and Christian chauvinists talk loud about national integration but they stand in reality for the exploiting classes that are the main sources of abuse and oppression. The main concern of the national minorities is land; the abuses of landlords, loggers and land grabbers and their exploitation in mines and plantations. A new type of leadership, a revolutionary one, must be encouraged to rise among them so as to supplant the traditional leadership that has failed to protect them and has merely contributed and participated in their exploitation. With regard to naturalized Filipinos and foreign nationals, the class approach must be firmly taken so as to do away with "Malay" racism and chauvinism. Residents or citizens of Chinese ancestry are very often the target of racist and chauvinist attacks launched by U.S. imperialists, modern revisionists, and other local reactionaries in line with their anti-China, anti-communist and anti-people policy. The Kuomintang comprador bourgeoisie should be thoroughly exposed and attacked for its class position and for the fact that it is an accomplice of U.S. imperialism, modern revisionism and all reactionaries.

10. The Problem of Foreign Policy:

The foreign policy of the Philippine bourgeois government is dictated by U.S. imperialism and the internal reactionary classes. The diplomatic relations and foreign trade of the Philippines is monopolized by the United States, together with its reactionary allies like resurgent imperialist Japan. Relations with revisionist states have been initiated only because of the permission granted by the United States which recognizes modern revisionism as its chief accomplice in maintaining neo-colonialism throughout the world, including the Philippines. The U.S. imperialists and the modern revisionists are maintaining an all-round co-operation to save puppet states like the bourgeois reactionary state in the Philippines. The only true basis for an independent and active foreign policy is the overthrow of the internal power of U.S. imperialism and its local lackeys in the Philippines, and the abrogation of all treaties, executive agreements and statutes that define "special relations" with the U.S. government and its imperialist allies. The People's Republic of China and all other countries willing to have relations in the spirit of mutual respect for nation sovereignty and mutual benefit. The people's democratic government shall give moral and material support to the revolutionary movements of oppressed peoples abroad and shall maintain the firmest alliance with genuine socialist states like the People's Republic of China and the People's Republic of Albania. It shall be inspired by the principle of proletarian internationalism and guided by the policy of the international united front. It regards the People's Republic of China as an iron bastion of the world proletarian revolution and as a reliable friend of all oppressed peoples, including the Filipino people.

III. OUR SPECIFIC PROGRAMME

Our general programme will remain unchanged during the entire stage of the people's democratic revolution. But from phase to phase during this general stage, our specific and immediate demands shall change.

Hereunder are our specific and immediate demands:

In the Political Field

1. Attack, isolate and destroy the bourgeois reactionary state, the U.S. imperialists, the landlords and all local tyrants until their doom in our country;
2. Establish the armed independent regime and develop the people's ability in the conduct of government in the course of armed struggle;

3. Purge our ranks of modern revisionists and all other opportunists who sabotage our revolutionary efforts, and expose the bankruptcy of bourgeois legalism and parliamentarism;

4. Campaign for a people's democratic constitution and demand the revocation of provisions in the bourgeois constitution, laws, executive agreements and treaties that are reactionary;

5. Expose the curtailment of the political rights of workers, peasants, intellectuals and patriotic citizens who fight against foreign and feudal oppression, and allow the free operation of or support every democratic party or mass organization;

6. Fight the rise of fascism and the use of murder and threats against the people and their revolutionary and democratic leaders and organizations;

7. Punish the evil gentry and corrupt government officials and subject them to public trial by the people's court whenever possible;

8. Replace or re-organize the barrio councils and promote the leadership of the poor peasants and farm workers through revolutionary barrio councils;

9. Cooperate with all organizations and groups that can help build up the national united front and isolate the die-hard enemies of the people's democratic revolution; and

10. Assure low-ranking officials and rank and file employes in the bourgeois government that they shall be re-integrated in the people's democratic government so long as they do not participate directly in the commission of public crimes and so long as they secretly cooperate with the revolutionary movement.

In the Economic Field

1. Render ineffective the Parity Amendment, the Laurel-Langley Agreement, the Economic and Technical Cooperation Agreement, the Agreement Relating to Entry Rights of American Traders and Investors, Agricultural Commodities Agreement and the Investment Incentives Law and all other such legal instruments that bind our country economically to U.S. imperialism and all its local lackeys, and reject the old and new loan agreements made by the bourgeois reactionary government, including the "aid" agreements;

2. Encourage the people and the national bourgeoisie to make a self-reliant economy and at the same time confiscate foreign goods that depress or eliminate the local production of goods by patriotic Filipino citizens while urging the broad masses of the people to boycott imperialist businesses and consumer goods;

3. Outlaw bureaucrat capital and all property gained through corrupt and criminal means;

4. Help improve the livelihood of workers, peasants, farm workers, fishermen and handicraftsmen by exercising price control in base areas and providing work for the unemployed and under-employed; and organize the peasants, fishermen and handicraftsmen into elementary cooperative units (mutual aid teams and labor exchange systems) and support every movement for the economic emancipation of the people.

5. Compel the reduction of rent and interest rates in guerrilla zone and abolish rent in the liberated areas, abolish exorbitant taxes and miscellaneous levies and establish a consolidated progressive tax, collecting an agricultural tax not exceeding two per cent of produce and also a fair business tax from the petty and the national bourgeoisie;

6. Help the workers in the factories, mines, plantations, transportation lines and offices to conduct strikes successfully;

7. Expose the deceptive and reactionary character of the Magna Carta for Labor, the Agricultural Land Reform Code and other such bourgeois

measures pretending to support the economic and social struggle of the exploited masses;

8. Protect and encourage Filipino-owned commerce and industry by providing market guarantees, protection, credit and tax relief;

9. Support the national minorities in their fight against landlords, land grabbers, mining companies, logging concessionaires and plantations; and

10. Safeguard the people's health and expand medical services.

In the Military Field

1. Organize and train units of the People's Army; armed propaganda teams, guerrilla units, regular mobile troops, militia and armed city partisans;

2. Campaign against the U.S. military bases and U.S. military assistance and all treaties (U.S.-R.P. Military Bases Treaty, Military Assistance Pact and Mutual Defense Treaty, the SEATO, etc.) that bind the reactionary government and army to the U.S. imperialists, and also against the anti-democratic intent of "civic action," the "Peace Corps" and other counter-insurgency projects of the U.S. imperialists;

3. Destroy the military units of the reactionary government and of the U.S. imperialists and capture useful military equipment;

4. Punish the spies and all subversive agents (especially members of the CIA and DIA) of U.S. imperialism and their local reactionary cohorts;

5. Campaign against the drafting of the youth, workers and peasants for military camp training and service and also against the PMT, ROTC and the Philippine Military Academy because of their reactionary orientation;

6. Eliminate cattle rustling and piracy, banditry and all other activities that prey on the poor;

7. Destroy the terror squads like the Home Defense Corps, the Monkees and the like, and disarm and disband the bodyguards of bureaucrat capitalists, civilian guards of landlords and strike-breakers;

8. Organize the oppressed national minorities to take up arms against imperialist and feudal oppression;

9. Wage a war of annihilation but exercise leniency on captured combatants so as to demoralize the enemy; and

10. Cooperate with all other armed movements or groups fighting against imperialist and feudal oppression.

In the Cultural Field

1. Develop a national, scientific and mass culture responsive to the needs and aspirations of the Filipino people;

2. Campaign against imperialist and feudalist or Church control and influence over the educational system and mass media;

3. Propagate the national language as the principal medium of instruction and communication;

4. Develop a people's democratic culture and put revolutionary content in art and literature while combatting the decadent literature of "universal humanism," pessimism, escapism, class reconciliation and all other pernicious bourgeois trends;

5. Combat Christian chauvinism against the national minorities;

6. Support the progressive movements and actions among students, teachers and all intellectuals;

7. Guarantee the better livelihood of teachers and other staff members of educational institutions and guarantee academic freedom;

8. Respect the freedom of thought and religious belief and use patient persuasion in gathering support for the people's democratic revolution;

9. Denounce imperialist study and travel grants;

10. Fight for free education at all levels and wipe out illiteracy and superstition among the masses and rouse them to a revolutionary scientific spirit.

In the Field of Foreign Policy

1. Base Philippine foreign policy on the Filipino people's sovereignty and self-reliance, and cooperate with all friendly revolutionary peoples, governments and movements on the basis of mutual respect and benefit;

2. Fight against all the unjust treaties and agreements imposed by U.S. imperialism;

3. Develop the firmest relations with the People's Republic of China, Albania and all revolutionary governments and peoples;

4. Support the revolutionary struggles of all oppressed peoples in Asia, Africa and Latin America: and all neighboring oppressed peoples of Vietnam, Laos, Indonesia, Thailand, Kalimantan Utara, Malaya, Burma, Korea and others;

5. Expose the United Nations as a tool of U.S. imperialism and their revisionist renegade accomplices in the crime of neo-colonialism;

6. Oppose every treacherous maneuver of all revisionist states and parties in their collaboration with U.S. imperialism;

7. Resist the attempt of U.S. imperialism to make use of Japan and the revisionist renegade clique led by the Soviet Union as tools in the exploitation of the Philippines;

8. Oppose such "regional" arrangements as the Asian Development Bank, Association of Southeast Asian Nations (ASEAN), the Asian Pacific Council (ASPAC), and the like that reinforce the SEATO and other longstanding instruments of U.S. imperialism in the region;

9. Campaign against the imperialist advisers and survey missions in the bourgeois reactionary government; and

10. Follow the spirit of proletarian internationalism and the policy of the international united front.

IV. CONDITIONS FOR REVOLUTION ARE EXCELLENT

The objective conditions for the implementation of our general and specific programme are excellent. U.S. imperialism, modern revisionism and all reactionary forces are receiving crushing blows from the oppressed peoples of the world and are in a state of disintegration. This is indeed the era when imperialism is heading towards total collapse and socialism is marching towards world victory.

Increasingly, armed struggles in the countryside of the world, Asia, Africa and Latin America, are ever intensifying and expanding to tear apart and destroy the over-extended power of U.S. imperialism and all its reactionary allies. In the close vicinity of the Philippines, the tide of people's war is ever rising under the powerful inspiration of Mao Tsetung's thought. The heroic peoples of Vietnam, Laos, Thailand, Indonesia, Burma, Malaya and others are fighting U.S. imperialism and feudalism. The Filipino people and the Communist Party of the Philippines are fortunate to be within the storm center of the world proletarian revolutions.

Because of its losses in the Vietnam war, because of its expensive but futile aid to its puppet governments and because of its failure to further expand its foreign trade, U.S. imperialism is rocked in its very heartland by a serious crisis that is now agitating the American workers and youth, both Afro-American and white, who refuse to be carried away into imperialist wars of expansion and to be abused economically and politically at home. The deepening internal and external crisis of U.S. imperialism is clearly depriving the Filipino reactionaries of a significantly great amount of imperialist protection and support.

The crisis of over-production severely afflicts the entire world capitalist system today and is profoundly agitating their own working class and youth whom they viciously exploit. All capitalist countries are now engaged in a cut-throat competition because each is trying to save itself from economic and political crisis at the expense of the other. Although all capitalist countries are united in manipulating the revisionist renegade states and parties and shifting the burden of their financial crisis on the backs of their colonies and semi-colonies, they only aggravate the hopeless situation of their puppets and intensify the aspirations of the oppressed peoples to be freed of their imperialist yoke.

Modern revisionism spearheaded by the Soviet revisionist clique is failing to be an effective accomplice of U.S. imperialism in their mutual crime of neo-colonialism. The Soviet revisionist renegade clique bloc is fast disintegrating. The Soviet aggression against the Czechoslovak people has demonstrated the treacherous character of modern revisionism. While U.S. imperialism and Soviet social imperialism collude in claiming their respective spheres of influence, they also struggle to redivide the same.

While U.S. imperialism and modern revisionism are in deep crisis, the People's Republic of China has consolidated itself as an iron bastion of socialism and the world proletarian revolution by carrying out the epochal and great proletarian cultural revolution and by holding aloft Mao Tse-tung's thought to illumine the road of armed revolution throughout the world. Also, in the Eastern European heartland of modern revisionism, the People's Republic of Albania stands forth as an advance post of the world proletarian revolution and Mao Tse-tung's thought and is encouraging all the oppressed peoples and Marxist-Leninists there to rebel against the ruling revisionist renegade cliques.

The most significant development in the entire history of the Filipino people so far is the reestablishment and rebuilding of the Communist Party of the Philippines as a Party of Mao Tse-tung's thought. This occurs at a time when world and national conditions are extremely favorable for revolution under the leadership of the proletariat.

The Philippine reactionary state can no longer rely on the "unlimited" support of the crisis-stricken U.S. imperialism and the world capitalist system. What the United States and other capitalist powers are vainly trying to do is to shift the burden of their economic and financial crisis on the backs of colonies and semi-colonies like the Philippines. This will only aggravate the foreign and feudal oppression of the Filipino people and will only goad them to take up arms.

The Philippine reactionary state is increasingly unable to rule in the old way. Armed opposition to it by the Filipino people under the leadership of the Communist Party of the Philippines is sure to doom foreign and feudal oppression. It is both a patriotic and internationalist duty to fight U.S. imperialism and all its reactionary allies. Defeat of U.S. imperialism and modern revisionism and all domestic reactionaries in the Philippines is bound to have far-reaching world significance because our country has long served as a bastion of all these evils in this part of the world.

Ratified by the Congress of Re-Establishment of the Communist Party of the Philippines, December 26, 1968.

V. MAIN TASK OF THE PARTY

The central task of any revolutionary movement is to seize political power. The Communist Party of the Philippines assumes this task at a time that both the international and national situations are favorable to taking the road of armed revolution against armed counter-revolution.

U.S. imperialism is over-extended throughout the world. It is now receiving the powerful blows of an ever rising tide of armed revolutionary movement in Asia, Africa and Latin America. It is wracked by internal crisis and by its contradictions with other capitalist powers. The revisionist renegade bloc in Eastern Europe, led by the revisionist renegade clique in the Soviet Union, which is relied upon by U.S. imperialism to peddle the "peaceful road" and disarm the fighting peoples of the world, is in the state of internal disintegration. Instead of confusing the proletarian revolutionaries of the world, the ruling revisionist cliques in Eastern Europe are in turn causing chaos among themselves and their stooges throughout the world.

On the other hand, the countryside of the world, Asia, Africa and Latin America, has a reliable well consolidated central base in China. The revolutionization of the Chinese people through the Great Proletarian Cultural Revolution has guaranteed the irrepressible advance of the world proletarian revolution, the collapse of imperialism and the worldwide triumph of socialism.

It is in the nature of things, however, that they change only on the basis of their internal unity of opposites. The people's democratic revolution in the Philippines can be achieved basically through revolutionary efforts of a truly Marxist-Leninist Party, the Communist Party of the Philippines, which applies concretely the universal truth of Mao Tse-tung's thought. At the core of the people's revolutionary movement is the most advanced detachment of the working class, the Communist Party of the Philippines. Through this party, the working class firmly allies itself with the peasantry to wage the people's democratic revolution on the basis of an agrarian war. Furthermore, it unites with the petty bourgeoisie, especially the urban petty bourgeoisie, and applies the revolutionary dual policy of unity and struggle with the national bourgeoisie against all the irreconcilable enemies of national freedom and democracy, U.S. imperialism, the comprador bourgeois, landlords and capitalist bureaucrats.

In the Philippines today, the ruling classes are in serious difficulties in ruling in the old way. They cannot prolong the present balance of forces indefinitely. As a matter of fact, armed opposition now will aggravate their difficulties and hasten the maturing of what is now discernible as a revolutionary mood among the people. What little but well consolidated strength we may have now will grow bigger in a series of waves in the long run so long as we launch a protracted armed struggle in the countryside.

Under its central task of seizing political power through armed revolution, the Communist Party of the Philippines takes up the three tasks of party rebuilding, army building and united front building. Only by raising these three banners, by achieving these tasks, can the internal weaknesses of the present exploitative system be fully taken advantage of by the Party and the people and U.S. imperialism and feudalism be overthrown to make way for a people's democracy.

A. Party Rebuilding

The Communist Party of the Philippines must rebuild itself with the guidance of the most advanced revolutionary theory, Marxism-Leninism whose acme in the present era is Mao Tse-tung's thought. Without a revolutionary theory, there can be no revolutionary party; without this revolutionary party there can be no revolution.

As the Party performs the first requisite of ideological building, it must do it in the spirit of rectification, of correcting the errors of the past and the present so that future ones will be avoided and so that the Filipino working class will succeed in its historic mission of leading the people's democratic revolution.

The Party rebuilds itself at a time that it has suffered serious defeats and has been isolated from the masses of the people for a long period of time. Efforts to make the Party of a broad mass character and national in scale must take into critical consideration the serious errors committed by previous party leaderships and still carried over into the present.

A summing up of Party experience must be made in the scientific spirit of criticism and self-criticism so that the Party will learn to be closest to the masses throughout the country as it leads and musters the forces that make for the people's democratic revolution. The Party is the nucleus of the proletarian dictatorship; it should be able to rectify itself, remould the world outlook of its cadres and cast away the pernicious influence of the bourgeoisie and petty bourgeoisie among them.

Efforts of subjectivism in ideology, errors of Right and "left" opportunism in politics and violations of democratic centralism in organization should be weeded out, no matter how long these tendencies may have been embedded in the thinking and actions of Party members. It is perfectly alright for old and young cadres alike who want to make revolution to seek the basic reasons for the serious defeats and the present isolation of the Party occurring despite the thirty-eight years of Party experience and the sacrifice of thousands upon thousands of party members and sympathizers.

Our Party history reveals that the black bourgeoisie line of right opportunism and revisionism has persisted longer than "left" opportunism. The most thorough exposure of this error must be made especially at this time that modern revisionism is trying to grow in it. The "left" opportunism of the Jose Lava and Jesus Lava leaderships during the year of 1949 to 1965 should be related to the longer line of Right opportunism as the reverse facet of bourgeois subjectivism.

In carrying out a rectification movement to weed out modern revisionism and all forms of opportunism, ideological building should be conducted at all levels with closest supervision of the Central Committee and the Higher Party School, the Revolutionary School of Mao Tse-tung's thought. This rectification movement should be carried out in the course of ideological Party members and the masses of the people of concrete struggles by which Mao Tse-tung's thought is put to practice in the concrete conditions of Philippine society.

In the organizational rebuilding of the Party, the principles of democratic centralism and taking the mass line should be established. Errors of liberalism and sectarianism should be eradicated. No Party member of mass organization should be repudiated or coddled for subjective reasons or without any clear basis in principle, No segment of the Party should consider itself superior to the Party and the principle of democratic centralism. Those who are scandalously waving the black flag of "noble lineage" and those who prevent criticism of serious errors of previous party leadership and current party work lose their status as communists. The handful of revisionists who falsify facts like they were fourth-rate detectives and spread intrigues to run down loyal party members are counter-revolutionaries.

Because the Party must be close to the masses, it is utterly wrong for some elements to form themselves as a group and foist themselves as the Party, even as they treat the affairs of the Party as merely a side-interest, a week-end hobby to be attended to by bourgeois academic experts and high bureaucrats who actually give their best hours and efforts in the service of the present bourgeois reactionary government, to their private interests and to the reform projects of the bourgeois reactionary government.

The tasks of the people's democratic revolution should be taken seriously by every Party member at every level. The Party leadership should reflect to the utmost the mass of Party members who are engaged in the main tasks of the Party. The complementary relationship between the struggle in the city and that in the countryside should be developed fully while placing principal stress on the development of armed struggle in the countryside. Legal and illegal forms of struggle in both the city and the countryside should be waged and coordinated by the Party as the general staff.

The Party should master the handling of its two weapons, armed struggle and united front. It should grasp them firmly, with one hand holding armed struggle as the weapon of offensive and the united front as the shield that parries and blunts the attacks of the enemy. In the people's democratic revolution, armed struggle and united front are inseparable. Any attempt to separate the two can only be done by Right opportunists and "Left" opportunists.

Aside from putting out a summing-up of Party experience the Communist Party of the Philippines should also put out now a Party Programme and Party Constitution that reflects the great advances of the theory and practice of Marxism-Leninism, Mao Tse-tung's thought and the long repressed aspirations of the masses of the Filipino people and that can guide the rebuilding of the Party and the revolutionary conduct of all Party members, cadres and leading organs in the struggle for a people's democratic revolution.

B. Army Building

The Communist Party of the Philippines can gain stature as a national revolutionary force only if it commands a People's Army. This truth has been proven since the establishment of the People's Army against the Japanese in 1942. Indeed, if the people have no People's Army, they continue to be the victims of national and class exploitation without let-up.

A movement is truly revolutionary when it has a People's Army. It is, therefore, the principal revolutionary task of the Communist Party of the Philippines to build up a People's Army. The People's Army is the principal weapon of the Party and armed struggle is the main form of struggle. It is only by taking the road of armed revolution that armed counter-revolution by the bourgeois state can be confronted and defeated by the people.

The Marxist-Leninist theory of the state and Mao Tse-tung's great thought that "optical power grows out of the barrel of a gun," must be grasped by every Party member. The people have nothing to defend themselves with and to advance their democratic interests if there is no People's Army. The ruling class will never surrender its power voluntarily: the bourgeois state will not disappear on its own accord. The proletarian revolutionary party at the helm of the people's democratic revolution must strike down and sweep it away with a People's Army.

The Party must build up a revolutionary army that is loyal and obedient to the Party, that is, close to the people and wherein officers and men share weal and woe and are welded together into one fighting faimly.

In accordance with the semi-colonial and semi-feudal conditions of the Philippines, the Party must build up a People's Army whose main support and whose main source of red soldiers is the peasantry. The proletarian revolutionary party welds the basic alliance of the working class and peasantry through the armed struggle. It is by waging a peasant war that the greatest number of masses are mobilized under revolutionary proletarian leadership. Necessarily, the Party and its Army must pay close attention to the implementation of an agrarian revolution that fulfills the struggle for land among the peasant masses. The struggle for land is, as a matter of fact, the main content of the people's democratic revolution.

It is in the countryside that the Party and the People's Army can establish an armed independent regime by pursuing the three integral components of armed struggle, agrarian revolution and rural bases.

It is in the countryside where the enemy can become over-extended, where it is weakest, where the peasant main force of the people's democratic revolution exists and can be mobilized, where the revolutionary forces enjoy the widest grounds of maneuver and where they can take the offensive. It is here where the strategic majority of the enemy at the beginning of the people's war can become so dispersed as to allow the revolutionary forces to concentrate superior forces tactically. It is here where the enemy can be lured in deep territory and among the people with the greatest uncertainty for him.

It is here where the fighting forces of the people's democratic revolution can retreat when the enemy advances, where they can harass the enemy when it is at rest, where they can advance when the enemy retreats. It is also here where the enemy campaigns of encirclement and suppression can be smashed with counter-campaigns of encirclement and suppression by the Red Army.

While the importance of urban revolutionary activity, both legal and illegal, should not be disregarded, it should be recognized as secondary but complimentary to the armed struggle in the countryside, until the People's Army in the countryside is ready to seize the cities, the role of urban revolutionary activity is mainly defensive because the counter-revolutionary forces are here most concentrated and strong.

The Party takes the strategic line in armed struggle of making the countryside encircle the cities, of defeating the counter-revolutionary forces in the countryside before taking the cities. It must develop its main armed forces in the island of Luzon where the main forces of the reactionary state are also concentrated but it must at the same time give strategic value to armed revolutionary activity in the other islands of Visayas and Mindanao, as capable of dispersing and weakening the enemy's armed forces now concentrated in Luzon, especially in Central Luzon and the Greater Manila area. This is in consonance with the archipelagic character of the Philippines. All the way, however, the Party and the People's Army are to take the correct class line in every island.

In pursuing the strategic line of developing the people's war in the countryside in every part of the country, the People's Army under the command of the Party must maintain the correct class line. It should arouse and mobilize the poor peasants, lower middle peasants and farm workers as its most reliable allies and sources of fighters. It should unite with the middle peasants while neutralizing the rich peasants. But it should constantly let the poor peasants, lower middle peasants and farm workers prevail in revolutionary barrio committees that replace the old barrio councils dominated by the rich peaasnts and landlords.

Agrarian revolution can be effected only through armed struggle and the growth of a People's Army. The Party guarantees the free distribution of lands to the poor peasants, lower middle peasants and farm workers only with the People's Army. Only the People's Army can be the effective weapon of the Party and the main pillar of the people in striking down the evil gentry and all other local tyrants and in effecting agrarian revolution. The armed struggle and the agrarian revolution in turn result in the establishment of stable rural bases where the people's democratic power is consolidated.

It is from rural bases where the people's democratic revolution can advance in a series of waves. It is here where the People's Army and the masses of the people can drown the reactionary forces. From here, guerrilla units and armed propaganda units can be dispatched to adjacent and other areas to expand the people's democratic revolution by first developing guerrilla ones which in due time mature into revolutionary base areas where the great masses of the people are fully mobilized.

By advancing in a series of waves, the People's Army avoids the military adventurism of the Jose Lava and Jesus Lava leadership which until now is manifested by roving rebel activities, sectarianism and the mountain stronghold mentality. Politics should be in full command of the People's Army and all its activities. Errors of the purely or mainly military viewpoint should be discarded. The Party and the People's Army should arouse, mobilize and involve great masses of the people in activities ranging from struggle meetings in guerrilla zones to armed campaign in what are to evolve as stable base areas. To develop the closest revolutionary intimacy with the masses, the People's Army should not be merely a fighting force. It should also be propaganda and productive force.

The Party should now zealously lay the groundwork for a more intensive and extensive people's war at a few but well-chosen and manageable areas in the countryside and in the whole archipelago. The present number of cadres who have already grasped Mao Tse-tung's thought and who can be disposed in the countryside is still small but it shall surely grow big and strong as it merges with the masses of people on a national scale.

C. United Front Building

A genuine national united front can exist only if the Communist Party of the Philippines can maintain its independence and initiative by developing a strong People's Army that is correctly guided by Mao Tse-tung's thought.

The experience of the Party in the Popular Front and Democratic Alliance should provide us with several good lessons. The lack of armed preparation in the anti-fascist struggle preceding the outbreak of World War II caused severe damages to the Party when the Japanese invasion came; and difficulties occurred even when the Party had already established the People's Army against the Japanese because of a persistent Right opportunist line that was the essence of the "retreat for defense" policy.

The Democratic Alliance as a formal united front organization was also put up as a part of the Right opportunist error of relying mainly on legal struggle after the anti-Japanese struggle. The importance of a consistent peasant war was not understood as the base of what could have been an effective people's democratic revolution against U.S. imperialism and feudalism. Even the promised return of U.S. imperialism had not been fully understood by the Party leadership in the course of the anti-Japanese war, and soon after its close.

The U.S. imperialists and the landlords did not spare all efforts to outmaneuver the Party and the People's Army even after the latter had become disarmed by Party decision during the period of 1945 to 1948. Instead of maintaining the armed vigilance of all units of the People's Army, the Party moved its central organs to the city, started to participate in bourgeois parliamentary activity and engaged in alliance with bourgeois political groups and personalities through the Democratic Alliance.

Again the modern revisionists in the Philippines are trying to lead the progressive movement into promoting the Movement for the Advancement of Nationalism beyond its limited tactical value, giving principal stress to the Agricultural Land Reform Code and Magna Carta of Labor of the bourgeois government and carrying the sedan chair for bourgeois personalities who do not even carry any definite mass following.

The Communist Party of the Philippines must make a thorough and comprehensive class analysis of Philippine society in order to determine its friends and enemies, and also in order to distinguish its reliable and unreliable allies, its long-run and temporary allies. The Party policy of national united front is essentially a class analysis in Philippine society.

The leading force of the national united front is the working class led by the Communist Party of the Philippines. In the people's democratic revolution, working class leadership is best, achieved in alliance with the peasantry, especially the poor peasants, lower middle peasants and farm workers through armed revolution. The basic alliance of the working class and the peasantry effected best and most deeply by armed struggle serves as the basis of a national united front against U.S. imperialism, the comprador bourgeoisie, landlords and bureaucrat capitalists.

The urban petty bourgeoisie is also an ally of the working class. It is less revolutionary than the peasantry but more revolutionary and more lasting as an ally than the national bourgeoisie.

The national bourgeoisie has a dual character, revolutionary and reactionary. To some extent, it can accept anti-imperialism and anti-feudalism. But it still has a bourgeois class character to which the working class and its Party must always be alert. The Party can cooperate with it within certain periods and to some limited extent but it must be on the alert for its betrayals and basically opportunist class character. Because of this dual character, the Party has to adopt consistently a revolutionary dual tactics towards it. The Party must be cautious towards it although concessions may be given to it without sacrificing the basic interests and principles of workers and peasants.

If the working class and the Communist Party of the Philippines do not firmly uphold and advance proletarian revolutionary leadership, the national bourgeoisie, with the assistance of the petty bourgeois leadership, misleads the peasantry and fosters directly or indirectly a Right opportunist or revisionist line within the Party.

If the Party allows itself to lose revolutionary leadership over the peasant masses, it is bound to suffer from right opportunism or modern revisionism as the principal political error. The danger of cooperating with the national bourgeoisie always lies in tendencies towards urban political activity as the main political activity. However, if the Party should unduly cut itself off from the national bourgeoisie, it can easily make the effort of "Left" opportunism as its main error.

But what certainly takes precedence over the question of cooperating with the national bourgeoisie is the development of the closest alliance between the working class and peasantry through armed struggle conducted by the Communist Party of the Philippines. It is this alliance that can only be the true foundation of a national united front. Without this it is senseless to give decisive importance to a formal organization like the Movement for the Advancement of Nationalism, consider it a united front and worry most of the time about the tolerance and attitudes of bourgeois allies for the sake of preserving some weak and artificial unity. It is not surprising then that the Movement for the Advancement of Nationalism is getting to be vapid ineffectual group like the National Economic Protectionism Association (NEPA), the Civil Liberties Union or the pre-war League for the Defense of Democracy.

The local revisionists who have been encouraged by the revolutionary mood of the people are busy capitulating to the enemy that uses an attractive phraseology and cheap gimmicks. They actually surrender themselves to the enemy like the liquidationist and Right opportunist Jesus Lava or they busy themselves begging for absolute pardons and amnesty, disrupting the armed struggle and building up bourgeois-controlled organizations as their parliamentary havens while they go about casting intrigues in privileged places as those they bewail as "upstarts" who question their sham authority as "veterans" and "born revolutionary leaders."

These local revisionist renegades copy the pseudo-principles and styles of their revisionist renegade counterparts abroad, led by the Soviet ruling clique. They are heavy baggage and disrupters within the communist and democratic movements in the Philippines today.

Their sinister links with the modern revisionists abroad, their active support for Philippine-Soviet relations, and their "united action" policy are nothing but a reflection of their deep-seated bourgeois character and their local revisionist line.

The Communist Party of the Philippines adheres to the policy of the international united front as an extension of its national united front. Its main guiding principle is proletarian internationalism.

By taking the road of armed revolution illuminated by Mao Tse-tung's thought, the Party contributes concretely to the collapse of U.S. imperialism, modern revisionism and reaction throughout the world. It clears the way for the world triumph of socialism and the liberation of all oppressed peoples.

The Party is fortunate that it is face to face in line and death struggle against U.S. imperialism, the No. 1 enemy of all peoples of the world. By fighting U.S. imperialism directly, it clearly performs its internationalist duty of giving support to all other oppressed peoples. U.S. imperialist control of the Philippines has too long been an important link in the chain of imperialist domination in Asia and throughout the world.

The Party must relate its national revolutionary efforts to the world proletarian revolution spearheaded by the People's Republic of China, the People's Republic of Albania and all Marxist-Leninist parties armed with Mao Tse-tung's thought.

In the countryside of the world which is Asia, Africa and Latin America where the Philippines is, the 700 million Chinese people have become consolidated with Mao Tse-tung's thought and have become an iron bastion for the world-wide efforts to defeat U.S. imperialism. The Filipino working class and people have all reasons to be optimistic, no matter how hard the difficulties and sacrifices that they must undergo to achieve the triumph of their people's democratic revolution and the world-wide triumph of socialism.

Annex C

THE NEW PEOPLE'S ARMY

(A CPP-NPA document captured by the Armed Forces of the Philippines in Capas, Tarlac, on June 9, 1969)

As surely as the Communist Party of the Philippines is being regenerated, reoriented and re-established under the supreme guidance of Mao Tse-tung's thought, the acme of Marxism-Leninism in the present era, the People's Liberation Army which the Party commands as its principal instrument in the Philippine Revolution is likewise being regenerated, reoriented and re-established under the supreme guidance of Marxism-Leninism, Mao Tse-tung's thought.

In the same way that the Party is undertaking a rectification movement in the spirit of "learning from past mistakes to avoid future ones" and of "curing the sickness to save the patient", the People's Liberation Army is likewise doing so in order to regenerate itself correctly, cast away degenerates and take in new blood, so as to carry out more firmly and vigorously the tasks of the people's democratic revolution against U.S. imperialism and domestic feudalism.

The New People's Army is definitely emergent, after twenty-seven years of hard struggle and sacrifice in the people's democratic interests. It can take pride in its splendid achievements and in the glorious martyrdom of its heroic soldiers. It can also learn bitter lessons from more than two decades of not yet having won the Revolution nor having preserved a single liberated area in the country. It is now arduously striving to intensify the armed struggle in a number of guerrilla zones and girding for the realization of agrarian revolution as the condition for establishing the rural base and the armed independent regime.

At this juncture, the universal truth of Mao Tse-tung's thought is now being consciously and thoroughly integrated with the concrete practice of the Philippine Revolution. After an extended process of rectification and self-criticism lasting for a number of years, reflected by the historic document, "Rectify Errors and Rebuild the Party," the Communist Party of the Philippines put out in its Congress of Re-establishment on December 26, 1968, a new Constitution and a new Programme for a People's Democratic Revolution in order to give new guidance, the guidance of Mao Tse-tung's thought to the People's Liberation Army and to the conduct of our revolutionary armed struggle.

The Party Constitution and Programme make it clear that the road of armed revolution is the only road for the Filipino people to take in order to liberate themselves from the exploitative and oppressive rule of U.S. imperialism, feudalism and bureaucrat capitalism. This basic stand of our Party recognizes the great role of the People's Army in the Philippine Revolution. Since armed struggle is the main form of struggle, the People's Army is the main form of organization in the People's democratic revolution.

As Comrade Mao Tse-tung has long pointed out, "Without a People's Army, the people have nothing." Neither can the Communist Party of the Philippines nor the Filipino working class lead the revolution, nor fight for the people's interests without the People's Army. Neither can a true united front be formed without armed struggle and the People's

Army welding together the workers and the peasants. The people and the Party can have political power only by taking up arms, only by having a genuine People's Army as the mainstay of all efforts to overthrow the reactionaries and consolidate revolutionary power. As Comrade Mao Tse-tung has said, "Political power grows out of the barrel of a gun."

Today, on March 29, 1969, on the occasion of the 27th anniversary of the founding of the People's Army, we have the best and happiest reasons for celebration. In line with the rectification, re-establishment and re-invigoration of the Communist Party of the Philippines under the powerful inspiration of the invincible thought of Mao Tse-tung, we the overwhelming majority of Red Commanders and soldiers are convened to formalize the adoption of the proletarian revolutionary line of the Party and Mao Tse-tung's thought, announce the creation of the New People's Army and approve the draft of the Basic Rules for submission to the Party Central Committee, proclaim our irrevocable repudiation of and triumph over the bourgeois headquarters in the Army which is lorded over by the Taruc-Sumulong renegade clique and express our resolute determination to combat and remove all vestiges of modern revisionism and Right opportunism, particularly Lavaism and Taruc-ism, which have besmirched the integrity and prestige of the Party and Army and have hindered for so long the advance of the people's democratic revolution against U.S. imperialism and domestic feudalism.

Today, we speak of the New People's Army because it is under the unified command of Mao Tse-tung's thought and the Communist Party of the Philippines, because it truly serves the most fundamental interests of the people by being the principal instrument in the agrarian revolution that we are to launch to mobilize the masses of peasants and farm workers and also in the united front against U.S. imperialism and feudalism, and because it has a style of being closely linked with the masses of the people by helping them in every possible way.

Our Army is new in two senses. It is new in the sense that it is fundamentally different from the reactionary puppet Armed Forces of the Philippines (and all its supplementary forces) that wages armed suppression of the people and defends the exploiting classes. It is also new in the sense that it is fundamentally different from the black bourgeois line that has persisted in the People's Army and has sabotaged the revolutionary armed struggle for quite a long time already.

That the New People's Army is resplendently new is beyond all doubt inasmuch as it has emerged as the fruit of inner Party struggle, the concrete result of the triumph of Mao Tse-tung's thought and the overthrow of the bourgeois headquarters in the Party and Army. Following the Marxist-Leninist leadership of the Communist Party of the Philippines, the New People's Army has arisen as the fresh formation of Red commanders and soldiers who have rejected the bourgeois army headquarters of "Commander" Sumulong and who have upheld Mao Tse-tung's thought against the pernicious black bourgeois line of Lavaism and Taruc-ism.

Within the Party, we the Red commanders and soldiers following the lead of proletarian revolutionary cadres and inspired by Mao Tse-tung's thought have set ourselves free from the two main sources of modern revisionism and Right opportunism in the Party and Army.

One main source is the city-based Lava clique which engages mainly in legalist and parliamentary struggle and whose principal leaders are in the payroll of the bourgeois reactionary government. This clique conceives of the national united front as something detached from the armed struggle. It is sponsoring a reformist peasant organization that limits its activities to arbitration within the narrow channels of the bourgeois reactionary government and systematically sabotages the activities of the People's Army and harbors surrenderees, swindlers, cattle-rustlers and other bad elements.

The other main source of modern revisionism and Right opportunism is lorded over by the Pedro Taruc-Sumulong clique that mis-appropriates the name of the Communist Party of the Philippines and the People's Liberation Army to advance the selfish counter-revolutionary bourgeois and feudal ends that are essentially no different from those of the Lava clique.

In dealing with the present situation in the Army, we have to deal at length with the Taruc-Sumulong clique which has since 1964 formally usurped the leadership over all those units of the People's Liberation Army that have heroically persisted in armed struggle against the enemy. Though we, the overwhelming majority of Red commanders and soldiers have already overthrown this revisionist renegade clique in the countryside, we must expose clearly its anti-Party and counter-revolutionary crimes so as to make them serve as negative examples and to show to all comrades and to the people that the Communist Party of the Philippines and the New People's Army are capable of rectifying errors and rebuilding themselves as genuine instruments of the people's democratic revolution against U.S. imperialism and feudalism.

The Taruc-Sumulong clique has deliberately encouraged the persistence of the ideology and activities of roving rebel bands for selfish counter-revolutionary bourgeois and feudal ends of its own. Though it has usurped the name of the Party and Army and even usurped high titles therein through a system of false appointments, it has outrightly taken the counter-revolutionary standpoint on many problems and issues of basic importance and has done so in open violation of the basic norms of a Marxist-Leninist Party and People's Army. Like the heirs and advocates of Lavaism, the Taruc-Sumulong clique has never found it necessary during the 1964-1969 period to put forward a new Party Programme and Constitution and other documents and directives to replace the outmoded ones put out during the 1946-1951 period and also those put out arbitrarily by Jesus Lava until his surrender. There has never been any attempt on the part of the heirs of Lavaism and Taruc-ism to apply the universal truth of Marxism-Leninism, Mao Tse-tung's thought, on the concrete practice of the Philippine Revolution. They have only consistently abandoned and violated it.

Despite its presumptions of leadership, the Taruc-Sumulong clique has wilfully failed to issue ample, clearcut and correct Party guide in order to give the proper direction to the armed struggle. It has completely shunned the principle of agrarian revolution and has never made any significant step to advance towards it. Instead, this clique has merely made use of armed units of the People's Liberation Army to compel mediation by this clique between the landlords and the peasants; and this mediation has been used mainly to favor the landlords who get what they want by making financial or grain contributions to the "revolutionary" fund. In this manner, the Taruc-Sumulong clique has criminally tried to cut off the Red Army from the peasant masses. The outlook of the roving rebel has been bred by this clique on the basis of its criminal refusal to base the growth and development of the People's Army on the peasants struggle for land and on the mobilization of the masses as the only true and strong basis for a people's democratic revolution.

On the other hand, this clique has systematically made use of the units of the People's Liberation Army to apply coercion more on the peasant masses than on the landlords whose friendship it would rather cultivate. It uses the flimsy reasoning that the landlords are needed in a "united front" against U.S. imperialism solely. But, when confronted with the specific case of poor peasants being ejected by the U.S. imperialists, landlords and capitalist bureaucrats as in Concepcion, Tarlac to make way for the gigantic radio installation of the Voice of America, this clique ordered the People's Army and the peasant masses to desist from fighting the ejection. In many instances, the Taruc-Sumulong clique has acted to discourage mass protest actions and labor strikes against the U.S. military on the counter-revolutionary ground that Angeles City would lose plenty of business if the U.S. imperialists were denounced and antagonized.

Shamelessly, this clique has on a big scale dictated the use of units of the Red Army as security guards for the landlords' fields and granaries again on the flimsy excuse of "actually helping out the peasants to cheat the landlords." This is a completely wrong orientation in the Revolution because the peasants do not have to cheat or be sly in fighting the landlords. The over-riding goal of the Party and Army is to arouse and mobilize the peasants into a revolutionary mass force capable of destroying the pillars of feudalism.

The peasants still voluntarily give support to the People's Army. That is because we the majority of Red commanders and soldiers have always tried to do our best in helping the peasant masses beyond the bureaucratic control of the Taruc-Sumulong clique. Being close to the masses of the people in the field, we the majority of Red commanders and soldiers have constantly sided with the peasants against the landlords, the armed agents and soldiers of the bourgeois reactionary government and such bad elements as cattle-rustlers, swindlers and bandits. In many areas, we have succeeded in reducing land rent and interest rates on loans beyond what the bourgeois Agricultural Land Reform Code promises. To reduce the bullying and abuses of the landlord class and the bourgeois reactionary government, we have used our weapons to wipe out both their big representatives and running dogs in many areas where the people now live in conditions better than elsewhere. We have also managed to help the peasants in their daily work and life.

But, whenever the Taruc-Sumulong clique is approached by landlords regarding agrarian disputes with peasants, the interests of the latter are sold out and, thereby, the good work of the People's Army is sabotaged. Thus, the peasants in particular areas become resentful over the fact that they have to give contributions to an army whose leadership takes the side of the landlords. Also in this manner are the reactionaries and counter-revolutionary reformists given the chance to malign the People's Army and prepare the betrayal and murder of Red fighters in the field, especially in those areas to which we are trying to expand for the first time.

In labor and student strikes in Central Luzon, the Taruc-Sumulong clique has also wantonly stood aside while the exploiting classes and their armed agents, the Philippine Constabulary and the local police wreak their vengeance on the strikers. In other cases, armed units have been scandalously used by the Taruc-Sumulong clique to coerce the strikers and their organizations to submit themselves to the capitalist owners of the hacienda, transportation company or school. This has been done in exchange for a paltry sum of money.

Class capitulation, class collaboration and class betrayal have been carried to the extremest point by the Taruc-Sumulong clique in several ways. Politically, it has kowtowed to the biggest representatives of the exploiting classes — such as Marcos, Nepomuceno, Cojuangco and the like, converted themselves into *compadres*, of these reactionary politicians and made agreements of "ceasefire" and "political support" with them. The folly of embracing the enemy, of collaborating with reactionary politicians has already cost the exposure and murder of so many comrades after the elections of 1965. This class betrayal is nothing but a political reflection of the counter-revolutionary bourgeois and feudal character of the Taruc-

Sumulong clique. In that regard, this clique has been blatantly spreading the philosophy of survival among the Red fighters. It has recently ordered the stopping of campaigns launched by revolutionary commanders to wipe out enemy detachments and agents in their field commands. To please the big reactionary politicians, this clique has also ordered, for monetary reasons, the surrender of a comrade to the reactionary government. Fortunately, this counter-revolutionary order to surrender a comrade has been frustrated.

The obvious reason for the counter-revolutionary revisionist policy of "peaceful co-existence" with the enemy is that the latter has promised to tolerate the landholdings, the investments in Angeles City and elsewhere and also the gang-style collections of this clique from businessmen, landlords and the peasant masses, which collections are under the one-man control and disposition of "Commander" Sumulong in the name of the Party and Army. This unprincipled compromise has always been falsely justified in terms of economism. Yet, the financial resources and property holdings accumulated by this clique have been privately appropriated by the clique-masters in the most rapacious manner and have been kept away mainly from the Party and Army.

The Taruc-Sumulong clique has deliberately restricted the growth of the People's Liberation Army and also smothered therein party life so as to maintain its selfish capitalist and feudal rule. There is no democratic centralism; there is only the centralism of one big shot, "Commander" Sumulong has criminally made one-man decisions involving the execution of "erring" comrades and other people, the disposition of huge amount of funds and the like. Without due process and on the flimsiest grounds that usually have something to do with finance collection or some business enterprise, many comrades have been judged by him as deserving of the death penalty and mass murders have actually been committed on his orders. The Taruc-Sumulong clique has been directly responsible more for the killing of comrades and other people in connection with some shady business enterprise than in connection with revolutionary armed struggle against the enemy. Following the old sectarian style of the Jose and Jesus Lava leaderships, cases of "finance opportunism" involving the smallest amount have often been concocted to discredit and justify the mass execution of comrades whose life histories as cadres are never considered.

Since there is absolutely no democracy practised by the Taruc-Sumulong clique, since there is no committee system, no system of political commissars, no report system and no accounting of funds, to clique-masters have been in a position to make arbitrary decisions, abuse the mechanical discipline of some comrades and armed units and to commit finance opportunism on a grand scale as scandalously manifested by their luxurious and corrupt living, by their having several wives and spending Party funds in such manner, by their lavish parties for their reactionary friends and "compadres" and also by having close relatives gain private titles over some sizeable property that properly belong to the Party and the people.

Consistently importing the style of the vagabond and the lumpen proletariat into the Party and Army and assuming a fascist gangster or petty warlord attiude, "Commander" Sumulong appoints goons and police characters to high responsibilities in his staff, mixes them up with dedicated comrades and thereby endangers these comrades, personally administers beatings to them alike and orders their execution whenever they fail to satisfy his financial demands. "Commander" Sumulong has also made use of the name of the Party and Army in practising usury among comrades and the people at the average rate of 50% a month, in forcing the sale of properties to him at the price he dictates and in extorting money and grain from the masses. He has actually manipulated units of the People's Liberation Army to conduct his evil business practices in the style of a protection gang. This man who has assumed the functions of commander-in-chief and national finance officer of the People's Liberation Army is one of the blackest scoundrels that has ever infiltrated into the Party and Army. Pedro Taruc has to assume full responsibility as his accomplice.

Because of its selfish counter-revolutionary interests, the Taruc-Sumulong clique is afraid to see the building of a Marxist-Leninist party within the People's Liberation Army. It is afraid of inner democracy and the use of criticism and self-criticism within the Party and Army. It is afraid of seeing Party cadres and Red soldiers raise their quality and the Party and Army expand under the guidance of Mao Tse-tung's thought. It is afraid of being exposed, criticized and repudiated. Thus, they would rather have themselves continue acting like crime ring-leaders. It is now clear beyond doubt why the Taruc-Sumulong clique has consistently practised sectarianism and a new brand of closed-doorism. It wishes vainly to prevent the expansion of the Party and Army and the emergence of revolutionary mass organizations in order to keep out the good and keep in the bad and maintain its counter-revolutionary renegade command and its system of privately appropriating wealth. This clique wishes to lord over the Party and Army in Central Luzon as if it were their "independent kingdom." It does this at a time when the urgent need is to rebuild the Party and Army as the intimate and conscientious servants of the people on a nationwide scale.

The black bourgeois line carried out by the Pedro Taruc-Sumulong clique in Central Luzon has its historical roots. It has the same root cause as the counter-revolutionary revisionism and Right opportunism of the Lava clique. It is merely a branch of the long line of Right opportunism that has run through the history of the Party and that has retarded the growth of the Party and Army and prejudiced the consistent advance of the Revolution. It is directly related to the Right opportunist line of Lavaism within the Communist Party of the Philippines for the last thirty-four years or since the mid-thirties. It is immediately related to that black bourgeois line carried forward by Jesus Lava, who, as already isolated from the masses of the people, the masses of Party members and masses of Red soldiers and already preparing to surrender himself to the enemy after failing to get the help of fraternal parties for him to escape from the country, made one-man appointments and decisions that benefited his close relatives and also his accomplice in counter-revolution, Pedro Taruc, who in turn appointed his close relative, "Commander" Sumulong as the Commander in Chief and National Finance Officer of the People's Liberation Army.

Just before he surrendered himself to Macapagal through the Social Security System medical officer, Jesus Lava gave himself the title of Party Chairman and appointed a number of secretaries to form the Party secretariat for peasants. Independent of the other secretaries of whom were in Manila, Pedro Taruc made his own one-man decisions and appointments, among which was the sanctioning of "Commander" Sumulong as military and finance chieftain of the Taruc-Sumulong clique. Sumulong was appointed to his position despite the fact that the case against him in 1963 in the Party for malversation and rape had never been properly litigated.

It is possible to make an exposure and rectification of errors in the Party and in the People's Liberation Army because we, the majority of Party members and Red soldiers, have remained steadfastly true to the Party and to the Philippine Revolution. The Party and Army have persisted under the most difficult conditions because among the masses of Party members and Red soldiers the vast majority have remained faithful to the interests of the toiling masses and have consistently taken the mass line. The Taruc-Sumulong clique which has usurped Party and Army leadership in Central Luzon has long acted as a hindrance to the advance of the Revolution and as a heavy burden on the masses of the people. Their crimes have been utilized by the enemy to discredit the Party and the People's Army. This clique has perpetrated the most grievous crimes inside and outside the Party and Army. It is best, therefore, that the Party and Army should wage a rectification movement, ideological, political and organizational, in order to cleanse the Party and Army and make them ever stronger servants of the masses of people.

Comrades who are passive to or who refuse the call for rectification will only endanger themselves because if the evil practices of the Taruc-Sumulong clique are not repudiated now, then the reactionaries can use them to isolate the Party and Army from the people. The Communist Party of the Philippines and the New People's Army cannot carry out the tasks of the Revolution without engaging in criticism and self-criticism, without engaging in a rectification movement and clarifying their revolutionary tasks, without arousing the people to feel free to say what they think and what they expect to be done. Certainly, not all the particular crimes of the Taruc-Sumulong clique can be included in this document. Only the full play of a rectification campaign among Party members and Red soldiers can unfold them most amply and clear the way for the proletarian revolutionary line of Mao Tse-tung's thought.

However, to be most profound and to be of the greatest benefit to the Party and to the New People's Army, the rectification movement should encompass not only the wrongs committed by the Taruc-Sumulong clique but the whole history of the Communist Party of the Philippines. With such a scope of criticism, then comrades will fully understand why the phenomenon of a Taruc-Sumulong clique has come to pass and why, for instance, many of those who entered the Party and Army at various stages have become passive, afraid and reluctant to carry out the tasks of the Revolution or have turned the other way around only to strike back at the Party and Army as counter-revolutionaries. To understand the present as something that develops into the future, with the true proletarian revolutionaries advancing and the degenerate capitalist-rogues being thrown away into the dustbin of history, we must know the past that has brought about certain wrongs and weaknesses and also that has brought about what is good and strong about us today.

An understanding of the whole history of the Party is necessary, especially because most of the Party members and Red soldiers who are now actively working for the success of the Philippine Revolution are literally a new generation. It is most important that we take advantage of the lessons of the past and of the positive and negative experiences of old comrades who now compose a minority within the Party and Army at the moment.

Hereunder we outline briefly the major stages in the development of the Party and Army, with special interest in the latter and with special emphasis on the causes of failure. For an ampler view of Party history, it is indispensable for comrades to adopt this document together with the more extensive document, "Rectify Errors and Rebuild the Party" issued previously by the Party.

For twelve long years, after its formal establishment on November 7, 1930, the Communist Party of the Philippines failed to create a People's Army to combat the U.S. imperialist regime and the puppet comprador-landlord government of Quezon. Without a People's Army, the Party was defenseless. A few months after its public founding, repressive measures were taken by the U.S. imperialists and the puppet government against the Party. In 1932, the Party and all the mass organizations associated with it were formally declared illegal by the reactionary government and all principal Party leaders were sentenced, imprisoned and banished to various parts of the country. While being completely illegal, the Party leadership still failed to recognize the importance of Party and Army building among the peasants in the countryside. Throughout the decade of the thirties, widespread agitation for independence and land reform was being conducted more vigorously by other organizations.

In 1937, the Party was again allowed to operate legally in line with the anti-fascist Popular Front and in 1938, a merger of the Communist Party of the Philippines and the Socialist Party was made under the influence of the Right opportunist leadership of Earl Browder in the Communist Party of the U.S.A. The Party leadership continued to concentrate on parliamentary work in the city and no armed preparations were undertaken in the countryside against the impending Japanese invasion. Only campaigns for the voluntary boycott of Japanese goods were made mainly by the trade union movement under the leadership of the CPP chairman Crisanto Evangelista. The cadres of the Socialist Party continued to engage in purely legal urban agitation. At this time, Party members of petty bourgeois orientation who stood out in advocating civil liberties and whose chief representative was Dr. Vicente Lava started to gain principal influence in the Party.

The People's Army in the form of the Hukbalahap was established under the leadership of the Party on March 29, 1942 in Central Luzon. Since then, confirming what Comrade Mao Tse-tung has said that political power grows out of the barrel of a gun, the Party and the people gained a certain amount of power and prestige in Central Luzon that they had never held before. Within one year of waging guerrilla warfare, the People's Army grew from a small force to a big one. It's strength grew rapidly as the peasants rallied around it under such favorable conditions as the evacuation of the U.S. imperialists and the Commonwealth government from the Philippines, the disintegration of landlord power in the countryside and the clear need among the people to take up arms against the Japanese imperialists.

But after the Japanese raid on the Mt. Arayat Base of the People's Army in the early part of March, 1943, the Party leadership of the Right opportunist Vicente Lava was overcome with pessimism and adopted the wrong policy of "retreat for defense" which was a passive military line, involving the dissolution of armed units and prevention of tactical offense against the enemy. The Lava leadership also entertained serious doubts about the working class being able to lead under conditions that the trade union movement in the city was in chaos. He did not recognize clearly that the Communist Party of the Philippines as the most advanced detachment of the working class was already in the countryside to lead the peasant masses.

The "retreat for defense" policy was rectified only sometime in September, 1944 when the U.S. military forces and their puppet forces were already starting to make their own offensive. Because of this Right opportunist policy, which covered more than half of the three-year Japanese occupation, the Red Army lost the opportunity of building up more massive fighting forces and of expanding as fast as it should have even beyond Central Luzon. On a national scale, the Party and Army failed to seize the leadership in the anti-fascist armed struggle. The plan to send out cadres to other parts of the archipelago to develop armed struggle had been called off even as early as 1942. Thus, the development of armed struggle under the leadership of the Party became limited to Central Luzon and to a small part of Southern Tagalog. Furthermore, the Party leadership failed to use agrarian revolution as the basis for its strength in areas securely held by the People's Army. It also glaringly failed to expose U.S. imperialism as an enemy. It utterly failed to implement the Communist Internationalist policy of using the anti-fascist struggle as an occasion to establish a people's democratic government.

As the U.S. imperialist and puppet forces were advancing, the Party leadership still mainly influenced by the Right opportunism of Dr. Vicente Lava and Luis Taruc relied on the word of American agents who contacted them that they could participate in the parliamentary life and economic reconstruction of the country. The Party leadership passed on to more outright Right opportunists like Pedro Castro and Jorge Frianeza who advocated an open and legal mass party in the style of bourgoeis parties and who carried out further the line of separating the gun from the Red soldiers, despite the atrocious crimes being committed by the U.S. imperialists and their puppets against Hukbalahap leaders who were being imprisoned by them, despite entire Hukbalahap squadrons being massacred by them and despite a sizeable force like the Banal Regiment selling out for American back-pay. The Party leadership failed to recognize that the U.S. imperialists and the landlords were systematically disorganizing the People's Army to strengthen armed counter-revolution and re-impose their control over the entire countryside and over the whole country.

True to its Right opportunist line, the Party leadership shifted its headquarters from the countryside to the city, launched the Democratic Alliance which was dominated by bourgeois personalities and engaged in the bourgeois electoral game only to discover too late that the U.S. imperialists, the comprador bourgeoisie and the landlords would violate parliamentary rules to get what they want, such as the Bell Trade Act, Parity Amendment and other reactionary laws, and would commit the most dastardly murders of revolutionary leaders and masses. During the period of the "democratic peace" line, the reactionaries were able to re-install themselves in positions of power all over the country while unhesitantly using their guns to suppress the people as in the regions of Central Luzon and Southern Tagalog.

As a result of the ouster of Party-supported members of Congress from their parliamentary seats, the murder of revolutionary leaders, Red soldiers and ordinary people, and the just clamor of the people for resuming armed struggle, the Right opportunist leadership in the Party was overthrown and the Party decided to launch the armed struggle in 1948. But, as no sufficient rectification movement was waged aside from organizational rejection of the Right opportunists, the Jose Lava leadership that tried to resume the armed struggle was not able to formulate correctly the ideological, political and organizational basis for a protracted people's war. While the Party was already bent on waging armed struggle, the Right opportunist Luis Taruc, who was commander-in-chief of the People's Liberation Army, was still allowed to negotiate the surrender and disarming of the People's Liberation Army in the same year of 1948.

Taking a dogmatic and sectarian attitude as clearly manifested by its PB Resolutions of 1950, the Jose Lava leadership adopted the impetuous petty bourgeois line of quick military victory within two years which underestimated the enemy and overestimated the revolutionary forces. It was a complete violation of Mao Tse-tung's strategic principle of a protracted people's war. It was merely a subjective conclusion reached by heavily relying on such external possibilities as a third world war, the absolute breakdown of the U.S. economy and the violent split among the local political factions in the country which were foretold to occur within two years. The putschist line of military victory in two years overstrained the limited revolutionary forces, made them leap over unstable area, instead of advancing wave upon wave, and impelled the imposition of bourgeois rules of war and sectarian punishments on the overstrained cadres, soldiers and masses. The more the Party and Army leadership waved the black flag of commandism, the more the Party and the Army became isolated from the masses on whom sectarian abuses were committed. These sectarian abuses were repeated in a big way by reactionary soldiers in civilian disguise and were blamed on the Party and Army, thus isolating them further from the masses.

The Left opportunist leadership of Jose Lava (PB-In and Secretariat) was isolated in the city from which it dictated its adventurist orders. It had a sub-command under Jesus Lava (the so-called PB-Out) which was likewise isolated in a physical base, not a political base, in the Sierra Madre vastnesses of Laguna, far away rfom the main military forces in the plains of Central Luzon. Even before half of the preliminary raids decided by the 1950 PB Resolutions could be implemented, the Jose Lava leadership was quickly smashed by only a few major counter-attacks such as the total capture of the central Party headquarters in the city, the massive encirclement of the Sierra Madre, the slicing-off of over-extended supply and communications lines, large-scale enemy imitation of the roguish sectarian activities of a big number of Party and Army units and heavy enemy infiltration of the central headquarters because of a liberal policy of recruitment in the city. The Jose Lava leadership was criminally responsible for the almost total obliteration of the People's Army within the short period of two years and for the most wanton sacrifice of the lives of Party cadres and Red soldiers in the entire history of the Communist Party of the Philippines.

After the enemy had smashed the Jose Lava leadership, Jesus Lava assumed the Party leadership and, together with Casto Alejandrino as Commander-in-Chief, continued the Left opportunist and sectarian line of his brother. Adducing the failure of the Jose Lava leadership to mere negligence and tactical errors of some comrades and to mere accidence, the Jesus Lava leadership carried further the line of his brother and failed to launch a much-needed rectification movement. Revealing its utter ignorance of the theory of people's war, this leadership asserted that the strategic phase that the People's Liberation Army had been in since 1949 was neither the strategic defense nor the strategic offense but what its muddle headedly called the strategic "counter-offensive." The Central Committee Conference of February-March, 1951 which elevated Jesus Lava to the general secretaryship did not find any substantial ideological, political and organizational errors in the previous leadership. Jesus Lava was more concerned then with outwitting and out-maneuvering the equally careerist renegade Luis Taruc to assume the Party leadership.

Taking advantage of the defeats suffered by the People's Army, Luis Taruc and his clique pushed forward the Right opportunist line of seeking peace negotiations with the enemy on the basis of weaknesses. This capitulationist line had disastrous results inasmuch as it encouraged the mood of many soldiers to surrender even in areas where the People's Army was still strong. In 1954, the renegade, traitor and scab Luis Taruc surrendered to the enemy under the auspices of the Central Intelligence Agency.

While the enemy launched a series of massive campaigns of encirclement and suppression during the period of 1951, the Party and Army were severely split between two factions and the Jesus Lava leadership failed to give the unifying ideological, political and organizational leadership for a protracted people's war. The relations between the Party and Army on the one hand and the people on the other, between Party officials and Army officers on one hand and soldiers on the other, and among soldiers worsened without let-up. The Jesus Lava leadership failed to grasp the mass line, failed to overcome but even increased the harsh sectarian activities of the previous leadership and continued to propagate a purely military viewpoint.

In 1955, the Jesus Lava leadership was overcome with pessimism about the armed struggle as a result of its ceaseless military defeats and its isolation from the masses. Its dogmatism, Left opportunism and sectarianism easily reversed into empiricism and Right opportunism. It was a result of the continuous military defeats that this leadership subsequently adopted the line of parliamentary struggle. In 1957, it went out of its way to dissolve those armed units of the People's Army that it had access to and converted them into "organizational brigades." As Jesus Lava himself prepared to abandon the armed struggle and the countryside, he dissolved his own security unit. During this period, the Khrushchev revisionist renegades of the Soviet Union were already waging a world-wide campaign for the "parliamentary road" and the possibility of "peaceful transition." In 1958, he took flight from the countryside and began his career of being General Secretary of his secluded city room from which he issued political transmissions and directives without the benefit of collective discussions and concrete experience. This flightism was imitated by other principal Party leaders, particularly by the Commander-in-Chief of the People's Liberation Army, Casto Alejandrino.

But not even the efforts of the Party in the parliamentary struggle directly bore fruit. Independent efforts of the leaders of the national bourgeoisie and urban petty bourgeoisie advanced the line of anti-imperialism and left behind the Jesus Lava leadership in political agitation. What crippled the Party most in this period was the one-man decision taken by Jesus Lava that the Party must take the single-file policy in organization. This is liquidationism pure and simple, destroying the collective life of the Party. The vast majority of Party members became disconnected and became passive as they were easily cut off from their single files due to the arrest of a single Party member, the increasing passivity and opportunism of others, or the infrequency of contacts. It would only be in 1960 that new Party members in both legal and illegal forms of struggle emerged to re-invigorate the Party and Army.

Carrying out further his flightist policy, Jesus Lava sought vainly to leave the country. After failing to do so, he tried to cajole President Macapagal with several letters of support for his bourgeois policy and finally wrote him a treasonous letter offering his surrender. Before his "capture" by the enemy in 1964, he alone made appointments to the Party leadership. These appointments were characterized by nepotism, thinly camouflaged by the appointment in name of Pedro Taruc as the secretary for peasants. The nepotistic character of the other appointments to the Party Secretariat was very obvious in that the beneficiaries were close relatives and had never before excelled in Party work or mass work.

The Right opportunist line of the Jesus Lava leadership resulted into two degenerate and counter-revolutionary trends. Feigning loss of contact with the People's Liberation Army and Party cadres therein led by Pedro Taruc, the heirs in leadership of the Lava family took the blessings of the Soviet revisionist renegade clique, held a conference of its own in April, 1967 to perpetuate the "noble image" of the Lavas and put forward formally the line of opposing those engaged in armed struggle, of accepting the leadership of the reactionary government in land reform, of contraposing the united front with the armed struggle and of repeating the old error of letting bourgeois personalities assume the leadership in what they conceive to be a formal united front organization. On the other hand, also feigning loss of contact with the barefaced city-based, local revisionist renegades, the Taruc-Sumulong clique defined a limited area in Central Luzon as its own "independent kingdom" and put forward its own line of Right opportunism and revisionist treachery in the countryside as explained previously. Pedro Taruc, acting on his own alone, committed the serious crime of appointing Sumulong as Commander-in-Chief of the People's Liberation Army and also as National Finance Officer despite the fact that the latter was still facing the serious charges of malversation and corruption made in 1963.

If there is a bourgeois headquarters within the Party and Army and also factions within the same bourgeois headquarters, the counter-revolutionary line they put forward is bound to be opposed by a revolutionary line put forward by the proletarian revolutionary headquarters within the same Party and Army. During the years of 1964 to the present when the one-man decisions and appointments made by the renegade Jesus Lava was creating confusion within the Party, those upholding Mao Tse-tung's thought led by Comrade Amado Guerrero rose up to criticize and repudiate modern revisionism, Lavaism and Tarucism, and thus, prepared the way for the reestablishment and rebuilding of the Communist Party of the Philippines under the supreme guidance of Mao Tse-tung's thought. At the same time, within the People's Liberation Army, Commander Dante, together with the late Commander Delio, struggled hard to put other Red commanders and soldiers on the revolutionary path, continued to wage armed struggle most militantly and fostered the revolutionary spirit of serving the people and making the Red soldiers and people like fish and water. Today, the efforts of the overwhelming majority of Red commanders and soldiers led by Commander Dante who remain ever faithful to the people's democratic revolution and to Mao Tse-tung's thought are crowned with the transformation of the old People's Liberation Army into the New People's Army under the supreme command of Mao Tse-tung's thought and the Communist Party of the Philippines.

Under the Marxist-Leninist principle that the Party commands the gun, the New People's Army follows the absolute leadership of the Communist Party of the Philippines and the supreme command of Mao Tse-tung's thought. The New People's Army is an instrument for implementing the Party Programme for a People's Democratic Revolution. It is, as a matter of fact, the principal organization under the command of the Communist Party of the Philippines, an organization for waging the main form of struggle, armed struggle in the people's democratic revolution.

The tasks of the New People's Army are comprehensively outlined in the Party Programme for a People's Democratic Revolution. Both the general and specific programmes are therein stated. But, in another comprehensive manner, we outline hereunder its urgent tasks:

1. The New People's Army Must Engage in Party Rebuilding

It is by propagating Mao Tse-tung's thought in the Army and among the masses, applying it in revolutionary practice and organizing Party branches and committees inside and outside the Army that the New People's Army engages in Party rebuilding. The New People's Army is not only a fighting force, it is also a propaganda and organizing force. It must propagate and apply Mao Tse-tung's thought as the highest development of Marxism-Leninism in the present era. Its cadres, commanders and soldiers must all alike instill themselves with Mao Tse-tung's thought by undertaking Mao Tse-tung's thought study classes under the direction of the Revolutionary School of Mao Tse-tung's thought, under the Army Political Department and under the Political Commissars appointed by the Party to supervise Party life and political education in every Red armed unit. All Party cadres in the Army, commanders and soldiers should in turn effect an ideological mobilization of the masses under Mao Tse-tung's thought and they should see to it that the most advanced elements among the masses, as among the Red soldiers, should be taken as members of the Communist Party of the Philippines in the course of mass struggle. All daily problems of the Party, Army and the masses in politics, armed struggle, culture and economic work should be solved by applying the universal truth of Mao Tse-tung's thought.

As an organized force, the New People's Army must see to it that Party branches at company level, Party groups in every platoon and every guerrilla unit and Party committees at every level from the company upwards are established. As an organizing force, it must establish Party branches and local Party committees among the people. The New People's Army must always be conscious that the Communist Party of the Philippines is at the core of the mass revolutionary movement.

In instilling itself with Mao Tse-tung's thought, the New People's Army instills itself with the spirit of serving the people and repudiating itself. It rejects modern revisionism and subjectivism in its dogmatist or empiricist form. Right and "Left" opportunism, sectarianism and liberalism, commandism and tailism and all other weaknesses and mistakes that have obstructed the advance of the people's democratic revolution. Mao Tse-tung's thought is the most precise instrument for rectifying and weeding out all the weaknesses and mistakes bred by Lavaism, Taruc-ism and all other evil sources of errors in the Philippine revolutionary movement.

The New People's Army and all its living components have a conscious iron discipline. It follows the principle of democratic centralism. Centralism is essentially the supreme command of Mao Tse-tung's thought. It is the content of the subordination of the minority to the majority, the lower organ to the higher organ and the individual to the Party. Inner democracy shall be fully enjoyed by all Red soldiers and shall serve as the means for the practical and concrete application of Mao Tse-tung's thought. Criticism and self-criticism shall be given full play in order to raise the political and the combat effectiveness of the New People's Army.

There shall be political democracy in the New People's Army with the soldiers having the right to hold meetings and speak out freely on any worthwhile subject or problem that confronts them.

There shall be economic democracy with all officers and men enjoying equal material conditions, such as allowances and rations, with the men having the right to elect representatives to assist the company leadership in managing their material conditions and with all officers and men having the right to look into the books of accounts at anytime.

There shall also be military democracy, with the officers teaching the soldiers, the soldiers teaching the officers and the soldiers learning from each other with regard to military plans, methods and techniques of fighting. As much as possible, meetings shall be held before and after battles in order to raise their fighting knowledge and effectiveness. Bourgeois and feudal practices between officers and soldiers, such as beatings and bullying, shall be absolutely prohibited. The best of relations shall therefore be developed between officers and men within the Army so that the Army as a whole shall always be oriented towards the maintenance and development of the best relations with the masses.

The officers and men of the New People's Army shall be strictly bound by Comrade Mao Tse-tung's Three Rules of Discipline and Eight Points of Attention and shall always go out of their way to serve the people, aside from performing well their fighting tasks.

2. The New People's Army Must Carry Out Agrarian Revolution, Build Rural Bases and Advance the Armed Struggle

Since the people's democratic revolution is essentially a peasant war under the leadership of the working class and the Communist Party of the Philippines, since the peasant struggle for land is the main content of the people's democratic revolution, the New People's Army must launch an agrarian revolution and mobilize the peasant masses, the vast majority of the Filipino people, for the people's democratic revolution. A revolution is a mass undertaking and so the New People's Army as a revolutionary army must rely on the masses for increasing its fighting strength, preserving itself, for winning battles, for winning the whole war and consolidating the power won.

It is only through agrarian revolution that rural bases can be created as great rears for the emergence of more rural bases and more guerrilla zones and that the great masses of the people are mobilized against U.S. imperialism, the comprador bourgeoisie, the landlord class and the bureaucrat capitalists. Only by destroying the feudal base of U.S. imperialism in the Philippines can the people's democratic revolution be won against both U.S. imperialism and domestic feudalism.

It is only by having stable base areas can the New People's Army wage a protracted people's war. From these stable base areas, it can advance wave upon wave against the enemy. By building stable base areas to encircle the city, the biggest graveyard of the enemy forces are created. It is here in the countryside that the enemy is compelled to spread out thinly, lured in and destroyed piece by piece over a long period of time. It is here in the countryside that the enemy becomes exhausted and defeated before the main forces of the New People's Army march in on the cities to seize power, finally with the help of workers in general strike or in general uprising together with the urban petty bourgeoisie.

It is now the urgent task of the New People's Army to establish the armed independent regime in the countryside on the basis of agrarian revolution. The armed independent regime shall become the focus of an ever expanding wave of guerrilla zones throughout the country. All commanders and fighters must learn from Party cadres how to raise the level of a guerrilla zone to a rural base.

The New People's Army must establish its main fighting forces in Luzon to defeat the enemy forces concentrated in Luzon and in the Greater Manila area and also big forces at certain points in Visayas and Mindanao to compel the enemy to disperse its forces at great costs across the archipelago. We must disperse the enemy in two ways: first throughout the countryside; and second, throughout the archipelago. Then we can destroy them piece by piece. For this purpose great rural bases must be created in Luzon, Visayas and Mindanao. The nationwide expansion of the Party and the Army should be made in the light of this consideration.

To carry out the armed struggle, the New People's Army should develop four types of armed units: the regular mobile forces, the guerrilla units, the militia or self-defense corps, and the armed city partisans. The New People's Army must learn from the experience of the Chinese and Vietnamese people's wars and must be trained to employ old and new methods of fighting and military technique. Aside from developing marksmanship with various types of guns, the New People's Army must train in night operations, bayoneting, using land mines, mortar fire, tunnel warfare and the like. It must also be able to muster all the indigenous methods of fighting that the workers, fishermen, peasants and national minorities know.

In building itself up, the New People's Army must be guided by the principle of self-reliance. So long as it is closely linked with the masses of the people and enjoys their support, the New People's Army shall find its efforts adequate for a protracted armed struggle. The Party committees in the Army and in local areas must unite in every way to carry out the tasks of the people's democratic revolution.

3. The New People's Army Must Build Up The National United Front

The New People's Army must build up the national united front by upholding and following the leadership of the Communist Party of the Philippines, by welding together through armed struggle the workers and peasants whose alliance serves as the basis of the national united front and by attracting the urban petty bourgeoisie and the national bourgeoisie to the fold of the people's democratic revolution.

Because of the anti-national, anti-democratic and corrupt character of the state that it seeks to destroy and replace, the New People's Army can easily attract the urban petty bourgeoisie which inevitably joins the ranks of the exploited in sentiment and material condition as the crisis aggravates. Because the New People's Army shall confiscate imperialist goods and deprive the imperialists of markets in the provinces, the national bourgeoisie and all small patriotic businessmen shall be encouraged to produce goods locally and to support the revolutionary forces.

In the countryside, the New People's Army must wage an anti-feudal united front to unite poor peasants, poor fishermen and farm workers as its invincible political base, win over the middle peasants and middle fishermen and neutralize the rich peasants.

The New People's Army shall be willing to establish a National Liberation Front as an armed united front of all patriotic and progressive classes, groups and individuals. It welcomes the formation of other groups of armed units that wage armed struggle against the enemy. The New People's Army shall extend to them as much support and cooperation as it can.

In every instance of cooperative unity, the New People's Army must take firm hold of the revolutionary class line. So long as the goal of any class or group is the destruction of the power of U.S. imperialism and feudalism, the New People's Army shall always be willing to extend its cooperation and helping hand. But it shall always be alert to enemy infiltrators and revisionist saboteurs of the armed struggle.

In performing its revolutionary duty of fighting U.S. imperialism, modern revisionism and all local reactionaries, the New People's Army is highly conscious that it is contributing to the development of the international united front and that it is upholding the principle of proletarian internationalism. Revolutionary armed struggle in the Philippines is certainly an effective party of the world-wide struggle of all oppressed peoples against U.S. imperialism, modern revisionism and all reactionaries. The overthrow of U.S. imperialism and all domestic reaction in the Philippines will be a great contribution towards the total collapse of imperialism and the world-wide triumph of socialism.

Long live Mao Tse-tung's thought!
Long live the Philippine Revolution!
Long live the Communist Party of the Philippines!
Long live the New People's Army!

Issued by the
MEETING OF RED COMMANDERS AND SOLDIERS
MARCH 29, 1969

Annex D

BASIC RULES OF THE NEW PEOPLE'S ARMY

(A CPP-NPA document captured by the Armed Forces of the Philippines in Capas, Tarlac, on June 9, 1969)

The New People's Army is under the supreme command of Marxism-Leninism, Mao Tse-tung's thought, and the Communist Party of the Philippines. It is the revolutionary army of the broad masses of the Filipino people against U.S. imperialism, the comprador bourgeoisie, the landlord class and the bureaucrat capitalists.

The New People's Army is the principal form of organization under the leadership of the Communist Party of the Philippines, which has taken the road of armed revolution in line with Mao Tse-tung's thought. It is the instrument for carrying out the Party's central task of seizing political power and consolidating it. It is the instrument for overthrowing the present bourgeois reactionary puppet government and for winning the people's democratic revolution. It is the instrument for helping in a big way carry out the Programme for a People's Democratic Revolution of the Communist Party of the Philippines.

The New People's Army is completely in the service of the people's democratic interests and is the mainstay of the people's democratic dictatorship. It defends the people from the evil forces of U.S. imperialist and feudal oppression and expolitation and always strives to help them in every possible way in their daily life. It abhors the least harm done to the masses of the people and it instills an iron discipline among its officers and men which prevents them from doing the least harm to the masses of the people.

Armed with the invincible Mao Tse-tung's thought, the New People's Army has emerged after shedding off the counter-revolutionary revisionist errors of Lavaism and Taruc-ism and other sources of modern revisionism and opportunism, "Left" and Right. It combats within its ranks the purely military viewpoint, ultra democracy, disregard of organizational discipline, absolute equalitarianism, subjectivism, individualism, the ideology of roving rebel bands and putchism. Now, the New People's Army includes the best fighters who persist in waging armed struggle and in propagating Mao Tse-tung's thought. It consistently integrates the universal truth of Mao Tse-tung's thought, the acme of Marxism-Leninism in the present era, with the practice of protracted people's war in the Philippines.

While following the absolute leadership of the working class and the Communist Party of the Philippines, the New People's Army incorporates mainly the armed peasants fighting for agrarian revolution which is the main content of the people's democratic revolution. In this sense, the people's democratic revolution is essentially a peasant war led by the working class. In the countryside, the New People's Army works and fights arduously to transform backward villages into the most advanced political, military, economic and cultural bastions of the people's democratic revolution. To carry out this great task, it relies mainly on the masses of poor peasants and farm workers and then wins over the middle peasants to neutralize the rich peasants. Such is its revolutionary anti-feudal class line in the countryside.

The main strategic principle of the New People's Army is a protracted people's war, with its armed units ever growing stronger in the countryside on the basis of agrarian revolution, armed struggle and the building of rural bases and consistently encircling the cities until such time that the enemy forces are finally exhausted after being defeated piece by piece in the countryside. The New People's Army is determined to build rural bases, establish local organs of people's government and advance wave upon wave until it can effectively destroy the remaining enemy forces concentrated in big cities and big military camps. It shall systematically create and elevate the guerrilla zones to the level of rural bases where local people's governments can operate fully. The rural bases shall serve as the great rears for the emergence and expansion of guerrilla zones and for the advance of all other forces of the people's democratic revolution.

The New People's Army shall undergo three strategic phases in the protracted people's war. The first phase is the strategic defense in which it always maintains tactical offense and initiative against the strategic military superiority of the enemy. The second phase is the strategic stalemate in which its fighting forces are already more or less equal to the enemy forces in strength. The third and final phase is the strategic offensive in which the regular mobile forces of the New People's Army have reached such a strength and scope to be able to take the offensive against the isolated enemy forces in their city and big camp fortifications. All throughout the protracted people's war, the New People's Army has the political initiative because it integrates revolutionary theory with revolutionary practice, because it is closely linked with the masses of the people and because it conducts self-criticism whenever it does wrong or carries weaknesses.

The New People's Army creates and employs several forms of fighting units in the course of the protracted people's war. The regular mobile forces defend the rural bases and destroy the enemy forces in a big way. The guerrilla forces defend the guerrilla zones, prepare the emergence or the advance of regular mobile forces or create new guerrilla zones. The militia and self-defense corps defend the masses in local areas without separating themselves from daily productive work. The armed city partisans perform special tasks of disrupting the enemy and punishing traitors in cities. All these fighting units of the New People's Army shall be coordinated and shall employ all kinds of warfare that they can develop and that are made available by the situation and the masses of the people.

The New People's Army is highly conscious that by performing its revolutionary duty of overthrowing U.S. imperialism, the comprador bourgeoisie, the landlord class and the bureaucrat capitalists in the Philippines, it is performing a great and noble task for the broad masses of the Filipino people, especially for the exploited masses of workers and peasants, as well as for the oppressed people of the world. It is both a patriotic duty and an act of proletarian internationalism for the New People's Army to fight for a people's democratic revolution as the transitional stage towards socialism. Armed struggle in the Philippines weakens and helps destroy U.S. imperialism, modern revisionism and all reaction in the countryside of the world and in the whole world in the same way that the armed struggle waged by all other oppressed people weakens and helps destroy the same in the Philippines. The New People's Army has the internationalist mandate to fight for the total collapse of imperialism led by U.S. imperialism and the worldwide triumph of socialism in the era of Mao Tse-tung's thought.

The New People's Army and the Communist Party of the Philippines

Point 1. The New People's Army shall always follow the leadership of the Communist Party of the Philippines and shall, therefore, be bound by the decisions, orders and directives of the Party National Congress, Central Committee and Military Commission.

Point 2. The Military Commission is the highest special organ of the Central Committee which shall receive regular and special reports from the lowest to the highest military command and shall issue appropriate policies, orders and directives.

Point 3. The Military Commission shall see to it that the Party leadership, Party organization and Party life are maintained within the entire New People's Army. The Party Branch shall be based at the company level and a Party Group shall operate in every platoon and guerrilla unit. All non-regular armed units shall be under the direct control of local Party committees.

Point 4. The Party Committees shall be created from the level of the Branch upwards and shall be responsible for the maintenance of the leadership of the Communist Party of the Philippines and the development of the best relations between the Army and the people, between the officers and men, among the men and between the Army and the local Party committees.

Point 5. The New People's Army shall have its own Political Department responsible for the revolutionary class education of all officers and men, for developing proletarian revolutionary cadres from the Army and for making mass mobilization, specially in new areas of armed operation.

Point 6. Political commissars shall be assigned to every unit of the regular mobile and guerrilla forces in order to educate all the fighters and maintain Party organization and Party life.

Point 7 Territorial and unit Commanders shall be responsible for internal military administration and combat operations in their respective areas and units but they shall be guided by the Party at every level. The number and special functions of Deputy Commanders shall be defined by the Military Commission.

Point 8. All district commanders and platoon leaders upwards shall have graduated from the Revolutionary School of Mao Tse-tung's Thought conducted centrally or locally.

Point 9. All non-regular fighting units such as the guerrillas, militia, self-defense corps and the armed city partisans shall be directly controlled by the local Party committees. However, they shall take orders from the Military Commission or the Military Command for purposes of coordination with regular mobile forces.

Functions of the New People's Army

Point 1. The main function of the New People's Army at present shall be to wage a protracted people's war to destroy the reactionary state power and the interventionist U.S. imperialist forces, protect the people and advance their national and democratic interests.

Point 2. The New People's Army shall help organize the revolutionary barrio committees and other revolutionary bodies as local organs of people's government.

Point 3. The New People's Army shall serve the people in every possible way aside from performing combat duties.

Point 4. The New People's Army shall engage in revolutionary propaganda and mass mobilization.

Resolution Electing Comrade Dante to the Central Committee

RESOLUTION TO ELECT NINE CADRES FROM THE NEW PEOPLE'S ARMY AND THE PEASANT MOVEMENT TO THE FIRST CENTRAL COMMITTEE OF THE COMMUNIST PARTY OF THE PHILIPPINES

Whereas, the New People's Army is the leading organization following the road of armed revolution in accordance with Mao Tse-tung's Thought;

Whereas, it is necessary to strengthen the Party in the countrysides and the armed peasants are the main force for the victory of agrarian revolution led by the Communist Party of the Philippines;

Whereas, the leaders of the New People's Army and the peasant movement have high political consciousness and are guided by Mao Tse-tung's Thought and have shown courage as proletarian revolutionary cadres;

Whereas, be it resolved as it is hereby resolved that 9 cadres from the New People's Army and the peasant movement be elected to the Central Committee of the Communist Party of the Philippines;

And be it further resolved, as it is hereby resolved that Comrade Dante, Comrade Melody, Comrade Goody, Comrade Eddie, Comrade Ruben, Comrade Elias, Comrade Juaning, Comrade Ben be the nine cadres from the New People's Army and the peasant movement be elected to the Central Committee of the Communist Party of the Philippines.

Point 5. The New People's Army shall help organize local Party Branches, local Party committees and revolutionary mass organizations.

Point 6. The New People's Army shall engage in construction, productive and economic work for its own needs as well as for those of the Party and the people.

Point 7. The New People's Army shall help keep public order and it shall arrest wrong-doers and submit them to the people's court for trial.

Point 8. Within the New People's Army, various sections of work shall be created such as staff work, training, internal order and security, intelligence, reconnaissance, supplies, ordnance and repair, medical care, communications, transport, construction, production and others.

Point 9. Short rest periods from combat shall be allowed for regular mobile and guerrilla forces only to undergo further ideological, political and combat training, to regroup, recuperate and replenish their forces and conduct local political work.

Membership in the New People's Army

Point 1. Any able-bodied person, irrespective of age, sex, color, nationality or religious belief, who is capable of combat duties and who is ready to participate in a protracted armed struggle against the reactionary state power may become a member of a fighting unit of the New People's Army.

Point 2. Those who wish to join the New People's Army shall inform any unit or office of the New People's Army, Party Committee or Party members or revolutionary mass organizations of their intention.

Point 3. Local Party Committees, armed units of the New People's Army and revolutionary mass organizations, shall take the initiative of accepting individual and collective requests for membership in the New People's Army or of directly recruiting fighters and of creating new fighting units of the New People's Army.

Point 4. The military command and the local Party committee immediately responsible for the area where recruitment of Red soldiers is being made shall direct and supervise the recruitment work.

Point 5. A higher military command or Party committee shall have the right to dissolve or reorganize any armed unit on valid grounds.

Point 6. Individual or mass deserters from the enemy side or captive soldiers may be incorporated into the New People's Army, provided they are re-educated and re-organized. Their incorporation shall be approved after a thorough investigation by the Military Command and Army Party committee of the provincial level at least.

Point 7. The New People's Army shall regularly check up the class origin, performance of duty and will to fight of all its fighters in order to raise consistently their proletarian revolutionary character.

Point 8. The vast majority of members of the New People's Army shall be armed combatants at all times, although some members may be assigned to non-combat functions which are directly related to the fighting effectiveness of the New People's Army.

Discipline

Point 1. The discipline of the officers and men in the New People's Army shall be a conscious discipline guided by Marxism-Leninism, Mao Tse-tung's thought, by the Communist Party of the Philippines and by the organizational principle of democratic centralism. The Army Party committees shall see to it that the line, policies and decisions of the Party shall be implemented by the military command at every level.

Point 2. The New People's Army shall be bound by the following discipline:

a. the individual is subordinate to the whole Army;
b. the minority is subordinate to the majority;
c. the lower level is subordinate to the higher level; and
d. the entire membership is subordinate to the Military Commission and to the Central Committee.

Point 3. All officers and men shall be prohibited to do the least harm to the people's interests and they shall be always bound by Comrade Mao Tse-tung's Three Main Rules of Discipline and Eight Points of Attention in order to keep high their revolutionary integrity.

a. Three Main Rules of Discipline
   1) Obey orders in all your actions.
   2) Do not take a single needle or piece of thread from the masses.
   3) Turn in everything captured.
b. Eight Points of Attention
   1) Speak politely.
   2) Pay fairly for what you buy.
   3) Return everything you borrow.
   4) Pay for anything you damage.
   5) Do not hit or swear at people.
   6) Do not damage crops.
   7) Do not take liberties with women.
   8) Do not ill-treat captives.

Point 4. Officers shall be absolutely prohibited from bourgeois and feudal practices in their relations with their men and with the people.

Point 5. Officers and men shall be strictly prohibited from getting drunk and from gambling.

Point 6. The Army Party Committee at the proper level or the military court it may create shall hear and decide cases against officers and men at the level where the alleged mistake or crime is committed and shall impose the following penalties according to the gravity of the offense committed.

a. reprimand and public apology to the offended party
b. reprimand and re-assignment
c. demotion
d. suspension and hard labor
e. expulsion
f. expulsion and execution

Point 7. In all kinds of penalty, excepting expulsion and execution, the offender or offenders shall receive re-education within a reasonable period of time and shall be required to make a public apology to the offended.

Point 8. The highest penalty, expulsion and execution, shall be meted out on offenders for the proven crimes of treason, betrayal, desertion in the face of the enemy, espionage, sabotage, mutiny, inciting to mutiny, murder, robbery, rape, arson and grave malversation of people's funds.

Point 9. All cases shall be fully investigated and all accused shall be given a fair hearing.

Democracy

Point 1. To be able to enjoy democracy yet maintain discipline and avoid ultra-democracy within the New People's Army, all officers, soldiers and Party cadres shall discuss and educate each other on Mao Tse-tung's thought and on the Programme, policies and decisions of the Communist Party of the Philippines.

Point 2. All officers and men shall together engage in periodic and special criticism and self-criticism sessions in order to improve their political and combat effectiveness. Ideological, political and organizational mistakes and weaknesses shall be corrected through the process of criticism and self-criticism.

Point 3. There shall be political democracy in that the officers and soldiers shall be free to hold meetings and speak out freely on how to raise their proletarian revolutionary consciousness, bring themselves closer to the people, improve their fighting ability, organize their non-combat work and improve their material conditions.

Point 4. There shall be economic democracy among the officers and soldiers in that they shall share weal and woe, enjoying equal material conditions such as equal rations and equal allowances, they shall have the right to manage together their supplies and mess with the soldiers electing representatives to assist the company leadership in management, and that anyone shall have the right to look into the accounts and supplies anytime.

Point 5. There shall be military democracy among officers and soldiers in that together they shall hold a series of meetings before and after battles and campaigns, whereby the officers teach the soldiers, the soldiers teach the officers and the soldiers teach each other concerning operational plans, methods and techniques of fighting and winning the fight.

Military Conferences

Point 1 A National Military Conference shall be called by the Military Commission at least once a year to discuss the political and military situation and tasks of the New People's Army. The Military Commission, the National Operational Command, the Regional, Provincial and District Commands shall attend the conference. The Chairman of the Military Commission shall preside.

Point 2. A Regional Military Conference shall be called by the Military Commission at least once in six months to discuss the political and military situation and tasks of the New People's Army within the region. Representatives of the Military Commission, the Regional Operational Command, the Provincial and District Commands and the Regional Party Committee shall attend the conference. The chief representative of the Military Commission shall preside.

Point 3. Provincial Military conference shall be called by the Provincial Military Command at least once in three months to discuss the political and military situation and tasks of the New People's Army within the district. Representatives of the Provincial Operational Command, the District Party Committee, the secretaries of Party sections, all unit commanders and all heads of Party groups in the Army shall attend the conference. The chief representative of the Provincial Operational Command shall preside.

Point 4. The above military conferences may formulate recommendations to be acted on by the Military Commission of the Central Committee.

System of Military Command

Point 1. The National Operational Command shall be responsible for the execution of national and inter-regional military policies and plans approved by the Military Commission and/or the Central Committee, shall command all forms of armed units of the New People's Army and shall make regular and special military reports and recommendations to the Military Commission.

The National Operational Command shall be composed of the Commander-in-Chief, his Deputy Commanders, the Regional Commanders and their Deputy Commanders.

Point 3. The Provincial Operational Command shall be responsi- for the execution of regional and inter-provincial military policies and plans, shall command all forms of armed units within the region and shall make regular and special military reports and recommendations to the Military Commission and to the National Operational Command.

The Regional Operational Command shall be composed of the Regional Commander, his Deputy Commanders, the Provincial Commanders and their Deputy Commanders.

Point 3. The Provincial Operational Command shall be responsible for the execution of provincial and inter-district military policies and plans, shall command all forms of armed units within the province and shall make regular and special military reports and recommendations to the Regional Operational Command and Provincial Party Committee.

The Provincial Operational Command shall be composed of the Provincial Commander, his Deputy Commanders, the District Commanders and their Deputy Commanders.

Point 4. The District Operational Command shall be responsible for the execution of district military policies and plans, shall command all forms of armed units within the district and shall make regular and special military reports and recommendations to the Provincial Operational Command and to the District Party Committee.

The District Operational Command shall be composed of the District Commander, his Deputy Commanders, company commanders, guerrilla commanders and commanders of militia units.

Point 5. The National Operational Command shall be constituted by the Military Commission and all Regional, Provincial and District Commanders and Deputy Commanders shall be appointed by the Military Commission with or without the recommendation of the National Operational Command. Commanders for strategic campaigns or special operations of national significance shall be appointed by the Military Commission or the Central Committee.

Point 6. The selection of all military commanders shall be made on the basis of their revolutionary class standpoint and fighting performance. However, commanders of non-regular units may emerge in local areas in the course of practical armed struggle.

Point 7. Territorial commanders shall be superior to unit commanders and their respective areas of command shall be set by the higher military command.

Point 8. The size and variety of the people's armed forces under any territorial command at any level shall depend entirely on the development of the people's war. Further disposition of these shall be decided according to the needs of winning battles, campaigns and the entire war.

Point 9. Unit commanders from the level of battalion upwards, shall be appointed by the Military Commission upon the recommendation of the National Operational Command and the local Party committees. Company commanders shall be appointed by the National Operational Command upon the recommendation of the Party committee in the company. Platoon and squad leaders shall be appointed by their company commanders upon the recommendation of the Party Groups in the platoon.

Point 10. In any coordinated operation of all forms of armed units, the regular mobile forces shall play the central role in destroying the enemy.

Point 11. The system of command shall in no case prevent the taking of any quick military action by any armed unit within a particular area unless it can be proven that it prejudices a current larger military operation against the enemy.

Point 12. The headquarters of the National Operational Command shall be decided by the Central Committee or the Military Commission and the headquarters of the lower command, regional, provincial and district, shall be decided by the higher command.

Forms of People's Armed Forces

Point 1. The New People's Army shall encompass the following forms of fighting units:

a. regular mobile forces
b. guerrilla units
c. militia and self-defense corps
d. armed city partisans

Point 2. The regular mobile forces shall be organized in the following manner:

a. Squad: 5 to 10 men plus Squad Leader
b. Platoon: 2 to 3 squads plus Platoon Leader
c. Company: 2 to 3 platoons plus Commander and Deputy Commanders
d. Battalions: 2 to 3 companies plus Commander and Deputy Commanders
e. Regiment: 2 to 3 battalions plus Commander and Deputy Commanders
f. Division: 2 to 3 regiments plus Commander and Deputy Commanders
g. Corps: 2 to 3 divisions plus Commander and Deputy Commanders
h. Army: 2 to 3 corps plus Commander and Deputy Commanders

The territorial commanders and unit commanders shall always strive to raise the size of the above regular units to the maximum limit.

Point 3. The size of guerrilla units shall be allowed to range between five and fifteen men, including their commander. As soon as the size of a guerrilla unit shall have reached the size of two full squads, it shall be converted into two regular mobile forces upon the approval or order of the Provincial Operational Command and the Provincial Party Committee.

Point 4. The militia and self-defense corps shall be composed of those who continue with their daily productive life. They shall play a mainly defensive role but they shall serve as the vast reserve and support for the regular mobile forces and the guerrilla units.

Point 5. Every unit of the armed city partisans shall consist of at least three combat members and shall specialize in city operations, in disrupting the enemy rule, in raising the fighting morale of workers and the urban petty bourgeoisie and in preparing in a long-term way for a general city uprising upon instructions of the Military Commission.

Point 6. The unit commanders and their deputy commanders shall constitute the unit operational command.

Point 7. The regular mobile forces shall distribute arms and ammunitions to the guerrillas, militia, self-defense corps and armed city partisans to raise their fighting capacity or integrate them as regular troops or create new fighting units of the same type. The guerrillas shall likewise distribute arms and ammunitions to the militia and self-defense units to raise their fighting capacity, or create new fighting units of the same type or raise them to a higher combat formation.

Point 8. Party cadres, officers and men in the New People's Army may be assigned to create the non-regular armed units mentioned in Points 3, 4, and 5 above.

Logistics

Point 1. The regular mobile forces and guerrilla units of the New People's Army shall receive a special appropriation in the regular budget of the local people's governments, the local Party organization and/or revolutionary mass organizations.

Point 2. The New People's Army shall take initiative in establishing production units such as farms, shops, transportation and other enterprises which are useful to the people and Army and which shall support the latter in kind or in cash.

Point 3. The central people's government shall sell war bonds or set aside a reasonable percentage of money issued by it to support the New People's Army.

Point 4. The New People's Army shall assist the people's government in the collection of taxes, business and agricultural, and shall be automatically compensated for its efforts.

Point 5. Units of the New People's Army shall work for the masses as a measure of paying back for the material support given to them.

Point 6. Contributions in kind or cash from allies and sympathizers which are specifically intended for the New People's Army shall be accepted.

Point 7. A certain percentage of the income derived from confiscated goods, capital and properties off the U.S. imperialists, comprador bourgeoisie, landlords, bureaucrat capitalists and traitors shall be allocated for the support of the New People's Army.

Point 8. The logistics shall always be accounted for by a committee created for the purpose.

Amendments

Point 1. The Central Committee, Political Bureau or Military Commission of the Communist Party of the Philippines may initiate any amendments to these Basic Rules of the New People's Army.

Point 2. The National Operational Command or any Regional Command may recommend any amendment it deems necessary.

Point 3. The Military Commission or the National Operational Command may issue rules and regulations to supplement these basic Rules.

Draft issued by the
MEETING OF RED
COMMANDERS
AND SOLDIERS
March 29, 1969

INDEX